T0277278

Japanese Perspectives
on the Death of Christ

Series Preface

Regnum Studies in Mission are born from the lived experience of Christians and Christian communities in mission, especially but not solely in the fast-growing churches among the people of the developing world. These churches have more to tell than stories of growth. They are making significant impacts on their cultures in the cause of Christ. They are producing 'cultural products' which express the reality of Christian faith, hope and love in their societies.

Regnum Studies in Mission are the fruit often of rigorous research to the highest international standards and always of authentic Christian engagement in the transformation of people and societies. These are for the world. The formation of Christian theology, missiology and practice in the twenty-first century will depend to a great extent on the active participation of growing churches contributing biblical and culturally appropriate expressions of Christian practice to inform World Christianity.

Regnum is supported by the generosity of EMW

Japanese Perspectives on the Death of Christ: A Study in Contextualized Christology

How Chuang Chua

First published 2021 by Regnum Books International

Regnum is an imprint of the Oxford Centre for Mission Studies
St. Philip and St. James Church
Woodstock Road
Oxford OX2 6HR, UK
www.ocms.ac.uk/regnum

09 08 07 06 05 04 03 7 6 5 4 3 2 1

British Library Cataloguing in Publication Data
A catalogue record for this book is available from the British Library

ISBN: 978-1-5064-8370-2

eBook ISBN: 978-1-5064-8392-4

Typeset by Words by Design

Cover image by JuniperPhoton on www.unsplash.com

Distributed by 1517 Media in the US, Canada, India, and Brazil

Dedication

To my beloved Kaori, and to my OMF colleagues
who work tirelessly to make the Risen Son
known in the Land of the Rising Sun

*God was reconciling the world to himself in Christ, not counting people's sins
against them. And he has committed to us the message of reconciliation.*

2 Corinthians 5.19

Preface

One would not normally expect to find fresh and thoughtful perspectives on Jesus Christ coming from Japanese intellectuals. After all, despite four centuries of Christian presence in Japan only about one per cent of all Japanese identify themselves as Christian. Although Japan today is one of the world's most modernized, technologically advanced, and literate societies, it retains values, beliefs and practices formed by centuries of Shinto, Buddhist and animistic folk traditions. Christian missionaries arrived in Japan in the sixteenth century, and although Japanese Christians have been a small minority ever since they comprise an important part of the social and intellectual landscape. The Japanese have long had a fascination with Jesus – simultaneously attracted to Jesus' ethical teachings while remaining deeply suspicious of Christianity as a "foreign" religion. And in spite of its size, the Japanese Protestant church is mature and strong, exerting much greater cultural influence than one would expect. Many twentieth century Japanese novelists incorporated Christian themes into their writings and many Japanese, while rejecting Christian faith as such, have some understanding of Christian teachings and values.

The death of Jesus has always elicited thoughtful reflection, both from Christ's followers and from those outside the Christian community who nevertheless see in the cross something of profound significance. The aftermath of World War II in Japan, with the utter devastation of the previous order and an opportunity of a fresh beginning, was a time of extraordinary ferment among Japanese intellectuals. Three Japanese Christians in particular -- a theologian, a missiologist, and a novelist – addressed the death of Jesus in creative and thoughtful ways which are relevant not only to the late twentieth century Japanese context but also to the global Christian community today. While the insights of Kitamori Kazo, Koyama Kosuke, and Endo Shusaku[1] reflect their particular post-war Japanese contexts, they also help to elucidate biblical and theological themes which transcend local particularities and speak to universal concerns.

This book, which sets out the views of Kitamori, Koyama and Endo on the death of Jesus Christ, is a revision of Dr. How Chuang Chua's 2007 PhD dissertation presented to Trinity Evangelical Divinity School (TEDS). I was

---

[1] In keeping with Japanese tradition, the family name is listed first.

Japanese Perspectives on the Death of Christ

privileged to chair his doctoral committee, which also included Dr. Tite Tiénou (TEDS), Dr. Robert Priest (then at TEDS, now at Taylor University), and Dr. Stephen Bevans, SVD (Catholic Theological Union). The committee all agreed that this is an outstanding piece of work which deserves publication. I am delighted that Regnum Publishers is publishing this important work, but in noting the reasons for some delay in publication I must first say something about Dr. Chua himself.

How Chuang Chua was born in Singapore in 1959. He came to faith in Christ as a child and was baptized at age fourteen. He earned the Bachelor of Science degree in mathematics from the National University of Singapore in 1983, where he was also active with the Varsity Christian Fellowship (an affiliate of the Fellowship of Evangelical Students). In late 1983 he went for a short-term mission trip to Japan, which instilled in him an interest in long term mission service in Japan. After serving in a variety of ministry contexts, in 1991 How Chuang earned a Masters of Arts degree in English and linguistics at the National University of Singapore. He then studied at Regent College, Vancouver, earning both the Master of Divinity (1995) and Master of Theology (1997), and serving as a teaching assistant to Dr. J. I. Packer.

How Chuang met his lovely Japanese wife Kaori at an International Fellowship of Evangelical Students East Asia Regional Conference in the Philippines in 1989. After corresponding for several years, they were married in 1995. From 1998-2002 How Chuang and Kaori Chua served with OMF International in church planting in Sapporo, Japan. How Chuang and Kaori then both studied at Trinity Evangelical Divinity School, with How Chuang earning the PhD in Intercultural Studies and Kaori the Master of Arts in Counseling. They returned to Japan, where Dr. Chua was involved both in church planting and theological education, teaching at Hokkaido Bible Institute, and Kaori developed a counseling ministry among churches. Although heavily involved in local church responsibilities as well as teaching and administration at a seminary, Dr. Chua always intended to rework his dissertation for publication. However, the immediate demands of ministry prevented his being able to do so.

In June, 2014, while in Singapore, How Chuang was diagnosed with advanced colorectal cancer. Just eight months later, on 5 March, 2015, the Lord called him home, leaving behind his wife Kaori and their three year old daughter, Airi. Upon hearing the news of his passing, my immediate thought was, Why, Lord? He was relatively young, exceptionally gifted, and he had such a promising ministry in Japan ahead of him. Why? We are reminded again that God's thoughts are not our thoughts, God's ways are not our ways (Isaiah 55:8-9). What makes perfectly good sense to us missiologically may not be in line with God's purposes. In times like these, we are called to walk in faithful obedience to what God has revealed and to trust him for what remains undisclosed. How Chuang's unflinching faith in God's goodness and love throughout his illness was a powerful testimony to many worldwide.[2]

In many ways Dr. Chua exemplified what Christian mission should be in our very challenging and globalizing world. He was a brilliant thinker and well educated, with advanced degrees in linguistics, theology, and missiology. Yet he was humble and unassuming, and eager to minister among ordinary people through the local church. He became fluent in speaking and reading Japanese, and this gave him access to untranslated materials from the writings of Kitamori, Koyama and Endo. I know that he could have secured a teaching position in a major seminary in the United States, but he wished to develop his missiological and theological perspectives while immersed in cross-cultural ministry in northern Japan. He was committed to developing mission theology "on the ground," from within the church and for the church.

With the publication of this book Dr. Chua continues to speak to us, challenging us theologically and missiologically. The last time I saw my friend How Chuang was in July, 2010, at a conference on Christology in an Asian context held at Tokyo Christian University. In his contribution at the conference Dr. Chua very effectively drew upon key themes from his dissertation. There was much anticipation among the participants concerning what he might contribute to an authentically Asian Christology in the years ahead. God, however, had other plans. Yet, Dr. Chua's life, and now his book, provide us with fine examples of how we are to do theology in our diverse and globalizing world. We are to listen carefully to brothers and sisters from around the world, learning from them and responding to them respectfully, all while remaining faithful to Scripture and sensitive to the Spirit. Dr. Chua would have it no other way. May the conversation continue.

Harold Netland
Trinity Evangelical Divinity School
November, 2020

---

[2] For something of the impact of How Chuang Chua's life and death upon others see Tan Lai Yong, *Twist and Wait* (Singapore: Fellowship of Evangelical Students, 2016).

Table of Contents

1. Research Problem

Early in my ministry as a missionary in Japan, a senior colleague told me the following story. A missionary was preaching the gospel in a public evangelistic meeting and, towards the end of his talk, he summarized his message with an impassioned plea: "Jesus Christ died on the cross for your sins. If you accept him as your personal Lord and Savior, you will have everlasting life. This means that after you die on earth, you will go to heaven where you will live forever." After the meeting, an elderly lady came up and expressed her myriad concerns to the missionary. "Teacher, how can someone else possibly die for the sins I have committed? And how can his death cause me to go to heaven? Besides, I don't want to live forever or go to heaven. When I die, I just want to be where my ancestors are." I have no way of telling if this story is true, but certainly even in my first term of missionary service in Japan, there were more than a few occasions when I encountered variations of that same anecdotal theme, namely, the great difficulty on the part of many Japanese people in making sense of the death of Christ.[1]

Obviously, the difficulty in understanding the death of Christ is not confined only to the Japanese.[2] The apostle Paul, writing to the church in Corinth, acknowledges that the Cross is "a stumbling block to Jews and foolishness to

---

[1] Contrary to what might be expected, most Japanese adults would immediately associate the name Jesus Christ with his death on the cross, even if they do not have the remotest idea why he died.

[2] The renowned Japanese writer Akutagawa Ryūnosuke (1892-1927) – after whom Japan's most prestigious literary prize is named – seemed to have believed that one of the reasons why Christianity could never sink its roots in Japan is that the image of the crucified Christ is particularly offensive to the Japanese mindset. He has written numerous short stories in which he portrayed so vividly the almost unbearable tension between Japanese culture and the Christian faith. See, for example, *Kamigami no bishō* (1922), *Ogin* (1922), *Oshino* (1923), and *Yūwaku* (1927). Akutagawa's cynicism notwithstanding, it must be said that the Cross is naturally offensive not only to the Japanese, but to all peoples. (Ironically, when his wife found Akutagawa unconscious from a deliberate lethal overdose of a sedative drug, she saw an open Bible lying on his chest. Akutagawa, then only thirty-five, never regained consciousness.) Oxford philosopher Sir Alfred Ayer calls the Cross "morally outrageous" (cited in Stott 1986, 43).

Gentiles" (1 Cor. 1:23).[3] In this sense, it is true that the scandal of the crucified Savior confounds human understanding and therefore cannot be "contextualized" (see Schnabel, 2004a: 546; 2004b: 1356, 1533). Yet, on another level, the factor of culture must be seriously considered. Sociologists and anthropologists tell us that the way people think and perceive reality is very much constrained by their socio-cultural conditioning (Hiebert, 1994: 35-51). Indeed, it is now widely-accepted that, even in the realm of biblical studies, it is impossible to approach theological truth without what Tite Tiénou calls "a prior allegiance or worldview" (1983: 90). Hence even the simple propositional statement, "Jesus died for the sins of all humankind" is appropriated differently by different people as a result of the different pre-existing conceptual grids that exist in their minds. These grids are constituted not only cognitively but also emotively, and as mentioned above, they are very much shaped by one's socio-cultural environment. Consequently, a common set of incoming external stimuli becomes filtered and processed differently by different grids. It is therefore not unexpected that Western people,[4] raised on Judeo-Christian moral foundations and modernist epistemological assumptions, should understand the death of Christ somewhat differently from people whose ethics and epistemology are founded on a radically different set of worldview underpinnings.

Hence in preaching the gospel, the problem of potential dissonance, both cognitive and emotive, is always present. This point, unfortunately, has not always been appreciated by missionaries. One of the more popular tools used in personal evangelism in Japan is *The Four Spiritual Laws* developed by Campus Crusade for Christ. Until the publication in 2002 of a revised Japanese version of the *Four Laws* – as it is commonly referred to – most people who used this tool simply did not realize that it was developed in the context of the American campus in the late 1950s, and that the "laws" presuppose a *particular* view of God, and of life. Instead, many missionaries unconsciously, hence uncritically, supposed the *Four Laws* to be relevant to the modern Japanese context, indeed believing the assumptions about God and human existence underlying them to

---

[3] All Scripture quotations in English are taken from the New International Version (1984), unless otherwise specified.
[4] The ideas denoted and connoted by the phrase "the West" and its modifier "Western" are admittedly easier to identity than define. See Abramsky's thought-provoking essay, "Defining the Indefinable West," in which the author problematizes the term "the West" as "a spectacularly vague and imprecise intellectual organizing tool" (2007: B7). The nebulous nature of the term notwithstanding, for the purpose of this book, "the West" is identified "with the philosophical and scientific legacy of the Enlightenment, with the questions asked and the answers generated by the leading thinkers of Europe and America over the past several hundred years, as well as with a historical narrative, a sense of shared destiny that leads back past the origins of Christianity and into the Greco-Roman world" (Abramsky, 2007: B6). I am indebted to Dr. Tite Tiénou for directing me to Abramsky's article.

be universal.[5] Therefore, when hearers of the *Four Laws* expressed difficulty in understanding and believing the "simple" gospel message as it was packaged and presented, these missionaries often responded by blaming it on the spiritual blindness of the people, lamenting that they have no concept of God or of sin. The real problem, however, lay with the missionaries themselves, in the way they confused their own cultural understanding of the gospel with the gospel itself (Priest, 1994: 291-315; Priest, 2006: 180-95).[6]

Of course, we are not advocating here a position of extreme cultural relativism in which universal truths about God and human existence are jettisoned altogether. The unity of humankind is a theological given. It is a necessary, indeed primary, assumption in anthropology; otherwise without it, it would be meaningless to even talk about cultural others.

---

[5] For instance, the *Four Laws* assume there is a supreme, personal God who relates directly with human beings, an assumption that many people from non-Western cultures find alien in the first place. When Japanese people are presented for the first time with the first law, "God loves you and has a wonderful plan for your life", they are often confused about which god is being referred to. The idea of a loving god who has a wonderful plan for a person is just too nebulous to grasp for one who is inculturated to see the world as populated by myriads of spiritual beings and governed by the impersonal mechanism of fate. The problem is compounded by the extremely complex and slippery Japanese word *kami* 神, which translates the English word "God". The word does not designate a unique order of being or a self-contained category of phenomenon, but refers rather to the "spiritualization of all things in the Universe" (*An Outline of Shinto Teachings*: 1958: 8). In fact, Shinto literally means "the way of *kami*". See McFarland (1967: 24) for seven categories of phenomena which have been, at one time or another, designated *kami*, and thus have been singled out for worship in Shinto: (1) fundamental life principles, such as fertility, growth and productivity; (2) celestial bodies, pre-eminently the sun and the moon; (3) natural forces, such as wind and thunder; (4) prominent topographical features, such as mountains and rivers; (5) natural objects, especially trees and rocks; (6) animals, especially the fox and the horse; and (7) spirits of the dead. Harada Tasuku has two more categories: manufactured objects and human beings (1914: 32). Conversely, the word *kami* is notoriously difficult to translate into English. To render it as "God" is to make a monotheistic assumption which may be unwarranted. Every instance of the word therefore requires a judgment call depending on the context. However, in the writings of Kitamori and Endō, it is often very clear when they use *kami* to refer to the Christian God. (Koyama writes mainly in English, so this problem does not arise in his works.)

[6] This is, of course, not to write off the *Four Spiritual Laws* completely as a totally ineffective means of sharing the gospel. Indeed, some have testified to its convenience and usefulness. The point stressed here is that like all means, it must never be regarded absolutely. Moreover, as alluded to earlier, the first of the *Four Laws* was changed from the traditional "God loves you and has a wonderful plan for your life", to "God loves us, and created us so that we may know him personally". The earlier statement assumes prior knowledge of God's creation of humankind. Realizing that this may not be intuitive to the Japanese psyche, the staff of the Japan Campus Crusade of Christ replaced it with the new statement. It cannot be overemphasized that the effectiveness of any evangelistic tool is a necessary function of its critical use.

According to the Bible, the problem of sin is universal, and so is the offer of salvation (Rom. 3:23-24; John 3:16). Culture is never such an insurmountable obstacle as to render a person impervious to the regenerative influence of the Holy Spirit and the transformational power of the gospel. However, for the gospel to make sense, it must be translated in a way that is culturally intelligible to its hearers. At the same time, the process through which the gospel takes root in people's hearts and minds necessarily involves its appropriation by its hearers using the innate cognitive categories of their culture. In contemporary missiological parlance, the cross-cultural transmission and appropriation of the gospel is known as *contextualization*. More will be said about this in the following chapter.

This work is concerned with the contextualization process, especially the appropriation part. In particular, this study seeks to examine the ways in which three leading Japanese Christian thinkers understand and interpret the death of Christ.

Research Concern

This volume is motivated predominantly by a desire to understand why it is so hard for Japanese people to come to faith in Christ.[7] Indeed, there has been no lack of attempt on the part of missionaries, missiologists, and scholars of Japanese religion, to offer reasons for the apparent lack of response to the gospel in Japan (see, for example, Yamamori, 1974; Ishida, 1994; Dale, 1998; Mullins, 1998: 156-200; Sadowitz, 2004). Studies can only uncover proximate causes for the situation at hand; hence, it is not possible to attribute the problem to *one* particular reason. This notwithstanding, it is not unreasonable to surmise the general failure of church planters and evangelists to understand the complexities of Japanese culture and Japanese ways of thinking as a major cause for the slow growth of the Japanese church (cf. Johnstone and Mandryk, 2001: 373; Sadowitz, 2004: 2). Many Japanese people continue to be put off by the foreign feel of Christianity. Even in my short time in Japan, not a few came confessing to me that they found the logic of the gospel as presented to them alien and difficult to grasp.

Surely missionaries are not unaware of the recent proliferation of writings arguing for the need of contextualization (e.g. Nicholls, 1978; Shorter, 1988; Whiteman, 1997; Bevans, 2002; Lee, 2005). Perhaps in their zeal to preserve the biblical integrity of the gospel, missionaries, notably evangelicals, have unwittingly sacrificed cultural intelligibility. In sum, it seems fair to say that missionaries in Japan have generally not done well in contextualizing the Christian message in its transmission.

---

[7] For this reason, this book is written with the missionary community in Japan as its primary readership in mind.

It is, however, encouraging to note that in recent years, some missionaries and missiologists who have had experience working in Japan, as well as Japanese pastors, have taken up the crucial challenge of studying ways to present the gospel using Japanese cultural categories. Interestingly, research on the contextualization of the gospel in Japan conducted so far has largely focused on the contrasting motifs of shame and guilt (Funaki, 1957; Baynes, 1980; Matsumoto, 1985; Kraus, 1987; Green and Baker, 2000: 153-70; Kraus, 2004: 205-46).[8] The general argument is that Western soteriology, constructed around the legal principle of guilt from the time of Augustine, does not fit in well with shame-based, communitarian cultures. Rather, it is argued, people from such cultures, for example, the Japanese, would better understand the concept of sin and the meaning of the Cross from the perspective of shame rather than that of guilt. This research approach to contextualization by way of a creative theological or missiological construction certainly holds much promise, and needs to be further encouraged.[9]

While it is certainly helpful to seek creative ways to transmit the gospel contextually, there is a second approach, which perhaps should be a primary approach, to study this problem of contextualization by examining how Japanese Christians *appropriate* the gospel theologically for themselves. For is it not true that unless we understand the latter, it would appear presumptuous to do the former? Yet the irony is that most discussion on contextualization seems to focus on missionary methods of transmission of the gospel rather than its native appropriation. This book seeks to address this second concern.

Research Rationale

At the beginning of his courses at the Trinity Evangelical Divinity School, anthropologist Robert Priest has the habit of quoting Proverbs 19:2, "It is not good to have zeal without knowledge, nor to be hasty and miss the way." When the subject of study involves direct human interest, it is all the more important to derive knowledge by paying attention to what people are saying. In the study of theological contextualization, for example, the necessity of listening to the native voice can scarcely be overestimated.

Despite the ground-breaking work of the scholars mentioned above in the area of contextualizing the gospel for evangelistic purposes, there is so much that remains to be done in studying and understanding how Japanese Christians have

---

[8] Raymond Song, a doctoral candidate at the Trinity Evangelical Divinity School, finished his dissertation entitled, "Shame and Guilt in the Japanese Culture: A Study of Lived Experiences of Japanese Emerging Generation and Its Relation to the Church Mission in Japan" in 2009.

[9] One must, of course, be careful not to fall into the trap of theologizing out of a single cultural principle, such as shame or harmony. The complexity of cultural reality is obscured by essentializing a single cultural trait.

appropriated the Christian faith for themselves. One may be surprised to note that, even though the Japanese church is more than a thousand years younger than her European counterpart, its theological output has been remarkably prodigious. Yet large volumes of original theological writings in the Japanese language are yet to be translated, and are therefore unexplored. These works are distillations of careful and intentional Japanese self-theologizing, and it will impoverish not only the missionary community, but more so the Japanese church, if they continue to be ignored for whatever reason.

   This work seeks to contribute to the ongoing research effort of interpreting and expositing Japanese theological thinking to the larger Christian community in and outside Japan. Because of my missionary interest and experience, my motivation for the study is clearly missiological. Since the centerpiece of the gospel message is "Jesus Christ and him crucified" (1 Cor. 2:2), this volume proposes to examine Japanese perspectives on Christ and his death.

Research Statement

Through an interpretative and evaluative study of the original writings of three leading modern Japanese Christian thinkers, Kitamori Kazō (1916-98), Endō Shūsaku (1923-96), and Koyama Kōsuke (b. 1929-2009),[10] this research seeks to uncover and explicate culturally- and theologically-emic[11] perspectives on the death of Christ. These viewpoints will be analyzed within the larger socio-historical contexts of the three writers and their works in an attempt to illuminate Japanese cultural themes, Japanese religiosity, and the nature of Japanese Christianity.

---

[10] The order of Japanese names is preserved according to Japanese convention, that is, with the family name first followed by the given name (or the so-called "first name"). Although a person is generally referred to by his or her family name, a few, especially famous or infamous figures (such as Oda Nobunaga, Toyotomi Hideyoshi, and Tokugawa Ieyasu), and children (such as Yanase Minoru on pp. 135-36), are called by their given names. In these cases, we follow the Japanese practice of using their given names.

[11] The term "emic", and its corresponding term "etic", were coined by the linguist Kenneth Pike in 1954. Pike created the words from "phonetic" and "phonemic", thus extending their meanings from their original conventional linguistic usage to cover the description of cultural phenomena. The terms are designed to describe behavior from two different standpoints: "The etic viewpoint studies behavior as from outside of a particular system, and as an essential initial approach to an alien system. The emic viewpoint results from studying behavior from inside the system" (Pike, 1967: 37). The twin concepts are today taken for granted as foundational to anthropological practice. For the purpose of this dissertation, I have taken the liberty to apply the word "emic" to theology: a theologically-emic perspective is the theological viewpoint of the insider – in our case, the three Japanese writers whom we are studying.

Research Questions

The book seeks to answer the following five questions:

- RQ 1. What is the nature and significance of the death of Christ in the writings of Kitamori, Endō, and Koyama? What are the similarities and differences between the three views?
- RQ 2. To what extent do the views of Kitamori, Endō, and Koyama reflect the perspectives on the Cross in Scripture?
- RQ 3. To what extent do the views of Kitamori, Endō, and Koyama reflect the perspectives on the Cross within classical Christian theology?
- RQ 4. To what extent do the views of Kitamori, Endō, and Koyama reflect themes and values generally identified with Japanese culture and religion?
- RQ 5. To what extent are the views of Kitamori, Endō, and Koyama shaped by their respective biographies?[12]

Research Methodology

The research for this project is wholly library-based. Primary and secondary sources are used as research material. All English translations of Japanese and other non-English texts are mine unless otherwise specified.

The data for this research are primarily textual, being derived from the original writings of Kitamori, Endō, and Koyama. The methodology employed in the analysis of these texts is adapted from *grounded theory*, an approach that was developed by sociologists to analyze ethnographic interview data (Glaser and Strauss, 1967; Strauss and Corbin, 1990). Although this approach is widely-used in sociological and anthropological research, its methodological framework is useful for analyzing literary data because of its inductive nature. Grounded theory simply refers to theory that is derived from – or grounded in – the textual data. Strauss and Corbin elaborate:

> A researcher does not begin a project with a preconceived theory in mind [...] Rather, the researcher begins with an area of study and allows the theory to emerge from the data. Theory derived from data is more likely to resemble the "reality" than is theory derived by putting together a series of concepts based on experience or solely through speculation [...] Grounded theories, because they are drawn from data, are likely to offer insight, enhance understanding, and provide a meaningful guide to action. (1990: 12)

The analysis of data is an iterative process by which potential analytic categories are identified (Bernard, 2002, 463). Data from these categories are thematically collated, compared and, where possible, linked together to build

---

[12] This fifth research question was not in the original dissertation proposal. In the course of the dissertation research, it became increasingly evident that personal biography indeed exerts a vital influence on the writings of the three men we are studying, hence the addition of this research question.

theoretical models (Bernard, 2002, 463). The process is a critical as well as a creative one (Patton, 2002: 513). It entails not only "conceiving and intuiting ideas (concepts) but also formulating them into a logical, systematic, and explanatory scheme" (Strauss and Corbin, 1990: 21).

Since all religious truth claims are necessarily motivated and constrained by subjective experience, cognitive habituation, and linguistic structure, grounded theory is appropriate for this book because the focus of this study is not to test theory, but to uncover theological patterns from textual data produced by cultural insiders themselves. Selected original texts pertinent to the research are studied, interpreted on their own terms, compared and contrasted, and critically evaluated. As themes emerge from the respective writings of Kitamori, Endō, and Koyama, they are described and interpreted in the larger contexts of their theological belief systems. We start with Kitamori, and when we move to Endō and later to Koyama, we will engage more intensively in comparing and contrasting some pertinent themes between these three writers. Each of their systemic conceptualization of the death of Christ is also compared and contrasted with biblical teaching as well as with the perspectives from classical theology.

As we shall see, theological works are in large measure influenced by prevailing socio-historical circumstances as well as personal biography. For this reason, a "thick description" of the history of Japanese Christianity is given in chapter 3.[13] Also, for each of the three Japanese thinkers we are studying, we provide an extensive biography, not simply as a drawn-out introduction to their works, but in order to show the intrinsic and profound nature of the relationship between who each person is and what he believes. And so, although this study is theological in orientation and missiological in intention,[14] it is inter-disciplinary in approach, drawing from history, biography, spirituality, literature, linguistics, and cultural studies.

The research was complimented by a one-hour telephone interview with Koyama on March 26, 2007. The purpose of the interview is threefold: to fill in

---

[13] The term "thick description" originates from Oxford philosopher Gilbert Ryle, but is famously utilized by the late anthropologist Clifford Geertz to highlight the microscopic and interpretive nature of ethnography. See Geertz, *The Interpretation of Cultures: Selected Essays of Clifford Geertz* (New York: Basic Books, 1973), pp. 3-30, for a sustained discussion on the methodological issues related to ethnographic research. In our context, a "thick description" of history simply refers to an historical account which is both microscopic and interpretive.

[14] The intrinsic relationship between theology and missiology is well captured by the Croatian missiologist Peter Kuzmič who, in a keynote address given on September 30, 2006 at the Lausanne Younger Leaders Gathering held in Kuala Lumpur, Malaysia, emphasized (again) that "[a]ll theology must be missiologically focused, [...] and all missions must be theologically grounded" cited in Judd Birdsall, "Ich bin ein Lausanner," Available at https://www.lausanne.org/gatherings/ylg/younger-leaders-gathering-2006-2 [accessed September 12, 2020].

some information gaps in his personal biography, to ascertain my interpretation of some of his key ideas, and to seek further clarification and explanation on a couple of pertinent points. The results of the interview are incorporated into the final presentation.

Research Significance

Once significant Japanese theological writings have been introduced and made accessible to the wider Church, one expects that they will contribute significantly to the rethinking and revitalization of the missionary task. This work hopes to make an original contribution to ongoing research on theological contextualization and global theologizing. More specifically, I hope to contribute toward a deeper appreciation of Japanese culture and theology, so that minimally, missionaries can be helped to understand the complex and dynamic interplay between culture and faith in the Japanese context. Hopefully, this in turn will lead to a better contextualization of the gospel in Japan and perhaps help missionaries and theologians working in Japan to develop a particular theology of the Cross that is not only biblically faithful and locally grounded, but also globally relevant for the Church of Christ.

Delimitation

The Japanese scholars we are studying are prolific writers in their own right. This research study hence scrutinizes only those of their writings that, directly and indirectly, relate to the death of Christ. Most of their other works, therefore, are omitted.

Limitations

The primary sources for our study are the written works of the three Japanese scholars in the original languages. Whenever a translation is used, it is indicated in the reference. Although secondary sources in Japanese are used, I am, regretfully, unable to use more because these, especially journal articles, are not readily available from American libraries. However, there are more than sufficient secondary sources in English which are both current and relevant so as to make this study viable.

Evangelical Presuppositions

It needs to be stated from the outset that this work is written from an evangelical perspective. The underlying theological presuppositions are set out below, albeit briefly.

First and foremost, evangelicals regard the sixty-six books that make up the Bible as the divinely inspired record of God's revelation. Scripture is infallible in all it affirms, being a totally adequate and reliable expression of God's will and purpose for humankind. There is, of course, the human aspect to Scripture in that God conveyed his[15] revelation to humankind through human writers who used culturally-conditioned words and imagery to record that revelation. This notwithstanding, evangelicals affirm the eternal and unconditional nature of that revelation and therefore regard Scripture as the authoritative guide for all people in all matters pertaining to life and faith. The divine inspiration of Scripture also means that the illumination of the Holy Spirit is required for the reader to understand the text and apply it appropriately to their specific context. In the theological task, evangelicals thus hold an unwavering commitment to the final authority of Scripture as well as to the necessity of the guidance of the Holy Spirit. Of course, this does not mean that there is one and only one way of interpreting Scripture, but at least in principle, evangelicals are agreed that theology can only be properly done when one maintains a posture of submission to the Word of God throughout the process.

Without going into detail, here are the key beliefs that evangelicals have derived from Scripture which they maintain without compromise: the infinitely-perfect and eternally-coexisting persons, the Father, the Son, and the Holy Spirit within the triune Godhead; God as the creator of all things; the problem of sin which corrupts all humankind, resulting in moral deviance, estranged relationships, and spiritual pollution; Jesus Christ as providing the only necessary and sufficient means of salvation through his death and resurrection; forgiveness of sin and salvation from death and eternal punishment by the sheer grace of God through the exercise of faith in Jesus Christ; the ministry of the Holy Spirit in convicting humans, regenerating believing sinners, and indwelling and empowering them for godly living and service; the responsibility of the Church to proclaim the good news of salvation so as to bring people from every part of the world to faith; and the visible and personal return of Jesus Christ to set up his eternal kingdom of righteousness and peace.[16]

Overview

As we can well see, this first chapter is a presentation of the research problem. The research statement and the five research questions are stated. The next two

---

[15] While it is beyond dispute that the nature of God transcends gender, in this dissertation, the divine pronoun is indicated by the masculine pronominal form, in conformity with biblical language and with most theological writings. When referring to human beings, inclusive language is used wherever linguistically possible.

[16] The key doctrinal beliefs of evangelicalism are well encapsulated in the twelve-article Statement of Faith of The Evangelical Free Church of America, posted on http://www.efca.org/about/doctrine [accessed September 12, 2020].

chapters deal with prolegomenal concerns relating to theology, missiology, and history. These are important insofar as they set the stage. Chapter 2 consists of three parts. First, it presents a review of the principal motifs of the death of Christ in the Bible, the New Testament in particular. Then, it provides an overview of the main theories of the Atonement in classical Western theology. Third, it discusses briefly the whys and wherefores of contextualization as they are understood in contemporary missiological literature. Chapter 3 presents the research context – first providing an overview of the history of Christianity in Japan, before examining, albeit summarily, the development of Christian theology in Japan, from its introduction until today. A short introduction of the three principal subjects of our study – Kitamori, Endō, and Koyama – is then given, followed by a brief literature review of scholarly research that has been conducted on these three Japanese thinkers. The next three chapters, constituting the heart of the project, deal with selected writings of Kitamori, Endō, and Koyama respectively, and provide an in-depth analysis of their perspectives on the death of Christ. Chapter 7 offers a summary evaluation of these three thinkers by working through the five research questions formulated in this chapter. Pertinent issues that are raised concerning theological content and method are then discussed, concluding with an epilogue where missiological implications are drawn with regard to the preaching of the gospel in the world today, and in Japan in particular.

A Note on Notation

The romanization of Japanese words follows the revised (or modified) Hepburn system – the system used by the Library of Congress.[17] Instead of duplication in the case of long vowels, macrons are used (e.g. *ō* instead of *oo*, *oh*, or *ou*). However, these macrons are omitted in the names of well-known places (e.g., Tokyo instead of Tōkyō). In the case of citation, the original words are cited as they are. In both popular and academic writings, for instance, "Endō Shūsaku" is often rendered as "Endo Shusaku," and "Kitamori Kazō" as Kitamori Kazoh. Words in the Japanese script are generally not given, except in pertinent instances, in which case they are given alongside their Romanized transliteration.

---

[17] The Hepburn system was originally developed by its namesake, Dr. James Curtis Hepburn (1815-1911), an American Presbyterian missionary who arrived in Yokohama in 1859. A decade after his arrival, Hepburn published the first modern Japanese-English dictionary.

2. Theological and Missiological Prolegomena

The Language of the Cross

In the New Testament, and in virtually all theological traditions following the era of the Early Church, the word "Cross" is often used as a metonym for the death of Christ. Indeed, the subjects of this study, Kitamori, Endō, and Koyama, use the word "Cross" unambiguously and invariably to refer to the physical death of Christ. However, the word often carries with it a distinctively theological signification that goes beyond the physical death of Christ. In this work, where such metonymy exists, its theological context is explicated as and when necessary. Care is especially taken to ensure that Western theological categories that are normally associated with the Cross, especially relating to the theological meaning and implications of the Atonement, do not influence *a priori* our interpretation of the Japanese perspectives on the Cross. However, should an ambiguous, or unwarranted, interpretation arise when the word "Cross" is used in a particular context, the phrase "death of Christ," or "Christ's death," is used instead.

The Cross in the Bible

The works of Kitamori, Endō, and Koyama are all derivative of a common faith commitment. All three associate themselves with the Christian Church, and all profess to believe in Jesus Christ as subject, although they may not necessarily agree on their understanding with regard to his nature.[1] Because of the Christian self-understanding and confession of the three men, we can reasonably assume that the Bible, the New Testament in particular, constitutes an important primary source of data for their reflections on the death of Christ, whatever their views may be with regard to matters relating to biblical inspiration and inerrancy. It is therefore fitting, from the outset, to consider, albeit briefly, some of the principal

---

[1] Kitamori had a lifelong ministry with the United Church of Christ in Japan (*Nihon kirisuto kyōdan* 日本基督教団, hereafter referred to simply as Kyōdan), the largest Protestant denomination in Japan. Koyama was sent out by the Kyōdan to serve as a missionary in Thailand, and later in Singapore. He spent his last years worshipping at The House of Hope Presbyterian Church in St. Paul, Minnesota, a church affiliated with the Presbyterian Church (USA) denomination. Endō was a member of the Roman Catholic Church all his life from the time of his baptism as a boy.

motifs that the New Testament writers employ to describe the death of Christ.[2] This section is necessary as a backdrop for our later discussion on how these three Japanese thinkers understand and interpret the biblical teaching on Christ's death.

It must be emphasized that the New Testament does not put forward any so-called theory of the Atonement.[3] Nonetheless, it cannot be denied that the Cross *is* the centerpiece of its theology (Warfield, 1950: 391; Morris, 1965: 365; Stott, 1986: 32-40). The New Testament writers employ a variety of modes when they write about the death of Christ, and these, taken together, provide such a complex and multifaceted picture that its interpretation, while determinable, can hardly be exhausted. These writers

> spoke in financial categories of redemption or release from slavery through payment of a price; in legal categories of advocacy, justification, and satisfaction; in cultic categories of sacrifice, sin-offering, and expiation; in political categories of liberation and victory over oppressive powers; in personal categories of reconciliation after dispute; in medical categories of being healed or made whole; in existential categories of freedom and new life; and in familial categories of becoming God's children by birth (John) or adoption (Paul). *The word salvation itself is one of these metaphors which in both its Hebrew and Greek forms connotes being rescued or snatched away from peril as well as being healed or preserved in well-being.* (Johnson, 1994: 3-4, emphasis added)[4]

For the sake of clarity, let us examine the biblical witness to Christ's death under three headings: (1) the nature of the Cross; (2) the achievements of the Cross; and (3) the ethics of the Cross.

First, the New Testament writers are unanimous in their view that Christ experienced unspeakable and unjust suffering that culminated in his crucifixion (e.g. Acts 2:23; 1 Pet. 2:21-25). Despite his complete innocence, Christ suffered capital punishment. Indeed, throughout the book of Acts, we find the chief apostles, first Peter and then Paul, emphasizing through their many sermons the point that the victimization of Christ is to be attributed to human wickedness, not his own (Acts. 2:14-39; 3:12-26; 4:8-12; 5:29-32; 10:34-43; 13:16-41; 14:15-17; 17:2-3, 22-31; 28:23-31). Yet, while wicked human agency was solely

---

[2] Needless to say, it is beyond the scope and purpose of this work to cover this topic in depth. For an excellent coverage on the subject, see the section "Atonement in the Old and New Testaments," in *The Glory of the Atonement*, ed. Charles Hill and Frank James III, (Downers Grove, Ill.: InterVarsity Press, 2004), pp. 23-208.

[3] It is instructive that the word "atonement" does not appear in most English translations of the New Testament. It occurs only once in the King James Version (Rom. 5:11), and three times in the New International Version (Rom. 3:25; Heb. 2:17; 9:5). The word, however, appears frequently in most English versions of the Old Testament.

[4] I am grateful to Dr. Stephen Bevans for directing me to Elizabeth Johnson's paper, "Jesus and Salvation," which was presented at the Forty-Ninth Annual Convention of the Catholic Theological Society of America in Baltimore, Maryland, in June 1994.

responsible for Christ's death, the New Testament writers also recognize that his was a divinely ordained death. Peter, in his first Pentecost sermon, could put it no more plainly: "This man [Christ] was handed over to you by *God's set purpose and foreknowledge*, and you, with the help of wicked men, put him to death by nailing him to the cross" (Acts 2:23, emphasis added). In a similar line of thought, Paul describes Christ's death both as voluntary self-surrender (Gal. 2:20) and as the Father's willed surrender of the Son (Rom. 8:32).

The fact that Christ's sufferings were designed to fulfill a divine purpose does not in any way lessen their actual intensity. In his 1977 classic work *Crucifixion*, Martin Hengel goes to great lengths to expose the sheer gruesome and inhumane realities of the crucifixion in the ancient world.[5] The cross was "an utterly offensive affair, 'obscene' in the original sense of the word," and no one, whether Greek, Roman, Jew, or barbarian, could be indifferent to it (Hengel, 1977: 22). Crucifixion was "a 'barbaric' form of execution of utmost cruelty" (Hengel, 1977: 22), "the supreme Roman penalty" (Hengel, 1977: 33), reserved for "rebellious foreigners, violent criminals and robbers" (Hengel, 1977: 46), and "the typical punishment for slaves" (Hengel, 1977: 51). Before a person was crucified, he would first be tortured, at least by flogging. The crucifixion invariably took place at a prominent location, and as the crucified person was nailed naked onto the cross, he suffered not only unspeakable physical pain, but also experienced uttermost humiliation (Hengel, 1977: 87). The cross was a symbol of absolute disgrace and abject failure; it was quite impossible to make a human being suffer more. The Gospel writers are all unanimous to the witness that Jesus was crucified under Pontius Pilate, the Roman procurator of Judea at that time. Moreover, each of the four Gospels devotes an inordinate amount of space to the Passion narrative, even much more than the Resurrection. The Gospel writers desired to emphasize not only the fact that Jesus died, but that he died an ignominious death.[6]

Besides the physical torments and emotional ordeal that were part and parcel of the crucifixion, Christ experienced spiritual agony of the profoundest kind, namely, total abandonment by his Father. Jesus foresaw and referred to his impending Passion as the "cup" (*poth,rion*) that the Father had prepared for him to drink from (John. 18:11; also Mt. 26:39, 42; Mk. 14:36; Lk. 22:42; Mt. 20:22, 23).[7] Indeed Jesus did drink deeply from that bitter cup while hanging on the

---

[5] I am grateful to Dr. Harold Netland for the reference to Hengel's magisterial work.
[6] This was why the Cross was such an unparalleled scandal, "a stumbling block to Jews and foolishness to Gentiles" (1 Cor. 1: 23). How could the preexistent Son of God die such a shameful death? It is not a wonder that Docetism should hold such an appeal in the early church, for it was a sensible "way of removing the 'folly' of the cross" (Hengel, 1977: 15).
[7] In Matthew 20:22-23 (and correspondingly in Mark 10:38-39), Jesus uses the words "cup" and "baptism" as metonyms for the sufferings that James and John would ultimately share with their Master. Indeed, we learn later that James suffered a violent death (Acts 12:2), and that John was sent into exile on the Island of Patmos (Rev. 1:9).

cross, and gave expression to his profound spiritual anguish through the words of Psalms 22:1, "My God, my God, why have you forsaken me?" (Mt. 27:46; Mk. 15:34). John Stott is right when he describes that painful utterance of Christ as "a cry of real dereliction" (1986: 81). No mortal could ever know the depth of Christ's sufferings.[8]

Christ's horrendous sufferings were therefore both a consequence of human brutality and a fruition of divine will. All the New Testament writers are agreed that within this paradox is embedded a profound theological truth, namely, that the death of Christ serves as a sacrifice made unto God. More precisely, it is a sacrifice for the sins of humankind (Mt. 26:28; Rom. 8:3; 1 Pet. 3:18). The writer to the Hebrews is careful to construct a correspondence between the different aspects of Christ's sacrificial death and the different Old Testament sacrifices (Heb. 2:17; 9:12-22; 13:11). The apostle Paul calls Christ the "Passover Lamb" (1 Cor. 5:7). It is not unexpected then to find in the New Testament the numerous references to the shedding of Christ's blood, symbolic of sacrifice (e.g. Acts 20:28; Rom. 5:9; Col. 1:20; Heb. 9:22). The sacrifice of Christ is also related to an effective sacrifice of atonement that satisfied divine justice (Rom. 3:25). Herein lies the basic meaning of the word *i'lasth,rion* in this verse, "propitiation", that is, the quenching of God's wrath (Black, 1973: 68; Packer, 1974: 23; Erickson, 1998: 827).[9] In other words, Paul regards Christ's death as atoning in the sense of propitiatory, in that it appeases God's wrath against sin. Moreover, in the epistle to the Hebrews, Christ is portrayed both as the perfect sacrifice and the perfect high priest who offers the sacrifice, whose death therefore obviates the need for any further sacrifice (Heb. 9:25-28; 10:10, 12-14). In other words, there is an efficacious finality in the sacrifice of Christ.

Besides suffering and sacrifice, the New Testament writers also understand Christ's death as substitutionary in nature. This can be demonstrated through a word study of the three Greek prepositions, with the genitive, that are used in the New Testament to show the relationship between the death of Christ and sinful humanity: *peri* (e.g. Mt. 26:28; 1 Pet. 3:18); *avntiv* (e.g. Mt. 20:28; Mk. 10:45); and the most frequently used of all, especially by Paul, *u'pe,r* (e.g. Rom. 5:6, 8; 1 Cor. 15:3; 2 Cor. 5:21; Gal. 2:20; Titus 2:14; cf. Lk. 22:19, 20; Jn. 18:14; 1 Pet.

---

[8] In the two instances where the cry of Psalms 22:1 is recorded in the Gospels –
Matthew and Mark – it is noteworthy that both Gospel writers should foreground their observation that Jesus uttered his cry in Aramaic such that it created a misunderstanding among the Greek speakers present at the scene of the Crucifixion (Mt. 27:47; Mk. 15:35). Jesus' expression of grief in his mother tongue surely attests to the reality and intensity of his suffering.

[9] C. H. Dodd famously argues that *i'lasth,rion* means expiation rather than propitiation (1935: 82-95). Expiation means the deliverance from guilt or removal of sin from God's sight (Dodd, 1935: 93-94). Of course, propitiation implies expiation, but the reverse relationship is not necessary. Biblical linguists generally today agree that *i'lasth,rion* means propitiation rather than simply expiation (see, for example, Hill, 1967: 23-48 and Erickson, 1998: 827-29 for a discussion on the semantics of *i'lasth,rion*).

3:18). In Matthew 20:28 and Mark 10:45, the context makes it plain that *avnti*, is substitutionary in meaning (cf. Mt. 2:22; Luke 11:11). The proof for *u`pe,r* is far more complex and technical. In at least two passages that do not have any theological overtones relating to Christ's death, Romans 9:3 and Philemon 13, the apostle Paul uses the preposition *u`pe,r* in an unambiguously substitutionary sense.[10] In other words, while a definite case cannot be made for *peri,*, it certainly can be for the substitutionary implications inherent in the other two prepositions *avntiv* and *u`pe,r*. It is therefore right to affirm that the translated English formula "Christ died for all" and its many variants point unmistakably, although admittedly somewhat mysteriously, to the substitutionary nature of Christ's death (so Rom. 5:6, 8; 1 Cor. 8:11; 15:3; 2 Cor. 5:15; Gal. 2:20; Eph. 5:2; 1 Thess. 5:10; 1 Pet. 3:18, etc.). To put it succinctly, Christ the sinless One died *in the place of* sinful humanity.

In sum, the fundamental nature of the death of Christ can be understood in terms of suffering, sacrifice, and substitution. Although the sufferings of Christ are unjust as they are in themselves, they are accepted by God as a just means of sacrifice on behalf of all humanity.

Now then, what exactly did the Cross achieve? First and foremost, the New Testament presents the death of Christ as imbued with *redemptive* significance. It is from here that Christians derive the primary titular reference of Jesus Christ as Redeemer.[11] Indeed, Christ speaks of his own death as providing a ransom (Mt. 20:28; 26:26-29; Mk. 10:45; 14:22-25; Lk. 22:19-20). In the New Testament, we find a range of terms used to describe the redemptive nature of Christ's death: *lu,w, avpalla,ssw* ("to release", "to set free"); *avgora,zw* ("to purchase", "to redeem"); *a;fesij* ("the process of setting free or liberating"); *evleuqero,w* ("to set free"). The motif of redemption is particularly prominent in Luke and Acts (Lk. 1:68, 77; 2:25, 38; 21:28; 24:21; Acts 7:35), and is presented "in such a way as to link the concept of redemption with the prototypical act of deliverance in the Old Testament: the liberation of God's people from Egypt" (Green and Baker, 2000: 100).

Specifically, Christ's death provides deliverance from sin's power and sin's penalty of death (Rom. 6:22-23; Heb. 9:26; 1 John 1:7; Rev. 1:5). It is noteworthy that the language of redemption that Paul uses, for example, in

---

[10] See Bruce Waltke's doctoral dissertation "The Theological Significations of *vAnti*, and `*Upe,r* in the New Testament" (Dallas Theological Seminary, 1958), pp. 267-390, where he constructs an elaborately argued case that is hard to refute, namely, that the preposition *u`pe,r* used in the genitive case does not only mean "in behalf of" (i.e. in the sense of representation), but it can also mean "in the place of" (i.e. in the sense of substitution).

[11] B. B. Warfield argues that, for the Christian, there is no more intimate or precious title of Christ than "Redeemer" (1950: 325). For this reason, Warfield calls Christianity "truly a 'Redemptive Religion'" (Warfield, 1950: 347). John Baillie attributes Christ's readiness to suffer for our sake to "the *redemptive passion* that filled His heart" (1996: 113, emphasis added).

Romans 3:21-26, Ephesus 1:7, and Colossians 1:13-14, is invariably related to the forgiveness of sins. Similarly, the apostle John describes Jesus as "the Lamb of God, who takes away the sins of the world" (John 1:29). Peter, like Paul, understands Christ as sin-bearer (1 Pet. 2:24). Through Christ's work of bearing the world's sin on the cross, sin's ransom is fully paid, and the sinner is liberated from its bondage. As the apostle Paul puts it, the redeemed are "bought at a price" (1 Cor. 6:20; 7:23).

Besides forgiveness of sin, another key result of the redemptive death of Christ is reconciliation (*katallagh,*). Reconciliation presupposes a former state of hostility that is subsequently resolved by the death of Christ. Through the death of Christ, not only are estranged sinners reconciled to God (Rom. 5:10-11; 2 Cor. 5:18-20), enemies are turned into friends (Eph. 2:16). Indeed, this is the basic sense of the English word "atonement," as its syllables "at-one-ment" visually indicate. The atonement of Christ brings about the unification, or reconciliation, of God and human beings who once were at enmity with each other. No wonder Basel theologian Georg Pfleiderer could unambiguously identify the Atonement as "the essence of Christianity" (2005: 127). It is interesting to note too that the Pauline concept of reconciliation carries not only personal and social meaning, but it includes a cosmic dimension as well (Col. 1:20-22). In the bifurcated divine scheme of salvation, cosmic reconciliation falls under the realm of the "not-yet," but as the apostle Paul puts it confidently, the eschatological moment will come when "the creation itself will be liberated from its bondage to decay and brought into the glorious freedom of the children of God" (Rom. 8:21).

In sum, redemption through Christ's death brings about liberation and reconciliation. Another way to understand this is to see redemption not only as a saving deliverance *from* a state of bondage, but also, necessarily, a movement *to* a new state of being. In other words, the redeemed are stripped of their old identity and conferred with a new one (cf. 2 Cor. 5:7). In the New Testament, we find a whole range of expressions employed to describe the new identity of those who, through Christ's death, are forgiven of their sins and reconciled to God and to each other: "children of God" (Jn. 1:11), "heirs of God and co-heirs with Christ" (Rom. 8:17), "a new creation" (2 Cor. 5:17), "the righteousness of God" (2 Cor. 5:21), "dead to sin" (Rom. 6:11), "alive in Christ" (Eph. 2:5), "sons of God" (Gal. 3:26), "called to be free" (Gal. 5:13), "fellow citizens with God's people and members of God's household" (Eph. 3:19), among others. This new identity of the New Testament [*laos theou*] (1 Pet. 2:10) is not to be thought of as radically separate from that of the Old Testament [*'am ᵉlōhîm*] (2 Sam. 14:13). Rather there is a profound theological continuity between the two (cf. Lev. 26:12; Jer. 31:33; Eze. 36:24-28; Rom. 12:3; 1 Pet. 2:10).[12] Suffice to say that the true and final basis by which the people of God are constituted is the death

---

[12] See N. T. Wright, *The New Testament and the People of God* (Minneapolis, MN: Fortress Press, 1992) for an excellent and scholarly treatment on the subject.

and resurrection of Jesus Christ, foreshadowed in the Old Testament and fulfilled in the New.

Indicatives of grace must lead to imperatives of conduct. Related to the achievements of the Cross are the ethics that necessarily flow from them. In other words, the new identity that is derived from appropriating the death of Christ must issue itself in a particular lifestyle. The New Testament writers teach this truth by first projecting a continuity with the Old Testament. They present the death of Christ as bringing about a new covenantal arrangement (Heb. 9:15). The curse of the law is broken (Gal. 3:13), and sins committed under "the first covenant" thereby forgiven (Heb. 9:15). Through Christ's death, God called a people out of darkness into light and reconstituted them as "a chosen people, a royal priesthood, a holy nation, a people belonging to God," whose proper response to God's mercy is to declare his praises to the world and to live "good lives among the pagans" (1 Pet. 2:9-12). Similarly, Paul teaches the Corinthians that they have not only been saved and set free from sin, but also that now they belong to the Lord and are therefore to walk in the newness of life characterized by freedom to love and serve him (1 Cor. 6:20; 7:23). In other words, a moral obligation awaits God's people who are made righteous as a result of Christ's death (2 Cor. 5:21): they are expected "to live for righteousness" (1 Pet. 2:24). The ethical demands placed on those who benefit from Christ's death are inescapable.

It is noteworthy that, in his first epistle, the apostle Peter elaborates at length Christian ethics in relation to suffering. He emphasizes the exemplary character of Christ's innocent sufferings, and based on this goes on to describe what he sees as model Christian conduct, one that is marked by non-violence and undeserved suffering (1 Pet. 2:21-25; 4:12-19). Of course, Peter's exhortation is not to be taken as simply a moralistic piece of advice, for it is predicated on his understanding of the efficacy of Christ's sacrificial death in restoring the sinner's fellowship with God (1 Pet. 1:2, 18-19; 3:19). The point is that the death of Christ places ethical obligations on the believer to live in a way consistent with the suffering example of Christ. In fact, both Paul and Peter would even go so far as to say that the calling of a Christian consists of suffering (Phil. 1:29; 1 Pet. 4:12-19).

The relationship between the Cross and suffering is not a new one. In the Synoptic Gospels, we see Christ himself teaching his disciples to deny themselves and take up their cross as they follow him (Mt. 16:24; Mk. 8:34; Lk. 9:23). The cross of Christ becomes paradigmatic of the cross that all his disciples are called to bear. Eugene Peterson makes this insightful comment on Mark 8:34:

> Two verbs leap from the sentence and pounce on us: deny yourself and take up your cross. Renunciation and death. It feels like an assault, an attack. We recoil.
>
> But then we notice that these two negatives are bracketed by the positive verb, "follow," first as an infinitive, then as an imperative. "If anyone wants to follow

(*akolouthein*)" opens the sentence; "you follow me (*akoloutheitō*)" concludes it. Jesus is going someplace; he invites us to come along. There is no hostility in that. It sounds, in fact, quite glorious. So glorious, in fact, that the great verb "follow" sheds glory on the negative verbs that call for renunciation and death. (2005: 196)

The point is clear. The element of suffering is always present in salvation. Whether it is imposed from without (2 Tim. 3:12), or whether it is a call to self-mortification from above (Col. 3:5), suffering is inevitable when one seeks to follow Christ. Not only is Christian salvation cruciform in shape; so is Christian discipleship.

Before we leave this section, a final word needs to be said on the resurrection of Christ. The New Testament writers are unified in their witness that death did not have the last word in the gospel story, for Christ rose from the dead on the third day. The New Testament takes pains to defend the Resurrection as a physical and historical reality, not a spiritual and mystical interpretation of a purported event that did not actually take place (e.g. Acts 2:24-32; 1 Cor. 15:3-8). Stott rightly points out that the significance of the Resurrection is determined by the nature of Christ's death (1986: 35). As it turns out, the Resurrection brought about "the divine reversal of the human verdict" (Stott, 1986: 35). However, this is not all.

Promoting him [Christ] to the place of supreme honor at his right hand, in fulfilment of Psalm 110:1 and on account of the achievement of his death, God made the crucified and risen Jesus 'both Lord and Christ', both 'Prince and Savior', with authority to save sinners by bestowing upon them repentance, forgiveness and the gift of the Spirit. Moreover, this comprehensive salvation is specifically said to be due to his powerful 'Name' (the sum total of his person, death and resurrection), in which people must believe and into which they must be baptized, since there is 'no other name under heaven given to men' by which they must be saved. (Stott, 1986: 35)

In sum, the resurrection of Christ is an important and integral part of the salvation story complementing the death of Christ, even though, as in the nature of the case, the Resurrection cannot stand on its own apart from the Cross.[13]

We have presented a sketch of the biblical record on the Cross by looking at some of the key motifs used by the New Testament writers to help their readers understand the meaning of Christ's death. In the next section, we shall look at some of the major theories of the Atonement in classical Western theology. These theories seek to answer the question of how the death of Christ could actually bring about redemption and salvation for sinful humanity.

---

[13] The converse is, of course, true. Without the Resurrection, the Cross becomes drained of its true meaning and significance (so 1 Cor. 15:1-28).

The Cross in Western Theological Tradition

Given what Kevin Vanhoozer aptly refers to as the "messiness of multiple metaphors" in the New Testament record on the death of Christ (2004 ;401), one can only expect that any discussion on the Atonement would be fraught with all sorts of theological difficulties. Western theology has traditionally understood the death of Christ in terms of what is known as the theories of the Atonement. Each theory claims to represent and interpret the biblical record on the subject best.[14] In his classic lecture, "What did the Cross Achieve? The Logic of Penal Substitution",[15] J. I. Packer classifies traditional Atonement theories into three types, according to how each views the nature of God and humanity's problem of sin, and the death of Christ as an effective means "to bring us to God in fellowship of acceptance on his side and faith and love on ours" (1974: 19).[16]

The first set of theories is known as "subjective" or "exemplar" theories. Proponents of these theories see the Cross

> as having its effect entirely on men, whether by revealing God's love to us, or by bringing home to us how much God hates our sins, or by setting us a supreme example of godliness, or by blazing a trail to God which we may now follow, or by so involving mankind in her redemptive obedience that the life of God now flows into us, or by all these modes together. (Packer, 1974: 19)

In a word, the redemptive power of the death of Christ is located completely in its subjective influence on human minds. So inspiring is Christ's death that the sinner is moved to respond in love and obedience. Although the most well-known of the subjective Atonement theories is in all probability the moral influence theory of Peter Abelard (1079-1142), Frank James III is right in his observation that it is only after the Enlightenment that these theories started gaining wide acceptance. The reason is that exemplar theories "comport well

---

[14] There are innumerable theological resources on Atonement theories. For good, in-depth discussion on the subject, see Colin Gunton, *The Actuality of the Atonement* (Edinburgh: T & T Clark, 1988); Paul Fiddes, *Past Event and Present Salvation* (Oxford: Oxford University Press, 1989); Hans Boersma, *Violence, Hospitality, and the Cross* (Grand Rapids, MI: Baker, 2004); Mark Baker, ed., *Proclaiming the Scandal of the Cross* (Grand Rapids, MI: Baker, 2006); James Beilby and Paul Eddy, eds., *The Nature of the Atonement: Four Views* (Downers Grove, IL: InterVarsity Press, 2006). In recent years, there is a revival in the study of the Atonement, with an increasing number of scholars, Protestant and Catholic, calling for a critical review of the traditional understandings of the Atonement (e.g. Winter, 1995; Dunn, 1998; Green and Baker, 2000; Bartlett, 2001; Weaver, 2001; Finlan, 2005; McKnight, 2005; and Schmiechen, 2005).

[15] Delivered at Tyndale House, Cambridge, on July 17, 1973.

[16] Since the publication of his Tyndale lecture, Packer's three-set classification has been used by evangelical theologians as a standard paradigm for understanding traditional Atonement theories. See, for example, James (2004); Boersma (2004); and Dever (2006).

with Enlightenment views of Christ as a mere human, although an extraordinary human" (James, 2004: 212).

The second type of Atonement account consists of "objective" theories that present the death of Christ "as having its effect primarily on hostile spiritual forces external to us which are held to be imprisoning us in a captivity of which our inveterate moral twistedness is one sign and symptom" (Packer, 1974: 20). The human predicament is interpreted as being held in bondage to Satan and his demonic hosts, and the Cross as the locus of God's cosmic war with the devil and his minions. Through his death and resurrection, however, Christ won a decisive victory over the forces of darkness, securing the release of human beings from their spiritual captors. The dramatic *Christus Victor* theories of the Atonement were particularly dominant among the early Church Fathers. A common variant of this Atonement account is the ransom theory. In this view, Christ offered himself as a ransom for the release of sinful humans from their bondage to Satan. The devil, however, did not realize that he could never hold the sinless Christ hostage. Consequently, Satan and all his demonic hosts were completely overpowered by the conquering Christ through the historic events of the Cross and the Resurrection.[17]

The third set of Atonement theories is also "objective" as such, but the focus is on the principle of "satisfaction" rather than on the image of the conquering Christ or the idea of ransom, although the former does not necessarily exclude the latter two. Anselm of Canterbury was undoubtedly the first to articulate a full-orbed satisfaction theory in his *Cur Deus Homo* (1098). The key thought in satisfaction theories is that by willfully sinning against God, human beings merit the righteous wrath of God that leads to eternal punishment. The sinless Christ, however, bore the punishment for human sin by offering himself to God on behalf of humanity. In so doing, the God-man did what humans should have done to appease God but did not have the ability to. The death of Christ became the perfect sacrifice that placated God's wrath and satisfied his righteousness. The penal substitution model of the Atonement emerged during the Protestant Reformation as a refinement of Anselm's satisfaction theory, and stresses that Christ vicariously bore the penalty of the sin of human beings as both their representative and substitute.[18] This view is held by most evangelicals today, and is rigorously defended by leading evangelical lights such as J. I. Packer, John Stott and Leon Morris.[19]

---

[17] For further discussion, see Gustaf Aulén, *Christus Victor* (London: SPCK, 1931).

[18] See Calvin's *Institutes* II, xvi, 1-7. Calvin writes, "[Christ] *in every respect took our place* to pay the price of our redemption. Death held us captive under its yoke; Christ, *in our stead*, gave himself over to its power to deliver us from it (*Institutes* II, xvi, 7, in Calvin, 1960: 511, emphasis added).

[19] Leon Morris, who passed away in July 2006 in Melbourne, Australia at the age of ninety-two, is remembered for his classic works on the Atonement such as *The Apostolic Preaching of the Cross* (1955); *The Cross in the New Testament* (1965); and *The Atonement: Its Meaning and Significance* (1983).

These three sets of Atonement theories are well established in Western systematic theology. It is clear that no one theory will ever do sufficient justice to the ineffable mystery of the Cross. For this reason, Mark Dever rightly refers to the Cross as a "many-splendored atonement" (2006: 32). Instead of pitting these theories one against the other, as one may be inclined to do, each of these theories should be seen as contributing to the understanding of a particular aspect of the Atonement. After all, the divine mystery of the Atonement will always be larger than the sum of all human theories that can be constructed to explain it.

In a sense then, the three sets of Atonement theories, even when taken together, do not contain all that there is to say about the Cross. In fact, in recent years, some scholars are calling attention to the Western cultural bias inherent in these theories. Green and Baker, in their book which has ruffled more than a few evangelical feathers, issue a call for our awareness to be raised "to the possibility, even probability, that our theological commitments with regard to Atonement theology do not simply speak to our culture, *but actually grow out of it*" (2000: 28, emphasis added). Green and Baker undoubtedly are driven by a missiological motivation, and are concerned that the significance of the Cross be articulated in a "living" (vis-à-vis "frozen") way to the contemporary contexts that we find ourselves in (Green and Baker, 2000: 214). In a similar vein, C. Norman Kraus argues that satisfaction theories of the Atonement are difficult to apprehend in cultures whose moral traditions are characterized by shame and social sanctions because the idea of vicarious suffering in these theories is derived from external – in this instance, Roman – categories of guilt and legal penalty (1990: 205-17). Using the terminology of Green and Baker, Kraus suggests that satisfaction theories do not constitute a "living" tradition for these cultures. Rather, in these contexts, he believes that it is more profitable to explain sin as shame, and to present the Cross as "the epitome of [Christ's] identification with us in shame" (Kraus, 1990: 217).

Roman Catholic theologian Elizabeth Johnson suggests that recent scholarship in theology, history and anthropology indicates that Christ's death

> was not something he sought or intended in a masochistic desire for victim status, but rather a consequence of the kind of ministry he freely practiced. In other words, he did not "come to die" [...] *However, historically he did so not as a preordained act of vicarious satisfaction but as part of his free, larger commitment to the flourishing of life in solidarity with others.* (1994: 14, emphasis added)

This "contingent historical" understanding of the Cross, as Johnson calls it, "discloses the hope that God intends to put an end to all the crosses of history (Johnson, 1994: 15). She elaborates:

> [A contingent historical] soteriology shifts from the model of God as perpetrator of the disaster of the cross to the model of God as participant in the pain of the world. In Jesus the Holy One enters into solidarity with suffering people in order to release

hope and bring new life. This construal brings us far from the satisfaction theory and correlative doctrines of the atonement. The cross remains, but its symbolic nexus changes. It stands in history as a life-affirming protest against all torture and injustice, and as a pledge that the transforming power of God is with those who suffer to bring about life for others.

Several comments are in order here. It is helpful to bear in mind that the different views of the Atonement are not mutually exclusive, for the inadequacies of each perspective are compensated by the strengths of others, and vice-versa. Second, every theory of the Atonement ultimately needs to be judged by how faithful it represents biblical revelation, and this task of theological validation is one that the whole Church needs to engage in. Third, while evangelicals may feel that Green and Baker, Kraus and Johnson, are sacrificing theological adequacy at the altar of missiological expediency, they cannot dismiss summarily the genuine contextual concerns these writers are trying to raise. Evangelicals, in the name of biblical fidelity, have for too long been insensitive to socio-cultural and political realities.

From a missiological standpoint, however, instead of crafting what the expatriate missionary or theologian believes to be a contextually relevant theology of the Atonement and introducing it to a community – especially one where there is already a viable church – would it not be better to encourage local Christians to develop a biblical understanding of the Cross for themselves? For otherwise, what began as a missiological introduction often becomes theological imposition. With the southward shift of global Christianity, the time has certainly come for the global Church to listen to non-Western Christians as they articulate their understanding of the Cross from the Bible.[20]

A note needs to be made that the traditional models of the Atonement as we have set out above, useful as they are for their own purposes, will not be imposed eisegetically onto the writings of the Japanese scholars we are studying. As we interpret how these scholars understand the death of Christ, we are mindful to let them speak on their own terms through their own theological categories. Their perspectives can surely complement and enhance the global Church's theological understanding of the Cross.

In the final section of this chapter, we shall discuss the meaning of contextualization, and examine its importance for doing theology in a globalizing world. A good understanding of the whys and wherefores of

---

[20] Constructing a contextually-relevant Atonement theory, of course, begs the crucial, but extremely tricky, question as to how normative the various biblical symbols and metaphors associated with the Cross for Christians are in different cultural settings. While there is a missiological imperative to utilize and highlight those symbols which bear special affinity within a local context, there may be theological and ecclesiological obligations for local Christians to strive toward appropriating all the various biblical perspectives as best as they can within their cultural framework.

contextualization will go a long way in helping us appreciate the need for doing theology in a cross-cultural mode.

Contextualization: The Whys and Wherefores

In its simplest terms, contextualization is the cross-cultural communication of the gospel and the application of the timeless truths of Scripture to specific contemporary contexts. From its earliest days, the Christian Church found itself embroiled in the tricky task of relating the gospel to culture as it communicated the Good News across language and cultural boundaries. [21] In today's increasingly globalizing and pluralizing world, it is not surprising that contextualization has become one of the most pressing concerns in mission. Indeed, given the very missionary nature of the Christian faith, the task of "contextualizing" the gospel is all but a necessary one.

The term "contextualization" is a relatively new one, having made its debut in the 1972 report of the Theological Education Fund (TEF) of the World Council of Churches.[22] The issues associated with the idea, however, are not new. Until the TEF report, the relationship between the mission agency and the local church plant was understood in terms of what is known as the "indigenization model." This model grew out of the so-called "Three-Selfs" principle,[23] a formula generally associated with three men: Rufus Anderson (1796-1880), Henry Venn (1796-1873), and John Nevius (1829-93). For more than a century, indigenization was the received approach to mission. Ironically, the weakness of the model is that insufficient attention was paid to the influence of culture on the gospel. The new emphasis on contextualization, while highlighting the cultural factor, seeks to go beyond it by taking into account "the process of secularity, technology, and the struggle for human justice, which characterize the historical moment of nations in the Third World" (TEF, 1972: 20).

According to the late TEF director Hwang Chong-Hui, better known as Shoki Coe, "contextualization" carries within it the notion of dynamic interaction with the diverse living contexts in which churches are founded, and is therefore to be preferred over the static, past-oriented character of "indigenization" (1976: 20-21). The "signs of the times" made it clear that it was not enough merely to elicit a passive response to the gospel, even if the response was made in terms of

---

[21] Andrew Walls provides an excellent treatment on the relationship between gospel and culture in the form of a historical capsule in "The Gospel as Prisoner and Liberator of Culture" (1996: 3-15). See also Dean Flemming's outstanding work on contextualization in the New Testament (2005).

[22] The title of the report is *Ministry in Context: The Third Mandate Programme of the Theological Education Fund (1970-77)*.

[23] The "Three-Selfs" principle provided the yardstick by which a missionary church plant was judged to have become an indigenous church: when it became self-supporting, self-governing, and self-propagating. The element of culture might have been implicit, but it was almost as good as absent.

the traditional culture. There was an increasing expectation that the gospel, when *truly* contextualized (that is, not merely indigenized), would bring about genuine and liberating changes and usher in a future of hope (Coe, 1973: 241-42).

It was also felt that despite the well-intentioned aims of the indigenization model, the old structures of Christendom still inherent in the modern missionary movement prevented the translation into practice of the "Three-Selfs" principle. As long as the status quo was maintained, the aspirations of the new, younger churches would never be met. It is a sad fact that even under the indigenization model, cultural resources which might have been utilized in evangelism and church planting were more often than not deployed and managed by the "enlightened" Western missionary. In the words of Wilbert Shenk, "the script [continued to be] provided from outside" (1999: 53).

However, the post-war reality of the worldwide growth of the non-Western church that increasingly demanded freedom from foreign cultural forms and control, and asserted the need for cultural diversity in theological reflection, could no longer be denied (Shenk, 1999: 56). At the same time, there was also the steady input of valuable anthropological insights into missiology through the work of top-notch missionary-scholars such as Kenneth Pike, Alan Tippet, Paul Hiebert, and Charles Kraft, among others, which contributed to the church's decisive abandonment of the notion of Western cultural supremacy. Even in evangelical circles, the missiological paradigm of the "Three-Selfs" was re-appropriated, but with a renewed focus on the socio-cultural context and a new awareness of the very real issue of power and the often-unwarranted foreign influence it wields on the context.

It should be clear by now that even though contextualization has today become a firmly entrenched missiological concept, the use of the term cannot be assumed to be uniform in all instances. Charles Kraft, for instance, treats "indigenization" and "contextualization" as synonymous (2005: xxiv-xxv; see also Kraft and Wisley, 1979). The Roman Catholic anthropologist, Aylward Shorter, on the other hand, prefers the word "inculturation" (Shorter, 1988).[24]

Shenk helpfully defines contextualization as

> a process whereby the gospel message encounters a particular culture, calling forth faith and leading to the formation of a faith community, which is *culturally authentic* and *authentically Christian. Control of the process resides within the context rather than with an external agent or agency.* (1999: 56, emphasis added)

---

[24] The same problem of terminology is found in Japanese as well. Apparently, the theologians at International Christian University (in Tokyo) use the phrase *bunmyakuka* 文脈化 to translate "contextualization" (e.g. Morimoto, 2004: 4), while those at Tokyo Christian University – and many Japanese evangelicals – use *bunkamyakuka* 文化脈化. This latter term, however, is more accurately translated as "inculturation."

Three observations can be derived from this definition. First, for Christianity to engage people effectively at the level of their deepest needs, it needs to be *culturally authentic*. The false notion in many parts of the non-Western world that Christianity is a white man's religion that has nothing to do with local, existential concerns must be rigorously combated. Second, a contextualized faith has to remain *authentically Christian*. As Paul Hiebert, the great anthropologist and mission theologian, so rightly warns us, an uncritical approach to contextualization can often lead to a syncretized faith in which biblical revelation dissolves without a single trace (1994: 84-85). Third, the control of the contextualization process must originate from within the context, not imposed from without.

In missionary practice, one can identify two essential questions that this particular definition raises: the first dealing with the actual propagation of the gospel, and the second with the reception and cultural shaping of the gospel message. The two questions can be phrased in this way:

1. How should the gospel be preached to a people in a way that is culturally intelligible to them, yet without compromising its biblical integrity?
2. How should a people who receive the gospel shape their theological understanding of divine revelation in a way that does not eliminate their cultural identity, but rather fulfills their cultural aspirations?

There are, of course, a whole host of related sub-questions, such as the way in which the gospel transforms culture, moral-ethical issues involved in contextualization, the meaning of Christian identity, and the problem of a culture's non-Christian past. These concerns are all variations of the same missiological themes of how to present the biblical message in way such that people can truly encounter Christ, and of how people respond to him in faith and obedience within their local cultural frame of reference. In sum, contextualization is to be understood as comprising two components: the *transmission* of biblical faith, and the *appropriation* of that faith by its recipients.[25] Stephen Bevans, in his valuable work, *Models of Contextual Theology* (2002), proposes six models to help us understand the contextualization process by showing how the Christian faith has been concretely transmitted and appropriated in various cultural contexts.[26]

---

[25] Indeed, Andrew Walls' central thesis in all his works is that the cross-cultural diffusion of Christianity in history must be understood not only in terms of its transmission, but also in the way it is received. Note the subtitle of his 2002 book, *The Cross-Cultural Process in Christian History: Studies in the Transmission and Appropriation of Faith* (Maryknoll, NY: Orbis, 2002).

[26] The six models are the translation model, the anthropological model, the praxis model, the synthetic model, the transcendental model, and the countercultural model. It is to be noted that while each model is distinct, they are not mutually exclusive. In practice, the use of one model may include several aspects of one or more of the other models (Bevans, 2002: 32).

David Bosch rightly points out that missionaries do not simply "take Christ" to other people and cultures, but they are "also to allow the faith the chance to start a history of its own in each people and its experience of Christ" (1991: 454). In other words, the gospel has to *incarnate* the very life of Christ in the culture where its seed is planted. In this respect, it is easy to see that the older model of indigenization has by and large concentrated on the cross-cultural transmission of faith, but neglected the incarnational appropriation of faith. Hiebert asks bluntly, "Do young churches have the right to read and interpret the Scriptures for themselves?" (1985: 196). By the rhetorical question, Hiebert is in effect saying that for the Christian faith to be authentically and incarnationally appropriated, local church leaders must be encouraged to study the Word of God *for themselves*, and apply it to their own historical and socio-cultural contexts. In other words, contextualization is more than just the creation of ecclesial structures which are self-governing, self-propagating and self-supporting, important as these are. Here, Hiebert helpfully provides the missing piece in the appropriation part of the contextualization equation by suggesting a "fourth self," that of *self-theologizing* (Hiebert, 1994: 46).

Indeed, it is this fourth self that provides the means through which the reality of the kingdom of God can be demonstrated in a particular context, by facilitating reflective and conscientious action that addresses social and cultural evils, and seeks to alleviate suffering. Self-theologizing as such will bring about not only the contextualization of Christianity, but also crucially, the Christianization of culture and society (cf. Bosch, 1991: 454).

The point is obvious – yet one that must not be taken for granted – that self-theologizing is best done in the vernacular by people who are subjects and agents of the culture. The outsider, whether a trained theologian or missionary, can, of course, provide a helpful extra-contextual perspective, but finally it is the people who must themselves own the results of their theologizing (Hiebert, 1994: 88-90). The importance of the vernacular in the theological process can never be overestimated, for it is the local tongue that provides the indigenous categories needed to facilitate a genuine and lasting dialogue between gospel and culture (Sanneh, 1989). Theologizing begins, when, as in that first Pentecost, people exclaim with amazement in Acts 2:11, "How is it that we hear in our own languages the wonders of God?" (Bediako, 1995: 59-74).

A biblical approach to contextualization must always take into consideration the ever-lurking dangers of syncretism and provincialism. The first danger is obvious enough, especially to evangelicals, whose fears of a cultural theology that can no longer be recognized as biblical are only too well known. The threat of provincialism is less obvious, but no less real. The universal Body of Christ is not built up if a local church develops a theology that serves no one else except herself. One must bear constantly in mind that which Walls calls the "indigenizing principle" and the "pilgrim principle" (1996: 7-9). The former refers to "the desire to 'indigenize,' to live as a Christian and yet as a member of one's own society" (Walls, 1996: 7), while the latter to the reality that the

Christian "has no abiding city and [...] that to be faithful to Christ will put him out of step with his society" (Walls, 1996: 8).

In other words, authentic theological contextualizing must contribute to the larger task of global theologizing (Ott and Netland, 2006). In a fast-shrinking world, yet one that is increasingly fractured along ethnic and cultural fault lines, the witness to the unity of the church has never been more urgent. The theological activities of the global Church are not exempt from the responsibility to bear such witness. In this regard, contextualized theologies, insofar as they do not explicitly compromise biblical integrity, are to be regarded as complementary, not contradictory and, together, they serve to challenge the whole church in its self-understanding. At the same time, the Church serves as an international hermeneutical community to which all contextualized theologies are to be subject and accountable. On this point, Bosch suggests that what the Church needs today is not just inculturation, but "*inter*culturation" – an "exchange of theologies" (1991: 456). While evangelicals need to guard their theological distinctives, they need to be open to what others are saying, critiquing and allowing themselves to be critiqued.

The case for the contextualization of the Christian faith in Japan can never be overstated. Indeed, unless Christianity sinks its roots deeply into Japanese soil, it will continue to be wrongly perceived as a foreign religion with little to offer a people who have their own rich cultural and religious heritage. In this respect, there are two pertinent challenges facing missiological scholarship and missionary practice. First, there is the constant need to look for ways to present the gospel that clear it of as much cultural foreignness as possible, so that Japanese people can understand it within their own phenomenological frame of reference. The second challenge is less obvious, but no less important. Theologians and practitioners need to learn from Japanese Christians how they themselves receive and internalize the truths of the gospel. One of the best ways to do this is to study, in the Japanese vernacular, the original theological writings of key Japanese Christians. This is what this work seeks to do, by examining three Japanese perspectives on the death of Christ.

3. The Historical and Theological Contexts of Japanese Christianity

Before we embark on the discussion of central themes, it is imperative that we take a sustained look at the historical and theological backgrounds of Christianity in Japan. This is what this chapter proposes to do. After the historical and theological presentations, a biographical introduction is provided of the three subjects of our study: Kitamori Kazō, Endō Shūsaku, and Koyama Kōsuke, followed by a summary literature survey of some key works on these thinkers and their writings.

History of Christianity in Japan

The history of Christianity in Japan is tied up in a large part with the history of Christian missions in Japan. Much of this section is thus focused on Japanese mission history. There are three distinct periods of missionary activity in Japan. The first was begun by Francis Xavier (1506-1552) and the Jesuit missionaries in 1549, and it was purely a movement of the Roman Catholic Church. The second wave of missionary arrivals occurred in the second half of the nineteenth century following the reopening of Japan to the West after more than two hundred years of self-imposed national isolation. The third period of missionary activity began in the aftermath of the Second World War. The second and third periods of missionary activity were predominantly Protestant, although Catholic and, to a much smaller extent, Russian Orthodox missionaries also participated in spreading the gospel in the country.

Christianity in Pre-modern Japan (1549-1639)

The Jesuit mission engendered Japan's very first encounter with Christianity.[1] It was a most dramatic encounter. By the time serious persecution broke out in

---

[1] Some have suggested that the Nestorians' presence in Japan predated that of the Jesuits by at least 300 years, but the evidence for that is ambiguous at best. It is true that Nestorian relics are found in Japan, but these were unearthed from the tomb of the envoys from Kublai Khan who were executed in 1280 (see Saeki, 1951: 444-47) as well as from the tomb of five men captured and executed during the failed Mongolian

1614 under the Tokugawa shogun Ieyasu – less than seventy years after the launch of the Christian mission by Xavier – there were no fewer than 300,000 baptized Christians in the country.[2] Nagasaki, the principal city on the southern island of Kyushu at that time, became so predominantly Christian that Luis Cerqueira, the second bishop of Japan, proudly referred to it as "the Rome of the Far East" (cited in Fujita, 1991: 9). Christian growth spread northwards along the populated coastal regions, both east and west, right up to the southern edge of what is today's Aomori prefecture. Historian C. R. Boxer was so impressed with the phenomenal growth of the church between the 1550s and 1630s that he coined the phrase "the Christian Century in Japan" for the title for his seminal work on the Jesuit mission to Japan (1967).[3] Equally awed by the Jesuits' achievements is Andrew Ross who hails the Society of Jesus as "the creative force in the growth of the Japanese Church" (1994: 87).

Ross attributes the phenomenal growth of a thriving indigenous Japanese church under the Jesuits to the culturally-sensitive philosophy of mission of the Italian Jesuit Father Alessandro Valignano, Papal Visitor to the East (1994: 88). Valignano developed a missionary theory and practice based on ideas which today we would call inculturation or contextualization. Yet, in spite of the spectacular growth of the church, Tokugawa Ieyasu's edict to expel all missionaries from the country in 1614 resulted in the church being ignobly persecuted, and within less than a hundred years, it was all but eliminated.

There are many reasons for the virtual disappearance of the church. To begin, the Jesuit mission took place in one of the most politically turbulent eras in Japanese history (see Fujita, 1991: 3-10). The first Jesuits arrived in Japan without the slightest inkling that the country was embroiled in a devastating civil war. Although the emperor was still reigning on his throne, he did not actually rule. Rather he found himself under virtual house arrest, while rival warlords fought for territorial supremacy. During the hundred years or so of Jesuit presence in Japan, political and military power changed hands, rather violently, first to Oda Nobunaga who was sympathetic toward the Christian cause, then to the temperamentally unpredictable Toyotomi Hideyoshi, and finally to the

---

invasion in 1281 (see Natori, 1957: 12-16). Nestorian missionary presence in Japan is plausible but improbable (Mullins, 2006: 116).

[2] Exact figures are notoriously difficult to establish. C. R. Boxer, relying on the 1605 report of the missionary Fernão Guerreiro, believes that by the turn of the seventeenth century there was already "a Christian community of about 750,000 believers, with an annual increase of five or six thousand" (1967: 197). Mark Mullins suggests that the ratio of Christians to non-Christians at that time was "probably several times higher than what it is today" (1998a: 12). The population of Japan then was somewhere between 15 and 20 million.

[3] It must be said that a good number of *daimyō* (samurai warlords) converted to Christianity, with the consequence that all the subjects in their fief also converted. Among the better known Christian *daimyō* are Ōmura Sumitada, Ōtomo Shūrin, Takayama Ukon, and Konishi Yukinaga.

staunch Buddhist shogun Tokugawa Ieyasu under whose rule the fate of the church was sealed.[4] Therefore, even though church growth exploded especially in the first half-century, it could never quite sustain itself through the entire course under these volatile socio-political circumstances.

The other reason for the collapse of the church, in all probability, has to do with the lack of free availability of the Bible in the Japanese vernacular. The earliest translations of the Bible were problematic because of the uncritical use of Buddhist terms for Christian concepts such as God and heaven, to the effect that many Japanese mistook Christianity for a new Buddhist sect. Some improved translations were later made of the Gospels for public ministry, but these were all virtually destroyed in the fire on the island of Takushima in 1563. Ironically, the loss of these materials coincided with the closing year of the Council of Trent in Europe. The Tridentine decrees which stipulated Latin to be the language of the Mass, and the Latin Vulgate as the only authoritative Scripture for public reading and doctrinal expositions, gave no encouragement whatsoever to anyone attempting to translate the Bible into Japanese.[5] Consequently, when the missionaries were expelled from the country, Roman Catholicism would suffer a catastrophic blow simply because the church did not have a good, standardized Japanese translation of the complete Bible to nurture the faith of subsequent believers.[6] The Jesuit mission ended dramatically in 1637 with the Tokugawa leaders declaring Christianity an "evil teaching" (*jakyō* 邪教), and effecting a total ban on it upon threat of a cruel death. It is estimated that altogether about five to six

---

[4] The decisive victory of Ieyasu in the one-day Battle of Sekigahara on October 21, 1600 ushered in the Tokugawa shogunate that would rule Japan until November 1867 when political rule reverted to the emperor. The Tokugawa period was also known as the Edo period because the shoguns relocated the seat of government from Kyoto to Edo (today's Tokyo). The imperial family, however, remained in Kyoto throughout the Tokugawa period.

[5] Some manuscript fragments of different Scripture texts in Japanese have indeed been found, but there is little evidence to suggest that these translated texts were widely circulated. Moreover, many were informal translations into which Buddhist terms were incorporated. See Kaiser (1996: 8-29) for an interesting discussion on the indelible influence of Buddhism and Buddhist terminology on these various translations. Apparently, the Jesuits did produce the "Newe Testament printed in the Japan Language" before 1613, according to a diary entry of the Englishman John Saris who spent two years in Japan (cited in Ebisawa, 1982: 80). However, no copy is extant. Bernardin Schneider offers this assessment, "In view of the general conditions of the time and the negative evidence of the contemporary literature, it seems very unlikely that this could have been a complete New Testament, including especially the writings of St. Paul and the Apocalypse" (2003: 206).

[6] In contrast, the Chinese church of the twentieth century grew phenomenally despite the communists' expulsion of all missionaries from the country in 1949 and the ensuing persecution of the church. This was due, in good part, to the existence of the Union Bible, a good and established translation of the whole Bible in the Chinese script that enjoyed wide circulation since its publication in 1909.

thousand European and Japanese Christians were martyred for their faith (Varley, 1984: 148). The persecutions finally drove the church underground.

The final straw for the Tokugawa regime came in the form of the Shimabara Rebellion, which the government (mis)interpreted as a revolt fueled by Christian militants. In desperation against the economic exploitation by the local feudal lords, the farmers of Shimabara and the adjoining Amakusa Peninsula in northwestern Kyushu rose up in rebellion in December 1637. Among these farmers were a number of Christian *rōnin* 浪人 (vagabond samurai) who had settled quietly in the region as a result of the ongoing persecutions. After a three-month holdout against the Tokugawa forces, the revolt ended with the slaughter of no less than 27,000 peasants. Although the revolt was more economically than religiously motivated, the Tokugawa shogun Iemitsu interpreted it as "an open attempt by the Christians to take over the country" (Fujita, 1991: 186).[7] The following year, 1639, the shogun enforced a stringent policy of national seclusion (*sakoku* 鎖国), allowing only a small number of Protestant Dutch traders to live and trade in Dejima, a small landfill at the head of Nagasaki Bay, under extremely restrictive conditions. Fiercely persecuted and completely cut off from the Christian West, the number of Japanese Christians dwindled rapidly.[8] Japan's doors would be closed to the West for two hundred years.[9]

Christianity in Modern Japan (1859-1945)

The crucial event that precipitated the end of Japan's national isolation was the ominous appearance of Commodore Matthew Perry and his four heavily-armed "black ships" at the mouth of Edo Bay one summer day in 1853.[10] Perry brought

---

[7] For a detailed account and analysis of the Shimabara Rebellion, see Andrew Ross, *A Vision Betrayed: The Jesuits in Japan and China, 1542-1742* (Maryknoll, NY: Orbis, 1994), pp. 101-104.

[8] The Jesuits organized two attempts to penetrate the closed country, in 1642 and 1643. Both ended in tragedy: the captured priests either apostatized under torture, or were martyred. The last missionary to enter Japan during this period of national isolation was the Sicilian priest Giovanni Battista Sidotti in 1708. He was arrested immediately – undoubtedly due to his Western face – and died in prison six years later. However, Battista was not tortured, a sign that overt persecutions had already ended by the turn of the eighteenth century.

[9] Contrary to what is popularly believed in the West, Japan's self-imposed exclusion did not result in complete isolation from the rest of the world. It was aimed at segregating Japan from the West. Apart from the handful of Dutch traders, Japan allowed a good number of Chinese traders to remain in Nagasaki.

[10] The bay was renamed Tokyo Bay shortly later. Perry's black-hulled steam frigate anchored at the port of Uraga in Yokosuka. Yokosuka is today home of the US Seventh Naval Fleet, including the forward-deployed USS Kitty Hawk. It is interesting to note that former primer minister of Japan Koizumi Jun'ichirō was born and raised in Yokosuka. This may explain in part his extremely positive impressions of America and American culture.

with him a letter from American President Millard Fillmore seeking diplomatic and commercial relations.[11] The sudden visit and request precipitated a prolonged political crisis within the Tokugawa government which by this time was already in an advanced state of decline. The crisis resulted in the reluctant reopening of the country's doors to the world the ensuing year through the signing of the unequal Treaty of Peace and Amity between the United States and Japan on March 31, 1854.[12] The samurai families who were unhappy with the poor handling of what they perceived to be American gunboat diplomacy decided to establish a new government centered on imperial rule. The internal tensions built to a climax in 1863, and a four-year civil war broke out between the supporters of the Tokugawa shogunate and supporters of the imperial family. The war ended with the unconditional surrender of all political power by Yoshinobu, the last Tokugawa shogun, to the emperor in November 1867, in a watershed event known as the Meiji Restoration.[13] The fifteen-year-old emperor

---

[11] It would be a mistake to think that Perry's was the first and only foreign naval expedition to visit Japan during her years of isolation. For half a century leading up to Perry's visit, the Tokugawa government was already feeling mounting pressure to end her policy of national seclusion. From 1797 to 1809, the Dutch hired American ships to trade in Nagasaki because their own vessels were engaged in the conflict against Britain during the Napoleonic Wars. With the advent of steam navigation at the turn of the nineteenth century, Western commercial interests in the Pacific began to grow further. Around the same time, rich whaling grounds were discovered off Japan's coasts, attracting many whalers in search of oil resources. A series of maritime attempts were made by the Russians to open up trade relations with Japan, including the 1804 expedition led by Nicolai Petrovich Rezanov in 1804; however, all were unsuccessful. In 1844, King William II of Holland sent a letter to the Tokugawa shogun warning him of the folly of continuing the policy of national isolation in the light of current world events. In 1846, the Americans sent a fleet delegation of two ships under Commander James Biddle, but trade negotiations failed. And in 1848, Captain James Glynn sailed to Nagasaki and, upon returning to the United States, recommended to Congress to force open Japan through a demonstration of force, thus paving the way for the Perry expedition. One of Perry's missions was to acquire the right – preferably by diplomacy; if not, by force – from the Tokugawa government to establish coaling stations in ports along the Japanese coast. These ports would serve as steppingstones for American merchant ships and liners, thereby enabling the United States to catch up with its rival, Britain, by expanding its own trade relations with China. Moreover, by establishing a visible presence in the West Pacific, the Americans sought to secure protection for their own whalers. For an illuminating perspective on Matthew Perry's expedition, see Fujimoto Masaru, "Black Ships of 'shock and awe'", in the online edition of *The Japan Times*, https://www.japantimes.co.jp/community/2003/06/01/general/black-ships-of-shock-and-awe/, June 1, 2003 [accessed September 13, 2020].
[12] Because the treaty was signed in Kanagawa Village, today's Yokohama, it is known popularly as the Treaty of Kanagawa.
[13] The immediate years following the Meiji Restoration were far from peaceful, however. Pro-Tokugawa forces and the imperial army were embroiled in the bloody Boshin War from January 1868 to June 1869. Then in 1877, Takamori Saigo led the Satsuma Rebellion, but that was also put down by the imperial forces. With Takamori's

moved his capital from Kyoto to Edo, which he renamed Tokyo ("Eastern Capital").[14]

Six years after Perry's historic visit, in 1859, the second wave of missionaries in Japanese Christian history started arriving.[15] Even though Japan was no longer a closed country, the practice of Christianity remained outlawed. In fact, almost immediately after the Meiji Restoration, the new government sought to nationalize Shinto in a carefully-designed plan to root the legitimacy of the imperial family in the cultural myth of the Sun Goddess so as to secure unquestioning allegiance from all its subjects. A renewed ban on Christianity was enforced, and anyone caught practicing the faith was prosecuted. So, although the early "missionaries" continued to operate in the country during the years of the ban, they had never been allowed to conduct religious activities openly. Virtually all of them worked as teachers.

Interestingly, it was the Western presence in Japan that prompted the Chinese word *shūkyō* 宗教 to be imported into Japanese language as a translation for the word "religion". The word apparently made its first appearance in the trilingual text of the Amity and Commercial Treaty between Japan and the North German Bund, signed on February 20, 1869 (Spae, 1971: 23; see also Tsuchiya, 2000: 14-15).[16]

---

defeat, the last vestiges of resistance to the emperor were decisively removed. Interestingly, America at this time had just come out of her own civil war between North and South over the issues of slavery and Southern secession. Although the Hollywood blockbuster *The Last Samurai*, which hit the big screen in 2003, fictionalized the events of the 1877 revolt, it nevertheless provides an interesting cultural window into the unstable political situation following the Meiji Restoration, from the perspective of an American civil war veteran.

[14] Although political power in theory reverted to the emperor for the first time since the fifteenth century, in truth the country was governed by an oligarchy of former samurai who understood the role of the emperor as no more than a high priestly one. The Meiji oligarchs sought urgently to modernize and militarize Japan so as to catch up with the West. Around the same time, however, the people's rights movement was launched which sought a greater participation in government, thus leading to Japan's tentative experimentation with parliamentary democracy. In 1885, a cabinet system of government was instituted with Itō Hirobumi as the country's prime minister. Itō studied Western constitutionalism, and in 1889 crafted the Meiji Constitution adapted from German constitutional theories.

[15] The focus of the rest of this section is on the Protestant church and missions in Japan. For a helpful overview of Catholic and Orthodox missionary activities from the nineteenth century, see Helen Ballhatchet, "The Modern Missionary Movement in Japan: Roman Catholic, Protestant, Orthodox," In *Handbook of Christianity in Japan*, ed. Mark R. Mullins (Leiden: Brill, 2003), pp. 35-68.

[16] The fourth paragraph of the treaty reads: "German subjects residing in Japan shall be allowed the free exercise of their religion" (*Jikoku no shūkyō o jiyū ni okonau no ri arubeshi* 自国の宗教を自由に行ふの理あるべし). Apparently, the word gained general acceptance as a result of Kozaki Hiromichi's 1881 translation of Julius Seelye's *The Way, the Truth, and the Life: Lectures to Educated Hindus* (1873), which Kozaki

One of the most striking discoveries of the early Meiji period was that, contrary to all expectations, there were sizable communities of Japanese believers who risked their lives and continued to practice their faith in secret throughout the years of Japan's isolation. These believers could trace the roots of their faith back to the Jesuit mission of the seventeenth century. Despite severe persecution and suffering, they preserved their faith identity, and even passed down their beliefs to the next generation. However, closer examination reveals that the religion of these secret Christians had metamorphosed into a barely-recognizable and highly-syncretized mix of Catholicism and Japanese folk religious beliefs that bore only a remote resemblance to orthodox Catholic faith.[17]

It was not until 1873, a full twenty years after Perry's visit, that the Meiji leaders finally caved in to intense diplomatic pressure from the Americans, and quietly lifted the country's long-standing ban on Christianity.[18] News that the ban had been lifted, however, could hardly be contained, and before long it opened the floodgates to Protestant, Catholic, and Orthodox missionaries, not only from the United States, but also from Europe. However, even after the ban was lifted, American Protestants of every denominational stripe and color constituted the bulk of missionaries working in the country. This is not surprising, not only because it was the Americans who forced open Japan's doors, but more so because America had just come out of the Second Great Awakening, spiritually energized through post-millennial theology and the spirit of voluntarism.[19] As Andrew Walls puts it succinctly, "The main missionary

---

named *Shūkyō yōron* 宗教要論 (*A Treatise on Religion*) (see Spae, 1971: 23-24). Kozaki's translation was used as "favored introduction to Christianity" in Meiji Japan (Spae, 1971: 23).

[17] These "hidden Christians" (*kakure kirishitan* 隠れ切支丹), as they are referred to, number about 30,000 today, and are mostly located in the southern island of Kyushu and its offshore islands. For further study, see Ann M. Harrington, *Japan's Hidden Christians* (Chicago, IL: Loyola University Press, 1993), a fascinating ethnography on the *kakure kirishitan*. See also Richard Drummond, *A History of Christianity in Japan* (Grand Rapids, MI: Eerdmans, 1971), especially pp. 109-125.

[18] The missionary intentions of the Americans were evidently part of their original desire to see Japan's doors open. In his report dated December 4, 1852 – a full six months before Perry's first visit to Japan – the Secretary of Navy wrote, "Christendom is constrained by the pressure of an increasing necessity to publish its wants and declare its rights to the heathen; and in making its power felt, will bring innumerable blessings to every race which shall acknowledge its mastery [...]. The opening of Japan has become a necessity, which is recognized in the commercial adventure of all Christian nations, and is deeply felt by every owner of an American whale-ship, and every voyager between California and China." For the full report, see *Report of the Secretary of the Navy, December 4, 1852* (Washington D.C.: Navy Historical Center, 1852), pp. 295-97.

[19] The Second Great Awakening lasted for about half a century from the 1790s to the 1840s, and it gave rise to personal piety, social activism, and evangelistic fervor. The

achievement of the nineteenth century was the Christianizing of the United States" (1996: 227). American Christians, revived in Word and Spirit, found the new opportunities to restart the stalled missionary endeavor in Japan too good to miss. In this way, the cross followed the Star-Spangled Banner into the country. The Meiji Era (1868-1912), which lasted nearly forty-five years, saw an unprecedented Westernization and modernization of Japan as well as the unhindered spread of Christianity throughout the country from the three mission centers of Kumamoto, Yokohama, and Sapporo.[20]

It is noteworthy that a significant number of the first generation of Japanese converts came from the samurai class. This was in all probability due to the collapse of the feudal system and with it the demise of the warrior class, the result of a series of sweeping socio-political changes brought about by the Meiji Restoration.[21] The samurai families, suddenly disenfranchised by the new political developments of Meiji Japan, saw that they had no choice but to lay down their swords and, for the sake of their future, acquire the knowledge and technology that had made the West strong. And of course, during the early Meiji years, the only people who could teach Western science and culture were the

---

Haystack Prayer Meeting at Williams College, Massachusetts, in 1806, was instrumental in fueling the missionary passion so characteristic of the Awakening. Coupled with a strong belief in the unity of the church, the spirit of voluntarism was born. Ironically, the revolutionary insistence on *sola Scriptura* free from traditional interpretations led to many groups breaking away from the mainline denominations and forming new ones. Christian voluntary societies were also organized not only to reform America, but also to evangelize the world. For further study, see Andrew Walls' chapter "The American Dimension of the Missionary Movement" in his *The Missionary Movement in Christian History: Studies in the Transmission of Faith*, (Maryknoll, NY: Orbis, 1996), pp. 221-240.

[20] Kumamoto – the birthplace of Kitamori – was a major port city on the southern island of Kyushu. Yokohama was the port city of Tokyo, the new capital of Meiji Japan. Sapporo was a newly-constituted city in the recently annexed northern island of Hokkaido. The Meiji government specifically sought American help to develop Sapporo, and in response to that, William Smith Clark (1826-86), President of the Massachusetts Agricultural College in Amherst and a devout Christian, spent eight months in Sapporo to set up Sapporo Agricultural College – the forerunner of Hokkaido University. It is noteworthy that all sixteen students of the pioneer class of the college converted to Christianity under Clark's influence. For a study on Clark's wider influence on the Japanese church, see David Michell's doctoral dissertation, "William S. Clark of Sapporo: Pioneer Educator and Church Planter in Japan" (Trinity Evangelical Divinity School, 1988).

[21] In fact, the decline of the warrior cult had already begun since the latter half of the Tokugawa period, when Japan entered a time of unparalleled peace and prosperity. There had not been any major conflict in more than a century. Uchimura Kanzō, the founder of the Non-church Movement, made this telling remark about his samurai grandfather, "He lamented that the land was in peace, and died with regret that he never was able to put his trade in practice" (1895: 8).

missionaries.[22] Many families from the now-defunct warrior class saw it politically and economically expedient to send their scions to acquire a Western education under the tutelage of these Christian teachers.[23] These young men, coming from distinguished families known for their prowess not only in the martial arts but also in the literary classics, were the best and brightest of the land. Many would later rise to become prominent Christian statesmen.[24] Not accidentally, the period between the Meiji Restoration and the early pre-war Showa Era saw an enormous output of indigenous Japanese Protestant theology. The range of discussion was wide, covering topics such as the relationship between faith and culture, the person of Jesus Christ, the mystery of the Trinity, and the meaning of the Church.

The Meiji period also saw concerted efforts in translating the Bible into Japanese. Missionaries played a principal role in organizing and leading translation committees. The so-called Committee New Testament was published in 1880, followed by the Old Testament in 1887. The translation of the New Testament was further revised using the Nestle text and completed in 1917. This revised translated text was to become the standard Protestant New Testament for the next thirty-seven years. Catholic and Orthodox missionaries also carried out their own separate translation projects.

The impact of Meiji Christianity on Japanese society was considerable despite the fact that it was still very much a minority religion. Ballhatchet observes that its influence "was particularly evident in intellectual circles and in areas such as women's education, work among the sick and disadvantaged, and movements for social reform" (2003, 58). Also, because of their marginal status

---

[22] The close relationship between Christianity and Western culture was not an unmixed blessing. Unlike Buddhism which came to Japan via China and Korea, Christianity wore a distinctively Western face. Even today, many Japanese view Christianity as a Western religion. It is not a wonder that Kitamori should comment that it is almost impossible for a Japanese person to read the Bible without feeling the tension between their own culture and Western culture (1995: 5).

[23] It appears that a number of these American Christians who came to Japan in the 1870s were either former soldiers who fought in the American Civil War (1861-65), or had some military training. The martial discipline and ethics of men like Captain Leroy L. Janes (1838-1909) in Kumamoto and William Clark in Sapporo were certainly not lost on their samurai charges, many of whom were converted to Christianity. Janes was a graduate of West Point. Clark attained the rank of Brigadier General because of his military accomplishments in the Civil War. It would make a fascinating study to explore the relationship between the American Civil War and the evangelization of Meiji Japan.

[24] Among the most prominent of Japan's early Protestant leaders who came from ex-samurai families were Ebina Danjō (1856-1937) and Kozaki Hiromichi (1856-1938) of the Kumamoto Band, Uemura Masahisa (1858-1925) and Honda Yōichi (1848-1912) of the Yokohama Band, and Uchimura Kanzō (1861-1930), and Nitobe Inazō (1862-1933) of the Sapporo Band. Missionary Daniel Greene (1834-1914) reported in 1889 that 30% of Protestant church members came from ex-samurai families, a high figure indeed considering that the samurai class accounted for only 6% of the total population (Ballhatchet, 2003: 45).

and visible foreign ties given their associations with the missionaries, Japanese Christians from the Meiji Era right through to the Early Showa Era felt compelled to assert their patriotism whenever the opportunity presented itself.[25] Uchimura Kanzō's famous proclamation in 1926 of his abiding loyalty to the "two J's" – Jesus and Japan – is a case in point. It is not a wonder that most Protestant leaders supported the government in the Sino-Japanese War (1894-95), which ended with the colonization of Taiwan, and the Russo-Japanese War (1904-05), which led to the annexation of the Korean Peninsula in 1910 – an event which Protestant statesman Uemura Masahisa interpreted as the will of God (Ballhatchet, 2003: 52).[26] Moreover, Japan's expansionist policies provided the Japanese church with overseas missionary opportunities. The early years of the twentieth century saw an outburst of missionary activity in Manchuria, Taiwan, and Korea. The intrinsic and intricate relationship between Japanese colonialism and missionary work proved to be a very tricky problem for Japanese Christians. As Hamish Ion rightly observes, "Because the Japanese missionary movement was effectively assisting the colonial administration and being subsidized by it, it was difficult or impossible for Christians to support missionary and to criticize colonial policy" (2003: 81).

An event of gargantuan proportions happened in 1923 which, curiously, is left unmentioned in virtually all works on Japanese Christian history. The Great Kanto Earthquake occurred about two minutes before noon on September 1, 1923, and brought about near complete destruction of Tokyo and Yokohama, Japan's two most important cities. An excess of 120,000 people perished, about 4% of the country's population. A quarter of a million were injured. Nine-tenths of all buildings were destroyed, including, obviously, churches, seminaries and universities, and mission hospitals (Prang, 1995: 203). In Tokyo, 67% were made homeless. Foreigners were among those who died and many survivors

---

[25] Notto Thelle insightfully suggests that the difference between Buddhist nationalism and Christian patriotism also fueled the charge that Christianity was incompatible with national polity (1987: 163-66). From the beginning, Buddhism was closely linked to the state, serving as "a spiritual and ritual guarantee for the state and [receiving] state protection and supervision", while Christianity combined patriotism with universal principles that transcend the state (Thelle, 1987: 164-65). Thelle (1987) is an excellent, in-depth study of the relationship between Buddhism and Christianity in nineteenth-century Meiji Japan.

[26] The reasons why the early Meiji Christians supported the government's war efforts so readily are complex. First, there is the obvious desire to appear at least as patriotic as, other Japanese, if not more so, especially in the light of a resurgent state Shinto. Second, it is highly conceivable that the Japanese Christians were influenced by the American understanding of "manifest destiny" that had led to American exerting her political and military powers beyond her shores, and indeed to Japan's opening her doors to the West. Third, considering that many of the Christian leaders came from families steeped in *bushido* 武士道 (way of the warrior), it is hardly surprising that they should not be troubled by Japan's ascent to militaristic nationalism. The lesson here is that faith alloyed with a nationalistic spirit yields a venomous potion.

were evacuated and sent home. It is not known how many missionaries stayed, but those who did were busily organizing relief efforts or burying the dead (see Prang, 1995: 201-19; Hammer, 2006: 241-42).[27]

In the hours following the earthquake, rumors spread that Koreans were setting fires, poisoning wells, and looting. This led to unprecedented group hysteria, and the consequent senseless massacre of six thousand Koreans and two hundred Chinese cast an incriminating blight on the history of Japanese social consciousness.[28]

The Great Kanto Earthquake "inflicted a trauma unmatched in [Japanese] history, until the firestorms and atomic bombs of the Second World War" (Hammer, 2006: 260). It is not known what lasting effects the seismic catastrophe had on the church and Christian mission in Japan. In his carefully researched work on the earthquake, Hammer argues that the disaster "created among many Japanese a sense of fatalism, a tendency to retreat inward, a desire to cling to ancient traditions and symbols of strength and absolute authority, such as the emperor and the army" (Hammer, 2006: 260). If Hammer is right in his assertion, then one can imagine the adverse effects the earthquake must have had on the Japanese church. Studies in this area are presently non-existent, hence needed.

What is undeniable is that the years following the earthquake saw a sharp rise in nationalistic fervor. Christian nationalism, which began in the Meiji period, took on a life of its own, to the effect that a politically-motivated, syncretized form of Japanese Christianity arose in the final years leading up to the Second World War. Seeking to justify Japan's role in the Second Sino-Japanese War that began in 1937, a small but vocal group of Christian nationalists insisted that "serving the emperor and cooperation in Japan's advance into China serves the advancement of the kingdom of God" (Sato 1997, 57). In April 1939, the Diet passed Law No. 77, the Religious Organizations Law (*Shūkyō dantai hō* 宗教団体法) to bring all recognized religions under government "protection". The National Christian Council responded to this thinly-veiled wartime ordinance by organizing a unified Protestant Church, comprising some thirty or so denominations. Thus, the United Church of Christ in Japan (*Nihon kirisuto kyōdan* 日本基督教団) was born.[29] In the main, the Kyōdan pledged allegiance to the emperor and supported the government in the Pacific War.[30] To be sure, there were dissident groups, such as the Holiness churches, the Non-church

---

[27] Prang has a chapter in her book, entitled, "Turning Earth's Smoothness Rough", which provides a fascinating account of the days following the earthquake from the perspective of Canadian missionary Caroline Macdonald (1995: 201-19).
[28] See Joshua Hammer, *Yokohama Burning* (New York: Free Press, 2006), pp. 149-70, for an incisive account of the infamous incident.
[29] As mentioned earlier, following Japanese convention, and for the sake of economy, the United Church Christ in Japan is referred to simply as Kyōdan. See p. 23, f.n. 1 above. This was the denomination that Kitamori and Koyama belonged to.
[30] See Koyama (1984: 17-24) for a penetrating theological critique of the war.

Movement, and the Seventh-Day Adventists, who resisted cooperation with the military. Many of their leaders suffered imprisonment; some were even tortured and killed (Yanagida, 1958: 670). The war came to a tragic end with the atomic holocausts of Hiroshima and Nagasaki in August 1945.[31] On September 2, 1945, Japan formally signed the unconditional Instrument of Surrender in the presence of General MacArthur on the deck of the USS Missouri in Tokyo Bay, an ironically tragic throwback to Commodore Perry's naval frigate that opened Japan to the world nearly a hundred years before.

Christianity in Japan after 1945

The immediate aftermath of the Second World War brought about the third wave of missionary arrivals into Japan. The war had resulted in widespread devastation. Suffering was rife as a result of massive bombings on no less than sixty Japanese cities.

Countless civilian lives were lost. [32] Along with the nation's humiliating surrender to the Allied Forces, the denunciation of the emperor of his divinity created a moral and spiritual disorientation among the people.[33] Needless to say, Christianity suffered a huge blow as well. Some four hundred churches were destroyed by the air raids. The Kyōdan fell into moral shambles because of her uncritical support for the emperor and the war effort of the defeated nation. It is not a wonder that Methodist missionary Charles Iglehart should describe early post-war missionary work as an expression of "love among the ruins" (1959: 256).

From the end of the war in 1945 until 1952, Japan was placed under the administration of the Allied Occupation, formally known as SCAP ("Supreme Commander, Allied Powers"), headed by General Douglas MacArthur. One of the first acts of the Occupation was to effect a separation between state and religion. Through an SCAP directive issued on October 4, 1945 – less than two months after the atomic holocaust – the Religious Organizations Law was repealed. All prisoners detained for their religious beliefs were released. This sudden turnaround of events prompted about one-third of the member churches leaving the Kyōdan to re-establish their former denominations or form new ones. Although the policy of the SCAP was one of religious neutrality, MacArthur did

---

[31] It is a tragic irony that Nagasaki, the "Rome of the Far East" (see p. 42 above), should suffer such an ignoble fate at the hands of a supposedly Christian nation.

[32] It is estimated that about 100,000 civilians died in the March 1945 firebombing of Tokyo. Five months later, another 200,000 would perish when the atomic bombs were dropped on Hiroshima and Nagasaki.

[33] When researching for his book *The Allied Occupation of Japan 1945-1952 and Japanese Religions* (1972), William Woodard studied pre-war writings on Japanese political philosophy and interviewed several Japanese businessmen, and came to the conclusion that as absurd as it might seem, that the emperor is *akitsukami* 現つ神 (God incarnate) was the "*orthodox view* for the Japanese people in the prewar and war years" (1972: 370, emphasis in the original).

not hide his personal bias toward Christianity.[34] In May 1947, undoubtedly through his influence, the SCAP implemented a policy that made it easier for Christian missionaries to come to Japan with their families. Churches in America were permitted to ship tons of food, prefabricated housing, clothing, motor vehicles, and other supplies for new missionary arrivals (Shorrock, 2004b: 1). Bibles and hymn books were also imported *en masse* from the United States.[35] And so, ironically, the SCAP became the political vehicle on which the gospel was transported into the very country in which it had so decisively effected the separation of state and religion. This is the second time in barely a hundred years that the cross should enter Japan following closely on the heels of the Stars and Stripes.

In any case, the dire physical and spiritual needs of Japan were more than enough to sound a Macedonian call, to which the American churches responded readily with much enthusiasm. Between 1946 and 1950, some two thousand American evangelists, teachers, and social workers arrived (Shorrock, 2004a: 1).[36] Many of these missionaries were young people fresh out of high school, Bible colleges, and even the military, full of zeal and courage. They flocked to Japan through independent mission agencies such as the Far Eastern Gospel Crusade (later known as SEND International), The Evangelical Missionary Alliance (TEAM), Navigators, Campus Crusade for Christ (CCC), Japan Evangelistic Band (JEB), Youth for Christ (YFC), and the China Inland Mission (later known as the Overseas Missionary Fellowship or OMF). Many of these missionaries would spend their entire lives in Japan. Also, in 1949, the

---

[34] As reported in the Religious News Service on April 6, 1964, MacArthur said, "I am a Christian and an Episcopalian, but I believe in all religions [...]. They may differ in form or ritual but all recognize a divine creator, a superior power that transcends all that is mortal" (cited in Woodard, 1972: 358). MacArthur's words seem to represent a slight shift from his earlier view of the non-Christian religions. In an interview with Charles O' Malley as reported on the Congressional Record dated July 12, 1949, MacArthur said, "We need religion in Japan. The people here are saturated with Shintoism and Buddhism, neither of which, in my estimation, is up to what we need in making better and nobler human beings" (cited in Woodard, 1972: 359). And in an earlier letter dated October 4, 1947, to missionary Elizabeth Whewell working in Gifu Prefecture, MacArthur wrote, "I think you equally realize the hope and belief I entertain that Japan will become Christianized. Every possible effort to that end is being made and, had I my way, I would hope for a thousand missionaries for every one that is now here" (cited in Woodard, 1972: 357). There is little evidence, however, to suggest that MacArthur ever issued a formal call for a thousand missionaries, as is commonly believed. Woodard's book contains eight appendices of copies of documents from war archives, including oral statements and writings of General MacArthur (1972: 285-363).

[35] MacArthur had himself requested the Pocket Testament League to distribute ten million Japanese Bibles. MacArthur claims that as a result of the Bible distribution, "a spiritual regeneration in Japan began to grow" (1964: 311).

[36] Because of the decline of the British Empire and the devastation of Europe as a result of the war, the United States and Canada became the main supplier of missionaries in the early post-war years.

missionary community in Japan found itself reinforced in size and strength as a result of many missionaries being re-assigned to Japan after being expelled from Mao's China. These missionaries tended to be older and more experienced. Their decidedly anti-communist stance was certainly much appreciated by the Occupation for obvious reasons. [37] While their overarching desire was undeniably to preach the gospel, the motivations of these post-war American missionaries to Japan were actually quite mixed: "[desire for] reconciliation with the former enemy, guilt for Hiroshima and Nagasaki, and sorrow for the Japanese-Americans assigned to relocation camps" (Shorrock, 2004a: 1). After the end of the Occupation in 1952, Japan welcomed hordes of new missionary arrivals from Western Europe, Australia, New Zealand, and South Africa.

Not surprisingly then, Christianity in post-war Japan is characterized by the flurry of missionary and evangelistic activities. In the year the war ended, the Far Eastern Broadcasting Company (FEBC) opened a branch in Tokyo (*Operation Japan*, 2000: 16). In 1947, two major evangelical organizations were founded: *Kirisuto gakusei kai* (KGK, or Japan InterVarsity Christian Fellowship), and the Evangelical Missionary Association of Japan (EMAJ) (*Operation Japan*, 2000: 16). In 1950, the Japan Evangelical Fellowship (JEF) was founded (*Operation Japan*, 2000: 16). Japan also hosted the visit of many important international Christian leaders, including Emil Brunner, John R. Mott, E. Stanley Jones, Paul Tillich, and Hendrik Kraemer. There was apparently such a marked interest in Christianity that some people refer to the Occupation years as a "Christian boom."[38] The conversion of former soldiers who fought for the imperial army was highlighted, including Fuchida Mitsuo, the commander who led the infamous air attack on Pearl Harbor (see Fuchida, 1953), as well as a number of

---

[37] There is reason to believe that MacArthur's keen support for Christian work in Japan was motivated in good part by his fear of a very real threat from left-wing radicals. In a field report to America by Paul Rusch in 1950, MacArthur was quoted as saying, "For more than all else, democracy as we interpret it, is the exemplification of the tenets of all Christianity" (cited in Woodard, 1972: 359). In an unpublished manuscript by Rusch, MacArthur was reported to have said, "Japan cannot be a democracy without Christianity" (cited in Woodard, 1972: 359). MacArthur must have known that the days of the Occupation in Japan were numbered, hence his unreserved support for Christian missionary work. Rusch writes, "'The door, [MacArthur] said, would be open for about ten years" (cited in Woodard, 1972: 359).

[38] James Phillips rightly points out that it is more accurately a "religions boom", as virtually all religious groups received a new lease of life with the emperor's denunciation of his divinity (1981: 20). Moreover, there was a sharp increase in the number of groups associated with the so-called New Religions (*shinkō shūkyō* 新興宗教) (Durgin, 1953: 17; Shimazono, 2003: 278). Indeed, by the end of the American Occupation in 1952, it was estimated that no less than seven hundred New Religions were being practiced in the country, an observation that prompted Neill McFarland to describe the immediate post-war years with the playful expression, "the rush hour of the gods" (1967: 4). Citing Byron Earhart, Morimoto Anri refers to Japan as a "living museum of religions" (2003: 164; cf. Kishimoto, 1961: 1).

high-profile war criminals on death row (see Hitt, 1965: 223-33). Christians even had access to the Imperial Household. Crown Prince Akihito – the present emperor – and several members of the Imperial Household were given an English tutor in the form of a Quaker lady from Philadelphia, Elizabeth Gray Vining, who taught them from 1946 to 1950.[39] For some years, a weekly group Bible study was held at the Imperial Palace for the empress and other women, led by a prominent Japanese evangelist, Mrs. Uemura Tamaki (Durgin, 1953: 17).[40]

The unbridled evangelical activism of post-war Japan was not without its downside, however. Furuya Yasuo, an educational minister of the Kyōdan, puts it bluntly, "[T]here was no time for Japanese Christians to repent of what they had or what they had not done during the war" (1998: 21). Furuya places part of the blame on the missionaries, who were overly busy working to "[rebuild] the ruined churches and to evangelize Japan" that they did not leave room for Japanese Christians to reflect on and repent of their responsibility for the war (Furuya, 1998: 21-22).[41] Moreover, according to Furuya, if missionaries during the pre-war period were known to be paternalistic, then post-war missionaries could be said to be indulgent (Furuya, 1998: 24). He laments that the *amae* relationship between Japanese and American churches in postwar Japan was such that missionaries simply did not see the need to help Japanese Christians face up to what happened during the war (Furuya, 1998: 24).[42]

---

[39] Vining's best-selling book, *Windows for the Crown Prince* (1952), contains interesting glimpses into the Imperial Household in the years immediately following the war. The book was republished by Charles E. Tuttle in 1990.

[40] It is indeed hard to gauge the level of genuine interest in Christianity among the general populace. That notwithstanding, Christianity was at least *acknowledged* to have widespread appeal, undoubtedly due to the fact that it had even penetrated the highest echelons of the imperial household.

[41] See Koyama (1984: 25-30) for an incisive critique of Japan's failure to repent and apologize for the war. There was actually a national campaign of repentance launched by the newly-installed prime minister, Prince Higashikuni Naruhiko, on August 30, 1945, the very day that General MacArthur arrived in Tokyo. The campaign is called *Ichioku sō zange* 一億層懺悔 (All one hundred million Japanese must repent). But as Koyama points out, there was nothing in the prime minister's so-called repentance speech that acknowledged any wrongdoing on the part of the Japanese government (1985: 27-28). The prime minister merely enumerated the reasons for Japan's defeat, and called on all one hundred million Japanese people to repent as "the first step to unite the nation" (cited in Koyama, 1985: 28). It sounded more like an expression of regret for Japan's defeat than a true repentance for the war. This is hardly surprising given the fact that the prime minister was a full military general serving in the Supreme War Council and the Home Defense Command through the years of the war.

[42] The concept of *amae* 甘え was popularized by a Catholic psychoanalyst Doi Takeo in his 1965 bestseller, *Amae no kōzō* (*The Structure of Amae*). Doi suggests that *amae* constitutes the basis of relationships among Japanese people. The psychological prototype of *amae* is the relation of dependence and presumptive love of infant to mother. It is a mutual relation, since the mother expresses her *amae* by indulging in the child. In the case of the relationship between missionaries and Japanese Christians,

It was not until 1965 that the Kyōdan took up the problem of the so-called "war responsibility". The catalyst for this was an incident in September 1965 when Ōmura Isamu, the then moderator of Kyōdan found himself ostracized by a large number of Korean participants at the General Assembly of the Korean Presbyterian Church to which he was invited to speak (Phillips, 1981: 33-34). Ōmura was taken aback by what he perceived to be genuine hostility on the part of the Koreans toward him and the rest of the Japanese delegation. On further probing, the Kyōdan leaders attributed the Koreans' reaction to the failure of the Japanese church to acknowledge the role she played in the war.

Two years later, in 1967, the Kyōdan issued a formal confession of its wartime sins to Asian Christians.[43] It appears that the confession came twenty-two years too late, at a time when war memories had begun to fade. Church leaders did not quite expect the turmoil and division that the apology would precipitate within the Kyōdan as a result of the confession. Conservative voices expressed indignation over several points of the statement of confession, one of which had to do with the deeply-rooted conviction held by some that, even though Kyōdan came into being by government order, it was ultimately God's will that it came into being at all. Any apology then would seem to nullify faith in divine providence. On the other hand, some others felt that the apology did not go far enough.[44]

Things came to a head over the contentious issue of the Christian Pavilion to be set up at the 1970 Osaka World Exposition. Radical students at the Tokyo Union Theological Seminary (TUTS) were vehemently opposed to what they perceived would be an ostentatious display at the Expo of Japan's wealth at the expense of other economically weaker nations, especially those nations Japan had invaded during the war. This being the case, the Christian Pavilion would render the Kyōdan's confession of its war guilt nothing more than an act of hypocrisy. In other words, the students interpreted the Pavilion as a symbol of "the church walking in hand in hand with imperialism and capitalism" (Sherrill, 2003: 171). An all-night meeting to address the issue was convened on September 1, 1969, between the Kyōdan Standing Committee and students opposing the Pavilion. It ended rather traumatically with Kitamori, the chairman of the theme committee of the Christian Pavilion, being struck in the cheek by one of the students. The TUTS faculty denounced the incident, and this led to the students barricading the seminary and boycotting classes. The impasse between faculty and students lasted six months, and ended only in March 1970 when riot

---

Furuya claims that *amae* is clearly evident since the former invariably accept the latter without criticism, and that the latter always expect to be accepted by the former without being criticized (1998: 24).

[43] The Japan Evangelical Association (JEA) issued its own statement of apology to Asian Christians in 1995.

[44] A standing committee headed by Kitamori was set up to resolve the differences between the various parties. It brought into careful consideration of all the points of contention, but the final report it produced pleased no one.

police was called in to disperse the students. Student upheaval spread to other campuses, leading to the permanent closure of the theology departments of Kanto Gakuin University and Aoyama Gakuin University.

These events of the late 1960s and early 1970s had two lasting effects on the church in post-war Japan. First, they led to a change in the distribution of the Protestant church. Sherrill reports:

> From 1970 to 1978, Kyōdan membership dropped from 205,051 to 188,409, and mainline Protestant churches as a whole experienced a 2.1 percent decrease in total membership. This is in stark contrast to the evangelical churches, which experienced a 29.6 percent increase in membership, and the Roman Catholic Church, which grew from 337,243 to 375,533 members, an increase of about 11 percent. (2003: 171)

The Kyōdan never quite recovered from the damage that it suffered. Evangelical Christianity, on the other hand, grew substantially.[45] The visit of Dr. Billy Graham in 1965, followed by the launching of three huge crusades in 1967, 1980, and 1994 provided some impetus to evangelical growth (*Operation Japan*, 2000: 16). Evangelist Honda Kōji (1912-2002) also organized big city crusades from the mid-1950s to the late 1990s, and these were instrumental in bringing about many evangelical conversions. Another major source of evangelical conversions, not often acknowledged, is to be found in the widely-read novels of Miura Ayako (1922-99) in which the gospel is explicated without reserve. Her award-winning *Hyōten* 氷点 (*Freezing Point*, 1964) was made into a television movie or drama series no less than ten times between 1966 and 2006, while her ever-popular *Shiokari tōge* 塩狩峠 (*Shiokari Pass*, 1968) was made into a motion picture in 1973.

Besides changing the face of the Protestant church, the student riots of the late 1960s exerted a second, and more undesirable, effect on the church. As a result of the unsatisfactory way in which the student riots were handled, the church became decidedly apolitical. Indeed, it is the political apathy and theological indifference of the church in post-war Japan – especially the evangelical church – that makes her so markedly different from the church of pre-war Japan. Moreover, with the pervasive pacifism that is all too characteristic of post-war Japanese society, the church too became thoroughly pacifistic – a sharp contrast with the nationalistic stance that the church adopted before the war.

There is another reason for the anomalous theological, and ecclesiological, discontinuity between the Christianity of pre-war Japan and that of post-war Japan, and this has to do with Furuya's earlier point concerning the church's responsibility of her wartime actions. Even though streams of statements of confession and apology have been issued since 1967, it does not seem that the

---

[45] For a study of Japanese evangelicalism, see Satoshi Nakamura, *Nihon ni okeru fukuinha no rekishi: Mō hitotsu no nihon kirisutokyō shi* (*History of Evangelicalism in Japan: Another Japanese Christian history*) (Tokyo: Word of Life Press, 2000).

church has *truly* evaluated and come to terms with her pre-war history. To be sure, the apologies that have repeatedly been offered for the war are genuine. Rather than disengaging herself from her pre-war history, the church needs to go all the way back to the Meiji period so as to assess all her expressions of nationalism since and all the attendant ramifications that unfolded over the years, beginning with the unqualified support the first Christians, imbued with the *bushido* spirit, gave for the nation's war with China, Russia, and for the colonization of Korea. At the moment, the absence of a properly-worked out theology of repentance in the history of the Japanese church is only too conspicuous.[46]

In retrospect, the gains made by Japanese evangelicalism in post-war Japan are effectively cancelled out by the losses inflicted on the Kyōdan and other mainline Protestant denominations during the same period. After more than sixty years of missionary and evangelistic work following the end of the war, Protestant Christians today still constitute a small minority, barely 1% of the country's 127 million people (*Operation World*, 2001, 370).[47] A key reason for this apparent lack of church growth is the perception that many Japanese people still have of Christianity as a foreign religion (Mullins, 1998a: 9). This is not surprising given the way Christianity came into the country uninvited – that is, on the sole initiative of the Americans – both in the 1800s and after the Second World War. The church did try once to shake off its Western image by aligning herself with nationalistic interests, but it was an experiment that ended in disaster. This, in turn, has unwittingly led to many evangelical Christians, Japanese and missionaries, preferring a conservative posture on matters pertaining to culture, a stance which obviously does not help at all in creating an environment conducive for the development of Christian theology that is both faithful to Scripture and rooted in the Japanese context. Many missionaries continue to preach a Western gospel, subconsciously equating it with the biblical gospel itself. Many promising Japanese evangelical leaders, especially those with English proficiency, continue to go overseas for what they perceive to be superior theological training in the West, returning to Japan only to perpetuate a

---

[46] Koyama has an excellent article on the dynamics of forgiveness, especially in relation to the war. The article, entitled "Father, Forgive…," is published in 1995 in *Ecumenical Review* 47(3), pp. 268-77. The Japanese translation is published in Koyama (1996: 189-207). However, Koyama laments that there is yet no serious theological reflection on the 1937 Nanjing Massacre and the atomic bombing of Hiroshima, let alone a theology of repentance relating to the war (personal communication).
[47] In the February 2006 report of the Gallup Survey, the percentage of Japanese Christians was estimated as 6% of the population. Later, it corrected the figure to 4%. The Church Information Service (CIS), whose annual surveys consistently show the Christian population to be around 1% of the general population, locates the discrepancy in the way the Gallup pollsters framed their questions. The Gallup Survey polled people who would consider themselves Christian, while CIS collected data from churches on baptism and membership figures (Hanazono, 2006: 3).

Western theological curriculum in the Japanese seminaries. Japanese theological works, especially those written by non-evangelical theologians as well as those produced before the war, are largely ignored.

In sum, despite her evangelistic fervor evident in the initial years following the war, the church has not transcended its marginal status in Japanese society. In fact, she has even come to accept it as inevitably such. Sherrill's assessment may be overly negative, although there is a grain of truth in his assertion that rather than engaging radically changing social realities, "it seems that the majority of pastors and congregations settle for the maintenance of the status quo" (2003: 177). There are indeed Christians who are beginning to see the need to engage with Japanese society and culture in a more proactive way.

As we leave this section on the historical overview of Christianity in Japan, a summary description of each of the three missionary periods is in order. The Catholic mission was a bold, pioneering endeavor that brought about the very first encounter between Japan and the Christian faith. In spite of the phenomenal growth of the church, the mission finally found itself sucked into the political mudswamp of seventeenth-century Japan.[48] The church suffered greatly, and contrary to Tertullian's dictum, *Semen est sanguis Christianorum*, the blood of the martyrs never quite became seed for the church.[49] The modern missionary movement of the nineteenth century provided the impetus for missionary work when Japan opened her doors to the world. Many of the early Japanese converts came from the elite, samurai class. The late 1800s and early 1900s saw a prodigious output of theological writings. Once again, however, the Church soon found herself entrapped in the political machinery of the times characterized by a blinding nationalism, resulting in her lending uncritical support for the expansionist military policies of imperial Japan. The church paid dearly for her actions. Finally, in the years following the war, missionary focus shifted to rebuilding the church from the ruins of war. Post-war Japanese Protestant Christianity is marked by a decline in mainline Protestantism, counter-balanced by a rise in an evangelical Christianity characterized by pacifism and political indifference, whose main focus is on evangelism and church building.

---

[48] See my paper, "Reinterpreting Endō Shūsaku's Swamp Motif in the Light of the Historical Jesuit Mission to Japan," presented at the 54th Midwest Conference on Asian Affairs in September 2005 at Michigan State University.

[49] Interestingly, David Bosch interprets what happened to the Japanese church in the seventeenth-century as a "confirmation" of Tertullian's words (1994: 75). See his thought-provoking article, "The Vulnerability of Mission," in *New Directions in Mission and Evangelization 2: Theological Foundations*, ed. James Scherer and Stephen Bevans (Maryknoll, NY: Orbis, 1994), pp. 73-86. I am indebted to Dr. Bevans for this reference.

Theology in Japan

This section provides a very brief overview of the historical development of theology in Japan from the advent of Christianity in the country until the present.[50]

Factors Inhibiting Theological Development during the Jesuit Mission

It may appear anomalous that no significant Japanese Catholic theology was produced during the whole century of Jesuit missionary work in feudal Japan. This theological barrenness is understandable when one realizes that there was no standardized Japanese translation of the complete Bible. Related to this was the inability of the fledgling church to develop a stable linguistic register of Christian terminology in Japanese. Kaiser (1996: 24) says it well, "The difficulties faced by the Jesuit mission in translating Christian terminology are symptomatic of a situation where there was virtually no tradition or previous work available."

Given that the vernacular is a necessary – although not sufficient – factor for doctrinal and theological development (cf. Sanneh, 1989: 51), it is not hard to imagine how theologically impoverished the church in Japan must have been under the leadership of Father Francisco Cabral, Superior of the Japan Mission from 1570 to 1581, when no proper provision was made for missionaries to study the Japanese language.[51] Moreover, Cabral's well-known condescending and arrogant attitude toward the Japanese and their culture cast a negative influence on the missionaries (see Elison, 1973: 55-56; Moran, 1993: 101). Under his leadership, the Jesuits developed a view of Buddhism as a totally false religion of demonic origin which needed to be refuted.[52] Their confrontational approach toward the Buddhist monks contributed to the impossibility of respectful dialogue, and this indeed would create a terrible backlash later when Christians were persecuted.

It is not a wonder that when Valignano visited Japan in July 1579, he was appalled by Cabral's strong-handed tactics, and sought in earnest a reversal of the latter's policies by developing a culturally-informed missiological approach.[53] In June 1580, the Visitor issued *Regimento para el Superior de Japon,*

---

[50] For a comprehensive bibliography of Japanese theological works produced over the years, see John England et al., eds., *Asian Christian Theologies: A Research Guide to Authors, Movements, Sources,* vol. 3: *Northeast Asia* (Delhi: ISPCK, 2004), pp. 302-474.
[51] Portuguese theological terminology was transferred into the Japanese language, and this was all but eradicated by the authorities during the years of persecution.
[52] Although it must be said that both Francis Xavier and Alessandro Valignano met Buddhist monks whom they had a profound respect for, even if they saw them as being severely misguided. Both men apparently developed a fascination with the practices associated with Zen Buddhism, undoubtedly because of their affinity with the *Spiritual Exercises* of Ignatius of Loyola (see Drummond, 1994: 28).
[53] It is easy to understand Cabral's leadership style and cultural attitude when one takes

a document redefining the rules governing the work of the Japanese Superior. This document was obviously intended to be a backhanded slap in Cabral's face. Valignano also crafted *Advertimentos e Avisos acreca dos Costumes a Catangues de Jappao*, "one of the most decisive documents of his career" (Ross, 1994: 62). The document, which specified in minute detail how missionaries should appropriate the Japanese way of life, lay the cornerstone for Valignano's policy of accommodation (see Ross, 1994: 63-64).[54] Incensed by Valignano's actions, Cabral resigned from his post and left for Macau in 1581. The Visitor then appointed the more agreeable Gaspar Coelho as the new Japanese Superior. However, with the assassination of Nobunaga, the pro-Christian overlord, the following year, and the seizure of power by Hideyoshi, the political tide began to turn against the church. The ensuing political turbulence simply did not afford the church the freedom to develop her theology.

During his third and last visit to Japan in 1603, Valignano implemented a program to teach all Jesuit missionaries the main teachings of Buddhism, Shinto, and Confucianism. However, Valignano's initiative came a little too late as political power had fallen into the hands of the Tokugawa family after the Battle of Sekigahara in the autumn of 1600. The new shogun, Ieyasu, under the advice of the Confucianist Hayashi Razan, the Buddhist abbot Tenkai, and the Zen monk Suden Konjin, adopted an ideology of Japan as *shinkoku* 神国, "the land of the gods".[55] And before the Japanese church could respond, persecutions began. In sum, the lack of Japanese theology during the Jesuit mission can be attributed to three factors: the absence of the Japanese Bible and the lack of a

---

into account the fact that Cabral was an ex-conquistador in the West Indies before he joined the Society of Jesus. It should be noted too that under his leadership the church in Japan experienced an explosive growth. Cabral actively encouraged mass baptisms and the "forced" conversions of whole fiefs whose feudal lords were Christians. Indeed, when he thought it necessary, he did not hesitate to advocate the use of physical force, "specifically that which was being used in Latin America or the Philippines" (Drummond, 1994: 26). Ross believes though, that there were many genuine conversions, as a result of the effective preaching of young Japanese evangelists (Ross, 1994: 51).

[54] Valignano altogether made three trips to Japan from 1579 to 1603, staying a total of ten years. See Josef Franz Schütte, S.J., *Valignano's Mission Principles for* Japan. Vol. 1, Parts 1 and 2 (St. Louis, MO.: Institute of Jesuit Sources 1980, 1985), and J. F. Moran, *The Japanese and the Jesuits: Alessandro Valignano in Sixteenth Century Japan* (London: Routledge, 1993) for an excellent documentation and discussion of Valignano's missiological thinking and achievements.

[55] The *shinkoku* ideology was first promulgated during the time of Hideyoshi. But it was the Tokugawa leaders who developed a Buddhist parish structure to enforce it. The same ideology was invoked during the Meiji period and the years leading up to the Second World War. As recently as on May 15, 2000, Prime Minister Mori Yoshirō whipped up a political storm by declaring Japan a divine country centered on the emperor (*tennō no chūshin to suru kami no kuni* 天皇の中心とする神の国). He retracted his statement May 26, but not after irreversible political damage had been inflicted. Mori resigned from office April 6, 2001.

stable religious vocabulary, the irreversible missiological harm caused by the Eurocentric policies of Father Cabral, and the political roller coaster that the Japanese church was subject to for most of the time the Jesuits were in Japan.

Development of Japanese Theology from the Nineteenth Century

In a true sense then, the history of Japanese theology began with the rebirth of the church in the late nineteenth century. For the sake of simplicity, the stages of theological development in Japan are classified according to the imperial eras: Meiji (1868-1912), Taishō (1912-26), early Shōwa (1926-45), and post-war Shōwa (1945-89), and Heisei (1989-present). [56] Again, at the risk of oversimplification, let me propose the principal traits that characterize each of these five stages as, respectively, acculturation, tension, testing, conservatism, and contextualization. These are obviously not intended to be carved-in-stone labels, for the reality is much more complex than is suggested by them. But they are useful insofar as they serve a heuristic function.

Theology in Meiji Japan: Acculturation

As we have noted above, the first Christian converts in Meiji Japan came from the now-defunct warrior class. These were the brightest young men of the land, and although their original motive was learning Western science and technology, many of them became converted through their missionary teachers. Because of their martial upbringing and staunchly Confucian background, these early Christians naturally struggled to harmonize their new faith with their cultural heritage. It is not surprising that Meiji Christianity should develop a heavy Confucian accent and a strong ethical component. For this reason, Nelson Jennings (2003: 185) refers to Meiji Christianity aptly as "Baptized Bushidō". [57] The emphasis on ethics became even more pronounced with the publication of Nitobe Inazo's *Bushido* (in English!) in 1900. And so, ironically, even though the samurai class was officially dismantled with the Meiji Restoration, the warrior code became the contesting site in which tension between the cultural and spiritual values of old and new was worked out. [58]

---

[56] This schema of classification is obviously an arbitrary one, chosen purely for convenience. Two things need to be borne in mind. First, the years spanning each era are of varying lengths. Second, the development of theology does not happen in discrete stages; rather it is a continuous process. There will therefore be overlaps between contiguous eras.

[57] *Bushidō* (武士道) is the ancient code of the warrior extolling the ethical virtues of justice, courage, benevolence, politeness, sincerity, honor, loyalty, and self-control. Although they might be constituted differently, these virtues are also biblical virtues. See p. 50, f.n. 26 above.

[58] Michael Foster rightly describes the Meiji period as "a time characterized by oppositions: old and new, native and foreign, irrational and rational, supernatural and scientific" (2006: 253). He adds insightfully, "Perhaps most striking about these various oppositions, however, is that they are so rarely mutually exclusive. Seemingly incomparable modes of interpreting the world exist simultaneously – distinct perhaps,

With their intellectual prowess, many Meiji Christian leaders came of age around the turn of the century and became theologians in their own right. Not unexpectedly, their central theological concern was *acculturation*. The aim was to reinterpret Japan's non-Christian past in the light of the new religious faith. Ebina Danjō, for instance, employed the ethics of the father-son relationship – one of the five basic moral precepts in Confucianism – as a way to understand the Christian's relationship with God (see Dohi, 1997: 13-14). Kozaki Hiromichi interpreted Confucianism as *preparatio evangelica* for Christianity in Japan. Christianity was understood as the fulfilment of Confucianism, and as such, its timely advent in Japan qualified it to provide the spiritual resources for a new, imperial Japan (see Dohi, 1997: 14-16). Uemura Masahisa, founder of Tokyo Theological Seminary (later renamed Tokyo Union Theological Seminary, or TUTS in short), regarded the Japanese traditions as the "Japanese Old Testament" preceding the gospel (Prang, 1995: 54). For Uchimura Kanzō, the problem was located not so much in culture, but in what he perceived to be the foreign jurisdiction of the Japanese church. In seeking to free the church from missionary control, Uchimura conceived the idea of the Non-church (*mukyōkai* 無教会) as a spontaneous, authentically Japanese expression of the Christian faith (Uchimura, 1901).

Theology in Taishō Japan: Tension
Japanese Christians during the Meiji period had virtually learned all their theology from American missionaries. However, at the turn of the century moving right through the Taishō period, Japanese theology became infused with a permeating influence of German liberalism. There are two reasons for this. The first has to do with the arrival in 1885 of the German liberal missionary society, *Allgemeine Evangelisch Protestantische Missions Verein*. Wilfred Spinner, the first missionary of the society, began publishing a magazine entitled *Shinri* 真理 (Truth), "an organ for the presentation of scientific theology and philosophy" (Heinrich Ritter, cited in Germany, 1965: 9-10).[59] The second reason for the shift to German liberal theology is related to the government's decision to adopt the German model of education at the end of the nineteenth century.[60] German

---

but always in the process of overlapping, intermingling, and coalescing. Indeed, this period of interaction with the West and the advent of new ideas is [*sic*] characterized by an often paradoxical collusion of opposites combining dynamically to create a unique whole. In a sense, the mystery that is the Meiji period can be found in the remarkable ability of people to simultaneously negotiate differing discourses and practices, happily embracing apparently contradictory ways of understanding the world around them" (Foster, 2006: 253).

[59] Many Japanese Christian leaders were influenced by the new and supposedly progressive ideas disseminated through the magazine. Even Uchimura was led to believe in Darwinism, and saw it as an important task to harmonize the biblical teaching on creation with the theory of evolution.

[60] Even today, junior high and high school students continue to don German military style uniform.

replaced English as the main foreign language in the state universities. It soon became a matter of prestige for graduates of these universities to pursue further theological studies in Germany, which many did, studying under theological luminaries of the day, such as Johannes Weiss, Ernst Troeltsch, Adolf Deissmann, Adolf von Harnack, Hans von Schubert, and Karl Holl. In the course of their studies, Japanese scholars drank deeply from the well of German theological liberalism. Returning to Japan, most of these scholars taught in seminaries and theological departments of the state universities, and continued to develop their own brand of Japanese liberal theology. However, the German influence was so pervasive that Methodist missionary Charles Germany could even say that Japanese liberal theology "reads with familiarity to a Western student" (1965: ix).

Although the theological landscape of Taishō Japan was heavily colored by liberalism, there were significant non-liberal voices as well. Many of these non-liberal scholars would have acquired their theological education in America or Britain rather than Germany. Takakura Tokutarō (1885-1934), who studied at Edinburgh, Oxford, and Cambridge, fought liberal theology by expounding what he called *fukuinteki kirisutokyō* 福音的基督教, an "evangelical Christianity" characterized by an unswerving faithfulness to the Bible as the Word of God (see Sato, 1997: 49).[61] Takakura also lambasted the humanistic focus of liberal theology by emphasizing the sheer grace of God (see Jennings, 2005: 258). His trilogy, *Onchō no ōkoku* (*The Kingdom of Grace*, 1921), *Onchō to shinjitsu* (Grace and Faithfulness, 1925), and *Onchō to shōmei* (*Grace and Calling*, 1926), and his *magnum opus*, *Fukuinteki kirisutokyō* (*Evangelical Christianity*, 1927), became classics in the world of Japanese theology. Besides Takakura, there were others, such as Uemura Masahisa and Uchimura Kanzō, who stood against the stream of liberal thought by holding fast to the authority of the Bible and the historic faith of the church. Uemura stressed the absolute deity of Christ and the total depravity of humanity whose only hope of salvation is in Christ. Jennings comments, "Amidst the plethora of imported-indigenous streams of thought, Uemura's 'evangelical' theological viewpoint had become the single most prevailing Protestant understanding of the Christian faith" (2003: 191). Uchimura's distinctive contribution in the battle with theological liberalism was his coinage of the phrase "Japanese Christianity", in English, and its Japanese equivalent, *Nihonteki kirisutokyō* 日本的基督教, to make a point that it is possible to develop an indigenous Christianity without capitulating to ideas that are alien to both the Bible and Japanese culture (Uchimura, 1920).[62] In sum, if

---

[61] Takakura is credited with introducing Calvin to Japan. Around the same time, Satō Shigehiko (1887-1935) introduced Luther to Japan with the publication of his *Wakaki Rūteru* (*Young Luther*) in 1918.

[62] See Uchimura Kanzō, "Japanese Christianity," *Seisho no kenkyū* (Biblical Studies), no. 245 (10 December 1920), in *Uchimura Kanzō Zenshū* (*The Complete Works of Uchimura Kanzō*) (Tokyo: Iwanami Shoten, 1980-84), vol. 25, p. 592.

theology during the Meiji period could be regarded as being characterized by acculturation, then theology during the Taishō period could be said to be marked by *tension*, between biblical orthodoxy and liberalism, and between indigeneity and foreignness.

Theology in Pre-war Shōwa Japan: Testing
The early Shōwa period saw the rise of social Christianity. The roots of this movement are to be found in the Christian socialism of Kagawa Toyohiko (1888-1960). But unlike Kagawa's socialism which was directed toward those outside the church, the Social Christianity of the early Shōwa period sought to develop a theological critique directed within the church. The main thrust, as Sato rightly understands it, "was to propose that a socialized Christianity take precedence over individualistic Christianity" (1997: 50). The leader of the movement was Nakajima Shigeru (1889-1949), who developed a hermeneutic of "redemptive love" as the means to bring about a new "communized" society of humankind that moves toward the realization of the kingdom of God (Sato, 1997: 51-53).

The other theological current that gained prominence in the pre-war Shōwa period was the dialectical theology of Karl Barth. The two theologians credited for introducing Barth into the Japanese theological landscape are Kumano Yoshitaka (1899-1982) and Kuwada Hidenobu (1895-1975). Kumano published *Benshōhōteki shingaku gairon* (*Introduction to Dialectical Theology*) in 1932, and in the following year Kuwada published *Benshōhōteki shingaku* (*Dialectical Theology*). Even though Barth had only begun to publish his *Kirkliche Dogmatik*, the intellectual depth of his earlier writings so impressed Japanese scholars that even Nishida Kitarō, Japan's leading philosopher at that time, became fascinated with him. Barthianism would occupy a central place in Japanese Protestant theology for a long time, even well into the post-war years. Also, the deep interest that the philosophers from the Kyoto School led by Nishida had in Christian theology led to a serious dialogue between philosophy and theology.[63] The relationship between the two became a hallmark in many theological works of the day.

As Japan entered the war years, the pressure exerted by Shinto nationalism on all aspects of Japanese society became extreme, to say the least, such that a bizarre form of "Japanese Christianity" grew in keeping with the spirit of ultra-nationalism of the times. Although the mainstream churches by and large rejected it, a small but highly vocal group of Christian nationalists propounded a patriotic version of Christianity with the following points, as summarized by Sato:

---

[63] The Kyoto School of Philosophy sought a way to build a philosophical system that maintains fidelity to Mahayana Buddhism and openness to Western thought at the same time. See pp. 101ff below.

1. Since *Mikuni* (kingdom of the emperor) and *Mikuni* (kingdom of God) are pronounced in the same way, serving the emperor and cooperation in Japan's advance into China serves the advancement of the kingdom of God.
2. The emperor and Christ are identical, otherwise Japanese would not believe in Christianity.
3. For the Japanese, if not for Westerners, Shintoist ancient writings such as Kojiki and Nihonshoki are the Old Testament.
4. Yahweh, the God of the Old Testament, and the god Amenominakanushinokami of Kojiki are identical.
5. As it is written in the Old Testament, especially in the book of Isaiah, the mission of the Japanese is to restore Israel, and the war against China is part of that mission. (1997: 57)

According to Sato, there were two groups of people who adopted this form of Japanese Christianity: those who were sold on liberal theology, and those who were associated with pietism (Sato, 1997: 58). The first group "had no orthodox faith as a brake upon their ideas," while the second believed that, as Japanese, they "should embrace the Japanese spirit" (Sato, 1997: 58). In any case, the gospel became grossly compromised and distorted beyond recognition. In sum, Japanese theology in the pre-war Shōwa period underwent severe *testing*, and sadly, despite the preached activism of Christian socialism and the radical intellectualism of dialectical theology, it was not able to provide a sound theological articulation against the rising tide of militarism and nationalism in the way that the *Bekennende Kirche* in Germany could.

Theology in Post-war Shōwa Japan: Conservatism
The war exposed the hollowness of liberal theology, reminiscent of the situation in Europe after the First World War. The end of the Pacific War brought about a pervasive sense of disillusionment with academic theology in the Japanese church. For, in spite of all that was written and published before the war, the church still could not appropriate a theological witness to her country on the brink of self-destruction. The lingering effect was that after the war, the church did not quite know how to develop a theological voice that could speak with relevance to contemporary society. Thus, began the ever-widening divide between the academy and the church. It is not a wonder that, when serving as visiting professor at the International Christian University from 1953 to 1955, Emil Brunner made this piercing indictment:

> What Japanese Christianity lacks is an interpretation of Christianity to the intellectual of this age. By this I mean an interpretation in terms of the Christian's questions about life, including problems such as ethics, culture, education, and so forth. (1954: 15)

Another reason for the overall theological apathy of the Japanese church is the theological conservatism of post-war missionaries, especially those of the evangelical persuasion. The theological posture of these missionaries reflected "a fundamentalist approach to scriptural interpretation and the work of mission" (Phillips, 1981: 155). Phillips elaborates:

> The missionaries were generally eager to engage in direct personal evangelism, and they had little patience with the vast expenditures of time by other mission groups in consultations with Japanese colleagues. The newer groups were generally suspicious of alleged theological liberalism among established Protestant churches and missions, both in Japan and overseas, and they sought to remedy the situation by emphasizing what they held was a return to the original Christian gospel. (Phillips, 1981:155)

The preoccupation with mass evangelism and church planting left missionaries with little time for sustained theological reflection. Moreover, as many of these missionaries were involved in training Japanese pastors, it is not hard to see how this conservative theological attitude was being perpetuated in the Japanese church.

Theological conservatism, evangelistic pragmatism, and the traditional Japanese tendency to exercise unwavering loyalty to a missionary or church leader added fuel to the frenzy of drawing as many people into the church in the shortest time possible, creating an atmosphere of competition among churches and mission agencies. The unfortunate outcome was that Christianity became cast "as a sectarian faith that called individuals to make an exclusive commitment to a specific church community, which made it difficult for Christians of one church to relate to Christians of another church" (Sherrill, 2003: 166). The results are enduring: Japanese churches today continue to be characteristically sectarian.

Perhaps the only area which has garnered substantial theological and missiological reflection among missionaries and Japanese pastors alike is the whole issue of the ancestors (e.g. Ooms, 1976; Fukada, 1984; Horikoshi, 1986: 81-85; Goodwin, 1989). This is not surprising since caring for the dead and revering the ancestors still constitute an integral part of the modern Japanese psyche (Mullins, 1998b: 42; Enns, 2001: 58).

In the academy, dialectical theology, which gained prominence in the decade before the war, continued to exercise a strong hold on Japanese theology even long after it, such that the period of post-war theology until around 1970 was often referred to as the period of "German captivity" (cf. Odagaki, 1997: 113). The neo-orthodoxy of Karl Barth especially had many faithful adherents. At the same time, however, dissenting voices were beginning to be heard. Kitamori published his *Kami no itami no shingaku* (*Theology of the Pain of God*) in 1946, in which he launched his first salvo against Barth. Even though the book gained a huge popular readership, Kitamori's contemporaries in the theological academy did not take kindly to his critique of Barth, a testimony to the latter's enduring influence.

Another post-war theological development in the academy was the engagement with the non-Christian religions. Takizawa Katsumi (1909-1984), a student of Barth, published *Bukkyō to kirisutokyō* (*Buddhism and Christianity*) in 1964, in which he offered a philosophical critique of both the Buddhism of the great Zen master Hisamatsu Shin'ichi and of traditional Christianity. Furuya Yasuo (1926-) published *Shūkyō no shingaku* (*Theology of Religions*) in 1985, in which he attempted a theological evaluation of the religions on their own terms without dissolving the inherent tensions between Christianity and the other religions.

While academic theology remained quite inaccessible to most Japanese Christians, the church found an intelligible theological expression through the medium of the novel. The novels of Endō Shūsaku, Miura Ayako, and Sōno Ayako continue to be widely read even today. As mentioned earlier, Endō was Catholic, and Miura was Protestant. Sōno still belongs to the Catholic Church, and was indeed given an award from the Vatican for her literary and humanitarian achievements. These three writers provided Christians with a vital means to reflect on the theological implications of living out the Christian faith in post-war Japanese society. Endō, in particular, produced some of his best and most creative works from the late 1960s to the early 1980s in an attempt to make Christianity indigenous in Japanese soil. During the last decade of his life, though, he moved toward a highly syncretistic and pluralist view of religious reality.

As an aside – and an important one– it was in the post-war era that Japanese theology began to draw attention from the rest of the world. The credit goes to American theologian Carl Michalson who, through his work *Japanese Contributions to Christian Theology* (1960), introduced indigenous Japanese theology to the world for the first time. In the book, Michalson explicated the theological ideas of five key Japanese theologians: Uchimura Kanzō, Watanabe Zenda, Kumano Yoshitaka, Kitamori Kazō, and Hatano Seiichi. Of the five, Uchimura and Hatano were the only pre-war figures; Watanabe and Yoshitaka wrote both before and after the war; and Kitamori wrote his theology after the war. In any case, so impressed was Michalson with what he had discovered that he was prompted to make the bold declaration that "of all the younger churches, it [the Japanese church] is apparently the first to have developed a significant theology" (1960: 9). It is interesting to note how ahead of his times Michalson was in recognizing the need for local, indigenous theologies to contribute constructively to global theologizing so as to break down "such walls of ignorance now dividing the church" (Michalson, 1960: 9).[64]

---

[64] Unfortunately, Michalson's work did little more than piquing the curiosity of Western theologians. The main reason for this is the language barrier. Other than Uchimura's English works and Kitamori's *Theology of the Pain of God* which was translated into English in 1965 – undoubtedly due to the publicity generated through Michalson's book – the other theologians whom Michalson dealt with in his book remain inaccessible to

A final comment is necessary before we move on to the Heisei period. The church in post-war Japan developed a missionary consciousness, undoubtedly due to the influence of the missionaries. More than three hundred missionaries have been sent out of Japan since the Second World War. Although more than half of the missionaries were sent out in the last twenty-five years or so, the pioneers of the Japanese missionary movement should not be forgotten. Among them is Koyama Kōsuke who was sent out by the Kyōdan in 1960 to serve as a missionary in Thailand. Because of their cross-cultural experiences, the contributions of these missionaries to Japanese theology when they return home can be expected to be substantial. Indeed, Koyama has already written extensively on the nature of the missionary task for the global church, and in the process, "he has been looking at Japan as an object from the outside, and has [therefore] been engaged in a sort of theology of Japan" (Furuya, 1997: 146).

Theology in Heisei Japan: Contextualization
The death of Emperor Hirohito on January 7, 1989 brings the nearly sixty-four years of a mostly tumultuous Shōwa period to a close.[65] The beginning of the Heisei period was marked with great controversy as civil and religious leaders debated the constitutionality of the religious nature of the funeral of the late emperor and the enthronement ceremonies of the new emperor Akihito.[66] In a real sense, the crisis surrounding the imperial succession gave Christian leaders and thinkers a fresh opportunity to reflect and respond biblically and theologically in context. Indeed, the Heisei period jolted the church out of her theological indifference and diffidence and gave a new impetus to the

---

those without any facility in Japanese. Even Michalson did not handle the primary Japanese texts himself. Rather, his research was the result of conversations with and translations by his bilingual Japanese students and friends. Michalson died prematurely in a plane crash near Cincinnati, Ohio, in November 1965, the year the English translation of Kitamori's magnum opus was released.

[65] The imperial family is the only family in Japan without a family name. Members of the imperial household possess a personal name and an imperial title. Now the Japanese would never refer to the emperor by his name, but by his title *Tennō heika* (His Majesty the Emperor). However, since the Meiji Restoration, the name of the imperial reign becomes the emperor's posthumous name which people would use. In case of Hirohito, the Japanese started referring to him as *Shōwa tennō* (Emperor Shōwa) only after his death.

[66] To maintain the separation of religion and state, and at the same time to preserve the religious heritage of the imperial system, the government actually organized two consecutive funerals for the late emperor: a Shinto funeral followed by a non-religious state funeral. However, both funerals were attended by foreign dignitaries, and both were televised live throughout the country. Similarly, there were two enthronement ceremonies. Although historically both have religious significance, the government carried out the first as a simple public ceremony, and the second as an elaborate, national ceremony with all the attendance religious paraphernalia intact. Both ceremonies were funded with public money. See Lee (1989: 16-19) for a background of the Japanese imperial system.

theological enterprise. Not surprisingly, the subject constituting the central theological concern for the church is contextualization. The year following Akihito's enthronement, the Tokyo Mission Research Institute launched the inaugural volume of its Occasional Series, entitled *Tennōsei no kenshō: Nihon senkyō ni okeru fukahi no kadai* (*The Japanese Emperor System: The Inescapable Missiological Issue*), a collection of theological and missiological essays on the Japanese imperial system. Closely related to the imperial system is the issue of the Yasukuni Shrine which has of late seen revived discussion among scholars especially in the light of the repeated visits of the former Prime Minister Koizumi Jun'ichirō despite continuing protests by China and Korea.[67]

Besides addressing politically charged issues such as the legitimacy of the Yasukuni Shrine, and the constitutionality of the national anthem and the national flag,[68] theologians are also working on the more down-to-earth issue of inculturation of the Christian faith. One such leading proponent is Takenaka Masao, known for his ecumenical views on religion. Takenaka's (1986) work, *God Is Rice: Asian Culture and Christian Faith*, was a huge success, though more so outside Japan than within it – undoubtedly because it was penned in English rather than Japanese. In the book, Takenaka reflects on the this-earthly aspect of the gospel as it calls us to live in contextual harmony with nature and with our culture. Takenaka follows up on the same theme, but this time focusing on Japan, with the publication in 2002 of *When the Bamboo Bends: Christ and Culture in Japan*.

In the 1990s, Kuribayashi Teruo, a theologian from Kwansei Gakuin University in western Japan, brought the task of contextualization into uncharted waters when he appropriated Christ's paschal suffering the experience of the burakumin, a group of people traditionally discriminated against by society because of their engagement with "unclean" occupations that involved the handling of corpses or the killing of animals, taboos associated with Buddhism. The status of butchers, leather tanners, and grave diggers, for example, as outcasts can be traced back to the four-class social structure of the Tokugawa period. [69] These burakumin were excluded from the four classes, and since then,

---

[67] The Yasukuni Shrine was constituted in 1879 as the national shrine commemorating Japan's war dead. Nearly two and a half million people who died in service for the emperor from the Boshin War (1868-69) until the Pacific War (1939-45) are enshrined here, including those who were convicted of war crimes committed during the Second World War. As a result of the 1951 San Francisco Peace Treaty, the shrine became a privately-funded religious institution. However, the legitimacy of its national status is still being deeply held and contested by many government leaders.

[68] The anthem and the flag have long been held with ambivalence by many because of their imperialistic connotations. It was only in 1999, under the initiative of the late Prime Minister Obuchi Keizo, that both were adopted as legal symbols of country.

[69] The four-class structure, hierarchically ordered as *shi-nō-kō-shō* 士農工商 (warrior-farmer-artisan-merchant), was abolished as part of the social reforms undertaken as part of the Meiji Restoration.

their status has become hereditary, and they continue to live in buraku hamlets segregated from mainstream society.[70] And so, even though they are now accorded equal status by constitutional right, the discrimination against them continues even today. In 1991, Kuribayashi published *Ibara no shingaku: Hisabetsu buraku kaihō to kirisutokyō* (*Theology of the Crown of Thorns: Liberation of the Discriminated-Against Buraku and Christianity*), a work based on his 1987 doctoral dissertation submitted to New York's Union Theological Seminary. It is essentially a Japanese liberation theology. Drawing his inspiration from *minjung* theology, Kuribayashi seeks to develop a Christology of suffering and liberation using the symbol of Jesus' crown of thorns.

Christian doctrine is another area where contextualization work has been attempted. Recently, Miyahira Nozomu, a young and upcoming Japanese theologian caught the attention of the academic world with the publication of his doctoral dissertation submitted to Coventry University, entitled, *Towards a Theology of the Concord of God: A Japanese Perspective on the Trinity* (2000). Judging the Nicene formula *treis hypostaseis kai mia ousia* (*sanmi ittai* 三位一体) to be opaque to Japanese cognition, Miyahira uses Japanese cultural categories to understand the biblical revelation on the triunity of God. The result is the original and creative trinitarian formula "three betweennesses and one concord" (*sangen ichiwa* 三間一和). The dissertation is written in English, and in it, Miyahira displays great facility in interacting not only with the ideas from Japanese philosophy and religion but also with the Church Fathers and classical Christian theology. However, given that the traditional trinitarian formula is already so deeply entrenched in Japanese theology, it is unclear as to the extent that Miyahira's contextualized formula will be accepted by the church. In any case, it is noteworthy that, with the shift of focus on inculturation or contextualization, Japanese theology finally achieved its release from its German – more specifically, Barthian, bondage.

The Heisei period also saw the development of a new historical awareness of Japan's Christian tradition. Odagaki explains,

> This historical consciousness insists that it is meaningless to evaluate the history of Christianity in Japan by the standard of European and American Christianity, and that there must be a history of Japanese Christianity written out of our own historical necessity. (1997: 138)

This trend is yet "another example of an exodus of Japanese theology from the Germanic Captivity" (Odagaki, 1997: 138). In truth, this development had already begun in the late Shōwa period. Even in the 1980s, church historian Dohi

---

[70] The word *buraku* 部落 means "excluded from the village," and *burakumin* 部落民 are members of this small group of people excluded from the rest of the "village." It needs to be borne in mind that the discrimination against them is not ethnic – for they are all ethnically Japanese – but purely occupational.

Akio had already raised an issue with the traditional Eurocentric model of understanding Christian history, and insisted that the history of the Japanese church cannot be divorced from her context (Odagaki, 1997: 138). Furuya's book, *Nihon no kirisutokyō* (*Japanese Christianity*), published in 2003, is an example of an academic exercise in the new direction. It offers a theological interpretation of the history of Christianity in Japan in context.

It is not surprising then to see a growing number of research projects undertaken to study the history of Japanese theology. Four scholars are worthy of mention. Miura Hiroshi worked at the Centre for the Study of Christianity in the Non-Western World in Edinburgh, Scotland, and in 1996 presented an insightful thesis on *The Life and Thought of Kanzo Uchimura*. Miura's research certainly helps to clear up the stereotypical misunderstandings that many people until then had of Uchimura and the Non-church Movement. Miura rightly shows that Uchimura was not anti-church, but that he was anti-institution. Indeed, Uchimura rejected the ecclesiastical institutionalism that he came to associate with the foreign missionaries, and sought to construct an indigenous ecclesiology that came to be known by its unfortunate appellation, "Non-church Movement."

The following year, Japanese theologian and Princeton doctoral graduate, Furuya Yasuo, translated and edited an immensely helpful work in English which traces the development of Japanese theology from the Meiji Restoration in 1868 until the close of the Shōwa period in 1989. In this volume, *A History of Japanese Theology* (1997), Furuya and four other eminent theologians – Dohi Akio, Satō Toshio, Yagi Seiichi, and Odagaki Masaya – contributed chapters in which they describe the context, methodology, and goals that have shaped Japanese theology in the last one hundred years. The value of this work can be seen in this blurb on the back cover of the book written by James Phillips: "Here is a book that seeks to open the 'bamboo curtain' that has hidden Japanese theology from non-Japanese readers. The dialogue that it invites is sure to be mutually helpful." Furuya and his colleagues have certainly done a remarkably good job.

Mark Mullins, a sociologist of religion at Tokyo's Meiji Gakuin University, has done much critical work on hitherto unknown indigenous Christian movements in Japan. Although his research methodology is oriented sociologically rather than theologically, Mullins' work casts a sharp light on the receptors' indigenous response to the gospel rather than on missionary efforts and intentions. By examining the complicated process through which Christianity takes root in Japanese soil, Mullins' seminal study, *Christianity Made in Japan* (1998), also teaches us much about Japanese culture and religiosity.

J. Nelson Jennings, former missionary to Japan and currently professor of missions at Covenant Theological Seminary in St. Louis, Missouri, introduced Takakura Tokutarō to the world through the publication of his (2005) doctoral dissertation, *Theology in Japan: Takakura Tokutaro (1885-1934)*. Jennings' work focuses on how Takakura utilized key ideas from Japanese Pure Land Buddhism as well as from British and German theology to rearticulate the historic, biblical, Christian faith for his generation.

Catholic Contributions to Japanese Theology

A brief word should be said on the place of Catholic theology in the Japanese church. Ernest Piryns has rightly perceived Catholic contribution to Japanese theology to be "weaker than the Protestant one" (1987: 547). Pre-Vatican II Catholic theologians in Japan, such as Iwashita Sōichi (1889-1940), Yoshimitsu Yoshihiko (1904-1945), and Matsumoto Masao (1910-1998), were distinctly Aristotelian-Thomistic in orientation. Interestingly, the conservative stance of these theologians could be traced back to the stubborn resistance of the Roman Catholic Church to the onslaught of modernity in nineteenth-century Europe, which culminated in Vatican I (1869-70). The Council occurred around the time of the second missionary movement to Japan, and was summoned and led by Pope Pius IX to ratify the hard-line position that he had taken in his Syllabus of Errors (1864) against liberalism, rationalism, and materialism. On August 4, 1879, Pope Leo XIII issued the encyclical *Aeterni Patris*, a disciplinary document "which became the *magna carta* of official Thomism within the Catholic Church" (McCool, 1977: 167; see also McCool, 1994: 25-42).[71] Japanese Catholic theology was deeply influenced by these events in nineteenth-century Europe, and even after Vatican II, found it hard to break away from its conservative mold.

Nelson Jennings is right when he suggests that "[p]erhaps more than in terms of philosophical discourse, creative Catholic thinking in Japan has developed within literature" (2003: 200). This is most evident in the case of Endō Shūsaku, whose novels have struck such a deep chord among so many people, both in and outside the church. Endō's novels, especially his earlier works, are not only professedly Catholic but also distinctively Japanese. It is interesting to note the theological conservatism of the Catholic Church in Japan from the rather ambivalent – even antagonistic – reaction to Endō's works shown especially by Catholic clergymen. This was not unexpected, however.

In recent years, there has been a growing interest among Catholic scholars in the subject of inculturation, especially the relationship between Christian faith

---

[71] For further study, see Gerald McCool, *Catholic Theology in the Nineteenth Century: The Quest for a Unitary Method* (New York: Seabury Press, 1977). Interestingly, the Protestant reaction to the Enlightenment is the opposite of the Catholic reaction. While the Catholic Church became decidedly anti-modern, the Protestant Church drank deeply from the wells of modernism. It is ironic that despite his Catholic faith, Endō would later allow liberal Protestant theology instead to shape his understanding of the Bible.

and Japanese religiosity. The works of Inoue Yōji (1990),[72] Kadowaki Kakichi (1997), and Okumura Ichirō (2001), among others, look very promising.

The Cross in Japanese Theology

The Cross is central to orthodox Christian faith. However, that does not mean that a systematic theology of the Atonement must be constructed and set in place before Christianity can sink its roots in a culture. Indeed, this does not seem to be the case in Japan. The Jesuits, for instance, did not focus so much on the Cross as they did on the resurrection of Christ and the power of the almighty God (Mase-Hasegawa, 2004: 11). Even in pre- and post-war Christian writings, the Cross was rarely taken as a subject of systematic study. Many Japanese Christians likely shared Takakaru Tokutarō's sentiments when he remarked that a theory of the Atonement is "troublesome, and perhaps unfathomable" (cited in Jennings, 2005: 334). Yet, as Jennings notes, Takakura did develop an elaborate theory of the Atonement that brings together the objective historical fact of Christ's death and the continuing subjective participation of the redeemed in the Cross (see Jennings, 2005: 334-42).

The relatively few instances of a systematic theological construction of Atonement theories should not obscure the fact that Japanese Christians have not infrequently referred to the death of Christ in their writings. As can be expected, there is a divergent range of views on the death of Christ among Japanese Christians. On the one end of the spectrum, we see the Meiji-Taishō Christian statesman Uemura Masahisa who defines Christianity as "a faith which recognizes the heart of God in the cross of Jesus" (1972: 297), and Uchimura Kanzō who, in his battle with the liberal theologians of his day, coins the English word "Crucifixianity" in order to emphasize that authentic Christian belief and experience must be predicated on the centrality of Christ's unique death (Tomioka, 2001: 160). In stark contrast, we have Nakajima Shigeru, the ideologue behind the Social Christianity movement, denying the traditional understanding of the Atonement as vicarious and sacrificial, but rather interpreting the Cross as an expression of Christ's love which brings about a transformation from one's old, egoistic self into a new, social self (, 1997: 51-53). As can be expected, we find a range of views between the two poles. What is telling is that many of these views are informed by already-held presuppositions about life and reality. The social reformer Kagawa Toyohiko, for instance, understands the Cross both as an act of apology to God on our behalf (1931: 102), and as a principle of redemptive love that enables us "to lay hold of our responsibility for the sins of Capitalism, and take upon ourselves the burden of redeeming the sins of capitalistic greed, bolshevistic destructiveness, and eroticism" (1935: 63).

---

[72] Together with Endō, Inoue was one of the earliest Japanese to study overseas after the war. In fact, both sailed on the same ship to France. And from that first encounter, both became lifelong friends. See p. 152, n. 19, and p. 171 below.

Japanese Theology: A Summary Assessment

New Testament scholar Ishida Manabu laments that in spite of more than a hundred years of Protestant witness, "the theological framework of the Protestant churches in Japan has been almost entirely that of Western Christianity" (1994: 55). As a result, "theological creativity in Japan has been limited because certain local cultural characteristics have been adopted into already existing Western theological concepts, or because specific problems have been dealt with in a Western theological framework" (Manabu, 1994: 55). From the overview of the development of Japanese theology as presented in the preceding pages, Ishida's comments need to be qualified. Considering the dearth of indigenous evangelical theology, Ishida's complaint is not a totally invalid one. However, it must not obscure the fact that a lot of self-theologizing has gone on for a long time among mainstream Japanese Protestants. Despite their heavy reliance on Western theological modes, Japanese theologians have consciously reshaped Western ideas, creating subtle nuances and accents that are quite recognizably Japanese, both in thought and in language.

There is an interesting paradox here. Even as missionaries kept on presenting the gospel in an unmistakably Western mode, Japanese Protestant thinkers have been appropriating the Christian message in a distinctively Japanese way. This curious state of affairs could be attributed to the irony of the vernacular principle. While few missionaries had the competency in Japanese to engage Japanese intellectuals theologically, many Japanese scholars were also not sufficiently proficient in English to do the same with their non-Japanese counterparts. The result was that the latter had little choice but to theologize in their native tongue.

In any case, given the small size of the Japanese church, its theological output is actually quite remarkable. In the third volume of *Asian Christian Theologies: A Research Guide to Authors, Movements, and Sources* (2004), the editors list 174 pages of bibliographic works by Japanese Christian thinkers, comparable to what was produced by their respective counterparts in China and Korea! These works were produced by mostly mainstream Protestants and some Roman Catholics. Evangelical writings are, sad to say, very few in comparison. It is also unfortunate that most Japanese theological writings are yet to be translated. Michalson correctly refers to this as "a miracle ... [that] is forced to exist in a shadow" (1960: 9). Now nearly half a century later, the situation has improved only slightly.

Thankfully, the situation is not a hopeless one. As we have seen above, there is now an increasing number of Christian scholars, Japanese and non-Japanese, who are proficient in a number of languages. Some scholars, mostly Japanese, are working on original theological constructions, while others are engaged in translating and interpreting the works of significant Japanese theologians to the world outside Japan. These two groups of scholars will undoubtedly lead in the facilitation of a mutually fruitful theological conversation between Japan and the rest of the global Church.

Moreover, with the many pressing socio-political issues at hand, and the increasing challenge of religious and cultural pluralism, Japanese Christians are rediscovering the importance of the theological task in addressing these issues. The JEA-sponsored Fourth Japan Congress on Evangelism held in Okinawa in June 2000 has, hopefully, provided the much-needed initial impetus to enable the church to be more theologically reflective and socially involved in all aspects of Japanese life. At the Congress, forty-eight papers were presented on a multiplicity of themes relating to contemporary Japanese society, besides the traditional topics of church planting and evangelism. The time has indeed come for the Japanese church to position itself to take on the challenges pertinent to Japanese society. With the present focus on contextualization and cultural engagement, Japanese theology has come full circle to its beginnings in Meiji Japan.

An Introduction to Kitamori Kazō, Endō Shūsaku, and Koyama Kōsuke

In this section, we shall briefly introduce the three subjects of our study and their key writings. More details in terms of their biography are given when we deal with each person in detail in subsequent chapters.

Kitamori Kazō 北森嘉蔵 *(1916-1998)*

Tokyo's International Christian University theologian Morimoto Anri says that no Japanese theologian enjoys a broader international readership than Kitamori Kazō (2005: 1). This is in all probability due to Kitamori's classic work, *Theology of the Pain of God*.[73] First published in 1946, only a year after the Second World War, the book has undergone seven editions since, the last in 1986. This edition had its twelfth printing run in 1995. Interest in Kitamori was generated after Carl Michalson introduced him to the English-speaking world through his book *Japanese Contributions to Christian theology* in 1960, such that the fifth edition of Kitamori's work was translated into English in 1965.[74]

[73] Morimoto initiated the republication of the English translation of Kitamori's *Pain of God Theology* in 2005, exactly forty years after its first release.

[74] The name of the translator is not given in the English version of the book, neither in the 1965 edition nor in the 2005 reprint. In his review of *Theology of the Pain of God* in the July 1966 issue of *Japan Christian Quarterly*, Norman Nuding identified the translator as "Canadian missionary Howard (W. H. H.) Norman" (1966: 224). Nuding also mentioned John Hesselink as having assisted Norman (Nuding, 1966: 224.). In an article published in Japanese in the 1966 Annual Report on Theology for The Japan Society of Christian Studies, missionary I. John Hesselink identifies Howard Norman as the principal translator of *Theology of the Pain of God*, with Hesselink himself and an unnamed "Japanese friend" as assistant translators (1966: 99). However, due to a major disagreement with John Knox Press over some translation issues, the translators' names were left out in the final publication. Hesselink lays the blame squarely on the publisher. (Howard Norman (1905-87) was born and raised in Japan by Canadian missionary

The following year, Kitamori earned the international recognition of "having produced the first indigenous Japanese theology" (Yamamoto, 1966: 40). The book has since been translated into German (1972), Spanish (1975), Italian (1975), and Korean (1987).

Kitamori was a pastor-theologian who did all his work in Japan. Although Lutheran by confession, he was associated with the Kyōdan all his life. For nearly forty years, he taught systematic theology at Tokyo Union Theological Seminary (TUTS), until his retirement in 1984. Throughout most of his years as seminary professor, Kitamori also pastored Chitose Funabashi Church, a church that he founded in 1950. He handed over his pastoral responsibilities in March 1996 to Kumazawa Yoshinobu (1929-2002), another distinguished pastor-theologian. Kitamori remained in the church as Pastor Emeritus until his death two years later.

Kitamori was truly a prolific writer, having penned some forty-three books and many more articles covering a broad range of topics in theology and biblical studies. His vital contribution to Lutheran scholarship is evident from his works *Shūkyōkaigaku no shingaku* (*The Theology of the Reformation*) published in 1960, *Ai ni okeru jiyū no mondai: Rutā "kirisutosha no jiyū" wo chūshin toshite* (*The Problem of Freedom in Love: Concerning Luther's "Freedom of the Christian*) published in 1966. It is curious that other than his *Theology of the Pain of God*, none of his other books has yet to be translated.

Endō Shūsaku 遠藤周作 *(1923-1996)*

Endō Shūsaku was born in Tokyo, but spent his formative childhood years in Manchuria. When he was ten, his parents underwent a divorce, a crisis that precipitated the conversion of his mother to Roman Catholicism. At his mother's urging, Endō received baptism the following year. The precocious Endō soon discovered his penchant for writing, and decided to pursue a literary career.

Endō's works are widely read throughout Japan. He is also extremely well-known outside his country, with many of his novels translated into various Asian and European languages, the most famous of which are *Silence* (1966), *The Samurai* (1980), and *Deep River* (1994).

Endō also published several non-fictional works centering on spiritual and theological themes, including *Iesu no shōgai* イエスの生涯 (*A Life of Jesus*)

---

parents, and indeed served as a missionary in Japan for many years. No mention, however, is made in the *Howard and Gwen Norman Papers* stored in the Special Collections of the University of British Columbia Library about the translation project.) For details on this "unfortunate incident," as well as Hesselink's unhappiness with the "frivolous, touristy design" on the dust jacket (a *torii*, the wooden gateway structure at the entrance to a Shinto shrine, against the backdrop of a huge rising sun), see Hesselink (1966: 99-100). In any case, the English translation of *Theology of the Pain of God* is a first-class piece of work, especially considering that Kitamori engaged in a lot of Japanese word play which is notoriously difficult to translate.

(1973) and *Kirisuto no tanjō* キリストの誕生 (*The Birth of Christ*) (1978). Through these apologetic treatises, Endō seeks to present the Christian faith in a way which is not only credible, but appealing to the Japanese mind.

Koyama Kōsuke 小山晃佑 (1929-)

Koyama Kōsuke studied at TUTS where he sat under the teaching of Kitamori among others. Upon graduation in 1952, Koyama left for the United States where he studied at Drew University, and then at Princeton where he obtained his doctoral degree for his work on Luther. In 1960, he and his wife were sent out to serve as Kyōdan missionaries in Thailand. For the next eight years, Koyama taught at the Thailand Theological Seminary in Chiangmai. From 1968 to 1974, Koyama took up a dual appointment in Singapore, as Dean of the South East Asia Graduate School of Theology and as Executive Director of the Association of Theological Schools and Colleges in South East Asia. He then taught at the University of Otago in New Zealand for the next five years, before moving to the Union Theological Seminary in New York in 1980 where he taught until his retirement in 1996. Now he lives in Minneapolis, Minnesota. So unlike Kitamori and Endō, Koyama has lived most of his life outside Japan.

James Phillips hails Koyama as "[a]n outstanding theologian among Japanese workers overseas" (1981: 132). Indeed, Koyama has developed a reputation as an eminent missiologist through his extensive, and provocative, writings, particularly on themes relating to Christ and culture. Koyama has also carried on a lifelong theological dialogue with Buddhism. Because Koyama writes primarily for an international audience, especially those engaged in cross-cultural missionary service, most of his writings are in English. To his credit, he has authored some twenty-one books and more than a hundred academic articles. Koyama's most famous work is *Waterbuffalo Theology*, first published in 1974, in which he offers an interpretation of history, the gospel as rooted in context, and of the Christian life, from an Asian perspective. The Catholic Foreign Mission Society of America (Maryknoll) honored Koyama with the publication of the twenty-fifth anniversary edition of the book in 1999.[75] Koyama's other key works include *No Handle on the Cross* (1976), *Three Mile and Hour God* (1979), and *Mount Fuji and Mount Sinai* (1984).

Unlike Kitamori who was converted through an active search for truth as a teenager, and Endō who agreed grudgingly to be baptized at the age of eleven just to please his newly-converted mother, Koyama inherited a solidly Christian faith from his family. His paternal grandfather had been the first in the Koyama clan to become a Christian in Meiji Japan. Indeed, Koyama's identity as a Japanese Christian has never been in doubt even though he has done most of his theological work overseas.

---

[75] The title of the 1999 reissue is *Water Buffalo Theology* (instead of *Waterbuffalo Theology*).

These three Japanese Christian intellectuals – Kitamori, Endō, and Koyama – are chosen for our study because they share the common experience of having suffered the aftermath of the Second World War, and gone through the political and cultural turbulences of the late twentieth century. They all have written extensively on theological themes. Furthermore, all have addressed, to different extents, the meaning and significance of the death of Christ. Although they all come from the non-evangelical tradition, their influence on Japanese theology is not inconsiderable. Kitamori's works continue to be published. Endō remains a best-selling novelist. Koyama is lesser known in Japan, having lived most of his life overseas, but his voice in the ecumenical world is not an insignificant one. Koyama's writings should become increasingly of more interest to Japanese theologians as they continue to work on theological contextualization but with global concerns in mind. Because of their different vocations, as theologian, novelist, and missiologist respectively, these men will provide us with interesting, and hopefully, weighty, perspectives on Christ and the Cross.

A Brief Literature Review of Studies on Kitamori, Endō, and Koyama

In the final section of this chapter, I shall present a brief review of some key studies that have been done on Kitamori, Endō, and Koyama respectively.

Studies on Kitamori

It is becoming common, perhaps even respectable, to cite Kitamori and his pain of God theology when writing a theological text touching on the question of the impassibility of God. Many of these citations, however, do not go beyond a passing mention (e.g. Moltmann, 1993: 47, 153; Ngien, 1995: 245; McGrath, 1997: 253; Lee, 2005: 522). There are, of course, articles which provide a more sustained treatment of Kitamori, such as McWilliams (1981: 184-200); Parratt, (2000: 141-51); Inagaki and Jennings, (2000: 98-114); Tang, 2004: 90-93); and Schwarz (2005: 510-512), among others. Even Koyama has a whole chapter in his *Water Buffalo Theology* (1999, 82-89) outlining his teacher's pain of God theology and interpreting "the theology of the analogy of suffering [as] a most comprehensive accommodational principle" (Koyama, 1999: 89).

Whole-book treatments of Kitamori are far fewer. The first extensive treatment of Kitamori is a 1955 doctoral dissertation by one of Kitamori's students, Noro Yoshio, entitled *Impassibilitas Dei*, submitted to New York City's Union Theological Seminary. When Noro finished his dissertation, Kitamori had only written ten of his forty-three books. It is not fair then to critique Noro's work against all that Kitamori has written. In the main, Noro finds the word "pain" problematic, and hence objects to Kitamori's assertion of divine pain as ontological. Noro may be overreacting when he claims that Kitamori's theology would upset the traditional doctrines of creation and justification (1955: 93), but his criticism that the ontological tendency in

Kitamori's theology, when pushed to its logical conclusion, would lead to an ahistorical Christianity and consequently to a docetic Christology, certainly needs to be reckoned with seriously even today (Noro, 1955: 88-91). It is curious that Kitamori never responded to Noro's charges directly, perhaps because Kitamori has already argued rather strenuously in his magnum opus that his theology would make no sense at all if the Christ were ahistorical and docetic (1986: 46-67). In any case, Noro's negative appraisal of Kitamori is hardly surprising, being aligned with the general attitude of most Japanese theologians toward Kitamori that persisted even well into the late 1960s.

Two recent studies on Kitamori are worthy of mention. Both are doctoral dissertations. The first is a massive 613-page work entitled, *Theology of the Pain of God: An Analysis and Evaluation of Kazoh Kitamori's (1916-) Work in Japanese Protestantism*, submitted by Lutheran scholar Hashimoto Akio in 1992 to Concordia Seminary in St. Louis, Missouri. Hashimoto provides a comprehensive theological analysis of Kitamori's concept of divine pain from the distinct perspective of Lutheran theological tradition. Curiously, Hashimoto comes to the negative and rather trite conclusion that Kitamori's theological formulation is probably "too prosaic to be examined with proper academic rigor," and that therefore it "suffers from the symptoms of theological monologue" (1992: 590). Hashimoto's strongest criticism is that, contrary to what most people might think, Kitamori's theology is a substantial, even syncretistic, deviation from authentic Lutheran theology (Hashimoto, 1992: 577). This assessment appears unduly harsh in the light of his acknowledgement that Kitamori was trying to indigenize Lutheranism in the spiritual soil of Japan (Hashimoto, 1992: 594). Hashimoto also finds the pain of God a contingent and negative value, and as such, "cannot be attributed to God as His eternal essence" (Hashimoto, 1992: 89).

A more sympathetic and favorable attitude to Kitamori is taken by Asakawa Toru in his dissertation submitted in 2003 to McGill University in Montreal. Asakawa's work, entitled, *Kitamori Kazō: Theologian of the Pain of God*, locates the idea of the pain of God helpfully in a wider soteriological context. This 285-page dissertation (with 1,044 footnotes!) is smaller than Hashimoto's, but no less rigorous. In it, Asakawa deals with Kitamori's understanding of creation, justification, and sanctification, and creatively superimposes these onto Kitamori's trilogical construct of divine love, matching creation with the immediate love of God, justification with the mediated love of God, and sanctification with divine love rooted in divine pain. In the middle of the dissertation, Asakawa discusses, albeit in way somewhat disjointed from the rest of the text, Kitamori's engagement with the Non-church Movement. Following that, he evaluates Kitamori's critique of three Japanese novelists, Natsume Sōseki, Chikamatsu Monzaemon, and Endō Shūsaku. In the section on Endō, Asakawa examines four of Endō's works, *The Sea and Poison*, *Silence*, *On the Shores of the Dead Sea*, and *Deep River*, and notes that while the salvation of sinners is a theme common to Kitamori and Endō, "Endō's interest is focused on

God's love at the expense of God's anger, whereas Kitamori deals with both God's love and God's anger" (2003: 178). As we shall see later in this dissertation, Asakawa's assessment is right. Asakawa is also convinced that Kitamori's notion of divine pain constitutes "an adequate touchstone that detects the authenticity of the paradoxical unity between God's love and God's wrath, *sola fide* and *sola scriptura*, grace and nature" (Asakawa, 2003: 260).

Studies on Endō

Given that Endō is a novelist rather than a theologian, it is to be expected that most of the studies done on him and his works should come from the literary guild rather than the theological world. Indeed, many in-depth scholarly studies have been undertaken on Endō's literature, such as Gessel (1979), Williams (1999), and Bussie (2003). Articles examining the place of religion in Endō's works are published in abundance, the more notable of which include Durfee (1989), Burkman (1994), Sano (1999), Netland (1999), and Holtrop (2000). Studies on Endō from within the Christian tradition are, understandably, fewer and generally shorter in length, and these include Matsuoka (1982), Hall (1987), Noble (1991), Noble (1992), and Willis (1992). Kitamori even has a chapter on Endō in his book *Ureinaki kami* (*Weeping God*), to which he gives the telling title, *Ashi no itami no bungaku* ("Literature of the Pain of the Foot") (1991: 304-40), alluding to the final agonizing scene in Endō's *Silence* in which Father Rodrigues places his foot on the bronze image of Christ as an act of renouncing his faith.[76]

Two doctoral studies by Christian scholars are worthy of mention. The first, entitled *The Dynamics of Shame in Japanese Chronically Absent Students: A Study of the Theological-Psychological Meaning and Pastoral Implications of Shame in Caring for Chronically Absent Students*, submitted to Luther Northwestern Theological Seminary in 1992, is not a study on Endō per se. Rather, the author, James Sack seeks to explore the psychology of shame and shaming as it relates to chronic absenteeism in Japanese adolescents. What is interesting for our purpose, however, is that Sacks also lays out a theological perspective of shame using Endō's presentation of a caring and accepting Christ who speaks to the Japanese. To all who suffer shame and pain, Christ offers understanding, companionship, and an empathetic companionship.

The next dissertation, written by Japanese Christian Mase-Hasegawa Emi, is entitled *Spirit of Christ Inculturated: A Theological Theme Implicit in Shusaku Endo's Literary Works*, and submitted to the Centre for Theology and Religious Studies at Sweden's Lund University in 2004. As is evident in the title, Mase-Hasegawa scrutinizes several of Endō's key works and discovers within

---

[76] Among Endō's works, the novel most written about in both secular and religious journals is *Silence* (1966) (e.g. Buss 1974; Hall 1987; Noble 1991; Cohen; Burkman 1994; Gessel, 1999; and Sano, 1999). Endō's last novel *Deep River* (1994) is also drawing increasing attention (e.g. Reinsma, 1999; Holtrop, 2000; and Williams, 2002).

them what she interprets as an inculturated spirit of Christ. Mase-Hasegawa argues that Endō's presentation of the growth of Christianity in Japan fits in with Stephen Bevans' anthropological model of contextualization and Takeda Kiyoko's grafting and apostatizing models of inculturation (2004: 121-25). Interestingly, Endō's honest struggles as a Japanese Christian find deep resonance with Mase-Hasegawa's own faith experience. She is prepared to go all the way with Endō, suggesting that when the gospel is really inculturated, it may not be overtly recognizable in form but is nonetheless the true gospel as long as it preserves the spirit of Christ, namely, a spirit of hope and love (Mase-Hasegawa, 2004: 165). The influence of Hick is unmistakable, which Mase-Hasegawa does not deny. According to her, the Cross, insofar as it presents Western domination, must give way to the spirit of Christ, which she interprets in psychological and moralistic terms (Mase-Hasegawa, 2004: 165-66).

Studies on Koyama

Although Koyama may not be as widely known among his fellow countrymen, he is certainly often cited in works of missiological interest published outside Japan (e.g. Bosch, 1979; Hesselgrave and Rommen, 1989; Newbigin, 1989; Hwa, 1997; and Kuster, 2001; Bevans, 2002; and Bevans and Schroeder, 2004). This is hardly surprising since he has lived and worked most of his life overseas. Japanese theologians, however, are beginning to take an interest in his writings (cf. Furuya, 1997: 146). Morimoto Anri has been instrumental in promoting a critical understanding of Koyama and other contemporary Asian theologians through his teaching at International Christian University. In his recent *Ajia shingaku kōgi: Gurōbarukasuru kontekusuto no shingaku* (*Lectures on Asian Theology: Theology in a Globalizing Context*), Morimoto devotes a chapter introducing Koyama and his key ideas, focusing on Koyama's characteristic use of the language of contrast between oppositions as a means to convey theological truth (e.g. Mount Fuji, which symbolizes polytheism, naturalism, safety, immanence, man ascending, etc., as opposed to Mount Sinai, which symbolizes monotheism, historicism, danger, transcendence, and God descending, etc.) (2004: 107-39). According to Morimoto, Koyama is illustrative of the need for Asians to theologize in a mode indigenous to their cultural and linguistic constitution (Morimoto, 2004: 138-39).

On the occasion of Koyama's retirement from Union Theological Seminary in 1996, his colleagues and former students presented him with a festschrift as "an outstanding tribute to the life and thought of this major twentieth-century Christian theologian" (Irvin and Akinade, 1996: xi). This fine book, *The Agitated Mind of God: The Theology of Kosuke Koyama*, contains fourteen essays covering three key themes that have been the focus of Koyama's work over the years: global community, the crucified mind, and neighborology. These missiological themes were first articulated in Koyama's *Waterbuffalo Theology*.

The first doctoral dissertation that involves a study of Koyama is a comparative study between three contemporaneous non-Western theologians: Gustavo Gutiérrez, John Mbiti, and Koyama, undertaken by Joseph Moody Martin in 1981 at Georgia State University. The work is entitled, *Gutierrez, Koyama, and Mbiti: Gaining Curriculum Insights from an Analysis and Comparison of Three Ways to Contextualize Theology*. As the subtitle suggests, Martin is not so much interested in the theologies of these three persons as he is in sieving the methodological distinctives of their theologizing for the purpose of developing culturally-sensitive curricula for Christian education.

The first piece of research wholly devoted to Koyama and his theology is in all probability the doctoral dissertation written by Merrill Morse at the University of Birmingham. It was published in book form in 1991, entitled *Kosuke Koyama: A Model for Intercultural Theology*, and serves as a good primer to Koyama. The book is divided into three parts. The first deals extensively with the cultural contexts of Asia at large, and Japan in particular, and identifies contextual influences that form Koyama's theological perspectives. In the second part, Morse lays out the key themes of Koyama's theology, namely his concept of the crucified mind, and his theological view of other religions. In the final part of the book, Morse discusses Koyama's stylistic contribution to the theological task. Morse observes rightly the paradoxical and symbolic use of language that has become a trademark of Koyama. He also suggests that since Koyama works outside Japan in a foreign language while operating in his native thought forms, his theology is better thought of not as Asian theology per se, but as "a bridge between East and West" (Morse, 1991: 269). For Morse, Koyama represents a good model of doing intercultural theology, not by confrontation, but by a constant wrestling with the tensions between Mount Fuji, "the symbolic mountain of Asian culture," and Mount Sinai, that of Western culture (Morse, 1991: 275). Of course, the world is more complex than the stereotypical East-West bipolarity, but Morse's point is well taken that authentic theological construction must be rooted in experience and characterized by relational openness.

More recently, in 2002, a Korean scholar by the name of Jaecheon Lee submitted a doctoral dissertation to Drew University entitled, *Toward an Asian Contextual Theology: A Critical Study of Kosuke Koyama's Theology and Ethics*. Lee's study is comprehensive and more nuanced than Morse's, in terms of explicating Koyama's theological contents and methodology. Lee takes the view that Asian theology is not to be regarded as something which is over and against Western theology, but as a phenomenon of cultural encounter between East and West. Therefore, Koyama is chosen for Lee's study because of his experiences with both East and West. Lee believes that the way Koyama does theology could constitute a "paradigm shift for the changing global context" (2002: 3). However, he seems to be uncomfortable with what he perceives to be the overly Christ-centered emphasis in Koyama's theology. For Lee, Asian theology has to be theocentric rather than Christocentric, not only because of the pluralist religious contexts of Asia, and also because the ethical obligations of theology demand that the "brokenness of the people" be the proper object of theology rather than the "brokenness of Christ" which Koyama often talks about (Lee, 2002: 286). He does appreciate, however, Koyama's interpretation of the Cross in term of self-denial as providing the basis for his vision for global theology and ethics. Nonetheless, in the quest for an Asian contextual theology, Lee advocates a methodological corrective to Koyama by appealing to the *minjung* theologians (Lee, 2002: 293-300). In this regard, Lee seems to have been influenced by the more liberal and pluralist views of his teachers, David Kwang-Sun Suh and S. Wesley Ariarajah.

The Distinctive Contribution of This Work

Although a number of research studies have been undertaken on Kitamori, Endō, and Koyama, there is still ample room for conversation with regard to their theological ideas and methodology. The evangelical voice in the discussion is conspicuously missing, and this publication seeks to fill this gap. Next, unlike the other dissertations which tend to be comprehensive – with the exception of the two dissertations reviewed on Endō – this work focuses on a single theological theme regarded by evangelicals to be central to the missionary task, namely, the death of Christ. Moreover, a comparative study of three seminal Japanese thinkers on the death of Christ has not been attempted before. Since the aim of this work is ultimately missiological, there is value in precisely a study of such nature, for it facilitates the foregrounding of common cultural themes. By no means does this imply the sacrifice of theological content and method. After all, good missiology must flow out of good theology. In our study, there is indeed substantial discussion on the relationship between theology and culture, and its attendant implications. In sum, the thematic focus of this work is singular, and its approach comparative. The driving question from beginning to end is: how can the message of the Cross be preached in a way that is respectfully intelligible to the Japanese without compromising its biblical integrity?

4. Kitamori Kazō and the Pain of God

One would be hard-pressed to find among Japanese theologians one who is more passionately crucicentric than Kitamori Kazō北森嘉蔵 (1916-1998). Indeed his magnum opus, *Kami no itami no shingaku* 神の痛みの神学 (*Theology of the Pain of God*), first published in 1946, is nothing less than a *theologia crucis*.[1] In this masterly work, Kitamori builds on Luther and provides a unique explication of the death of Christ using the motif of divine pain.[2] Kitamori would spend the rest of his life composing variations of his theological theme of the pain of God. This undoubtedly would be Kitamori's seminal contribution to the Church's understanding of the Atonement.

Extrapolating from the words of the apostle Paul in 1 Corinthians 2:2, Kitamori insists that "the Christ of the Cross is the starting point from which to understand all things" (1986: 74). Kitamori did not develop such a Cross-centered orientation by gradual degrees over the course of his life, for by

---

[1] The term *theologia crucis* probably made its first appearance in Martin Luther's commentary on Hebrews 12:11. It refers to more than simply the doctrine of the Atonement, but points to an understanding of the whole of Christian theology as theology of the Cross. See Martin Luther, "Lectures on the Epistle to the Hebrews 1517-18," in *Luther: Early Theological Works*, translated and edited by James Atkinson (Philadelphia, PA: Westminster, 1962), pp. 233-34; and also Conclusions XX and XXI of Luther's Heidelberg Disputation in the same volume, pp. 291-92. In this dissertation, however, the term *theologia crucis* and its English equivalent, "theology of the Cross", are used to describe any particular theological understanding of the death of Christ.

[2] *Theology of the Pain of God* is one of the very few Christian books published by the prestigious Kōdansha Academic Library (*Kōdansha gakujutsu bunko* 講談社学術文庫). The text used in this dissertation is the Kōdansha pocketbook edition published in 1986, and shall be notated as such. This is the seventh edition of Kitamori's original work. Apart from the publisher and pagination, this edition is essentially the same as the fifth – and sixth, the Kōdansha hardcover – edition. When citing directly from the Japanese text, I shall use my own translation. The English translation, published by John Knox Press in 1965 and republished by Wipf and Stock in 2005, is based on the fifth edition of the Japanese text published in 1958, and so is essentially a translation of the seventh edition as well. As noted earlier, this is a translation *par excellence*. Hence, I also use the 2005 English translated text liberally insofar as it represents the original text faithfully. In this case, I shall provide alongside it the equivalent reference to the 1986 Japanese text. The actual Japanese text runs short of 300 pages, while the English translated text is about 170 pages.

the time he graduated from the Japan Lutheran Seminary in the spring of 1938, at just the age of twenty-two, he had already come to full agreement with Luther's epigram, *Crux probat omnia* (*Weimarer Ausgabe* 5.179.31). For the rest of his life, Kitamori would embrace uncompromisingly the Cross as theologically axiomatic, "the only grid with which to perceive the whole counsel of the Godhead" (1968: 85). Indeed, his seminary graduation thesis, *Kirisuto ni okeru kami no ninshiki* キリストにおける神の認識 (*Knowledge of God in Christ*), completed on Christmas Day 1937, was his first theological manifesto on what he refers to as "the gospel of the Cross" (1999: 169).[3]

However, Kitamori goes beyond Luther by positing a *necessary* relationship between *theologia crucis* and *theologia doloris Dei*. This chapter seeks to examine Kitamori's understanding of the meaning and significance of the death of Christ through the pain of God. Certainly more than other theologians, Kitamori utilized the experiences of his late teens and early 20s – subconsciously, no doubt – as material for his theological construction. Hence in his case, particularly, without a proper understanding of the key events at this crucial stage of his life, it is impossible to appreciate Kitamori's rather unorthodox apprehension of the death of Christ through the leitmotif of the pain of God without lapsing into a stereotypical judgment of his theology. In the next section, we have hence adopted the methodology of a biographical study in order to trace the development of Kitamori's idea of divine pain.[4] The focus is on his spiritual pilgrimage and theological formation in the first thirty years of his life. At the age of thirty, Kitamori published *Theology of the Pain of God*; since then, his theology has remained largely unchanged.

---

[3] Kitamori's graduation thesis was published posthumously in 1999 as part of a bigger book by Chitose Funabashi Church, the church he pastored for forty-five years. The title of the book is *"Kami no itami" no rokujūnen: Kitamori Kazō bokushi kinenshi* 「神の痛み」の六十年―北森嘉蔵牧師記念誌 (*Sixty Years of "The Pain of God": In Memory of Pastor Kitamori Kazō*).

[4] Kitamori's two-volume autobiography, *Shingakuteki jiden* 神学的自伝 (*Theological Autobiography*), published in 1960 and 1968 respectively, is the main source of information of his early life. Other than the first section in Volume 1 in which the adult Kitamori recalls his childhood years until his conversion, the rest of the volume is a commentary on his diary entries and note jottings from 1934 to 1936. The second volume continues from the first, covering the period of 1937 to 1940, just before his graduation from Kyoto Imperial University. Kitamori calls his autobiography a "theological autobiography" because he wants to declare the unmistakable work of God in his life through the telling of his story (1960a: 20-21).

The Faith Journey of Kitamori Kazō

Early Years (1916-1935)

Kitamori was born into a pious Pure Land Buddhist family in Kumamoto on the southern island of Kyushu on February 1, 1916, during the fifth year of Emperor Taishō's reign. At that time, Kumamoto was one of the three centers of Christianity in Japan. In fact, exactly forty years earlier, Captain Leroy Janes had led some thirty-five of his students from the Kumamoto Western School where he was teaching, and together they climbed atop a small hill where they pledged to preach the gospel throughout the Empire "in order to dispel ignorance and enlighten the people" (Varley, 1984: 220). From this famous incident was birthed the Kumamoto Band of Japanese Protestantism, which produced eminent Christians such as Ebina Danjō, Kozaki Hiromichi, and Kanamori Tsurin (see pp. 48-9 above, esp. n. 24). The landmark hill, Hanaokayama, was near Kitamori's home, and as a boy, he used to climb it "almost every day" (1960a: 7). In his adult years, Kitamori would recall the mysterious bond he had in his childhood years with this hill as if it was prophetically symbolic of his spiritual vocation, but he would at the same time lament the irony that throughout those years he heard not a single word about the Christian faith (Kitamori, 1960a: 7). With hindsight, Kitamori attributed the anomalous state of the latter to the tragic loss of relevance of the Christian faith to the ordinary populace (Kitamori, 1960a: 7).

Kitamori felt the same way about Buddhism too. As a boy of six or seven, he would often follow his mother or grandmother to hear the monk preach at the local Buddhist temple. But the precocious child could see no relationship between the proclaimed mercy of the Amida Buddha and the everyday lives of believers. Jealousy and hatred continued to be rife even among the most devout Buddhists. To the young boy, it made no difference whatsoever whether one was fervently Buddhist or indifferently non-religious (Kitamori, 1960a: 8).

Conversion: From Existential Uncertainty to Providential Faith

Kitamori's four years in middle school were largely uneventful, except that the elitist environment of the school only boosted the ego of the exceptionally brilliant boy. In 1932, after finishing middle school, he entered the prestigious Fifth High School in his hometown.[5] Despite the clouds of political gloom hanging over the

---

[5] Compulsory education for both boys and girls in Japan at this time was limited to six years of elementary education. Beyond that, education tended to be selective and elitist. Middle school ordinarily lasted five years. Those who wished to pursue a university education went on to another three years of high school. Kumamoto's Fifth High School was one of the eight numbered elite high schools set up by the government in the country to prepare the brightest students to enter the few imperial universities. Lafcadio Hearn (also known as Koizumi Yakumo), who introduced Japanese culture to the Western world through his writings, taught at Fifth High School from 1891 to 1894; so

country as a result of the Manchurian Incident the year before, and the assassination of Prime Minister Inukai Tsuyoshi in the so-called Five-One-Five Incident eight months later,[6] Kitamori was curiously unperturbed by these events. Rather, he found himself occupied and assailed with "a completely different, but huge, problem" (Kitamori, 1960a: 12), a problem that led to his first encounter with Christianity. The sixteen-year-old was deeply bothered by what he perceived to be the sheer contingency (*gūzensei* 偶然性) of life. Kitamori explains,

> I had a kind of intuition that in the final analysis, life is but a series of contingencies. Birth, life, and death happen by chance. Indeed everything happens by chance. There could be no secure knowledge of being sustained by anyone. I felt a sense of nothingness within me. (Kitamori, 1960a: 12)

Paralyzed by deep feelings of despondency, the young boy went out to buy a copy of the New Testament from a secondhand bookstore. A short while afterwards, he attended a public lecture given by the visiting Christian social activist, Kagawa Toyohiko. It was a lively meeting which left a positive and lasting impression on Kitamori. For the first time in his life, Kitamori felt attracted to Christianity. He set himself down to read his newly-acquired New Testament, beginning with the Gospel of Matthew. When he came to these words from Jesus' agonizing prayer at the Garden of Gethsemane in Matthew 26:39, "Yet not as I will, but as you will", Kitamori felt a deep stirring within his spirit and came to the realization that contrary to what he had thought, there was indeed a God who sustained his very life by His will. This realization constituted Kitamori's conversion experience as he turned his heart to God. The young Kitamori wrote the conclusion he had arrived at in his diary – that the answer to his existential question about the contingent nature of life consisted in giving of himself "completely to be possessed by the Supreme One" (1960a, 14). In other

---

did the acclaimed novelist Natsume Sōseki from 1896 to 1900. (Natsume died the year Kitamori was born.)

[6] On September 18, 1931, the Japanese Kwantung Army conducted clandestine operations and bombed the railway tracks north of Mukden (today's Shenyang). Under long-standing agreements as a result of the Russo-Japanese War (1904-05), the Japanese were supposed to be guarding these tracks. Blame was assigned to the Chinese, and this led to the realization of the Army's true intention behind the bombing plot, namely, the founding of the puppet state of Manchukuo on March 1, 1932. Two months later, on May 15, 1932, eleven radical naval officers – most of them just turning twenty – launched a failed coup d'état by assassinating the prime minister in a bid to end the parliamentary democracy that had evolved from the middle of the Meiji Period. (The assassination plan supposedly included the killing of extremely popular Charlie Chaplin who was visiting Japan at that time, but he was with the prime minister's son away from the scene of the murder when it happened.) Although the coup d'état did not achieve its aims immediately; it increased the momentum of the country's descent into the abyss of military fascism. For the background on the political intrigues behind these two incidents, see Gordon (2003: 186-92).

words, salvation from life's uncertainties was to be attained by living within the will of God, and this was what Kitamori resolved to do. He began to attend the local Lutheran church in Kumamoto.[7] Kitamori calls the faith he had at this time of his life "providential faith" (Kitamori, 1960a: 16).[8]

Indeed, divine providence would lead Kitamori to seek further spiritual help from his chemistry teacher, Kondo Seijirō. As a student at the First High School in Tokyo in the early 1890s, Kondo had witnessed first-hand the so-called *Fukeikan* 不敬漢 (Irreverence Incident) involving Uchimura Kanzō, and as a result became rather antagonistic toward Christianity for a long time.[9] However, around the time when he was turning fifty, his wife, a Christian, became terminally ill. Until her death, she had displayed a remarkable and steadfast faith that eventually led Kondo to his own conversion. By the time Kitamori met him, Kondo had become a fervent Christian. Through his teacher, Kitamori was introduced to Uchimura's writings. His theological appetite whetted, the voracious reader visited the local library and devoured the works of Pascal, Koeber, Amiel, and Hilty, among others.

---

[7] Kumamoto had been the center of Lutheran missionary activities since the 1890s. A small Lutheran seminary was also founded in the city in 1905.

[8] Kitamori uses the word *setsuri* 摂理 (providence) to mean the will of God (1960a: 14-16). For him, to live within God's will is to be sustained by God's providence.

[9] Uchimura was a teacher at First High School at that time. In December 1890, to counter what the government perceived to be the threat of over-Westernization of the country, the Ministry of Education issued an Imperial Precept on Education, with the seal of the emperor affixed to it. Every school was given a copy of the precept, and told to hang it beside the emperor's portrait. On January 9, 1891, Emperor Meiji's birthday, a special school assembly was called, and all the students and faculty members were instructed to bow their heads before the precept hung next to the emperor's portrait. Among the sixty teachers in the school, three, including Uchimura, were Christians. Uchimura's Christian colleagues, however, absented themselves on that fateful day of the assembly. When it came to Uchimura's turn to bow, he went up the platform, hesitated for a moment, and then in the presence of all the teachers and some 1,000 students, stood still. Uchimura's refusal to bow created an instant uproar, and he was labeled a traitor to the country. According to Harvard historian Andrew Gordon, Uchimura repudiated his action and bowed to the rescript on several other occasions, but just could not turn back the tide of criticisms from the press (2003: 112). Needless to say, he lost his teaching position. Suddenly Uchimura became famous – or rather, infamous – throughout the country, and he had to take on an assumed name when traveling in order to prevent identification. Even though Uchimura's act of civil disobedience had the almost immediate effect of reinforcing ultimate imperial authority, John Howes, retired professor of Japanese studies at the University of British Columbia, believes that it became "one of the most important events in modern Japanese intellectual history," for it raises the important question of the place of personal conscience and integrity in an otherwise harmonious society governed by Confucian ethics (personal communication). This incident continues to be mentioned in many Japanese textbooks today.

Repentance: From Providential Faith to Faith in the Crucified Christ

Before long, however, the seventeen-year-old Kitamori found himself tormented by a new problem. Try as hard as he could to live in conformity to the will of God, he nevertheless found himself "imprisoned by disobedience" (Kitamori, 1960a: 17). His providential faith had become a "burden" (Kitamori, 1960a: 16). From his earlier existential problem of life's contingency, Kitamori now struggled with feelings of alienation as a result of his inability to live in such a way that he thought would please God. He read Uchimura and Barth, but found no help (Kitamori, 1960a: 19). Kierkegaard was over the head of the seventeen-year-old; although what left a deep impression was the Kierkegaardian expression "Either/Or" (*areka koreka*), which Kitamori took to be a constant imperative to seek God, the very thing he found painfully difficult, if not impossible (Kitamori, 1960a: 24-25).[10] For the next eighteen months or so, Kitamori found himself languishing in the depths of despair and depression, finding only occasional relief in the lament psalms of the Old Testament and the writings of Dostoyevsky (Kitamori, 1960a: 37-38).

In February 1934, Kitamori started reading Kumano and Kuwada and was inducted into the world of dialectical theology. Although he found the dialectical method appealing, he did not know how to bring it to bear on his inner struggles (Kitamori, 1960a: 33). A few weeks later, he visited the city library again, and this time his eye caught Satō Shigehiko's latest book *Ruttā no konpon shisō* (*Luther's Elemental Thoughts*).[11] Kitamori likens his experience of reading this book with the biblical episode of Jacob wrestling with the angel of God (Kitamori, 1960a: 19). Through the book, he made two startling discoveries which revealed the deficiency of his "providential faith". Firstly, he was struck when he read that "it is sin, not faith, to seek God for the sake of one's peace" (Kitamori, 1960a: 51). Kitamori came under the conviction that the root of his problem was the sin of self-love, for he had sought God not for his sake but for his own desire to be delivered from obsessive fear and anxiety. Secondly, he changed his view of Christ. Until then, Christ had been for him a moral example *par excellence* on how to live within the will of God (Kitamori, 1960a: 60). Now he learned about the unique mediatory role of Christ without which it was

---

[10] Kitamori admitted however that the way he appropriated Kierkegaard's phrase *Either/Or* was probably different from what Kierkegaard had intended it to be. Even though Kitamori confessed that he could not understand Kierkegaard, ironically, Kitamori's inner turmoil reminds one of Kierkegaard's own existential struggles.

[11] In all probability, this is the book adaptation of Satō's doctoral dissertation published a year earlier in 1933, the full title of which is *Rōmasho kōkai ni arawareshi ruttā no konpon shisō* 羅馬書講解に現われしルッたーの根本思想 (*Luther's Elemental Thoughts on Romans*). Satō had written a popular book *Wakaki Rūteru* 若きルーテル (*Young Luther*) in 1918 which caught the attention of Lutheran missionary J. M. T. Winther who then invited him to teach at the Lutheran seminary in Kumamoto (see p. 64, n. 61 above). Satō taught at the school for about two years from 1920 to 1922 before leaving for further theological studies in Germany.

impossible to love God, let alone do his will. Indeed, Kitamori discovered that the ability to love and obey God is a divine grace given only to the person reckoned righteous, that is, justified, in God's sight (Kitamori, 1960a: 59). One is granted such a standing in righteousness only through the mediatory work of Christ. In other words, it is only through Christ that "those who have been abandoned are lifted up" (*suterareta mono ga hiroiagerareru* 捨てられた者が拾い上げられる) (Kitamori, 1960a:41).[12]

It now dawned upon Kitamori that the "providential faith" that he had for the past two years was really an exercise in "immediate religiosity" (*chokusetsusei no shūkyō* 直接性の宗教) (Kitamori, 1960a: 17). What this means is that his was a religion in which he sought God *directly*, that is, unmediated by Christ – a sheer impossibility, hence his deep frustration. Although Kitamori had already considered himself converted from the time he discovered God's will and providence, what had been lacking all along was repentance of sin, and the consequent reception, through faith in Christ, of the forgiveness of sin, deliverance from self-love, and the grace to love and obey God (Kitamori, 1960a: 54, 58).[13] And so, Kitamori gave up his egocentric search for peace in divine providence, and put his faith in Christ and his redemptive work (Kitamori, 1960a: 59). Having moved from existential uncertainty to a formal, legalistic faith in providence, and now finally to what we might call an evangelical faith in Christ, all within a period of two years, Kitamori, now eighteen, received

---

[12] This phrase has a poetic ring and visual beauty to it. The Chinese character for the verb "to abandon," 捨 resembles the character for the verbal phrase "to pick up," 拾. And in this expression, the word "abandoned" is in the past perfect tense, sute*rareta*, while "lifted up" is in the present perfect, hiroiage*rareru*. Literary aesthetics is certainly a key characteristic of Kitamori's theology.

[13] Kitamori makes a clear distinction between *kaishin* 回心 (conversion) and *kuiaratame* 悔改め (repentance) (1960a: 54; 2000: 134-47). Pointing out that *kaishin* literally means "the turning of one's heart," Kitamori (2000: 135) defines conversion as "the turning of one's heart from a state where God was not to a state where God is." Put simply, it is turning to God with one's heart and mind. Conversion, according to Kitamori, is often motivated by suffering, fear, or even self-love (Kitamori, 2000: 135). It does not need to be, and is often not, accompanied by repentance, as evidenced from the later part of Hosea 5:15, "[I]n their misery they will earnestly seek me [God]." Kitamori also gives the example of Martin Luther, pointing out that what happened during the thunderstorm of July 2, 1505 was a conversion experience, for Luther turned to God only because he feared for his life (Kitamori, 2000: 143). Luther only understood the meaning of repentance much later. Kitamori defines repentance as a deep sense of remorse and hatred for one's sin before God and the consequent turning away from it (Kitamori, 2000: 142). It normally presupposes conversion, but never happens unless God exercises his kindness and shines his light into one's heart (Kitamori, 2000:; Rom 2:4). In other words, repentance is completely a gift of God's grace. Kitamori does not discuss at all how his understanding of conversion and repentance fits into the whole classical debate on the *ordo salutis*, especially with regard to the concepts of effectual calling and regeneration in Reformation theology.

baptism from Pastor Ishimatsu Ryōzō at the Japan Evangelical Lutheran Church in Kumamoto on August 19, 1934.[14]

Smallpox Outbreak
A few months after his baptism, Kitamori faced the first test that exposed the fragility of his faith (Kitamori, 1960a: 65-66). There was a smallpox outbreak in different parts of the city toward the end of that year. Kitamori's neighborhood was particularly affected. Three of his immediate neighbors were infected, and Kitamori feared greatly for his life. Kitamori's family members were evacuated to live with relatives in the western part of the city, while he moved into the Christian youth dormitory of his school. He and his family were spared from what he thought was an immutable death sentence from God, but through the episode he became deeply saddened by his own sin of unbelief. He had not been able to pray as his Lord prayed in Matthew 26:39. However, unlike previously, this experience did not plunge Kitamori back into existential despair; rather it strengthened his conviction of his utter need to follow Christ and depend on his grace.

"First Evangelistic Mission"
At the school dormitory, Kitamori became fast friends with three Christian boys. One of them, Nakatsu Yoshisuke, came to him one evening with a problem. Kitamori learned, to his great surprise, that Nakatsu had been contemplating suicide because he could not keep God's commandments as he understood them from the Sermon on the Mount. In particular, Nakatsu was distressed by Jesus' warning in Matthew 5:28, that "anyone who looks at a woman lustfully has already committed adultery with her in his heart." Nakatsu told Kitamori that if he could find no help from him that evening, he would kill himself the next day. (Kitamori later discovered that Nakatsu had obtained a pistol for that purpose.) Nakatsu's dilemma reminded Kitamori of his own earlier struggles, so much so that he was able to respond to Nakatsu readily:

> It is perfectly right to want to glorify God by keeping every part of the law. However, isn't the biblical gospel given for the purpose of saving those who cannot keep God's law? Are you not trying on your own to achieve righteousness through the law? But the Bible teaches that there is no one who is able to do that. In Psalm 78:57, humanity is described as a "mangled bow." It is only to be expected that the arrow that is released from a mangled bow will never be able to hit God's target of righteousness. You are just attempting the impossible. But God promises to save mangled bows like us. This is the good news. Even if your arrow cannot hit its target, God can still regard you as a perfect bow. The gospel is the grace of God which makes righteous those who have no ability to do what is good or right. All you need to do is to simply believe and accept this grace offered to you. If you do that, God will grant you the gift of righteousness. (Kitamori, 1960a: 70-71)

---

[14] Besides Kitamori, one other person was baptized at the service: the mother of the future dramatist Kinoshita Junji, Sassa Mie.

Kitamori then drew Nakatsu's attention to the wounds of the crucified Christ, which Kitamori later reflected to be very much similar to what Johann von Staupitz did when he counseled the anguished Luther to seek salvation in Christ's blood (Kitamori, 1960a: 72). To Kitamori's great relief, Nakatsu received his counsel gladly and gave up the idea of suicide altogether. On his part, Kitamori gained fresh insights into the power of the gospel, and became more convinced than ever that apart from Christ, no one has any means whatsoever to keep the law and win God's righteousness. The conviction that the initiative to save utterly helpless and sinful humans and make them righteous has to come totally from God would later become the foundational tenet of his theology of the pain of God.

In any case, as a result of this momentous encounter with Nakatsu, which he describes as his "first evangelistic mission" (Kitamori, 1960a: 72), Kitamori decided to give up his dream of an academic career in linguistics, but to think seriously instead about a vocation in theology so as to help people understand the gospel clearly as *truly* good news (Kitamori, 1960a: 73). It was a painful decision, for he had to sever "the bonds of gratitude and love" (Kitamori, 1960a: 75) with his family who had expected him to enter either of the two prestigious imperial universities in Tokyo or Kyoto.[15] Since it was Satō's book which had led Kitamori to a profound encounter with Christ, Kitamori wanted to study under Satō. After consulting with his pastor, he discovered that Satō was teaching at the Japan Lutheran Seminary in Tokyo. Without hesitation, Kitamori enrolled at the seminary to begin studies in April 1935.

Seminary Years (1935-1938): The Beginnings of the Pain of God Theology

Three incidents over the next month were to exert a profound effect on Kitamori's life and prompted him to reflect on the whole idea of a suffering God. The first two incidents had to do with the death of another person, while the third involved a mystical vision that Kitamori had of Christ suffering a miserable death on the cross.

A Tragic Death

At the end of March 1935, Kitamori left for Tokyo with his good friend Nakatsu to begin a new chapter of his life as a theology student.[16] Shortly after the train they were riding on left Kumamoto Station, it ran over and killed a small child who had wandered away from her mother onto the railway tracks.[17] The train screeched to a halt, and everyone in Kitamori's carriage heard a loud wailing.

---

[15] Kitamori calls his change of vocational plans as a kind of *shukke* 出家 (1960a: 75), a term used to describe a person entering Buddhist monkhood.

[16] Nakatsu's family was in Tokyo, and had invited Kitamori to stay with them at least until he had moved into the dormitory of the seminary.

[17] Kitamori thought that the child was a girl, but could not be completely sure (1960a: 78).

Peering out of the window, Kitamori saw a woman sitting beside a lifeless body, beating the ground with both her hands and crying inconsolably. The first instinctual thought that came to Kitamori's mind was that this was a bad omen, and he wondered if he should return to Kumamoto to begin his trip afresh.[18] The next moment he felt ashamed that he should even harbor such a selfish and superstitious thought, and he reaffirmed his calling to minister the gospel to "the lowest of humanity" (*donzoko no ningen* どん底の人間) such as this bereaved mother (Kitamori, 1960a: 79). After some delay, Kitamori and Nakatsu proceeded on with their journey, and made a stop at Yawata City in Kyoto where they spent the night at an Anglican church. It was only then that the shock of what Kitamori had witnessed earlier that day sank in. The next day, Kitamori and his friend continued eastwards with their train journey, and passing through Shizuoka Prefecture, they caught the wondrous beauty of the snow-capped Mount Fuji. But Kitamori quietly thought to himself, "Such beauty that is Mount Fuji's – but so far removed from the reality which is to be mine" (Kitamori, 1960a: 80).

An Unexpected Death
Kitamori's first days in Tokyo were memorable. He walked the streets of Ginza and took in the glamour and glitter of its bustling sights.[19] Entering the famed bookstores of Kyōbunkwan and Maruzen, Kitamori proceeded to the Western section and could not contain his excitement when he saw the many German theological texts that were on display on the shelves. He also managed to attend an evening lecture by the visiting John R. Mott, but more than the contents of Mott's speech, Kitamori was deeply moved by the sheer size of the Christian gathering, which he had never experienced before, and by the impressive linguistic ability of Mott's translator, Abe Mitsukame.

A week or so after arriving in Tokyo, Kitamori called on Satō Shigehiko at his home in Ikebukuro, a visit he had so eagerly been looking forward to. However, he was shocked and saddened when he saw was greeted with Satō on his sickbed, barely recognizable from the time they met in Kumamoto just a year earlier. The esteemed professor whom Kitamori had sought to study under was now fighting a losing battle against stomach cancer. Two weeks later, on the day of the entrance ceremony of the Japan Lutheran Seminary, Satō died. The grief-stricken Kitamori felt that God was mocking him, and that it was now meaningless to study theology without Satō. However, after a brief struggle with his conflicting emotions, on the same day, April 16, 1935, after the entrance ceremony, Kitamori made a fresh commitment to look to "Christ alone as Lord and Teacher," vowing "never to absolutize any other human authority"

---

[18] Kitamori uses a common Buddhist phrase *engi o katsugu* 縁起をかつぐ to describe his natural desire to undo the bad omen by starting the trip all over again (1960a: 78).

[19] It would have been hard for anyone to imagine that only ten years earlier, Tokyo and its environs were completely devastated by the Great Kanto Earthquake (see pp. 51ff above).

(Kitamori, 1960a: 86). He came to this momentous decision after discerning that Satō was "forcibly taken away from him" so that he might learn to live for "Christ alone" (Kitamori, 1960a: 86).[20]

Vision of the Crucified Christ: A Pathetic Death
Over the next two weeks as he began classes at the seminary, Kitamori wrote in his diary of an ongoing inner, mystical, dialogue with God which ended with God's wrathful condemnation of his sin (Kitamori, 1960a: 87-88). As he felt his frightful soul being cast into the bottomless pit of darkness, Kitamori captured a vision of the crucified Christ.

> A shaft of light came out of the deep darkness toward me. I saw a man crucified on a cross. He was filled with abject misery, and I saw his spirit being utterly crushed (by God's wrathful condemnation). The man on the cross said, "Look at me." I looked, and saw these words written on the cross: "This man hanging on this cross has received the sentence of eternal condemnation." I felt that the sentence which was mine was now being borne by this wretched man. With his last ounce of strength, this man said to me, "Did you see me? Did you read the sentence on the cross? Do you understand why I have become like this? My son, I am Christ. I died for you. It is only for your sake that I have become like this. For you alone, I have taken upon myself the sentence of eternal condemnation. My son, I have already received your punishment. For your sake, I have become wretched…. Salvation has been prepared for you, and you are now free from God's condemnation. I am Jesus Christ." (Kitamori, 1960a: 88-89)

Kitamori adds, "I certainly heard these words. I know for sure now that the wretched man Jesus Christ, alone, died for me" (Kitamori, 1960a: 89). From this mystical experience, Kitamori came to a confirmed understanding of his utter helplessness as a sinner and the necessary mediation of Christ's vicarious suffering and substitutionary death for his salvation. He also came to perceive the distinction between "subjective faith" and "objective faith" (Kitamori, 1960a: 90-91). The former is generated from within oneself, and even though it is directed to God, it does not make a person righteous, hence cannot save; the latter, on the other hand, is a pure gift from God that confers justification on the sinner. Because "subjective faith" conveys the illusion that one is seeking God when in fact one may be seeking one's own interests, Kitamori points out that such faith can be extremely dangerous to one's spiritual welfare (Kitamori, 1960a: 90). Subjective faith on its own leads to theological amnesia: one forgets that it is the sinner who has killed Christ, and that it is Christ who gives righteousness and life to the sinner (Kitamori, 1960a: 92).

It was only six months earlier that Kitamori feared for his life because of the smallpox outbreak in his hometown. Now within the short space of one month,

---

[20] Kitamori comments that his decision to focus absolutely on Christ insulated him from falling victim to the "Barthian captivity" that was to ensnare Japanese theology a few years later (1960a: 86).

he had three totally unexpected encounters relating respectively to the tragic death of the small child hit by the train, the premature death of Professor Satō, and the vision of the sorrowful death of Christ. These experiences in all probability had a huge impact on the life of the nineteen-year-old Kitamori, and subsequently gave his theology its characteristic tenor. In a way, these encounters created in him, rather prematurely, as it were, a sense of resignation that life is but a "valley of tears" (Kitamori, 1960a: 80). More positively, through them he developed a special sensitivity to the grace of the gospel, learning never ever to take it for granted.

The Visitation of the "Pain of God"
Barely two months after his mystical vision, in June 1935, Kitamori coined the expression *Kami no itami* 神の痛み ("pain of God"), as if it came to him "from heaven" (Kitamori, 1960a: 109). Reflecting on Jesus' question to his disciples in Mark 8:21, "Do you still not understand?", Kitamori employed the phrase "pain of God" for the very first time in his writings, in this July 1935 diary entry:

> The people whom Jesus calls "disciples," "children," and "friends" are those whose understanding is perpetually dull. It is beyond anyone's comprehension why the Son of God should keep on lavishing his love on men and women so utterly vulgar and sinful. Why does he not give up on them? One may think that it brings no honor, but rather loss, to God when he takes such an interest in trivial humanity, but God obviously thinks otherwise. He could have left sinful humanity alone; on the contrary, for the sake of rebellious and hateful sinners, he allows himself to be killed and hanged on the cross. How incomprehensible the love of God! How unfathomable the *pain of God*! God does not abandon the hopeless. And he loves even to the end those very ones who are to be detested. (Kitamori, 1960a: 107, emphasis added)

The concept of the "pain of God" produced for Kitamori an unprecedented clarity into the meaning of the death of Christ. Divine pain is generated through the act of divine self-negation when God chose, unnaturally, as it were, "hateful sinners" as the very objects of his love. The pain of God is unfathomable because the love of God that leads to it is incomprehensible.[21] Kitamori decided then that the concept of divine pain could be profitably developed and theologized "in service of the gospel" (Kitamori, 1960a: 110).[22]

Kitamori experienced a second "visitation" (*otozure* おとずれ) in November of the same year (Kitamori, 1960a: 128). Once again, he saw the inseparable relationship between divine grace and divine pain. Kitamori asks rhetorically, "What else can the grace of God be, if not the pain of God, when Christ should hold to himself rebellious sinners standing against him 'with spears in their

---

[21] In his interpretation of Kitamori, Koyama remarks that God suffers pain because in his love, "he refuses to give up on humanity" (personal communication).
[22] At this time, Kitamori had not yet come across Jeremiah 31:20. The verse only became the *locus classicus* of his pain of God theology almost two years later.

hands'?" (Kitamori, 1960a: 129).[23] This time, Kitamori became convinced that the ability to perceive God in pain is but a mark of "authentic spirituality" (Kitamori, 1960a: 129).

Three months later, in February 1936, Kitamori took a bold step further by positing the pain of God as *the* pivotal principle in Christian theology, to which all other theological concepts must be subordinate (Kitamori, 1960a: 179).[24] "What does Scripture proclaim, if not the pain of God?" he asked rhetorically (Kitamori, 1960a: 179). Convinced that this was indeed the whole counsel of Scripture, Kitamori started to look for key biblical texts to prove that his idea was more than just a hunch. A year later, in March 1937, as he came to the end of his second year in seminary, Kitamori found what he needed in Jeremiah 31:20. He did an exegesis on the text, and became assured that the pain of God is a concept that is indeed "ascertained from and supported by Scripture" (Kitamori, 1960a: 12). This verse would become the key – although not the only – text upon which to build a biblical theology of the pain of God.[25] In this sense, the discovery of Jeremiah 31:20 was instrumental in launching Kitamori's pain of God theology into the next stage of its development (Kitamori, 1960a: 12). It is no surprise that Kitamori should now decide to write his graduation thesis on the pain of God.[26] For the rest of 1937, he devoted himself to developing and fine-tuning his theological construction of the pain of God.

Another Unexpected Death
That summer of 1937, yet another tragic incident happened that showed Kitamori once more the total depravity of his sinful self. While on vacation back home in Kumamoto, Kitamori received the shocking news that a fellow student at the seminary had suddenly died of encephalitis lethargica. Matsumura Tadashi, a year Kitamori's senior, was the favorite student of the late Satō Shigehiko; indeed he "reminded everyone of Professor Satō by his manner of talking, walking, and even writing" (Kitamori, 1960a: 101). While Satō was still alive, Matsumura was a tenant at his home and commuted to seminary from there. After his teacher died, Matsumura moved into the dormitory. One day, Kitamori visited Matsumura in his room and was astounded to find that he had inherited Satō's whole library. For the following two years, Kitamori struggled with feelings of envy toward Matsumura. Therefore, when the news of Matsumura's death reached him, Kitamori reacted with mixed feelings of smug

---

[23] Kitamori acknowledges that the phrase "spears in their hands" is taken from P. T. Forsyth. Indeed, the double theme of "God's love of His bitter enemies, and [of] His grace to them in repaying their wrong by Himself atoning for them on the cross" is strong in Forsyth (1948: 81).

[24] Interestingly, Kitamori even defines conscience as "the place where the pain of God is revealed" (1960a: 180).

[25] See pp. 113ff below for Kitamori's biblical exegesis on the pain of God.

[26] Even today, virtually all universities and seminaries in Japan require all graduating students to submit a graduation thesis.

relief and stark horror. When he reflected on why he felt the way he did, he realized that he had secretly wished for Matsumura's death (Kitamori, 1960a: 104). That thought gave him a hellish fright at the state of his own soul. Kitamori writes, "I am unforgivable. I have fallen into the abyss of darkness. I had wished for Matsumura's death, when in fact, I am the one who should have died instead" (Kitamori, 1960a: 104). The incident served only to humble Kitamori, and strengthened his conviction that the unwavering act of God loving depraved sinners can only engender pain in the divine heart.

Kitamori's First Theological Manifesto

On Christmas Day, 1937, Kitamori completed his graduation thesis, entitled *Knowledge of God in Christ*, his first theological manifesto on the pain of God as revealed in the death of Christ. The overarching theme of this fine essay can be found in two sentences written on its cover page: a question from Mark 9:12 in New Testament Greek, *kai. pw/j ge,graptai evpi. to.n ui`o.n tou/ avnqrw,pou i[na polla. pa,qh| kai. evxoudenhqh/|;* followed by Kitamori's answer in the form of a statement from Luther in Latin, *In Christo crucifixo est vera theologia et cognitio Dei* (1999: 71).[27] Kitamori, following Luther, insists that true knowledge of God comes only through the crucified Christ.[28] The necessity of the cross and the impossibility of knowing God other than through Christ are predicated on nothing less than the revelation of God given through Scripture (Kitamori, 1999: 76-79). But Kitamori goes beyond Luther by asserting that to know God through the crucified Christ is to know the pain of God (Kitamori, 1999: 83-86). The knowledge of divine pain is also derived from divine revelation (Kitamori, 1999: 169-71; cf. 1986, 34).

"The gospel of the Cross is the vehicle which carries the pain of God," declares Kitamori (1999: 169). He unpacks this theme by breaking it down into four points:

1. In Christ alone, God is the God of sinners.
2. In Christ alone, God's love becomes the love for sinners.
3. God's love in Christ is the love for those who should not be loved.
4. God's love in Christ is the love manifested in the cross of Christ. (Kitamori, 1999: 86)

Each of these sub-themes is theologically dense in itself, but ultimately what Kitamori wants to convey is that there is no other way God and sinful humanity can relate with each other except through the painful mediation of God in the crucified Christ. In other words, no salvation is to be found in a direct approach to God, apart from the death of Christ.

---

[27] On the same cover page, below the two statements, Kitamori provides the Japanese translation of the statements. His handwritten thesis covers 148 sheets of Japanese writing paper, each sheet containing four hundred character squares.

[28] The thesis is strongly Lutheran in orientation, even though Kitamori breaks new ground when he introduces the pain of God as a theological concept. Luther is cited fifty-five times in the thesis.

After arguing for the uniqueness of the crucified Christ as *the* means to know God and receive his salvation, Kitamori proceeds to the second half of the thesis where he displays remarkable dexterity in his extended interaction with theological luminaries such as Friedrich Schleiermacher, Albrecht Ritschl, Wilhelm Hermann, Paul Althaus, Andreas Nygren, and Karl Barth, critiquing them in the light of his *theologia crucis* (Kitamori, 1999: 134-75).

Transition: From Seminary to University
Kitamori graduated from seminary in March 1938. His graduation prayer was, "Lord, grant life to your servant so that I may preach your love" (1968: 54). It is telling that in his autobiography, Kitamori hardly mentions his seminary teachers – three Americans and two Japanese. He says in a matter-of-fact way that seminary life, "on the outside", was "sparse lonely, poor, and cold" (Kitamori, 1968: 55). But recalling that he had come to the school theological illiterate only three years before, Kitamori was grateful for the deep spiritual and theological growth that he had experienced "within himself" at the seminary (Kitamori, 1968: 55). Indeed, it was here at the school that he cultivated the powerful faculty of independent thought (Kitamori, 1968: 55). However, judging from the many references to his university professors later in his autobiography (see Kitamori, 1968: 60-68), one can only surmise that the young man was too precocious for his seminary teachers. His pastoral theology teacher, Miura Inoko, however, recognized Kitamori's genius and strongly encouraged him to continue further studies at the prestigious Kyoto Imperial University. Miura, who was at that time the Chairman of the Japan Evangelical Lutheran Association, then made arrangements for Kitamori to live in the neighboring town of Ashiya where he could serve as an interim pastor at the Lutheran church plant while studying at the university.[29] Consequently, in the spring of 1938, Kitamori entered the philosophy department of Kyōdai, as the university was commonly referred to, to pursue graduate studies under Tanabe Hajime (1885-1962), the brilliant and extraordinarily popular scholar who would later inherit the Chair of Philosophy from his master Nishida Kitarō.

Yet Another Death
Barely two months after he assumed pastoral responsibilities at Ashiya, Kitamori faced the first death in his tiny congregation. On June 24, 1938, Yanase Minoru, an elementary fifth grader, died suddenly of acute pneumonia. Kitamori, caught totally by surprise, found himself not only having to comfort the bereaved parents but also to put together the funeral service. Reflecting on this incident later, Kitamori writes,

---

[29] The pastor of the church plant had just left to fight in the Second Sino-Japanese War that broke out in July 1937 as a result of the Marco Polo Bridge Incident. It is not clear if he was conscripted or if he had joined the Imperial Army on his own. Whatever the reason, the Ashiya church plant was now without a pastor.

In whatever age and place, it is almost too much to ask a young clergyman to assure the dying and comfort the bereaved, in short, to deal with humanity's gravest problem of death. I was no exception, having only a paltry twenty-two years of human experience. (Kitamori, 1968: 72)

Kitamori also came to the realization that until then his theology had only resided in the realm of thought; now he saw that his pastoral practice had to be theological as well (Kitamori, 1968: 72). However, he was faced with a difficult problem: the ten-year-old boy had not displayed any evidence of faith in Christ before he died. Kitamori decided to regard the dead boy as one who had *yet* to possess faith (*mishinkōsha* 未信仰者) rather than one who had no faith (*fushinkōsha* 不信仰者) (Kitamori, 1968: 73). But with even the subtle change in terminology – which invariably raises huge theological questions – how would that comfort Minoru's grief-stricken parents? What would he say in his funeral sermon?

Reflecting on what practical implications his theology of the pain of God could bring to bear on this situation, Kitamori develops two points for his sermon:

1. Without the enabling power of God, we can neither truly love another person nor grieve the death of that person. To love and grieve on our own strength only breeds deception.
2. When we receive God's power, we are also given the responsibility to keep walking in the love of God. As we walk in God's love, we must consciously practice what His power enables us to do, namely, to love others and enter into their sorrow (Kitamori, 1968: 73).

Kitamori then defines God's love, for the first time, as "the love of God rooted in the pain of God" (*Kami no itami ni kisozukerareshi ai* 神の痛みに基礎づけられし愛) (Kitamori, 1968: 73).

It is only when we abide in "God's love which is rooted in his pain" that we are able to entrust the spirit of the deceased (indeed especially the spirits of those who do not believe in Christ and those who cannot believe in Christ!) to God's bosom. The more we abide in the love of God, the more we will abide in his pain as well; conversely, the more we abide in his pain, the more we will find ourselves abiding in his love. The most important point to note is that we can only abide in the love of God to the extent that we abide in his pain. And this is because *all things depend upon the cross of Christ.* (Kitamori, 1968: 73 emphasis added)

What Kitamori means to say is that, even though the unbeliever is outside the grace of God, he or she is embraced by God's intentional love rooted in his pain (Kitamori, 1968: 73). He admits that at this point, however, that the thought behind the expression "God's love rooted in God's pain" is still not completely clear (Kitamori, 1968: 73). But Minoru's funeral gave him the occasion to reflect on this theme. Not long after, Kitamori would encounter the philosophy of Nishida which would give him the intellectual resources to develop this theme into a key idea in his theology. Minoru's death also precipitated in Kitamori's mind the idea of *soto* 外 ("outside") in relation to God's love, and the attendant thought of God "embracing" the outsider into himself. Kitamori would develop these ideas over the next few years as a student at Kyōdai.

University Years (1938-1941)
The Structural Development of the Pain of God Theology

Kitamori thoroughly enjoyed his student days at Kyōdai. In fact, he fondly refers to Kyoto as his "second home" (Kitamori, 1968: 57). Under the rigorous tutelage of Tanabe, Kitamori encountered what he calls "intense thought," which led him to judge the prevailing idea that "theology is based on divine revelation whereas philosophy is based on human speculation" as a "frighteningly empty" one (Kitamori, 1968: 62). The ethos of scholarship at the philosophy department was such that students were encouraged to read both Western and Eastern writings at the same time, and so Kitamori would have his mind stretched through the exposure to Buddhist thought (especially of Zen and Pure Land traditions), Kantian and Cartesian philosophy, "aesthetics, psychology and education" (Kitamori, 1968: 65). However, it was in the philosophy of Nishida Kitarō that Kitamori found what he needed to give his theology a cohesive and enduring structure. The next subsection provides a necessary excursus on Nishida and the so-called Kyoto School so that we can better understand how Kitamori modified and incorporated Nishida's philosophy into his theology.

Nishida Kitarō and the Kyoto School

Nishida Kitarō (1870-1945) is arguably the most well-known and influential modern Japanese philosopher. His earliest work, *Zen no kenkyū* 善の研究 (*An Inquiry into the Good*), published in 1911, secured a permanent place for him in academia's hall of fame.[30] The cornerstone of what is famously known as *Nishida tetsugaku* 西田哲学 (Nishida Philosophy) is encapsulated in the formulaic expression that Nishida devised, *zettai mujun teki jiko dōitsu* 絶対矛盾的自己同一, most commonly translated in the literature as "Self-Identity of the Absolute Contradiction".[31] This phrase is as barely intelligible in Japanese as

---

[30] The work was translated into English by Abe Masao and Christopher Ives, and published in 1990 by Yale University Press. Abe is a disciple of both Hisamatsu Shin'ichi and Nishitani Keiji, who in turn were students of Nishida.

[31] The word *mujun*, translated here as "contradiction," consists of two Chinese characters, 矛 (*hoko*), which refers to the weapon pike, and 盾 (*tate*), which means shield. Taken together the word *mujun* 矛盾 originally meant war or quarrel. In the 1880s, with the advent of philosophy as an academic discipline, the semantic range of the word became enlarged to include the logical relation of contradiction, i.e. "both A and non-A." However, it must be borne in mind that in everyday usage, the word *mujun* is a rather slippery one, and depending on context, it can also refer to a paradox, a discrepancy, an incoherent argument, or even a conflict.

it is in English, and Japanese and Western philosophers today continue to debate its meaning and nuances (Kopf, 2004: 74). At the high risk of sounding overly simplistic, one may think of Nishida positing a fundamental unity of reality which the mind is able to intuit as a union of opposites (Heisig, 2004: 58).[32] Nishida sought to overcome what he saw to be the fictitious dualism of ordinary experience by unifying subject and object through the cultivation of direct, intuitive consciousness, which he calls "pure experience" (*junsui keiken* 純粋経験) (1990: 3-10).[33] Later, developing what he refers to as "the logic of *topos* (or place)" (*basho no ronri* 場所の論理), and utilizing the classical Buddhist concept of Nothingness (*mu* 無), Nishida posits a self-negating Absolute Nothingness (*zettai mu* 絶対無) as the "place" that transcends (*koeru* 超える), embraces (*daku* 抱く), and enfolds (*tsutsumu* 包む) both subjective and objective polarities of reality, as well as their identity and difference (cf. Kitamori, 1956: 146). It is obvious that Nishida philosophized within a Zen Buddhist framework, hence the distinctly kenotic characteristic of his philosophy and his optimistic belief in the ability of the mind to perceive ultimate reality of Absolute Nothingness and reach enlightenment unaided.[34] Indeed, Bernard Faure describes Nishida's philosophy as "a 'Zen philosophy' based on the notion of 'pure experience'" (1993: 76). In stark contrast with the essentializing tendencies of his contemporary and good friend Suzuki Daisetsu – better known as D. T. Suzuki – Nishida's distinctive contribution to Zen scholarship could be said to be his effort "to systematize Zen insights in a way compatible with Western philosophy" (Faure, 1993: 76). Philosopher and former missionary to Japan Harold Netland agrees, explaining that what Nishida tried to do was "to incorporate certain Western themes in German idealism and the pragmatism of William James into a kind of Buddhist ontology and epistemology, a fusion of West and East" (personal communication).[35]

---

[32] Perhaps as an illustration of Nishida's principle of "Self-Identity of the Absolute Contradiction", one may look at the Christian doctrine of the Trinity where we have the unique identity of the one God who exists in three Persons. Whether this principle can indeed be applied to the Trinity or not is a totally separate matter, and may prove to be an interesting study.

[33] Kitamori has a helpful chapter on Nishida's philosophy in his book *Kami to ningen* 神と人間 (*God and Humanity*) (1956: 115-50). The English reader is directed to the chapter entitled "Nishida Philosophy" in Inagaki and Jennings, *Philosophical Theology and East-West Dialogue*, (Amsterdam: Rodopi, 2000), pp. 47-66. For a more detailed exposition of Nishida, see the English translation of Nishitani Keiji's work, *Nishida Kitarō* (Berkeley, CA.: University of California Press, 1991), as well as Robert Wargo, *The Logic of Nothingness: A Study of Nishida Kitarō* (Honolulu, HI: University of Hawai'i Press, 2005).

[34] On the comparison between Nishida's idea of self-negation and the Pauline idea of *kenosis* in Philistines 2:5-8, see Inagaki and Jennings (2000: 59-61).

[35] Nishida's agenda to formulate a philosophical system fusing East and West likely influenced Kitamori to some extent, as is evidenced by the integration of Western and Japanese insights so characteristic of Kitamori's theology. It must be noted, however,

Contrary to what is popularly believed, Nishida did not actually found the Kyoto School (cf. Faure, 1993: 74). In fact, the Kyoto school is by no means a formal school of philosophy. The term *Kyōto gakuha* 京都学派 (Kyoto School) was actually coined in 1932 by Tosaka Jun, a student of Nishida and Tanabe with Marxist leanings, who not only noted the stark differences between the philosophical systems of the two men, but also expressed disgruntlement at what he perceived to be his teachers' common bourgeois speculation that ignores the material and historical realities of society (see Tosaka, 1932: 171-76).[36] In all probability, that label would not have stuck had Tanabe, Nishida's most prominent disciple, not taken critical issue with Nishida's philosophical idealism, for then there would be no Kyoto School, only Nishida Philosophy.

Tanabe, who was privately tutored by Martin Heidegger in Germany for about two years from 1922 to 1924, thought that Nishida's method of overcoming the problem of dualism ends up dissolving all distinctions, rendering a monistic view of reality that is ultimately meaningless. In contrast to the Zen influence in Nishida's philosophy, Tanabe's philosophy draws heavily from True Pure Land Buddhist teachings. Expressing skepticism about the ability of the human mind to achieve pure experience on its own, Tanabe advocates an epistemological methodology which he calls *zangedō* 懺悔道, or "metanoetics" (from the Greek word *meta,noia*). This approach "implies, on the one hand, a self-awakening through a 'way' of repentance, a 'thinking-afterward' (*meta,noia*), and on the other, suggests a self-conscious transcending of intuition and contemplation (*metano,hsij*)" (1986: 3). The entire "process" is mediated by the transformative grace of absolute mediation of an Other-power (*tariki* 他 力) (Tanabe, 1986: 3). The sharp philosophical differences between Tanabe and his teacher ended in what amounts to a severing

---

that even in his seminary graduation thesis written before his entering Kyōdai, Kitamori was already interacting competently with non-Japanese theologians (see p. 99 above).

[36] Ironically, Tosaka is today considered part of the left wing of the Kyoto School.

of ties between the two men.[37] Nishida retired from the university in 1943, and his chair was assumed by Tanabe.[38] Two years later, Nishida died.[39]

In any case, over time, the term "Kyoto School" came to designate the "philosophical movement centered at Kyoto University that assimilated Western philosophic and religious ideas and used them to reformulate religious and moral insights unique to the East Asian cultural tradition" (Clark, 1991: vii).[40] One may add three more characteristics to the Kyoto School. First, the philosophical interactions of the School are always related to either Nishida's philosophy or Tanabe's critical response to it, or both. Second, while being open to new ideas from outside, the School takes an approach to philosophy which is faithfully rooted in Mahayana Buddhism, especially the traditions of Zen and Pure Land. For that reason, the Kyoto School is sometimes referred to as the Kyoto School of Buddhism. Third, unlike Western philosophy where its primary ontological focus privileges it to start with the conceptual problem of the nature of "being," the Kyoto School, reflective of its Eastern tradition, takes a *me*ontological (from the Greek negative particle *mh,*) approach which starts with the concept of "non-being" (*mu* 無) as "the ground of being," to use Paul Tillich's phrase.

---

[37] The conflict between Nishida and Tanabe could be traced back to the latter's publication of an article in May 1930 entitled, with a tinge of sarcasm, *Nishida sensei no oshie o aogu* 西田先生の教えを仰ぐ (*A Humble Request for Clarification and Guidance from the Teachings of Professor Nishida*). In the article, Tanabe basically expresses grave reservations concerning his teacher's philosophical methodology: "[T]o postulate a final universal that is incomprehensible, and then to interpret reality as the self-determination of that universal, would lead to the negation of philosophy itself" (cited in Yusa, 2002: 231). By the time Kitamori entered Kyōdai in 1938, Nishida and Tanabe were hardly on talking terms, even if "they actually never lost respect for one another and maintained their professional relationship" (Yusa, 2002: 288). Kitamori mentions *three* times in his autobiography his utter ignorance, as a new student, of the silent but ongoing feud between Nishida and Tanabe (1968: 60-61). For a detailed account of how the scholarly differences between the two men led to the formation of the Kyoto School of Philosophy, see Yusa (2002: 227-32).

[38] Nishida had actually retired from teaching in 1938, but held on to his chair for five years before giving it up in 1943.

[39] Tanabe offers a radical critique of Nishida's philosophy in his book *Zangedō toshite no tetsugaku* 懺悔道としての哲学 (*Metanoetics as Philosophy*), published in 1946, the year after Nishida's death. However, not even once in his book does Tanabe mention the name of his teacher. It is also interesting to note that Kitamori's *Kami no itami no shingaku* was released the same year as Tanabe's book.

[40] For a good introduction, see Bret Davis, "The Kyoto School" (2006), a very helpful but extremely long article on the subject in the online version of *Stanford Encyclopedia of Philosophy*, http://plato.stanford.edu/entries/kyoto-school/ (accessed April 5, 2007). Kitamori has a whole chapter on the Kyoto School in his *Nihon no kokoro to kirisutokyō* (Christianity and the Soul of Japan), (Tokyo: Yomiuri shimbunsha, 1973), pp. 125-64.

Indeed, the word *mu* is more accurately translated as "nothingness," since the term "non-being" implies the priority of "being" which it then negates.[41]

The Influence of the Kyoto School on Kitamori's Pain of God Theology

By the time that Kitamori came to Kyōdai, Nishida had already retired from teaching even though he was still occupying the Chair of Philosophy. Kitamori was hence never taught by Nishida. Although, not long after he entered the school, Kitamori was able to attend a three-part Monday Lecture Series, entitled, *Nihon bunka no mondai* 日本文化の問題 ("The Problem of Japanese Culture"), that Nishida gave at the university on April 25, May 2, and May 9, 1938.[42] Kitamori confessed that the lectures were too difficult for him to understand at that time, but observed that most students, including himself, came to these lectures for "the experience of seeing Nishida rather than listening to him" (1968: 75). However, Kitamori read the book into which the lectures were edited and compiled two years later,[43] and learned that Nishida was in effect applying his principle of the "Self-Identity of the Absolute Contradiction" to explain the tumultuous events of the world at that time (Kitamori, 1968: 75-76). In particular, Nishida sought to provide a philosophical justification for a national polity (*kokutai* 国体) based on the *historical* evolution of the imperial house – rather than its mythical origins – while at the same time emphasizing the global role Japan could play in combining the modernity of the West and the traditions of the East.[44] Kitamori later commented that the engagement with

---

[41] The concept of *mu* 無 (nothingness) is akin to the *Tao* 道 of ancient Chinese philosophy. Note the opening lines of the *Tao Te Ching*:
道可道。非常道。名可名。非常名。無名天地之始。有名萬物之母。
(The *Tao* that can be spoken of is not the eternal *Tao*.
The Name that can be named is not the eternal Name.
The Nameless is the origin of heaven and earth.
The Named is the mother of all things.)
Here in the first chapter of the *Tao Te Ching*, the *Tao* is described as the profound identity of being and non-being. And in the fortieth chapter, it is defined as "non-being from which all being issues."

[42] The lecture series was convened to counter the growing anti-intellectualism and emotional nationalism of the times by presenting a sounder perspective of Japanese culture and its place in the world. Nishida has always believed that the best in Japanese tradition can only be appropriated by interacting with the West, not by isolating itself. See Faure's and Netland's comments on p. 103 above.

[43] The book bears the same title as the lecture series, *Nihon bunka no mondai* (*The Problem of Japanese Culture*) (1940). Excerpts from the book, translated into English, can be found in *Sources of Japanese Tradition*, (New York: Columbia University Press, 1958), pp. 857-72. For an explanation and critique of Nishida's key ideas in this book, see Inagaki and Jennings (2000: 62-66).

[44] Because of his critiques of the fallacies in *both* Occidentalism *and* Orientalism, Nishida was, understandably, attacked as pro-Western during the war (cf. Minoda, 1938: 3-22), and as uncritically nationalistic after it (cf. Hashimoto, 1992: 136-38). It would be fair to say that during the war years, Nishida represented the attitude of many

human destiny on the historical plane is not only a philosophical problem but an important theological task as well (Kitamori, 1968: 76). However, at the time when the Pacific War was breaking out, Kitamori had virtually nothing to say, for or against, the rising nationalism of his country.

In any case, over time Kitamori was able to grasp Nishida's ideas enough to critique them, and even incorporate some of them into his theological method.[45] To begin, Kitamori does not reject the ontology and language of "being" the way Nishida did. In other words, unlike Nishida and his colleagues, Kitamori does not adopt a meontological approach to the problem of truth. Needless to say, then, the content of Nishida's philosophical project, namely, Absolute Nothingness, is completely different from that of Kitamori's theological construction, which is the pain of God. Kitamori expresses relief that the "passion" of what he had discovered in the gospel "protected [him] from the powerful allurement of Nishida's philosophy" (Kitamori, 1968: 76). That notwithstanding, he was able to benefit from "the purely formal and logical structure of Nishida's philosophy" which he appropriated for his theological ends (Kitamori, 1968: 60). Specifically, Kitamori adopted Nishida's structural principle of the "Self-Identity of the Absolute Contradiction", interpreting it as the dialectical unity between two contradictory, or paradoxical, poles. Applying this principle to his theology, Kitamori saw that when the opposing poles of divine love and divine wrath are brought together in unity, what is generated is a new identity of love, namely, divine love rooted in divine pain.[46] This clarified for Kitamori what he had first intuited at Minoru's funeral on the love of God rooted in the pain of God but was not able to articulate formally at that time (see p. 99 above).

Kitamori also utilizes Nishida's language from his theory of place, while critiquing his concept of Absolute Nothingness. Concerning the latter, Kitamori thinks that Nishida's Absolute Nothingness embraces both the contradictory poles of subject and object in a rather "ordinary, non-descript manner" (1956: 144). Referring to Hegel and Kierkegaard, Kitamori notes that Hegel's quality of contradiction (*mujun*) is comic and painless since his subject is a universal Spirit which manipulates individuals as if on the stage of a cosmic drama, whereas Kierkegaard's contradiction is tragic and painful for it deals with the paradoxical

---

Japanese academics that, on the one hand, were concerned about the rising nationalism of the country and the potential suppression of academic freedom, but on the other, did not manage to rise to challenge the threat. Before long, the threat became reality. Left-wing scholars, such as Tosaka Jun, lost their university jobs.

[45] Indeed, Kitamori would publish a number of articles on Nishida after the latter's death. These articles were later compiled, edited and published in the book *Tetsugaku to kami* 哲学と神 (*Philosophy and God*) in 1985.

[46] Here we encounter the tricky problem with the concept of *mujun* (see p. 101, n. 31 above). Rather than treating divine wrath and divine love as logical contradictions which cancel each other out in the manner of Nishida, Kitamori seems to view these more as entities which exist in tension, albeit an almost unbearable one, with each other.

experiences that are part and parcel of human reality (Kitamori, 1956: 143-47). In contrast to these two diametrically opposite sets of contradictions, the contradiction of Nishida is formal and idealistic, as the Absolute Nothingness that he posits transcends both pain and non-pain.[47] Put in mathematical terms, if one takes the quality of Hegel's contradiction to be positive and that of Kierkegaard's to be negative, then the quality of Nishida's logical contradiction is a bland zero (Kitamori, 1956: 145). For that reason, surmises Kitamori, Nishida's Absolute Nothingness cannot accommodate the extraordinary, such as the "contradiction" between divine love and divine wrath, the union of which does not dissolve into nothingness (Kitamori, 1956: 144; cf. 1985: 154). In this sense, Kitamori's pain of God does not fit exactly into the dialectical approach of synthesizing thesis and antithesis. For Kitamori, the pain of God is *not* a synthesis that resolves completely the contradiction between divine love and divine wrath. Rather, divine pain is altogether a different, and unresolved, "third thing" or "tertium" that is generated by the chemistry between divine love and divine pain (Kitamori, 1986: 27).[48]

In spite of his critique of Nishida's Absolute Nothingness, Kitamori employs Nishida's philosophical schema of "place" to explicate his understanding of God as the true Absolute. The word "absolute" *zettai* 絶対, literally means "the severing of opposition" (*"tai" o "zetsu" suru* 「対」を「絶」する) (Kitamori, 1981: 148). In contrast, the word "relative," *sōtai* 相対, literally means "mutual opposition" (Kitamori, 1981: 148). God, being the true Absolute, therefore cannot stand over against any relative opposition; either he eradicates it completely, or he *embraces into himself* (*tsutsumikomu* 包み込む) all opposition (Kitamori, 1981: 148). To embrace opposition is an act of self-negation, and to do so while at the same time maintaining divine transcendence implies the necessity of mediation of sorts. The only situation in which the absolute God relates without mediation is within the Trinity, where the three Persons exist in direct, eternal bliss with each other. Other than this singular instance, without mediation, the absolute would become reduced to the level of the relative. So, in the case of the absolute God embracing his enemy, the sinner, to himself, the love he displays in the process is indeed mediated by his wrath. (If that were not the case, God would have lost his transcendence.) The qualitative expression of such extraordinary mediation, according to Kitamori, is pain (Kitamori, 1981: 149). This is the pain that Nishida's pure experience cannot perceive.

---

[47] It must be noted here that Kitamori's use and interpretation of the word *mujun* in Kierkegaard, Hegel, and Nishida does not conform to the strictly philosophical meaning of logical contradiction. Rather, he is using it in a literary or metaphorical sense.

[48] If one may use the Korean concept of *han* 恨, one could say that God's love for the sinner and God's wrath against the sinner produces *han* within the heart of God. For an introduction to the concept of *han*, see A. Sung Park, "Theology of *Han* (The Abyss of *Han*)," *Quarterly Review* 9(1), (1989), pp. 48-62.

Kitamori also critiques Nishida's Absolute Nothingness as embracing all things *within* itself from the outset. There is nothing extraordinary about this (1985: 152-53). In contrast, Kitamori's absolute God painfully embraces into himself those who are *outside* (*soto* 外) (1968: 177). Here Kitamori picks up the initial thought he had of the "outside" as he was preparing for Minoru's funeral (see p. 99 above). Applying these insights from his dialogue with Nishida's philosophy to his understanding of the death of Christ, Kitamori identifies Calvary as the "place" where the absolute God negates himself by embracing in love the sinner from the outside into himself, in an act mediated by his transcendent wrath. The love that is generated as a result is identified as God's love rooted in God's pain. In sum, it would be right to say that Kitamori utilizes the linguistic resources, rather than the content, of Nishida's philosophy, for his theological construction. This is evident from the words that Kitamori uses in his theological formulation, such as "place," "negate," and "embrace," and "envelope". These are words from Nishida.

Kitamori does not say very much about the influence of Tanabe's philosophy on his theology. One's first impression may be that Tanabe's particular emphases on mediation and the grace of an Other-power are already present in Kitamori's theology. It is certainly true that Tanabe's philosophy had served to strengthen Kitamori's prior conviction on the utter helplessness of humanity and the need for external, mediatory grace, but Kitamori (1981: 206) alludes to subtle snares in Tanabe's teaching that the believer needs to be aware of (1981: 206). For, according to Tanabe, when people undergo tremendous suffering, they are often brought to a place of nothingness where they find that their only recourse is to repent and rely on an Other-power to save them. Kitamori remarks that, in contrast to the high premium that Tanabe places on the personal experience of coming or being brought to a state of nothingness, the Bible reveals a Savior who willingly experienced nothingness on behalf of all humanity by being utterly forsaken by God (Kitamori, 1981: 206). In other words, Tanabe's focus is on the pain of the person who needs to be saved rather than the pain of the One who saves. Moreover, it is not the nullifying pain of humans, but rather, God's kindness, that leads to repentance (Rom. 2:4), emphasizes Kitamori (Kitamori, 1981: 207). Still, Kitamori never failed to hold his teacher up with profound respect. According to Kitamori, the rigorous mental training that he received from Tanabe enabled him to build his theology on a firmer intellectual foundation (1968: 63).

Lord of the Cross

Through the course of the following year, 1939, armed with his new philosophical insights, Kitamori refined his theological agenda through a series of ten articles that he wrote for *Rūteru* るうてる (*Lutheran*), the monthly publication of the Japan Evangelical Lutheran Church. The overarching theme of his articles, as he named it, is telling: *Jūjika no shu* 十字架の主 (*Lord of the*

Cross).⁴⁹ But perhaps because of his youth, Kitamori's effort created scarcely any ripple within the church or the theological community. Kitamori would often lament that no one understood what he was saying (Kitamori, 1968: 167, 171-72). That notwithstanding, these ten articles were collated and published the following year, in 1940, as *Jūjika no shu: Kyōgigaku no tame no kakusho*十字架 の主一教義学のための覚書 (*Lord of the Cross: A Primer in Dogmatics*). This is the first of forty or so books that Kitamori would publish in the course of his theological career. He was barely twenty-four years old.

Unfortunately, Kitamori's first published work did not enjoy a wide readership, in all probability due to the subtitle which smacks of arrogance of a theological upstart. That notwithstanding, this initial work would lay a strongly Christological and cruciform foundation for the development of a full-orbed theology of the pain of God.⁵⁰

Scholar, Churchman, and Pastor (1941-98)

Kitamori graduated from Kyōdai in 1941, but remained at the university over the next two years working as a teaching assistant. In 1943, he received an academic appointment in the systematic theology department of Tokyo Union Theological Seminary (TUTS). Kitamori taught at the seminary until his retirement in 1984. He never married. Morimoto Anri, who studied under Kitamori at TUTS in the early 1980s, and who initiated the republication of the English translation of Kitamori's *Theology of the Pain of God* in 2005, has this to say, "I admired his ability to spin complex Hegelian thoughts into perfectly organized and sometimes even memorable sentences. But what I saw outside the classroom was a rather solitary figure amid much international acclaim" (2005: 1).

Kitamori's labor from his student days at the seminary and at Kyōdai finally bore fruit when *Theology of the Pain of God* was released in 1946, a year after the end of the Second World War. It generated monumental interest both in and out of the church, so much so that Kitamori was overtaken by feelings of "astonishment and bewilderment" (1986: 3). The central thesis of this work is essentially unchanged from that of his graduation thesis and his first published theological treatise, namely, that the historical death of Christ is the phenomenological expression of the pain of God (Kitamori, 1986: 41). This is indeed Kitamori's *theologia crucis*. It is not a wonder that Kitamori should posit the death of Christ as "the *axiom* of all theological thought" (Kitamori, 1986: 41 emphasis in original), which, when compromised, would render the gospel completely unintelligible (Kitamori, 1986: 41). Indeed, with the publication of his magnum opus, Kitamori hoped to issue a dire warning against the tendency

---

⁴⁹ These articles appeared in *Lutheran* from January to December 1939. Kitamori did not write for the May issue, and for one other month between August and November (inclusive) which I was not able to ascertain.
⁵⁰ The title *Lord of the Cross* captures Kitamori's emphasis that theology should not be vaguely Christocentric but concretely cruciform.

in modern Protestantism to do away with what Luther calls the *tragica verba* of John 3:16 (Kitamori, 1986: 67).[51]

After the war, Kitamori helped reorganize the whole Kyōdan denomination and drafted its Confession of Faith. Kitamori firmly believed in the unity of the Church, and remained committed to the Kyōdan for the rest of his life even though he was unwaveringly Lutheran in his theology. He was often called upon to settle ecclesiastical problems and theological controversies within the Kyōdan. During the years of student unrest in the 1970s, a student slapped him at a public meeting (see p. 56 above). Kitamori practiced what he taught: forgiving the unforgivable and embracing those who cannot be embraced.

Throughout most of his years as seminary professor and even beyond, Kitamori also pastored Chitose Funabashi Church, a church that he founded in 1950. He stepped down from the pastorate in 1996 after serving for forty-six years. He remained in the church as its Pastor Emeritus for the next two years until his death on September 29, 1998 in Takasaki. He was eighty-two.

Theology of the Pain of God

We shall now scrutinize Kitamori's *theologia crucis* by looking at the systemic features of his pain of God theology. We begin by reviewing the way Kitamori grounds his theology of divine in the written Word of God. Next, we shall look at how he relates divine pain with the living Word of God, Christ himself. Finally, we shall examine at length how Kitamori puts together his *theologia crucis* using what Asakawa Toru calls a "trilogical structure" (2003: 2).

The Pain of God in the Word of God

It was through the Old Testament prophet Jeremiah that Kitamori was led "to see the heart of God most deeply" (1986: 24). Interestingly, Kitamori draws an interesting parallel between Jeremiah and Paul, calling Jeremiah "the Paul of the Old Testament," and conversely, Paul "the Jeremiah of the New Testament" (Kitamori, 1986: 24). Moreover, "'God on the cross' as revealed to Paul is for Jeremiah 'God in pain'" (Kitamori, 1986: 24).

The verse that ignited Kitamori's thought on divine pain was Jeremiah 31:20. In the Japanese Literary Version (*bungoyaku* 文語訳), it reads,

---

[51] There are always Christians who want to do away with the cross. According to the news story "Rev. Moon and the black clergy: Taking down the cross (and taking trips) part of an unlikely alliance with local pastors" reported in the November 6, 2006 (Sunday) edition of *The Chicago Tribune*, some African American ministers in the Chicago area have taken down the cross from their churches because the cross reminded them of "this country's history of racism and brutality." Rev. Joseph McAfee, pastor of Central United Community Church on Chicago's South Side, reportedly said, "Why would you want to come to church every Sunday and look at a dead man killed on a piece of wood?" given the history of lynching in the USA.

エホバいいたまう、エフライムは我が愛するところの子、悦ぶところの
子ならずや、我彼にむかいて語るごとに彼を念わざるを得ず、是をもて
我が腸かれの為に痛む、我必ず彼を恤むべし。[52]

Kitamori saw immediately that the text spoke unambiguously of the pain of God. The expression *Waga harawata kare no tameni itamu* 我が腸かれの為に 痛む literally means, "For his sake, my insides are in pain." The expression "my insides are in pain" is translated from the Hebrew (*hāmû mē 'ay*), comprising two lexical items: the verb (*hāmâ*), and the noun (*mē 'eh*). The latter refers literally to one's intestines or inward parts. In this context, it is used figuratively to refer to the seat of emotions, and is appropriately translated into English as "heart."[53] According to the Theological Wordbook of the Old Testament, the verb (*hāmâ*) means to "cry aloud, mourn, rage, roar, sound; make noise, tumult; be clamorous, disquieted, loud, moved, troubled, in an uproar" (BibleWorks, 2018: 7). In the context of this verse, Kitamori sees this verb (*hāmâ*) as describing the heart of God in an emotional state of turmoil, anguish and restlessness (1986: 259). Kitamori's particular interpretation can be validated from the way (*hāmû mē 'ay*) is rendered as *mein Herz bricht mir* (literally, "my heart is breaking") in *Lutherbibel* (1545). Kitamori also cites a German paraphrase of the verse, which has *ich empfinde den heftigsen Schmerz* (literally, "I feel the most severe pain") (Kitamori, 1986: 263).[54]

Through a further word study on (*hāmâ*) from Jeremiah 4:19; 48:36, Psalms 39:6; 55:17; 77:3, and Isaiah 16:11, Kitamori concludes that divine revelation has made it possible for the very heart of God to be apprehended analogically from human emotions, even though human pain is qualitatively different from divine pain, "as a dog is different from the Dog Star" (Kitamori, 1986:288). Kitamori's approach may appear Thomist, but in fact, he rejects Thomas Aquinas' notion of *analogia entis* which, presumably to Kitamori, borders on natural theology (Kitamori, 1986: 261). Rather, insists Kitamori, it is "the very mercy of God" that has ordained the human experience of pain as the only means by which to understand, albeit imperfectly, the pain of God (Kitamori, 1986: 261-62). The tragic love of Hosea for his prostitute wife, according to Kitamori,

---

[52] In the King James Version, which is the closest in linguistic style with the Japanese Literary Version, the verse reads: "Is Ephraim my dear son? is he a pleasant child? for since I spake against him, I do earnestly remember him still; therefore my bowels are troubled for him; I will surely have mercy upon him, saith the Lord."

[53] The Japanese word *harawata* 腸 means intestines or guts, and hence corresponds exactly to the Hebrew word (*mē 'eh*). The use of one part of the human body to characterize the whole person is a common poetic device found in the Old Testament. Hans Walter Wolff calls this "stereometric thinking" (1974: 8). In Jeremiah 31:20, the use of (*mē 'eh*) – and its translated *harawata* – is intended to emphasize that the person's innermost being is being affected. As in Hebrew, the Japanese expression translated "my insides are in pain" is a poetic description of the pain that one experiences in the depths of one's heart.

[54] The source of this German paraphrase is unfortunately not documented.

is an example of how it serves the "glorious function" of revealing the grieving heart of God which we otherwise would not have known (2002: 38-39). Also, in the New Testament, we

> have the Parable of the Prodigal Son, a story given by Jesus so that "we are permitted to know the heart of God by means of events that happen in the human world" (1986: 261).

It is interesting to note at this point that the Church Father Irenaeus resolves the problem of the *analogia entis* – undoubtedly an anachronism here – by using God's revelation in Christ as the perfect *imago Dei* as the grounding of a "similarity within dissimilarity" (Boersma, 2005: 4; Behr, 2000: 89-90). Kitamori, however, chooses to resolve it very specifically through the foundational motif of pain. Kitamori's approach can be aptly described as predicated on the notion of *analogia doloris*. Here, of course, we face the limitations of human language in expressing divine realities. We will discuss this point at length when we address methodological issues in chapter 7.

Returning to Jeremiah 31:20, Kitamori comments, "Jeremiah must have seen in God the same condition of the heart which the prophets and psalmists themselves experienced. What kind of condition? The pain! The pain of God!" (2005, 153 = 1986, 262). In other words, Jeremiah saw the severest compassion of God's love toward sinners, and appropriately used the word "pain" to describe it. Kitamori justifies his interpretation of Jeremiah by citing from John Calvin's commentary on this verse:

> God enhances the reconciling grace further by saying, 'therefore my bowels are troubled for him; I will surely have mercy upon him.' Here God attributes human feelings to himself; for our bowels are shaken and roar under extraordinary 'pain' (*dolor*), and we sigh and groan deeply under the pressure of great sorrow. God, therefore, expresses his feelings as an affectionate father: 'my bowels are troubled' [literally "roar"] in accepting his people back in his grace.... *God's nature is to feel this way.* (Kitamori 2005, 154 = 1986, 264, emphasis added)

To strengthen his case, Kitamori quotes a host of other commentators, including C. F. Keil's comment that "God suffers pain on account of Ephraim his son" (1986: 265). In sum, Kitamori's exegesis led him to the insight that the pain of God is engendered when God refuses to stop loving those who turn against him. Kitamori is quick to point out that divine pain is therefore not to be understood in the substantive sense (*jittai gainen* 実体概念), that is, as a divine attribute in itself, but only in the relational sense (*kankei gainen* 関係概念) (Kitamori, 1986: 11).

Next, Kitamori observes that the word (*hāmâ*) is also used in Isaiah 63:15, but in this context, it refers not to divine pain but to divine love (Kitamori, 1986: 269-70). He concludes that the Hebrew word (*hāmâ*) carries the semantic content of pain and love simultaneously (Kitamori, 1986: 270).[55] This linguistic fact is "not simply a mystery of language, but also a mystery of grace" (Kitamori, 1986: 270). Kitamori also observes that in the Japanese language, the word for "sorrow", *kanashimi*, although commonly written as 悲しみ, could also be written as 愛しみ, that is, using the Chinese character for "love," 愛 (Kitamori, 1981: 166-67). Kitamori suggests that even if this is a linguistic accident, the relationship between love and pain is not a counter-intuitive notion in the realm of human experience (Kitamori, 1981: 166-67).[56]

The Dialectal Relationship between Divine Pain and Christology

Kitamori perceives a "purposeful structure" between Christ and divine pain (Kitamori, 1972: 84). Here, he constructs a dialectal relationship between divine pain and Christology by tracing a double movement between the pain of God and the historical Jesus. The first movement is that of Christology reflecting theology. Kitamori argues that it is only when we recognize the birth and death of Jesus Christ as "the pain of God", and his resurrection as "the love rooted in the pain of God" that the facts of the historical Jesus become "the fact of the gospel" (1968: 47-48). Indeed, the Christmas story is a story not only of joy, but also of intense suffering. The Slaughter of the Innocents and the flight of the Holy Family to Egypt (Mt. 2:13-18) are very much part of the Christmas narrative, and it is through these episodes that we catch a glimpse of the reality of divine pain (see pp. 123ff below). Moreover, the resurrection of Christ makes sense only in the light of the Crucifixion, that is, the pain of God. Only then can we appreciate the Resurrection not just as victory over death, but as love rooted in the pain of God.

The reverse movement from the pain of God to the historical Jesus is equally important. Following William Wrede, Kitamori insists that belief in the heavenly Christ must precede belief in the historical Jesus (Kitamori, 1968: 49). In other words, the historical Jesus did not become Christ by virtue of what he did; rather the divine Christ, the eternal Word of God became flesh and dwelt among humans (John 1:14). Through the Incarnation, the pain of God entered the historical plane as a person. In fact, Kitamori further argues that the pain of God implies the *necessity* of the *historical* Jesus (1986: 51). Referring to Luther, Kitamori (1986: 51) stresses that the pain of God deals with "real sin" (*verum*

---

[55] At this point, it is important to note that, contrary to what some have supposed, Kitamori did *not* construct his whole theology on just one or two verses (cf. Dyrness, 1990: 143). While it is true that Jeremiah 31:20 is pivotal to Kitamori's thought, he is careful to interpret that verse in the context of the whole Scripture. Throughout *Theology of the Pain of God*, a total of 327 different Scriptural texts from thirty biblical books were cited.

[56] According to linguist Eugene Nida, there is a word for "love" in the language of the Miskito Indians of Nicaragua which literally means "pain in the heart" (cited in Michalson, 1960: 174).

peccatum), and not "imaginary sin" (*fictum peccatum*). Since the historical world is the world of real sin, the only way for the divine Christ to personify the pain of God is by becoming a real, historical person (Kitamori, 1986: 51). For only a real, historical person can bear the responsibility of real sin. This point certainly presents a potent argument against the pluralist notion (common especially in Asia) that truth has to be ahistorical in order to be universal (cf. Ramachandra, 1996: 126-30). The scandal of historical particularity is that it serves the universal purpose of salvation. Moreover, as Kitamori points out, it is only the decisive mediation of divine pain in the context of human history that can refute every sort of docetism (1986: 52).

The whole life of Jesus Christ – from his birth to his death and even extending to his resurrection – is the phenomenological expression of the pain of God on the plane of human history. It is in the Crucifixion, however, that we see the clearest and climactic manifestation of divine pain. For that reason, Kitamori often speaks of the pain of God as synonymous with the death of Christ (e.g. Kitamori, 1986: 47, 74). Yet on the other hand, he is careful to maintain that the pain of God is ontologically prior to the Incarnation (Kitamori, 1986: 41). That is why the life of Jesus from the time of his birth was one of *via dolorosa*, the way of pain (Kitamori, 1986: 67). Jesus was born in order to die. "The very act of God coming into the world already implies his death in itself. The pain of God is not only located in Christ's death, but also in his birth (Kitamori, 1986: 67). For this reason, argues Kitamori, John 1:14 is incomprehensible without John 3:16 (Kitamori, 1986: 67). How then should we understand the relationship between the love of God as expressed in John 3:16 and the pain of God? Here is where Kitamori's theological creativity becomes most evident.

The Three Orders of Divine Love

Using Augustine's concept of *ordo amoris*, Kitamori suggests that the love of God can be understood as comprising three orders: (1) the immediate love of God, (2) the pain of God, and (3) the love rooted in the pain of God (1986: 201).

The Immediate Love of God
(chokusetsu teki naru kami no ai 直接的なる神の愛)

The immediate love of God is not to be construed in the temporal sense; rather it is to be understood as "a love poured out directly on its object in an unhindered manner" (1986: 202).[57] The object of the immediate love of God is the person who is *completely* worthy of receiving it. Such a person is loved directly by God without mediation. This is the love that exists ontologically within the trinitarian

---

[57] The word "immediate" is deliberately chosen to translate *chokusetsu teki naru*, partly to conform to the English translation of *Theology of the Pain of God*. Moreover, the word "immediate" seems to capture in a positive way Kitamori's intended emphasis here, namely, the direct and unmediated nature of this first order of divine love.

Godhead. The Father loves his completely obedient Son with a full and immediate love. God's love for Adam and Eve in their pre-Fall state was also an immediate love. Sin, however, betrayed that love. And because sin has come in between God and humans, God is no longer able to love human beings with an immediate love. Moreover, mediated by sin, divine love can only turn into divine wrath (Kitamori, 1986: 203). As a result of the universal effects of sin on humankind, all humans have now become objects of his wrath.

The Pain of God (Kami no itami 神の痛み)

The righteousness of God demands that sin should never be forgiven. In fact, Kitamori defines forgiveness as "the act of forgiving the unforgivable" (2000: 38).[58] As such, forgiveness involves sacrifice (Kitamori, 2000: 38). Here is where the scandal of the gospel comes in. God paid the high price of sacrifice by acting in an "ungodlike" and "improper" way (1986: 204). Instead of repulsing those who must be repulsed, God wills to forgive sin, enfold (*tsutsumu*包む) and embrace (*daku* 抱く) them against whom his wrath is directed (Kitamori, 1986: 204-205).[59] The gospel is indeed hard to believe, but it is true: God *still* loves the sinner who has lost all claims to be loved. However, as Kitamori points out, divine love is not smooth and easy, but rather obstructed and choked, for it is "the love for the enemy" (Rom. 5:10) (Kitamori, 1986: 155).[60] Here, Kitamori locates the enemy, whom he also describes as "the hateful" (*nikumu beki mono* 憎むべき者), at the bottom (*donzoko* どん底) of humanity, the furthest away from the reach of God's transcendent love and awaiting the sentence of his wrathful judgment (1981: 144-45). It is this humanity that God chooses to love and embrace. Hence, in John 3:16, when the beloved apostle writes about God loving the world so much that he gave his only Son, he is essentially talking about God loving the world, his enemy, to whom God handed his Son over to be killed.

God's decision to love those whom he hates creates a situation of "absolute contradiction," to use Nishida's term.[61] It causes God to experience fission within himself. However, because this inner conflict, intense though it is, cannot and does not destroy his fundamental unity, it engenders perpetual divine pain (Kitamori, 1981: 201). Kitamori coins a new term to describe this divine phenomenon: "the principle of fission-in-unity" (*bunretsu tōitsu ronri* 分裂統一論理) (Kitamori, 1981: 201). In trinitarian parlance, the immanent Trinity becomes the economic Trinity. The Father who begets the Son now causes the Son to die (Kitamori, 1986: 74). The pain of the God as perceived through the

---

[58] Here is another memorable expression from Kitamori: *yurushi to iu no wa yurusenai mono o yurusu koto desu* 赦しというのは赦せないものを赦すことです.

[59] Note the language borrowed from Nishida (see p. 108 above).

[60] The influence of Forsyth is evident here (see p. 117, n. 23 above).

[61] One often hears the saying that "God loves the sinner but hates the sin." Kitamori, however, does not make that distinction: God hates the sinner because he hates the sin.

principle of *opera trinitatis ad extra* is played out through the three stages of God's salvation plan.

First, the divine decision to love and save sinful humanity gives rise to a real conflict within God himself between his love and his wrath, for it is theologically impossible for God to make a sinner righteous first before embracing him or her (cf. Rom. 5:8). The act of a perfect and righteous God embracing an imperfect and unrighteous humanity engenders pain. Kitamori elaborates:

> God who must sentence sinners to death fought with God who wishes to love them. The fact that this fighting God is not two different gods but the same God causes his pain. Here heart is opposed to heart within God. (2005: 21 = 1986: 28)[62]

Kitamori uses the illustration of a seamless piece of cloth folded around a sharp object to show the pain that God experiences when he enfolds and embraces his enemy (1981: 244).

Second, the pain of God is played out in the realm of human history through the Incarnation of the Son of God, where it reaches its climax at the Crucifixion. Indeed, the pain of God is made manifest most fully at Golgotha, the very place where "God fought with God" (1986: 28). For on the cross, not only was the love of God for sinners supremely revealed, but so was the wrath of God in the sacrifice of his only begotten Son. In this regard, Kitamori believes that the biblical record, especially in Paul's writings, testifies to Jesus Christ bearing the full penalty of God's wrath as a substitute for sinful humanity (1981: 197-205). The punishment Jesus underwent constitutes the third aspect of the pain of God: the desolate experience of complete abandonment of the Son by the Father.

The Lord [Jesus] wants to heal our wounds, which were caused by God's wrath; this

> Lord suffers wounds, himself receiving his wrath. "[…] with his stripes we are healed" (Isa. 53:5) […]. The Lord was unable to resolve our death without putting himself to death. God himself was broken, was wounded, and suffered, because he embraced those who should not be embraced. By embracing our reality, God grants us absolute peace. *But the peace has been completely taken away from the Lord who grants us absolute peace.* "My God, my God, why hast thou forsaken me?" (2005: 22 = 1986: 28, emphasis in text)

In sum, in order to secure atonement for humankind, it was necessary for God to experience the threefold pain of embracing rebellious sinners at enmity with

---

[62] Kitamori presents the conflict within God and the pain that it engenders using such language of raw human emotions that some people may find objectionable. It has to be constantly borne in mind that such language is highly metaphorical and intended to be provocative lest we create God in our psychological image. Kitamori warns that it is ultimately impossible to know what the pain of God is; we can only sense through the historical event of Calvary that the divine plan of salvation caused something of unimaginable proportions to happen within the Godhead (1986: 261).

him, the searing pain of the Father giving his Son over to a most violent and unjust death, and the pain of the Son being forsaken by the Father. The salvation achieved through the victory of God's love over God's wrath on the cross must therefore never be regarded as without suffering and pain, for it was in truth mediated through the ultimate sacrifice of the object of God's immediate love, his Son. Through the shedding of Christ's blood, "divine love placates divine wrath, and in the process is wounded by it" (1981: 127). In other words, the love by which God loves sinners in Christ is always marked by divine pain. For, while it is true that on the cross Christ suffered *for* sinners, the pain of God provides a potent reminder that he suffered *because of* sinners. Citing Theodosius Harnack's interpretation of Luther, Kitamori concludes that divine pain is the "*tertium* that unites the wrath of God and the love of God" (1986: 27).

The Love of God Rooted in the Pain of God
(Kami no itami ni kisozukerareshi ai 神の痛みに基礎づけられし愛)
Herein lies a profound mystery. The death of Christ results in *mors mortis*, the death of death (Owen, 1959). For the resurrection of Christ vindicates his death, and provides the irrefutable evidence of the victory of divine pain: divine love has indeed conquered divine wrath! Forgiveness of sin is no longer just a possibility; it has become an actuality. God is now able to welcome sinners back as his reconciled children, in the same way the waiting father welcomes the prodigal son home. Our wounds have been healed by Christ's wounds, and our pain saved by God's pain. The victory of divine pain is "the love of God rooted in the pain of God" (Kitamori, 1986: 161). Yet, argues Kitamori, while God is now able to love us freely, he is still not able to love us immediately (Kitamori, 1986: 210). For God's love for us will always be mediated by divine pain. The reason is that the intentional and persistent love of God is "constantly being shipwrecked" by sin (Kitamori, 1986: 210). By this Kitamori seems to mean that even though we who are forgiven are delivered from the penalty and power of sin, we are still not delivered from the presence of sin. The reality of sin's presence continues to pose a constant threat to our faith, seeking to drive a wedge between us and the love of God. For this reason, it is important for Christians to live a crucified life (Gal. 2:20), remembering always "Jesus Christ and him crucified" (1 Cor. 2:2).

Translating the knowledge of "Jesus Christ and him crucified" into the language of divine pain, Kitamori stresses that it is only within the love of God rooted in the pain of God that we are sheltered and protected from the wrath of God (1986, 212). "God's pain is truly our peaceful abode [... for it] results from the love of the one who intercepts and blocks divine wrath from us" (Kitamori, 1986: 212). Kitamori tells this fascinating parable to illustrate his point:

A traveler is walking across a field in summer, when suddenly a thunderstorm breaks out above him. There is neither tree nor habitation; the traveler must walk on alone, in danger of being struck by lightning at any moment. Around him the lightning is striking here and there; in a minute it may strike him dead. But look! A mysterious hand is stretched over the traveler, covering and protecting him. Guarded by this loving hand, he can safely walk on through the thunderstorm. Because of that wonderful hand the lightning will not touch him. But look further. Like a linen cloth pierced by countless bullets, the hand which protects the traveler is being repeatedly struck by the lightning. This protecting hand is catching and intercepting the thunderbolts, which should fall on the traveler. (2005: 126 = 1986: 217)

In other words, the forgiven and reconciled sinner is called to trust and fear God at the same time. When we put our wholehearted trust in God's secure love, a love rooted in his pain, we can be fully assured of God's love protection to the point of knowing that "even the very hairs of [our] head are all numbered" (Luke 12:7). Yet it is this same God that one needs to fear. Outside of God, there is power that is capable of destroying us, but it can never destroy us completely the way that only a wrathful God can (Luke 12:4-5). It is hence imperative that those who have been forgiven as a result of the pain of God live their lives in such a way that they are always within the protection of his secure love.

Although Kitamori does not say if the love of God rooted in the pain of God ever becomes an immediate love, he does mention the theological reality of an incomplete and unfulfilled sanctification as long as we are in this world (1986: 245). The fact is that as long as sin is present, the love of God will remain in an unresolved condition. But that is not a critical problem, for we do have an eschatological hope in a glorious End, when the suffering of the world, corresponding to the pain of God, has "reached its fullness" (*tetteiteki to naru* 徹底的となる) (Kitamori, 1986: 241). It is not quite clear what Kitamori means by this. Presumably, only when suffering, human and divine, has "reached its fullness" will humans once again become the objects of God's immediate love.[63]

Kitamori's Soteriological Construct

Asakawa makes the insightful observation that Kitamori's three orders of love – the immediate love of God, the pain of God, the love of God rooted in the pain of God – corresponds directly to a soteriology constructed with the "trilogical structure" of creation, justification, and sanctification (2003: 2). We shall look at each of these stages briefly.

Creation and the Immediate Love of God

First, Kitamori understands *creatio ex nihilo* in terms of God creating by his self-giving love (1959a: 26). The immediate love that animates the perichoretic life shared by the three Persons in the trinitarian Godhead is what brought

---

[63] Kitamori draws an interesting correlation between the diffusion of the gospel throughout the world (Mt. 24:14) and the final fulfilment of the world's suffering and divine pain (1986: 240). The global spread of the gospel is an eschatological sign pointing to the end of the world's suffering. It is not clear though how the suffering of the world is related to divine pain.

humanity into existence. Until the Fall, God related with Adam and Eve with an unalloyed, unmediated love. Yet inherent in this immediate love is the risk of pain, for humans are created as free agents who could choose to obey or disobey their Creator (Kitamori, 1959a: 12). The Genesis record is clear that the first humans did rebel against God, and chose to become what they should not have become. Consequently, sin, which Kitamori defines as "the betrayal of God's love," infected the whole human race (Kitamori, 1959a: 16). As an aside, one may say that it is a brilliant move on the part of Kitamori to use the culturally intelligible concept of "betrayal" to explain "sin," which for many Japanese, is an abstract theological concept. It is not difficult then to see how the betrayal of God's immediate love arouses his wrath, such that God and humans can no longer relate with each other directly. The dire consequence is that sinful humanity has fallen *outside* God's will and God's love.

Justification and the Pain of God

The restoration of fallen humanity requires nothing less than the forgiveness of sin. The forgiveness of sin necessitates the mediation of blood sacrifice (Kitamori, 2000: 36), a theme which is prototypically repeated right through the Old Testament from its center in the Aaronic priesthood, and which foreshadows the supreme sacrifice of the perfect God-man on the cross.[64] In a word, God cannot relate with sinful humanity other than through a blood sacrifice mediated on the boundary between God and sinners who are outside. The good news of salvation is that God did take decisive action to love and embrace the sinner on the outside into God himself through the wrathful punishment meted out to the sinless Son of God. There on the cross, the Mediator became the perfect blood sacrifice. The divine action engenders divine pain, thereby securing the redemption and justification of the embraced sinner (Isa. 53:5).

Sanctification and the Love of God Rooted in the Pain of God

Taiwanese theologian Choan-Seng Song grossly misinterprets Kitamori when he claims that Kitamori's theology has no place for the Resurrection since the Cross is "the final station of God's journey" (1991: 78). On the contrary, Kitamori understands the Cross as the *kontei* 根底 (foundation) of the Resurrection, and the Resurrection as the *kiketsu* 帰結 (conclusion) of the Cross (1991: 75). Consequently, on the basis of Christ's resurrection, argues Kitamori, the justifying work of the crucified Christ must lead to the sanctifying ministry of the Spirit of the risen Christ (2002: 138-55).[65]

---

[64] Indeed, even way before the institution of the Aaronic priesthood, we read in Genesis of how God made "garments of skin" to clothe Adam and Eve soon after they sinned (Gen. 3:21). Such provision would have entailed animal sacrifice, in all probability the first such sacrifice after the Fall. The killing of an animal in the Garden of Eden could be said to symbolize simultaneously the wrath of God and the grace of God.

[65] Song's critique of Kitamori was first published in the original edition of his *Third Eye Theology* in 1979. When the revised edition of the book was released in 1991, Song's comments were kept intact. Kitamori's writings on the person and ministry of

For Kitamori, an understanding of the meaning and significance of Christ's death is not complete without a theology of sanctification; although he is careful to emphasize that sanctification is a necessary consequence, not condition, of justification (1950: 37-38). Sanctification is a necessary soteriological category because even though the sinner is justified by God's mediated love in Christ, they are not yet fully transformed into the image of Christ. Being *simul iustus et peccator*, the justified person continues to struggle with sin, and does not yet become the object of God's immediate love. However, the Holy Spirit now lives within the justified person, and effects a continuing work of transformation within that person while sustaining them with the secure love of God rooted in the pain of God (Kitamori, 2002: 146-47). Kitamori also warns that until the day when God's salvation is fully consummated, believers are not to grieve the Holy Spirit by the way they live (Eph. 4:30) (Kitamori, 2002: 150-51). "The day of consummation of salvation is the day of the victory of God's love, the day of redemption," says Kitamori (Kitamori, 2002: 151). Until then, the sanctifying work of the Spirit is necessarily mediated by the love of God rooted in the pain of God.[66]

A key area in the Christian's sanctification is learning how to deal with human pain. Here, Kitamori points out that one of the wondrous implications of the Incarnation is that, in the person of the God-man Jesus, we see the unity of divine pain and human pain (1986: 90-91). This means that God knows our pain and suffering. For not only is the Son the object of God's pain but, through the Son, all human beings have become the objects of God's pain as well (Kitamori, 1986: 91). Kitamori would even go so far as to say that "since God is the "Father of all humankind, he also experiences pain as our Father when we suffer" (Kitamori, 1986: 91). In the light of divine pain, how then should humans deal with their pain? Kitamori focuses on three areas in this discussion: service to God, mysticism, and service to others, that is, ethics.

Service

According to Kitamori, there are two key passages in the Gospels which not only offer us a glimpse into the paschal mystery of the Cross, but teach us how God often uses human suffering to serve the pain of God by testifying to it. The first

---

the Holy Spirit as cited here were first published in 1964 in his book *Seisho hyakuwa* (A hundred lessons from the Bible), fully fifteen years before the publication of Song's book. Kitamori's book was republished in 2002 as a Kōdansha pocket book. According to Kitamori, John 20:23 "reveals clearly that the Holy Spirit is the spirit of Jesus the Risen One" (2002: 140). Moreover, the Spirit lives in believers to transform them anew (Kitamori, 2002: 146-47). It is a pity that Song should evaluate Kitamori's *theologia crucis* by referring only to his *Pain of God Theology*, when in fact Kitamori had already published no less than thirty-six books by the time *Third Eye Theology* was first released (cf. Song, 1991: 78).

[66] Paul's warning against grieving the Spirit in Ephesus 4:30 implies that the Spirit allows himself to be inflicted with pain. Here, we see the possibility of a pneumatological, and trinitarian, theology of suffering.

passage relates to Herod's slaughter of the Innocents in Matthew 2:16-18. This text is set in the context of the Christmas story, but is almost never read during Christmas. Because of the violence inherent in this episode, it has become somewhat of a taboo to the Christmas spirit. The question is often asked as to why God, in his power, did not prevent such senseless bloodshed. Indeed, we do not know why such suffering was not prevented, but Kitamori suggests that, in this instance, the untold suffering as echoed in the haunting cry of Rachel reveals to us the suffering heart of God (2000: 22-28). The extreme contrast between the irenic scene of the Nativity and the following scene of the Slaughter of the Innocents is indicative of the unparalleled significance of the birth of Jesus. For the birth of Jesus is related to his death. The goal of Christmas is nothing less than the Passion. For all human beings, death is the final result of birth, but in the case of Jesus, death was the very *purpose* of his birth (Kitamori, 2000: 207). And so, along with the blessed news of the birth of Jesus, Matthew foretold his violent death, through the Slaughter of the Innocents. More than this, Kitamori suggests that the Slaughter of the Innocents expresses the unrelieved pain and grief of the Father who refuses to be comforted, like Jacob at the loss of his son Joseph (Kitamori, 2000: 26-27). The lament of the mothers in Bethlehem over the senseless slaughter of their sons points to the lament of the Father who would similarly witness the cruel slaughter of his own Son on the cross. For this reason, insists Kitamori, without the pain of God, the Christmas story becomes meaningless sentimentalism (Kitamori, 2000: 22).

A similar observation can be made of Luke 2:28-35. The words that Simeon pronounced to Mary about a sword piercing her soul were difficult words to say the least. Indeed, Mary would experience the full import of these words when she saw her son, Jesus, brutally beaten and then crucified. At the foot of the cross, Mary must have felt utterly lonely, that no one understood the hellish pain that she was going through. For who could empathize with her unique situation of losing a perfect son, a son who was miraculously conceived, the promised Savior, and who was now being subjected to the greatest injustice in history? This is where Kitamori's genius comes in. Kitamori points out that Jesus was not only the son of Mary, but he was also the Son of God, and therefore the very same sword that pierced Mary's soul would also pierce the soul of the Father (1988: 53). For Jesus died on the cross not only as the son of Mary, but as the Son of God. And so, just as Mary, *Mater dolorosa*, suffered the indescribable pain of losing her son on the cross, God the Father too became *Pater dolorosa* as he saw his Son being cruelly put to death. Both Mary and God the Father lost the same son on Calvary. In this sense, Mary's pain was not unique. Simeon's prophetic words hence were not only for Mary, but they were intended to give a glimpse of what God would experience at the Crucifixion.

For Kitamori, buried in these two Gospel passages that we have just considered is a theological pearl of great price. The pain of God is an inherent and essential part of his salvation plan, a point that must not be forgotten in the proclamation of the gospel. Kitamori understands well that the divine hospitality offered to sinners comes to us only through divine pain suffered.

Therefore, Kitamori calls all Christians to "serve the pain of God" by following the Lord of the Cross (1986: 78). By this he means that we are to accept our pain and use it as a testimony to divine pain (Kitamori, 1986: 84). According to Kitamori, the Bible teaches two ways in which humans can render service to divine pain. The first is "to let our *loved ones* suffer and die" (Kitamori, 1986: 137, emphasis in text). In so doing, we are witnessing the pain of *God*, since we experience the pain of God the Father who let his beloved Son suffer and die. The thought here is that because God knows precisely the pain involved, we need to trust him when our loved ones suffer and die, and not demand healing as if it were our intrinsic right.[67] Kitamori upholds the prime example of Abraham to show how the latter served God by his willingness to obey God and let his son die even though it would have been a most painful ordeal for him (Kitamori, 1986: 79-80). For this reason, Kitamori calls Abraham not only the "father of faith," but also the "father of divine service" (Kitamori, 1986 79). When we accept our suffering willingly as from God in the spirit of Abraham, says Kitamori, "our pain is transformed into light, and becomes meaningful and fruitful" (1986: 83). On the contrary, if we fixate on our suffering, we will end up committing suicide or becoming mad (Kitamori, 2000: 28). God wills to heal us of our pain, and he does it only by using our pain to serve his pain by testifying to it (Kitamori, 2000: 28).

The second means by which to render service to the pain of God is "for *us* to suffer and die" (1986: 137, emphasis in text). When we allow ourselves to suffer, we are witnessing to the *pain* of God because we are identifying with God the Son entering pain and dying. In sum, to serve the pain of God with our pain is, in biblical jargon, to deny ourselves, take up our cross and follow Jesus (Mt. 16:24). It is to recognize first and foremost that the central message of the gospel is not salvation from suffering – that would be Buddhism – but salvation from sin, and it involves suffering. It is to accept that our calling as Christians is *necessarily* one of pain and suffering (1 Pet. 4:12-19). In the words of Dietrich Bonhoeffer, "When Christ calls a man, he bids him come and die" (1995: 89).

---

[67] The idea of accepting one's pain willingly runs counter to the promise of "this-worldly benefits" (*genze riyaku* 現世利益) that is characteristic of the approximately 23,000 new religions in Japan today. The term "New Religions," or *shin-shūkyō* 新宗教 in Japanese, came into currency first in journalistic literature in the early 1950s, reflecting the explosive growth of the new religions in the immediate postwar years (see p. 54, f.n. 38 above). Although Kitamori is silent about the proliferation of these new religions, it is not hard to imagine how radical his message must have been in the immediate years following the war. Of course, as a modern application, to use one's pain to serve the pain of God, however one construes it, is indeed a powerful theological counterpoint to the health and healing industry so rampant in the church today.

Indeed, suffering is "the fruit of an exclusive allegiance to Jesus Christ" (Bonhoeffer, 1995: 88).

Mysticism

Next, there is a mystical dimension in sanctification as the Christian grows one's experience of God's love rooted in one's own pain. Both Paul and Peter speak of our union with Christ in his suffering, death and resurrection (Rom. 6:3-5; Gal. 2:20; Gal. 5:24; 2 Cor. 1:5; Phil. 3:10; 1 Pet. 2:21; 1 Pet. 4:13). Indeed, the expression "in Christ", scattered throughout Paul's letters, assumes this mystical union. Kitamori applies this spiritual reality to relate human pain to divine pain: the Christian "is dissolved in the pain of God and becomes one with him in pain" (1986: 118). Kitamori believes that this is what Paul means when he teaches that "we who have been baptized into Christ were baptized into his death" (Rom. 6:3) (Kitamori, 1986: 118). The union that the Christian has with Christ *in mysticam mortem* is the "mysticism of pain" (*itami no shimpi shugi* 痛みの神秘主義), says Kitamori (1986: 120).

Here, Kitamori anticipates a problem in his theological system. The defining characteristic of mysticism is in its experience of immediate intimacy with the divine. However, because the love of God rooted in pain is not an immediate love, in what sense can we claim a mysticism of pain, of becoming one with God in pain? Kitamori resolves this problem by appealing to his Lutheran heritage. A "healthy mysticism" (*kenzen naru shimpi shugi* 健全なる神秘主義), he argues, must be based on the doctrine of justification (Kitamori, 1986: 121-22). True faith is solafideist. Citing Galatians 2:20, Kitamori shows that justification necessarily leads to a biblical mysticism, which he then defines as "the mysticism of pain" (Kitamori, 1986: 124). The doctrine of justification by grace through faith implies that it is only through the mysticism of pain, that is, through being one with Christ in his death, that "we become immediately at one with the God who denies immediacy" (Kitamori, 1986: 123). All other mystical experience which claims a relationship of immediate intimacy with God, according to Kitamori, must therefore be treated with suspicion, for it can only lead to disobedience to God (Kitamori, 1986: 124). Despite his creative theologizing, however, Kitamori's explication of the mysticism of pain unfortunately remains rather opaque to understanding.

Ethics

What is clear, however, is that the mysticism of pain creates an ethic of pain. That is, union with Christ places ethical demands on the believer. First, the Christian is called to put to death all that belongs to the flesh (Col. 3:5; Gal. 5:24). This is essentially the same point made earlier when Kitamori exhorts Christians to serve the pain of God by being willing to suffer and die. Here he suggests that "the most effective way of eradicating sin is to constantly lay the pain of God on ourselves" (1986: 129). What this means in practice is that we are to remind ourselves constantly of our oneness with the crucified Christ and His pain. When we do that, the lusts and desires of the flesh will lose their grip on us.

But we do not overcome sin with our own strength. For the love of God rooted in the pain of God produces the gift of ethical sanctification through the empowering of the Holy Spirit (Kitamori, 1986: 130). Our response is to "walk by the Spirit" (Gal. 5:16), "be filled with the Spirit" (Eph. 5:18), and live such that we "do not grieve the Holy Spirit" (Eph. 4:27; cf. Kitamori, 2002: 150-51).

Second, because of the unity and commonality of humankind, we can feel our neighbor's pain as intensely as our own (Kitamori, 1986: 146). Kitamori defines "neighbors" to include both believers and non-believers (Kitamori, 1986: 152). Pain and suffering are existential human realities everywhere, but only those who have a living faith in Christ are able to make sense of pain and suffering because they have allowed their pain to serve the pain of God. And having suffered, they now understand the meaning of the pain of God, and can therefore comfort those suffering (cf. 2 Cor. 1:3-5). For this reason, the believer has the ethical responsibility of showing the way to the unbeliever. Kitamori elaborates, "When the believer who has laid upon himself the pain of God loves his unbelieving neighbor as earnestly as himself, the unbeliever is borne on the body of the believer into God's pain" (Kitamori, 1986: 153). In the process, the unbeliever is "transferred from darkness to light" (Kitamori, 1986:). It must be admitted that once again Kitamori is rather opaque to understanding here. Suffice to say that when Christians share their neighbor's pain and relate it to the pain of God, they are truly living out their calling as "light of the world" (Mt. 5:14; Kitamori 1986: 153). Here we see divine pain realizing an ethic of pain, which in turn leads to faith (Kitamori, 1986: 146-47).

The Death of Christ in Kitamori's Trinitarian Schema

It is no coincidence that a cohesive theological patterning exists behind Kitamori's pain of God theology. The three orders of love that provide the theological scaffolding for his soteriological construct is unmistakably trinitarian. The immediate love of God can be said to belong to the proper realm of God the Father, the Creator of all things. The pain of God is most obviously expressed through the death of God the Son on the cross, a death which brought about the justification of sinners. The pain of God also represents, not the immediate love of God which now has become impossible, but the love of God mediated by the cross. The intentional love of God rooted in the pain of God sustains the believer in the process of sanctification, the primary agent of which is God the Holy Spirit. According to Kitamori, the salvific work of God as understood through the lens of the pain of God is the proper understanding of the Trinity (1943: 12).

Of course, Kitamori subscribes unconditionally to the classical Nicene formulation of the Trinity as *treis hypostaseis kai mia ousia*. However, he refuses to speculate about the metaphysics behind such concepts as "substance," "generation of the Son," and "procession of the Spirit." To Kitamori, the immanent Trinity, as characterized by *opera trinitatis ad intra*, is a mystery

(1986: 75-77). Taking the cue from Calvin, Kitamori is content to say no more about the immanent Trinity other than to affirm the incommunicable otherness of each of the three divine Persons within the singular Godhead, and the relation of immediate love that exists between them (1960b: 224). What Kitamori is in effect saying is that the immanent Trinity provides limited theological mileage that can only be extended by the economic Trinity, the theological key here being the cross of Christ.[68]

Scripture, however, consistently reveals a God who relates with his creation *outside* of himself (Kitamori, 1959b: 38). Hence, Kitamori prefers to understand the nature of the trinitarian God not through the abstract essence of the three divine Persons, but through their work in salvation, *opera trinitatis ad extra*. The economic Trinity should be the proper focus of trinitarian theology, declares Kitamori (Kitamori, 1959b: 38). The key thought in Kitamori's understanding of the economic Trinity is that the Cross is not only a Christological event, but a trinitarian one.[69] The vital relationship between the Father and the Son, according to Kitamori, is captured in the gospel axiom, "The Father causes the Son to die" (1986: 75). Indeed, Kitamori accords precedence of these "primary words" over the traditional formulation, "The Father begets the Son," which he describes as "secondary words" (Kitamori, 1986: 75). In other words, Kitamori locates the death of Christ in the Trinity. It is first a theological act grounded in God himself before it becomes a historical fact (Kitamori, 1986: 70). This is why Kitamori understands the pain of God to be prior to the cross of Christ, describing the latter as the historical, phenomenological expression of the former (Kitamori, 1986: 41).

The question arises then as to whether the death of Christ within the Trinity is a supralapsarian or infralapsarian act. Unwilling to compromise God's sovereignty, Kitamori insists that since the initiative to save an utterly helpless humanity has to come from God alone, it must therefore involve supralapsarian sacrifice and pain on the part of God. Indeed, Kitamori cites Forsyth's statement that "the cross was the reflection (or say rather the historic pole) of an act within Godhead" (Forsyth, 1909: 270, in Kitamori, 1986: 70), and interprets it – a little

---

[68] In this regard, Kitamori does not subscribe to Rahner's rule which posits "the axiomatic unity of the 'economic' and 'immanent' Trinity" (Rahner, 1997: 21). According to Rahner, the economic Trinity *is* the immanent Trinity, and the immanent Trinity *is* the economic Trinity (Rahner, 1997: 22). I am indebted to Dr. Kevin Vanhoozer for directing me to Rahner. See Karl Rahner, *The Trinity* (New York: Crossroad, 1997).

[69] This is where Nomachi Shinri's explanation of Kitamori's pain of God in Christocentric terms misses the center of Kitamori's *theologia crucis*. See Nomachi's graduation thesis, *"Kami no itami" no shingaku no kirisuto chūshinteki rikai: Kirisutosha no seikatsu ni okeru kunan no sekkyokuteki no imi o motomete* ("A Christocentric Understanding of 'The Pain of God Theology': Seeking Positive Meaning in Suffering in the Life of a Christian") (Nagoya: Tokai Theological Seminary, 1999).

tenuously – to mean that the Cross is primarily an internal divine act before it becomes an external historical event. Kitamori asserts, "The divine tragedy of the cross of Christ *precedes* all human tragedy. Before humanity could suffer any pain, God had already suffered pain for all humanity" (1968: 127, emphasis added). In other words, before embracing the outsider in Christ historically, God has already effected the act of embrace theologically within himself even before the creation of the world. This, of course, begs the question why God should even suffer before he created the world (Hashimoto, 1992: 248).

In Kitamori's trinitarian schema, the divine tragedy is now moved onto the plane of eternity. As mentioned earlier, God created humans as free agents who could choose to obey God and continue to enjoy an immediate relationship with him, or to disobey God and consequently inflict suffering and pain on themselves as well as on God (1959a: 12). However, Kitamori seems to have unwittingly fallen prey to the Aristotelian notion that God is pure actuality when he decides that eternity implies necessity (1986: 71). In other words, *potential* pain cannot have any place in the eternal Godhead (cf. Kitamori, 1953: 30). The only way for Kitamori to formulate the concept of divine pain such that it fits into the logic of classical scholastic theology is to essentialize pain as a divine attribute.[70] Kitamori does not see any problem with this, pointing out that Christ, the First and the Last, is indeed described in the Apocalypse as "the Lamb that was slain from the creation of the world" (Rev. 13:8) (1986: 71). Here, one is confronted with a real contradiction, for in the preface to the fifth edition of his magnum opus – written in 1958 – Kitamori insists that divine pain is not to be understood as divine substance (*jittai* 実体) but in terms of relationship (*kankei* 関係) (1986: 11). Kitamori seeks to resolve the dilemma by using another word, *honshitsu* 本質 (essence), which he defines as "God's true heart" (*Kami no mikokoro* 神の御こころ) (1986: 72). In other words, according to Kitamori, even though pain is not to be understood as divine substance, it is to be thought of as an essential attribute of God's own heart! Kitamori's linguistic proposal only serves to complicate the theological morass that was already created from the very instance when he located divine pain inside the eternal Godhead.

At this juncture, one notes that Kitamori's understanding of the trinitarian relations runs afoul of Cappadocian trinitarianism. The Eastern Orthodox theologian John Zizioulas rightly shows the transition from an ontology of substance to an ontology of love as necessary for understanding the inter-relationships within the Godhead, by referring to how Basil the Great (330-397) rejected substance as an ontological category in describing the Godhead, and in its place used the concept of communion:

> Instead of speaking of the unity of God in terms of His one nature, [Basil] prefers to speak of it in terms of the *communion of persons*: communion is for Basil an

---

[70] Interestingly, while Kitamori adopts the scholastic framework of classical theology, he rejects the traditional notion of divine impassibility that arises from it.

ontological category. The *nature* of God is communion. (1985: 123, emphasis in the original)

The implication is that since the communion between the three trinitarian persons is one of perfect, immediate love, there cannot be eternal pain within the Godhead, contrary to Kitamori's assertion.

However Kitamori construes it, the notion that pain is a necessary attribute of God is highly problematic. This is Noro Yoshio's main critique of Kitamori, that in granting *dolor Dei* an ontological status, the "freedom of the grace of God" is invariably compromised (1955: 92). Noro is, of course, right here. Moreover, positing pain as an essential divine attribute ultimately implies that the historical cross of Christ is but a temporal manifestation of the eternal cross of the Trinity. It is hard not to treat this as a theological aberration.

One can also see how Kitamori's *theologia crucis* can easily be accused of patripassianism. Indeed, Noro does not understand how Kitamori can escape the charge of patripassianism if he keeps insisting that "the Father suffered with the Son" (Yoshio, 1955: 51). Kitamori, of course, denies the charge of patripassianism on the grounds that divine pain is to be understood relationally, not substantially (1986: 11, 199). He also defends himself by positing the argument for the incommunicable properties that give each of the three trinitarian Persons his unique identity (Kitamori, 1984: 284). It was not the Father, but the Son, who died on the cross (see Kitamori, 1959b: 53-54). In all of his writings, Kitamori does not use the theologically inflammatory phrase "crucified God" to describe the death of Christ, even if he acknowledges that the phrase was used at least once by Luther himself (cited in Kitamori, 1986: 196, and in Moltmann, 1993: 47). However, insists Kitamori, it was impossible for God the Father not to suffer pain when his one and only Son was being put to death (1986: 198).[71] Moreover, even though the Father did not suffer on the cross, to locate the pain of God *only* in the death of Christ is to divide the Trinity. Kitamori's pain of God theology is therefore more appropriately classified under the category of theopaschism rather than patripassianism. This, of course, altogether subverts the traditional understanding of divine impassibility as well.

Kitamori's Views on the Traditional Theories of the Atonement

Many people in Japan have pointed out the similarities between Christianity and True Pure Land Buddhism. Like Christianity, True Pure Land Buddhism teaches salvation by grace through faith. However, the fundamental difference is that in Pure Land there is no atonement (Kitamori, 2000: 98). This is why the Church bears the crucial responsibility of explaining the meaning of the Cross to the world, hence the importance of the theories of the Atonement (Kitamori, 2000: 98). Moreover, says Kitamori, for the fact of the Atonement to be actualized in

---

[71] Moltmann shares essentially the same view: "In the suffering of Christ, God himself suffers" (1993: 47).

the life of the believer, it has to be subjectively appropriated, and that cannot happen unless one engages in the theological exercise of seeking to understand the Atonement as much as possible (1981: 190).[72]

According to Kitamori, there are three main Atonement theories that merit study: Anselm's satisfaction theory, Gustav Aulén's *Christus Victor* theory, and the punishment theory of the Reformers (Kitamori, 1981: 192). Fundamentally, Anselm's theory consists of a "rational necessity and a logical compromise" (Kitamori, 1981: 194).[73] First, the problem of the loss of divine honor as a result of human sin is framed in a way that conforms to a rational necessity of binary relations: the execution of divine justice precludes the exercise of divine love. Second, the solution is provided through a logical compromise using the concept of compensation: if an adequate compensation is made to meet the terms of divine justice, then divine love will be freely operative. Kitamori describes Anselm's theory, not inaccurately, as "legalistic" (Kitamori, 1981: 195).

In the main, Kitamori agrees with the formal structure in Anselm's theory as he interprets it. According to Kitamori, Anselm has rightly identified the intrinsic "contradiction" (*mujun*) between divine love and divine justice to be the problem that needs to be overcome for salvation to be achieved (Kitamori, 1981: 195). However, even though Anselm's solution may be "right in form," it does not possess "rightness in quality" (Kitamori, 1981: 195). Without an element of "intensity" (*gekiretsusa* 激烈さ) which is inherent in Christ's death, Anselm's theory becomes nothing more than a mathematical procedure or commercial exercise (Kitamori, 2000: 100-101). Kitamori suggests that the missing element of "intensity" in Anselm's theory is the pain of God (1981: 195).

Aulén's theory can be traced back to the Church Fathers. In this theory, God waged a cosmic battle against the demonic hosts on the cross, and triumphed. The Atonement is therefore understood as an act of divine victory, with the crucified Christ emerging as Victor. Kitamori appreciates Aulén's portrayal of God as dramatic subject, not passive agent, in the Atonement, and the divine display of a non-rationalistic pathos (*higōriteki patosuteki seikaku* 非合理的パトス的性格) that is rightly characteristic of the event of the Cross (Kitamori, 1981: 196). However, Kitamori points out that when the focus is singularly on the victorious result of the battle at the expense of understanding the very nature of the battle itself, the Cross becomes emptied of its true significance (Kitamori, 1981: 197). The victorious love that emerges at the end of the battle on the cross is, insists Kitamori, "the love of God rooted in the pain of God" (Kitamori, 1981: 197).

Kitamori believes that the punishment theory of the magisterial Reformers best represents the biblical record. In this theory, God placed on his own beloved

---

[72] Interestingly, Kitamori cites the example from quantum mechanics to show the crucial role subjective involvement plays in shaping physical reality (1981: 261).
[73] The English terms "rational necessity" and "logical compromise" are Kitamori's own.

Son the full burden of human sin, punished him on the cross as the substitute for all humanity, and through his atoning death, forgave human beings their sins.[74] The prime difference between this theory and Anselm's theory is, in the former, the focus is on the redemption of sinful humanity while the latter focuses on the satisfaction of God's honor. Kitamori believes that the punishment theory possesses the existential element of "intensity", and for this reason, it has brought deep comfort to many suffering believers (Kitamori, 1981: 198).

Kitamori, however, puts his own theological spin on the structure of the punishment theory, using Kierkegaard's language of *areka-koreka* (Either/Or), the Hegelian all-encompassing notion of *aremo-koremo* (Both/And), and his teacher Tanabe's concept of nothingness, *aredemonaku-koredemonai* (Neither/Nor) (Kitamori, 1981: 203-207). Here is a fine example of creative contextualized theologizing.[75] God's righteousness *within* the law demands that sinful human beings be judged; otherwise, divine justice will be miscarried. In other words, the nature of the law creates a situation of *areka-koreka, either* God *or* humans. This in effect means that no salvation is possible within the law. However, the good news is that "a righteousness from God, *apart from law*, has been made known" (Rom. 3:21, emphasis added). This, according to the gospel, is divine righteousness, the *iustitia Christi aliena* in Luther's doctrine. This is altogether another righteousness, the content of which is the death of Christ (Rom. 3:25). Romans 3:26 then reveals the basic structure of redemption: "In Christ, God is proved just and (*kai,*) humans are proved justified" (Kitamori, 1981: 204). In other words, Christ opened the way for *both* God *and* humans to be reconciled. In contrast with the *areka-koreka* nature of the law, the way of the gospel is one of *aremo-koremo*. It must not be forgotten, however, that the gospel contains within itself the uncompromising requirements of the law (Kitamori, 1981: 205). In order to open the way to accommodate both God and humans *aremo-koremo*, Christ must necessarily fulfill "the law of opposition" of *areka-koreka*, on behalf of all humanity. In the process of the atoning act, Christ became utterly forsaken to a place where neither God nor humans are, a state of total loneliness, *aredemonaku-koredemonai* (Kitamori, 1981: 205). The way of punishment that Christ trod is one of profound pain, *via dolorosa*. Kitamori adds that since Christ is not man who became God, but rather God who became man, the pain that he experienced is ultimately the pain of God rather than the pain of a mere man (Kitamori, 1981: 205). In sum, the Redeemer willingly allowed himself to suffer pain and be abandoned to a desolate place of *aredemonaku-koredemonai* in order to bring about reconciliation, *aredemoari-koredemoaru*, between God and humanity. This, according to

---

[74] The punishment theory that Kitamori refers to is essentially what evangelicals would call penal-substitution theory.

[75] It must be noted, however, that here Kitamori is only using the language of Kierkegaard, Hegel, and Tanabe for his theological purposes; he is not utilizing their philosophical ideas in any substantial way.

Kitamori, is "the fundamental structure of the mediatory work of the Redeemer" (Kitamori, 1981: 205).

Kitamori's theological insights can hardly be said to be original, but the way he articulates them is novel and appeals to Japanese literary sensitivity. It is admittedly difficult for a person who has no knowledge of the Japanese language to appreciate the literary creativity and beauty that Kitamori brings to his theological construction. Perhaps the lesson to learn here is the importance of the vernacular in theologizing: it makes the gospel touch the heart of the native speaker.

The Dolor Dei *"Model" of the Atonement*

Although Kitamori affirms penal-substitution as his preferred theory of the Atonement, it would also be right, perhaps even more accurate, to say that he embraces an eclectic model of the Atonement, one that consists of an objective and a subjective aspect. Objectively, Kitamori accepts the biblical record of the divine punishment suffered by Christ on behalf of all humanity. His concept of the pain of God provides the subjective element in his understanding of the Atonement. One can almost imagine Kitamori appropriating Aulén's structure of the *Christus Victor* but modifying its contents. Aulén conceives of a cosmic battle on the cross where God triumphed over all the forces of evil. In contrast, Kitamori conceives of a cosmic battle where "God fought against God" on the cross (1986: 28). The outcome in Kitamori's scenario is the triumph of divine love over divine wrath. It is important to note that Kitamori does not see love and wrath as moral opposites – that is, love as good and wrath as evil – but rather as existing in an ontological tension. Two points are pertinent here. First, the possibility of the victory of divine love over divine wrath avails itself only because the former belongs to the realm of the *opus proprium Dei* (i.e. the work which belongs to God's very nature), while the latter to the *opus alienum Dei* (i.e. the work which is alien to God's nature) (Ps. 30:5). Here, Kitamori puts a creative spin to the dialectic between the *opus proprium* and the *opus alienum* that Luther introduces in his exposition of the sixteenth thesis of the Heidelberg Confession (Luther, 1962b: 288-89).[76] Second, the unity of divine wrath and divine love on the cross is not achieved without conflict; rather it is "a unity of victory gained after an awfully fearsome conflict" (Kitamori, 1986: 193). In other words, divine love and divine wrath are mediated by divine pain. It must be said, however, that Kitamori has no intention of putting forward a new theory to explain *how* the Cross saves; his interest is primarily in pointing to the immensity of the love of God that expresses itself in pain. That notwithstanding,

---

[76] Kitamori takes the liberty of defining God's love and God's wrath as *opi Dei*, even though, strictly speaking, they are not "works" as such. In Luther's understanding, by "making" a person a sinner in order to make them righteous, God is using the *opus alienum* as the means to bring about the *opus proprium* in the end.

we can still describe Kitamori's theology of the Cross as the *Dolor Dei* "model" of the Atonement.

The Primary Influence of Luther on Kitamori

The unmistakable and decisive influence of Luther on Kitamori's theology of the pain of God should be obvious by now. We shall therefore not belabor the point beyond a brief word. Luther is the most quoted theologian in Kitamori's works, being cited no less than fifty times in his 1937 seminary graduation thesis *Knowledge of God in Christ*, as well as in his magnum opus *Theology of the Pain of God*. John Hesselink's description of Kitamori's theology as "Luther's theology of the Cross garbed in Japanese kimono" (1966: 97) may be exaggerated, but it expresses well the seminal impact exerted on Kitamori by the magisterial Reformer.

Following Luther, Kitamori understands the death of Christ to be *the* central principle animating and informing all Christian theology.[77] In his classic work, *Luthers Theologia Crucis*, Walter von Loewenich lists five defining features of Luther's theology of the Cross, all of which can also be said to characterize Kitamori's theology of the pain of God:

1. The theology of the Cross is derived from divine revelation, not human speculation.
2. The revelation of God in Christ is an indirect, concealed revelation, in that Christ on the cross is not immediately recognizable as God.
3. This revelation is apprehended neither by good works nor in the created order, but is recognized only in the passion and cross of Christ.
4. The knowledge of God hidden in his revelation can only be discerned by faith.
5. God makes himself known particularly through suffering. (1954: 18)

Each of these five themes is deeply and intricately woven into Kitamori's theology of the pain of God, although not in a systematic way:

1. The pain of God cannot be believed in unless it is revealed by God (1986: 34).
2. On the cross, God, hidden in his pain, cannot be apprehended as such by the natural senses (Kitamori, 1986: 196; 1 Cor. 1:23).
3. God becomes truly revealed to sinners (*Deus revelatus*) only through his pain, that is, on the cross (Kitamori, 1986: 196).

---

[77] Hundreds of books have been written on Luther. Among them, two relatively recent titles offer particularly helpful and critical expositions of Luther's theology: Alister McGrath, *Luther's Theology of the Cross* (Grand Rapids, MI: Baker, 1990), and Gerhard Forde, *On Being a Theologian of the Cross: Reflections on Luther's Heidelberg Disputation* (Grand Rapids, MI: Eerdmans, 1997). A good English translation of Luther's Heidelberg Disputation is found in Luther (1962b: 276-307).

4. The only means by which to see the "revealed God" in the "hidden God" is faith, conferred on the believing sinner by the Holy Spirit (Kitamori, 1986: 197; 1 Cor. 12:3).

5. The definitive word of the gospel is the pain of God, which God communicates to us particularly through human suffering. (Kitamori, 1986: 74)

It is obvious that despite the structural mirroring of Luther in Kitamori, the latter departs radically from Luther by bringing the whole of his *theologia crucis* under the singular rubric of divine pain – a theological tour de force! Employing Luther's concept of *Deus absconditus in passionibus*, Kitamori asserts, "The death of God the Son was real death, and its darkness real pain. God the Father who hid himself in the death of God the Son is God in pain" (Kitamori, 1986: 198). For this reason, the theology of the Cross will always confound human wisdom, and will therefore always remain "outside" the *theologia gloriae* (Kitamori, 1986: 11). Despite his rather unorthodox appropriation of some of Luther's ideas, Kitamori's theological position remains basically Lutheran in orientation, and his posture is in full conformity with Luther's understanding of what it means to be a "theologian of the Cross" (Theses 20 and 21 of the Heidelberg Confession; see Luther, 1962b: 290-92).

Secondary Impetuses behind Kitamori's *Theologia Crucis*

We have thus far identified four primary influences that shaped Kitamori's understanding of the death of Christ: his own personal experiences from his years in high school through university, Scripture, Nishida's philosophy, and Luther's *Theologia Crucis*. We shall discuss first the Western influences on Kitamori, and then the Japanese influences.

Western Influences on Kitamori

In the course of developing his theology, Kitamori interacts with many other theologians as well as his own cultural traditions. We have seen the positive influence of P. T. Forsyth, who is cited five times in Kitamori's magnum opus (1986: 61, 67, 70, 95, 206).[78] Another key theologian with whom Kitamori interacts substantially is Karl Barth. Although there is much in Barth's theology that he appreciates, Kitamori takes issue with Barth on essentially two points.[79]

---

[78] The first three citations are from P. T. Forsyth, *The Person and Place of Jesus Christ* (London: Independent Press, 1909); the fourth reference is not documented; and the fifth is from Forsyth, *The Justification of God* (London: Independent Press, 1917).

[79] It is interesting to observe how in this instance Kitamori delivers a stinging critique of Barth's theological methodology without overtly mentioning Barth's name (1986: 29-31). The reader, however, would know that it is Barth who has come under attack from the two bibliographic references to Barth cited by Kitamori in his critique (Kitamori, 1986: 29, 31).

First, he faults Barth's theology for being legalistic since it is built upon the First Commandment as its axiom (1986: 30). Kitamori explains, "Even though the content of this theology is said to be the "gospel," in truth, the form governing the content is strictly the law, the First Commandment" (Kitamori, 1986: 30). In other words, the prolegomenon that reveals the true intention of this theology is the law. Next, Kitamori critiques Barth for proposing an overly distant God who does not embrace (Kitamori, 1986: 31). A God who does not embrace, says Kitamori, is a God who knows no pain (Kitamori, 1986: 31). The implication here is that an utterly transcendent God can only experience a monism of wrath against sinful humanity.

It is curious that over the course of his theological career, Kitamori never quite got over his fixation with these two points relating to the early Barth. As a consequence, he failed to appreciate Barth's methodological shift of emphasis from the Word of God to the Son of God. Indeed, Barth's Christocentric orientation was already evident by the time that he published the second part of the second volume of his *Church Dogmatics* on the doctrine of God in 1942 – four years before the publication of Kitamori's *Theology of the Pain of God*.[80] While it is right that Barth places a high premium on the First Commandment, it must not be forgotten that he understands God's revelation to be given through "the incarnation of the eternal Word, Jesus Christ" (Barth, 1956b: 1). "In the reality of this event," Barth declares, "God proves that He is free to be our God" (Barth, 1956b: 1). Later as he surveys the doctrine of reconciliation, Barth would pen these moving words in Thesis 58 of *Church Dogmatics* VI/1:

> The love of God in Jesus Christ is decisively, fundamentally and comprehensively His coming together with all men and their coming together with Him. This coming together is not deserved by man, but forfeited. Yet it has been accomplished by God in His free grace, defying and overcoming the sin of man. As this coming together the love of God active and revealed in Jesus Christ is the fulfilling of the covenant by Him. *It embraces realiter both the world and the community, non-Christians and Christians.* (1956a: 103, emphasis added; Barth, 1960: 48-49)

Moreover, the Incarnation, as Barth understands it, reveals the astounding truth that God's deity includes his humanity, a theme that he develops in the essay with the telling title, "The Humanity of God" (1960: 37-65). This is a remarkable departure from the transcendentalist position of the early Barth.

It is therefore extremely curious that Kitamori never understood Barth's theology as anything more than a theology "born in the face of the global tragedy [of the First World War]," hence its "thoroughgoing motif of a fundamental opposition between God and humankind" (Kitamori, 1986: 29). It is a pity that in his failure to interact with the subsequent developments of Barth's theology,

---

[80] See, for example, Thesis 33 of *Church Dogmatics*, II/2 for a deeply stirring account of the election of Jesus Christ for the salvation of humankind (Barth, 1957: 94-194, 306-40).

notably on the themes of divine grace and the humanity of God, Kitamori did not allow his own theology to be otherwise enriched by the later Barth. Given the predominance of Barth in Japanese theological circles in the pre-war and immediate post-war years, it is no wonder that during the first few years of its publication, Kitamori's magnum was not well received by Japanese theologians even though it was popular outside the church (Yagi, 1997: 88).

Kitamori has much to say about liberal theologians who care more about the life of Jesus than the death of Christ. In contrast with Barth, theirs is a monistic love which knows no wrath, hence no pain. For this reason, Kitamori rejects outright the sentimentalized notion of the painless love of God posited by the liberal theologians Schleiermacher, Ritschl, Hermann, and Harnack whom he describes as "nothing more than a bunch of happy people singing the soprano of God's love" (1986: 32). Moreover, theological liberalism seeks a natural, immediate love relationship with God, thereby draining the Cross of all its meaning and significance (Kitamori, 1986: 57-58). To prove his point, Kitamori points out that Schleiermacher himself confessed that he could believe neither in Jesus as the eternal God nor in His vicarious death (Asakawa, 2003: 59). There is hence no gospel in liberal theology. It is clear from his argument that Kitamori seeks to show that the only way to avoid a monism of wrath or a monism of love is to apprehend the pain of God.

Japanese Influences on Kitamori

Interestingly, Kitamori finds some theological resonance with the pain of God in Buddhism (2005: 26 = 1986: 36). Here he refers to *Notes on the Yuimakyo* written by Prince Shōtoku[81] in the late sixth century:

> There we find the earth-shaking sentence: "Man's real sickness springs from foolish love; Buddha's responding sickness arises from great mercy." Buddha's sickness-in-response "comes from his suffering mercy. His suffering mercy is man's vice – man's sickness. The sickness of the great mercy saves people by absorbing their sickness. Sickness is saved by sickness." The thought closest to the gospel which claims "the wound is healed by the wound" is found in the expression "Sickness is saved by sickness." We are exceedingly grateful to the revered religious ancestors of our native country who entertained these ideas. I believe that Japanese thought became deeper after the adoption of the above idea. (2005: 26 = 1986: 36-37)

However, since the Buddha has no wrath, Kitamori concludes that he cannot possibly have real pain (1986: 37). This, of course, begs the question as to

---

[81] Prince Shōtoku (574-622), the son of Emperor Yōmei, made Buddhism the state religion and orchestrated its spread throughout Japan in the late sixth century. He is also credited with the creation of Japan's first constitution, the Seventeen-Article Constitution which prescribed the philosophical and religious principles on which the imperial government was to be based.

whether the experience of pain is really not possible for one who has no capacity for wrath.[82] In any case, if we grant Kitamori's assumption as right, then the sickness of the Buddha cannot be not a real sickness, but always a responding sickness (Kitamori, 1986: 37). The most one could say of the Buddha is that he has great mercy or sympathy, but not pain (Kitamori, 1986: 27). Indeed, enlightenment for the Buddha is freedom from pain, but for the Christian God, the existential reality that he assumes is one of pain. This notwithstanding, Kitamori is impressed that "[the] idea that the Buddha himself becomes ill to save the illness of the people seems very close to the Christian idea of the savior who is wounded to save the wounded people" (1984: 26).[83]

Turning to Hegel, Kitamori picks up the thought that reason rules the world and spiritualizes it to mean that divine providence rules the world (1986: 38). Kitamori, however, is convinced that Hegel turned it the other way around. That is, Hegel, operating in a Christian context, used the theological idea of providence and converted it to the philosophical idea of reason (Kitamori, 1986: 38). In any case, Kitamori views the notion of God completely embracing human reality as the theological parallel to Hegelian teleological determinism (Kitamori, 1986: 38). Kitamori's problem with Hegel, however, is that Hegel's God does not suffer even though he embraces (Kitamori, 1986: 39).

Despite the inadequacies of the various systems of thought, Kitamori observes that the opposition between (the early) Barth and the liberal theologians, and between Buddhism and Hegelianism, mirror the opposition between divine wrath ("Barthianism") and divine love (liberalism), and between divine suffering (Buddhism) and divine embrace (Hegelianism) respectively (cf. Otto, 1991: 35). From his acute analysis and observation, Kitamori locates the theological meaning of the pain of God.

Kitamori also sees a vital point of contact between Christian theology and Japanese culture. He notes that the basic principle in Japanese tragedy is *tsurasa* 辛さ, an emotion that is often realized in the classical dramas when "one willingly suffers and dies, or makes his beloved son suffer and die, for the sake of loving and making another person live" (1986: 231).[84] The concept of *tsurasa* is rooted in personal relationships, and is a common emotion that any Japanese can readily identify.

---

[82] Since Kitamori defines pain in relational terms, it is highly plausible that unless one has the capacity for wrath, one has no capacity for pain.

[83] It is unclear where Kitamori gets this idea of the Buddha becoming ill from. It could be related to the legend of extreme self-mortification that the Buddha subjected himself to in order to achieve Enlightenment. See *The Middle Length Sayings (Majjhima Nikaya)*, vol. 1 (London: Pali Text Society), p. 107.

[84] The English translator of Kitamori's *Theology of the Pain of God* defines *tsurasa* helpfully as "the feeling of inevitable fate and sorrow that overhangs human life" (Kitamori, 2005: 177).

The depth of a truly Japanese man may be determined by his understanding of this *tsurasa*. According to the Japanese way of thinking, a man of depth, a man of understanding and intelligence, is one who understands *tsurasa*. One who does not understand *tsurasa* is shallow-minded and jejune – he is not like a true Japanese. (Kitamori, 2005: 135 = 1986: 230)

Tsurasa is both similar and dissimilar to the pain of God. It is similar in the sense that it understands the heart of God who sacrifices his only beloved Son for the sake of others (1986: 235). But it is different in that God experiences pain when he loves the unworthy and unlovable, while *tsurasa* is pain that arises only out of one's love for another who is deserving of love and respect (Kitamori, 1986: 235). This notwithstanding, the Japanese experience of *tsurasa* and the Christian understanding of the unconditional love of God for his enemies, says Kitamori, mean that Japanese Christians have a vital role to play in proclaiming the love of God rooted in the pain of God, not only to Japan but to the whole world (Kitamori, 1986: 233-34).

The heightened sensitivity toward pain and suffering seems to be a particularly – although not uniquely –Japanese cultural trait. In this regard, the idea that God had to suffer unspeakable pain in order to open the way of salvation for humankind is not absent prior to Kitamori. The suffering God is a prominent theme in the writings of Uemura Masahisa (e.g. 1932, 331, 403), which Kitamori obviously utilizes for his own theology (1986: 38, 69). Even twenty-five years after publishing his *Theology of the Pain of God*, Uemura's influence on Kitamori is still not lost, as evident from this quotation from Uemura's 1901 work, *Reisei no kiki* (*The Spiritual Crisis*) that Kitamori uses to conclude his article, "The Problem of Pain in Christology":

How does God save man? See, whoever will save another must himself go the way of pain [...]. It is a basic truth of Christian teaching that this also holds good for the saving action of God. This is basically the essence of love – to send oneself into pain, to sacrifice oneself and thereby to save oneself. *God who for man's sake can take pain upon himself* [...]. What else would be the Gospel we have from Christ? (cited in Kitamori, 1972: 90, emphasis added)

Uemura's notion of the suffering God, of course, does not compromise Kitamori's theology, for both the expression "pain of God" and the sustained development of a *theologia crucis* around that theme are unique to Kitamori. Uemura's words serve only to support Kitamori's contention that pain is neither an unnatural nor unbiblical way of understanding the work of God in Christ.

Kitamori's Pain of God and Jürgen Moltmann's The Crucified God

A word must be said, albeit briefly, about Jürgen Moltmann's theological construal of the crucified God which, on the surface, bears such an uncanny resemblance to Kitamori's pain of God theology that one might wonder if there was any dependence of one on the other. When Kitamori's magnum opus was first published in 1946, Moltmann was barely twenty years old. One would therefore not expect Kitamori to make any reference to Moltmann or his theology. It is curious, however, especially in the light of the many similarities between Moltmann and his theological senior, that Moltmann's seminal work on the Cross, published twenty-six years after Kitamori's work, should only contain two references to Kitamori: a passing remark in the main text and a comment in a footnote. It is also interesting to note the year of publication of the original German text *Der gekreuzigte Gott*, 1972, the same year that the German translation of Kitamori's *Theology of the Pain of God* was released. One should not read too much into this, however; it is evident that the two scholars hardly interacted with each other.

Kitamori, however, did write a review of the English edition of Moltmann's *The Crucified God* in 1976. While appreciating Moltmann's work as "revolutionary to the Western theology [...] controlled by the doctrine of *impassibilitas Dei*, being influenced by the Greek idea of God," Kitamori points out that there is no place for the wrath of God in Moltmann's theology (1976: 389). This is indeed no small criticism. Besides this, and the subtle theological accentuation that each author places on other different sub-themes, the contents of Moltmann's *The Crucified God* and Kitamori's *Theology of the Pain of God* are so similar that criticisms launched against one can mostly be used against the other. Even the language in Moltmann recalls the language in Kitamori. Here is a striking example from Moltmann's treatise on the "experience" of the trinitarian God in the redemption of humankind:

> Through his love for the Son who suffers from sin and who experiences sin itself in his death on the cross, God has an "experience" which belongs essentially to the redemption of the world. *It is the experience of pain.* In the night of the death on the cross, in the isolation of the Son from the Father and of the Father from the Son, God himself experiences the sacrifice in the form of death and rejection. One can add that here God has a new experience because he has decided from eternity for seeking love [*sic*], and in his decision to go *outside* of himself lie the conditions for the possibility of this experience. (1975: 644, emphasis added)

Also, arguing for the final, definite consummation of history, Moltmann writes, "If there is no new creation of all things, there is nothing that can withstand the *Nothingness* that annihilates the world" (1985:79, emphasis added). Describing the event of the Cross, Moltmann passionately explains, "[E]schatological faith in the cross of Jesus Christ must acknowledge *the theological trial between God and God. The cross of the Son divides God from God* to the utmost degree of enmity and distinction" (1993: 152, emphasis added). The point is well labored: Moltmann and Kitamori share a remarkably similar theological conceptualization of the suffering God on the cross.

Indeed, both Moltmann and Kitamori assert the centrality of the Cross in Christian theology. Moltmann (1993: 7) declares, in a fashion reminiscent of Kitamori, "In Christianity the cross is the test of everything which deserves to be called Christian" (Moltmann, 1993: 7). Kitamori's *Pain of God Theology*, however, is a singular work, while Moltmann's *The Crucified God* is really a sequel to his *Theology of Hope* published originally in 1964. In the latter, the focus is on "the *raising* of the crucified Christ," and in the former, "the *cross* of the risen Christ" (Moltmann, 1993: ix). Taken together with his next work, *The Church in the Power of the Spirit* (1975), these form a trilogy exploring the theological and socio-political implications of a crucified Christ for the Church seeking to witness to an eschatological hope in a world wracked by violence and suffering. For Moltmann, "[a] Christian theology which sees its problem and its task in knowing God in the crucified Christ cannot be *pure theory*" (1993: 69, emphasis in the original). Moltmann's comment might have intended to be an implicit criticism of Kitamori, for in contrast to his own theology, Kitamori's focus is indeed much narrower, moving barely beyond the theological metaphysics of divine pain. To Kitamori, the suffering of the world is secondary to the pain of God. In this sense, Kitamori's understanding of Christ's death can be rightly described as a mysticism of the Cross, while Moltmann's explication borders on a socio-political theology of the Cross. It is evident that the key problem which each man addresses is subtly different: for Kitamori, it is the existential problem of sin; for Moltmann, it is the universal problem of suffering. Moltmann acknowledges that his theology of the Cross is influenced by the liberation Christology of the Spanish Jesuit Jon Sobrino who has worked for many years in El Salvador (Moltmann, 1993: xi).

It is also noteworthy that Kitamori simply assumes that God can suffer, while Moltmann, working in a Western context, has to argue laboriously against the impassibility of God (Moltmann, 1993: 267-78). Another characteristic common to both is the rigorously trinitarian nature of their respective theologies. The subtle difference here is that Moltmann moves toward a unity of the Godhead, hence his ease in using the phrase "crucified God," while Kitamori consistently maintains the incommunicable properties of the three divine Persons.

Evaluative Summary

Kitamori's theology is truly a theology of the Cross. His construction of the Atonement is fundamentally Lutheran in orientation, but includes an unconventional, although not necessarily unbiblical, element, namely, the pain of God. According to Kitamori, the death of Christ is to be understood within a specific soteriological framework comprised of three stages. First, God created perfect humans whom he loved with an immediate, that is, unmediated, love. However, Adam and Eve, the first humans, sinned against God by betraying that love of God, and that act of treason drove a wedge between God and the whole of humanity. Sinful humanity became utterly removed from God. Human beings, once the objects of God's immediate love, now become his enemies, hence the objects of his immediate wrath. However, the scandal of the gospel is that God still desires to love sinful humans and forgive them of their sins. God therefore puts into effect the plan of salvation in which he causes his own Son to die as a representative and substitute for all humanity. On the cross, God embraces his enemy, sinful humanity, to himself. There, divine love and divine wrath find their unity, and the result is divine pain. In other words, the salvation of humankind is not achieved through a cold, calculated, commercial transaction, but with an intense divine pathos.

One can picture Kitamori's theory of the Atonement using a modified version of Aulén's *Christus Victor* theory: On the cross, the God of love fought and triumphed over the God of wrath. However, since the God of love *is* the God of wrath – there being only one God – the redemptive outcome that obtains comes therefore at the expense of divine pain. The process of justification constitutes the second stage of Kitamori's soteriological construct. Finally, the justified believer undergoes the process of sanctification by the Holy Spirit. During this third stage, however, the love with which God loves redeemed humanity is no longer immediate, but is always rooted in the pain of God. This soteriological construct can properly be called Kitamori's *Dolor Dei* understanding of the Cross. In sum, rather than explicating the mechanics of how salvation is achieved through the death of Christ, Kitamori is more concerned about demonstrating how that death reveals intensely the painful love of God for humankind. On the cross, Christ not only suffered *for* us; he suffered *because of* us. Kitamori's *theologia crucis* can hence be described as a soteriology of passion.

The structure of Kitamori's theology is undeniably eloquent. There is an aesthetic beauty to it, theologically and linguistically. Lutheran pastor Okada Tsuyoshi affirms that regardless of whether one agrees with it or not, Kitamori's theology is "quite congenial with the psychic [*sic*] and mental make-up of the Japanese" (cited in Hashimoto, 1992: 568). It is not a wonder then that for more than half a century since its inaugural publication in 1946, *Theology of the Pain of God* has never gone out of print.

The assessment of Carl Michalson is that "Kitamori in his discernment of the 'pain of God' provides the [theological] system with a soul" (1960: 125). This is hardly disputable. For Kitamori, however, the pain of God is not simply an aesthetic option but a theological imperative without which one is prone to fall into one of two errors: a monism of love or a monism of wrath. The former breeds a maudlin sentimentality, and the latter a suffocating legalism. The concept of the pain of God is undoubtedly a valuable theological insight (Watanabe, 1986: 69-70), but the difficulty with Kitamori's theology is its configuration of divine pain in ontological terms, even though Kitamori repeatedly denies this charge. The distinction that he makes between *jittai* (substance) and *honshitu* (essence) does not resolve the problem at all. In any case, his insistence that the death of Christ be regarded as an internal, hence eternal, act within the Trinity, leads him to the conviction that pain is an intrinsic part of the divine essence, "God's true heart" (Kitamori, 1986: 72). Granting his reasoning as right, the theological premise of Kitamori's claim is biblically unwarranted, hence rendering his conclusion theologically suspect.

Kitamori's theology is certainly fraught with tensions. His is certainly a theology of paradox. However, perhaps that is what an authentic *theologia crucis* should be, for it seeks to be witness to an ineffable divine mystery of God's salvation of humankind through the instrument of ultimate disgrace: the cross (cf. 1 Cor. 1:18-25). In contrast to the *theologia gloriae* which "ends in a simplistic understanding of God" (Forde, 1997: 13), the *theologia crucis* is necessarily characterized by "a certain suspicion and polemical edge" (Forde, 1997: 14). The story of the Cross, as the New Testament writers and the magisterial Reformers understood it, is sheer scandal to the natural human mind. For this reason, Kitamori insists, the theology of the Cross must always remain "outside the gate" (1986: 4). In other words, it should never become a so-called "'reigning' theology" (Kitamori, 1986: 257). It is obvious that Kitamori is here drawing a parallel from Luther's distinction between the theology of the Cross and the theology of glory.

It is easy to attribute the theme of Kitamori's theology to the suffering of the Japanese as a result of their country's defeat in the Second World War (McWilliams, 1980: 43; Ro, 2001: 883; Schwarz, 2005: 512). This is, however, a mistaken perception. The fact is that Kitamori reflected on the pain of God fully ten years before the end of the war, and many of his theological insights were gleaned from deep personal experiences, and as we have seen, many of these had to do with pain and death.[85] This explains the presence of a strong mystical dimension in Kitamori's theology.

It is true that when *Theology of the Pain of God* was published in 1946, the circumstances surrounding the war gave greater relevance to Kitamori's ideas and brought them into sharp focus. Even then, Simon Baynes expresses his disappointment that Kitamori's theology is so "pure" that it is "unencumbered by events" of the war (1980: 146). There is certainly more than a grain of truth in Baynes' comment. Kitamori had largely been indifferent to socio-political events. He had neither been critical of Japan's rising nationalism before the war, nor did he address the resulting devastation of the country after the war. Kitamori never made any apology for his silence, for his overriding concern was to explicate the divine mystery of the cross directly from Scripture rather than from the prevailing socio-cultural circumstances. On this matter, Kitamori offers this telling comment in the preface to the third edition of his magnum opus, "The theology of the pain of God is concerned literally with the pain of God. Hence the primary theme of this book is to behold the pain of God [...]. *The role of our*

---

[85] Morimoto (2005: 3) is not right when he seems to suggest that Kitamori did not personally experience pain until after the publication of *Theology of the Pain of God*, that is, after the war.

[human] pain should only be to serve the pain of God" (Kitamori, 1986: 6, emphasis added). It is beyond any dispute that Kitamori holds the singular conviction that divine pain is the fundamental, uncompromising biblical theme that constitutes "the very heart of the gospel" (Kitamori, 1986: 24). In his theological reckoning, the death of Christ is the "historical concretization of the pain of God," through which the salvation of humanity is definitely and fully achieved (Kitamori, 1986: 50).

In the final paragraph of his 1937 graduation thesis, Kitamori, then only twenty-one, describes God-talk as necessarily "lacking in permanence and stability" (Kitamori, 1999: 182). The implication is that every theology is essentially *theologia viatorum* (*tabibito no shingaku* 旅人の神学) (Kitamori, 1999: 182). Put another way, a theology is but an intermediate cognitive model to understand God and his work in the world. It cannot pretend to have the final word. Kitamori is, of course, completely right about the nature of theology. Yet strangely, barely ten years later, Kitamori seemed to have forgotten his earlier conviction when he made the extravagant claim in his magnum opus that the pain of God is *the* heart of the gospel (1986: 24). He has certainly overextended himself by interpreting the whole of Scripture in terms of a single principle, namely, divine pain. The mystery of God is far greater than we can ever fathom, and reducing it to a single theological principle smacks of epistemic arrogance. Such is the ever-present danger of theological essentialization: single-issue Christianity. Putting aside the way he essentializes divine pain, theologically and methodologically, Kitamori's theology of the pain of God is otherwise a fine piece of theological construction which helps us understand and appreciate better the divine mystery of the Cross.

5. Endō Shūsaku and the
Eternal Companionship of Christ

In this chapter, we shall explore the theological perspectives of Endō Shūsaku, focusing on his understanding of the meaning and significance of the death of Christ. Besides Endō, there are very few novelists in Japan whose works are consistently infused with Christological themes. In the main, the Cross for Endō is the supreme expression of Jesus' identification with suffering humanity. As a result of his passion, Christ becomes reborn in the hearts of men and women as their eternal companion, drawing alongside them in their every trial and suffering.

Endō Shūsaku 遠藤周作 (1923-96) is one of three Christian novelists whose works are widely read throughout Japan, by both Christians and non-Christians alike.[1] Along with his fellow Catholic, Sono Ayako (1931-), the wife of one of Endō's closest friends, another well-known novelist, Miura Shumon, and the Protestant writer Miura Ayako (1922-99), Endō characteristically uses the medium of the novel to explore the intricate, and often frustrating, struggles between a Christian faith and Japanese culture.[2] Given that these themes are quite alien in a country where Christians constitute less than one percent of the population, the wide readership of their works is indeed quite remarkable.[3] Of the three writers, Endō is without a doubt the most well-known.

---

[1] There are an inordinate number of baptized Christians among novelists and playwrights in post-war Japan, such as Ōhara Tomie, Takahashi Takako, Miura Shūmon, Yashiro Seiichi, Inoue Hisashi, Ogawa Kunio, Moriuchi Toshio, Tanaka Sumie, Shiina Rinzō, and Takadō Kaname. Most of these writers are Catholic. See Endō, "At the Baptism of One Friend after Another ..." in *Japan Christian Quarterly* 43(4) (Fall 1977), pp. 208-10.

[2] Within the genre of the modern Japanese novel (*shōsetsu*), Endō and Sono, and Miura, belong to a coterie of writers known as the *Daisan no shinjin* 第三の新人 (Third generation of new authors). The art of these post-war writers is characterized by what Mark Williams refers to as "the vision of the divided self" (1995: 5). An exemplification of this trait is the "[depiction of] composite individuals as protagonists" (Williams, 1995: 5). See Williams (1999: 1-24) for an introduction to the literary distinctives of the *Daisan no shinjin* authors.

[3] Endō himself acknowledges, "It is no simple matter for a Christian in Japan to write novels on Christian subjects. What has bothered me most is the uneasy feeling that my readers who are unfamiliar with Christianity will completely miss what I am saying.

Endō's popularity as a novelist is not only restricted to his native land. Just as Kitamori is the best-known Japanese theologian outside of Japan, Endō is, in all probability, the best-known Japanese novelist outside of Japan, considered by many to be even more famous than 1994 Nobel Laureate Ōe Kenzaburō. Endō's works have been translated into no less than twenty-five languages, many with glowing endorsements by such literary luminaries as Graham Greene, Irving Howe, and John Updike appearing on the books' dust jackets. In a memorial eulogy composed three years after Endō's death, American literary critic Jewel Brooker recalls that Endō was revered by many in the West as "Japan's greatest living writer," who left his legacy as "one of the [twentieth] century's finest writers" (1999: 41). Among Endo's award-winning works are *Shiroi hito, kiiroi hito* (*White Person, Yellow Person*) (1955);[4] *Umi to dokuyaku* (*The Sea and Poison*) (1958); *Obakasan* (*Wonderful Fool*) (1959); *Kazan* (*Volcano*) (1960); *Watakushi ga suteta onna* (*The Girl I Left Behind*) (1964); *Ryūgaku* (*Foreign Studies*) (1965); *Chinmoku* (*Silence*) (1966);[5] *Shikai no hotori* (*On the Shores of the Dead Sea*); *Kuchibue o fuku toki* (*When I Whistle*) (1974); *Samurai* (*The Samurai*) (1980); *Sukyandaru* (*Scandal*) (1986); and *Fukai kawa* (*Deep River*) (1994). Except for *White Person, Yellow Person* and *On the Shores of the Dead Sea*, the other novels on this list have all been translated into English, not a few by Roman Catholic missionaries.

Besides novels, Endō has also written many short stories, some professedly autobiographical, such as *Haha naru mono* (*Mothers*) (1969); *Watakushi no mono* (*Mine*) (1972); *Gojussai no otoko* (*A Fifty-year-old Man*) (1976); and *Rokujussai no otoko* (*A Sixty-year-old Man*) (1983).[6] All in all, Endō's literary

---

What I sense at once because I have known it intimately for years may elude them completely [...]. *This is not true in the West*" (Endo, 1974 [1973]: 184, emphasis added).

A word on notation is in order here. Many of Endō's fictional works have been excellently translated into English. When his Japanese works are referred to in this dissertation, the English translation is often cited. In this case, the year in brackets in the bibliographical information refers to the year of publication of the original Japanese text. Where a single year is stated, the reference is to the citation of the original text. Also, the orthography of "Endō," or "Endo" as the case might be, conforms exactly to the bibliographic information of the work cited. In all his translated works, the name is consistently rendered as "Endo," that is, without the macron marking the long vowel.

[4] Although published together in a single volume in 1955, *Shiroi hito, kiiroi hito* is actually comprised of two separate works: *Shiroi hito* (*White Person*) and *Kiiroi hito* (*Yellow Person*). The former was awarded the prestigious Akutagawa Prize.

[5] It was *Silence*, Endō's most famous novel and the winner of the Tanizaki Prize, which won him international acclaim. A movie was made in 1971 based on the novel, directed by Shinoda Masahiro. Endō met with Martin Scorsese in the US in 1991 to discuss the possibility of remaking the movie (Endō, 2006: 267). This second movie finally came out in 2016.

[6] All the short stories in this list have been translated into English: the first two in the Fall 1974 issue of *The Japan Christian Quarterly*, and the last two in the book *The Final Martyrs* (1993), a collection of nine other of Endō's short stories translated into

output is prodigious, with no less than two hundred and thirty published works, including novels, short stories, essays, and plays.

Besides literature, Endō was passionately involved in drama. He founded the theatrical company *Kiza* 樹座 in 1968, which he directed until his death. Besides performing frequently within Japan, the troupe staged two major international performances: *Carmen* in New York in 1980 and *Madame Butterfly* in London in 1986.[7]

The Theological Dimension of Endō's Writings

Sometime in the middle of what had been a prodigious career as a novelist, Endō began to write serious non-fictional works centering on spiritual and theological themes, including *Iesu no shōgai* (*A Life of Jesus*) (1973); *Watakushi no Iesu* (*My Jesus*) (1976); *Nihonjin wa kirisutokyō o shinjirareru ka* (*Can the Japanese Believe in Christianity?*) (1977); *Kirisuto no tanjō* (*The Birth of Christ*) (1978); and *Watakushi ni totte kami to wa* (*What God Is to Me*) (1983). Through these quasi-theological treatises, Endō seeks to provide a way out of the dilemmas of faith raised in his novels by reconstructing the Christian faith in a manner accessible to his fellow countrymen and women.[8]

Perhaps more than anyone else – certainly more than academic theologians and philosophers – Endō has contributed to the exploration of a religious vision that seeks to be both Christian and Japanese, and this he has done creatively through the field of literature. A recurring theme in Endo's novels and non-fictional works is theological dissonance – between European Christianity and Japanese religiosity, Western monotheism and Asian pantheism, and between religious triumphalism and the inescapable reality of deep suffering. Unwilling to renounce his personal Catholic faith, and at the same time unable to shake off the cultural underpinnings of that faith, Endō strives to find a way to reconcile Christian faith and Japanese culture. Mark Williams' description of Endō's works as "a literature of reconciliation" is indeed fitting, although it must be said that Williams uses that label primarily to highlight the process of growth and "reconciliation of the self" invariably experienced by the various protagonists in Endō's novels (1999: 57).

In any case, Endō's writings clearly reflect his lifelong struggle with the diametrically opposite religious values of East and West. In almost every one of his novels, these polar opposites are masterfully played out, but left unresolved. Yet, despite these almost unbearable tensions that stubbornly refuse to go away, Endō's protagonists always find redemption through an unexpected personal

---

English by Van C. Gessel. It is noteworthy that a number of Endō's short stories are written in the first person, and include many of his own real-life experiences.
[7] The company disbanded in November 1997, just over a year after Endō's death.
[8] Other than *A Life of Jesus*, none of Endō's other non-fiction books have been translated into English.

encounter with a compassionate Christ figure and, in the process, come to terms with the harsh reality, thereby experiencing the growth and inner reconciliation that Williams talks about.

However, in his last novel *Deep River* written nearly thirty years after *Silence*, Endō surprises his readers by allowing the cultural and theological tensions that have so characterized his preceding works to dissolve altogether in a religious vision that is unabashedly pluralist, very much resembling John Hick's. It would not be off the mark to say that Endō's attempt to contextualize Christianity in Japan began with a clear, although somewhat unconventional, faith in Christ but ended with a syncretistic belief in "a god with many faces" (Endō, 1994: 201).[9] Even then, in *Deep River*, as in virtually all his preceding works, Endō could not hide his deep and abiding fascination with the person of Jesus Christ, especially with the image of his shrunken, emaciated body on the cross. The confession of Ōtsu, the failed seminarian in *Deep River*, is in all probability Endō's own: "I am being held captive by Jesus" (Endō, 1994: 310). When Endō published *Silence* in 1966, he had already come to the conviction that the only means by which Christianity could take root in Japanese soil is for people to come to a new, existential encounter with Jesus Christ: not the powerful and resplendent Jesus as presented by the European missionaries, but rather a reversed Jesus who knows nothing but utter weakness, pain, humiliation, and ultimately death on the cross. It is not a coincidence then that many of Endō's novels are sustained by the underlying Christological themes of suffering, sacrifice, and servanthood. Unlikely Christ figures that offer solace and comfort to the weak and suffering are commonplace, for example, the awkward, horse-faced Frenchman Gaston Bonaparte in *Wonderful Fool*, the jilted, loveless country girl Mitsu who dedicates her life to serve in a leprosarium in *The Girl I Left Behind*, the trampled-on bronze image of the powerless Christ in *Silence*, even the mynah bird in *Deep River*,[10] or the mongrel with "moist, grieving eyes" in *Kagebōshi* (*Shadows*) (Endo, 1993 [1968]: 36).

Endō is by no means an uncontroversial figure among Japanese Christians. This is hardly surprising given his rather unconventional views that are consistently at odds with official Catholic dogma. Once again, Endō expresses himself through the character of Ōtsu in *Deep River*: "All my life I have always been reprimanded by the Church" (Endō, 1994: 299). Here is a telling incident. Shortly after the publication of the highly-acclaimed *Silence*, Endō was cross-examined by a panel of Catholic priests at Sophia University in Tokyo in

---

[9] For an excellent treatment on how Endō's religious vision evolved over the course of his lifetime, see Mase-Hasegawa (2004: 59-85).

[10] In this novel, the writer Numada keeps a pet mynah bird to which he constantly confesses the secrets of his heart. Then Numada undergoes a major surgery during which his heart stopped for a time, but miraculously recovers. When he wakes up four hours later, he discovers that his mynah has died. It then dawns upon Numada that the mynah might have died in his place (Endō, 1994: 132-33).

an open forum described later by his wife Junko as resembling an "inquisition" (Endō Junko, 1999: 146). Two years before his death, in an interview with Jesuit theologian William Johnston – the translator of *Silence* – Endō again complained that his works constantly got into trouble with his fellow Catholics (Johnston, 1994: 18). If Endō's works could arouse such discomfort among Japanese Catholics, one should not be surprised that evangelical Protestants would express a far greater hostility toward Endō for what they view as his extreme theological liberalism.[11] In spite of the religious controversy generated by his works, it would not be wise to dismiss Endō summarily. However one may regard them, his works are seminal, not only in the field of Japanese literature, but also in religious studies. This provides a good enough reason for us, through this chapter, to embark on a sustained study of Endō from an evangelical perspective.

A Methodological Note

A word on methodology is in order here. In literary criticism, one faces the immediate dilemma as to whether one could infer the true theological intent of the author through the characters that they have constructed in the novel. After all, as Kitamori wittingly comments, a *shōsetsu* 小説 (novel, literally "small theory") is not a *daisetsu* 大説 (literally, "big theory") (1991: 331).[12] In other words, Endō is writing literature, not theology as such. Williams (2003: 296) says it well: "Stories could not be shaped to conform to a specific authorial theology – for, as authors, they [are] in no position, either to take charge of their characters or to intervene arbitrarily in their destinies."[13] Williams' point is well taken. Yet, it is instructive to note that as a Catholic writer, Endō's expressed aim is to "find God on the streets of Shinjuku and Shibuya, districts which seem so far removed from Him" (Endō, 2000a/12: 381, cited in Williams, 2003: 300).

---

[11] On his visits to Japan in 1997 and 2000, both times speaking to evangelical churches on a lecture circuit, Philip Yancey, a huge fan of Endō, had this to say: "Whenever I mentioned him in one of my lectures, a Japanese Christian would come up afterward and solemnly advise me that Endo might not be the best example to use" (2003: 281).

[12] The word *daisetsu* 大説 is coined by Kitamori by combining the Chinese characters for "big" (大) and "theory" (説) in order to make a point about the novel, or *shōsetsu* 小説. The character 小 means "small."

[13] In a 1994 interview with Van C. Gessel, for example, Endō expressed his annoyance with Western critics who were constantly debating the meaning of the famous "mudswamp of Japan" statement in *Silence*. Endō said, "The most frequent question I am asked by foreign journalists is, 'Why do you call Japan a "mudswamp"?' It's always 'mudswamp, mudswamp.' That's actually a term used by one of the characters in the novel, not by me" (Gessel, 1999: 150). Endō's exasperation is understandable, but transferring the blame to one of his characters does not relieve him of the responsibility for developing the mudswamp motif, not only in *Silence* but also in his other novels such as *White Person, Yellow Person* and *Wonderful Fool* as we shall see later.

The tension between theological veracity and artistic integrity perhaps can never be fully resolved. But all is not lost. As mentioned earlier, Endō has also produced substantial works of non-fiction through which his theological position is clearly expressed and defended. Three such works are of particular interest for our purposes: *A Life of Jesus* (1973); *My Jesus* (1976); and *The Birth of Christ* (1978). These three works, taken together, spell out explicitly the latent Christological assumptions underlying Endō's fiction, and offer us an unambiguous understanding of Endō's views on the person and mission of Jesus.

Moreover, a literary analysis of Endō's fiction reveals that many of his novels indeed contain autobiographical or semi-autobiographical elements. Van C. Gessel, who translated *The Samurai* into English, makes this insightful observation:

> The scene in *The Samurai* in which Hasekura is baptized in Madrid is an eerily accurate reproduction of the ceremony in which Endō participated at the age of eleven. Like Hasekura, Endō did not choose Christianity of his own volition, but initially had it thrust upon him, and for some time he felt very distant from it. (1982: 272)

There are at least two characters in Endō's novels who are writers by profession, and who have undergone three major surgeries, very much like Endō himself: Suguro, who appears in the short story *Mine* and in the later novel *Scandal*, and Numada in *Deep River*, whose childhood experiences in Dalian, including the subsequent divorce of his parents, were undoubtedly Endō's own. It is obvious that Endō has projected his personal thoughts, struggles and experiences onto so many of his characters. Indeed, as we listen to the voice of these characters, we get the distinct impression that we are listening to Endō himself.

Endō, however, is not doing something original here. The fact is that literary works are never produced *in vacuo*, for every piece of creative work bears the marks of the writer's own life experiences. In the case of Endō, the formative years of his life from his childhood, including his conversion to Christianity, up to the time he returned to Japan from his studies abroad are crucial for consideration. A summary account of that period is therefore given in the next section. Following that, we will provide a chronological overview of Endō's key writings and, in the process, trace the development of a discernible theological theme that runs through virtually all of his works. This is necessary for our purposes since Endō is by vocation not a theologian but a writer. As such, his views on the Christian faith and on Christ in particular, can only be appropriately appraised within his total literary context. Only after we have attained a level of understanding of his literature will we be able to explicate the core theological themes that underlie his writings. We will look specifically at Endō's views on the nature of God and the person of Jesus Christ, and discuss his perspective on the Cross against the backdrop of his broader understanding of God and of the meaning and significance of the life of Jesus.

Of course, one needs to be careful not to treat a person's ideas as if they are static. We certainly see in Endō a religious vision which was constantly evolving throughout his life. Nevertheless, there are several identifiable themes that consistently appear in his works, particularly the core theological and Christological beliefs that form the bedrock of his religious vision. However, considering the unexpected but definite turn that Endō took toward the later part of his life in the direction of syncretistic pluralism, it is only appropriate to round up this chapter by taking a brief look at *Deep River*, his last novel, and discuss how his construal of the relationship between Christianity and the other religions fits in with his final religious vision in general and his Christology in particular.

Endō's Formative Years[14]

Early Years and Conversion (1923-1941)

Endō was born on March 27, 1923, in Tokyo, six months before the Great Kanto Earthquake. He was the younger of two boys. His father was an employee at Yasuda Bank (now Fuji Bank), and his mother was a violinist by training. At the age of three, his father's work took the whole family to Dalian – Dairen in Japanese – in the Japanese-occupied territory of Manchuria in Northeast China. When Endō was ten, his parents divorced, and his mother brought her two sons back to Japan to live with her sister in Kobe. Suffering from the shame and social rejection of a divorce, Endō's mother found solace in the devout faith of her sister, and soon converted to Catholicism. Shortly after that, Endō and his brother gave in to the persistent urging of his mother and aunt, and were baptized on Easter Sunday at the Shukugawa Catholic Church in the neighboring city of Nishinomiya. Endō had just turned eleven. He was given the baptismal name Paul, but never used it.

Throughout his teenage years, Endō faithfully attended Mass every morning, and at one point even considered the clerical vocation. Years later, however, Endō would reflect on his baptism as a frivolous event, an act taken to please his mother than of his own volition (2000a/10: 374). This notwithstanding, Endō could not deny the decisive sacramental imprint that his baptism had on his life: he felt a deep change within, although a very uncomfortable one. In an early essay entitled *Awanai yōfuku* ("Ill-fitting clothes"), Endō compares his conversion experience to donning a set of ill-fitting clothing:

---

[14] A detailed chronology of Endō's life is found in Endō, *Endō Shūsaku essei senshū* I (Selected Essays of Endō Shūsaku, Vol. I) (Tokyo: Kōbunsha, 2006), pp. 254-71 as well as in his *"Fukai kawa" sōsaku nikki* (Diary of the making of *Deep River*), (Tokyo: Kōdansha, 2000), pp. 193-211.

About ten years after my baptism, it dawned upon me for the first time that Christianity was like a western suit that my mother and aunt made me wear when I was growing up [...]. I suffered from the fact that this western suit did not fit. Some parts were too baggy, and others too loose. To my body this was a western suit and not an eastern dress. How often have I thought of throwing away this suit! How often have I tried to wear something which fitted my body [...]. But I was unable to discard this western suit because it was given to me by those who loved me. And it was also this suit that sustained me and gave me strength through my growing up years [...]. I did not mind the criticisms from others about my western suit because I had nothing else to wear. (Endō, 2006b: 189; cf. Endo, 1974 [1973]: 179; 2000a/10: 370)

Elsewhere, Endō likens his faith to an arranged marriage, a forced union with a woman decided by his parents (Endo, 1974 [1973]: 179). As Philip Yancey notes with characteristic insight, "[Endō] could not live with this arranged wife and he could not live without her. Meanwhile, she kept loving him, and to his surprise eventually he grew to love her in return" (2001: 277). Despite the intensity of the inner conflict between his faith and his cultural identity which he had felt so keenly from the time he was baptized, by the time he entered adulthood, Endō could never deny that Catholicism had become an inseparable part of him. When he became a writer, he resolved to let this ill-fitting faith of his direct his entire literary career.

The fact that it [Catholicism] had penetrated me so deeply in my youth was a sign, I thought, that it had, in part at least, become coextensive with me. Still, there was always the feeling in my heart that it was something borrowed, and I began to wonder what my real self was like. This I think is the 'mud swamp' Japanese in me. From the time I first began to write novels even to this present day, this confrontation of my Catholic self with the self that lies underneath has, like an idiot's constant refrain, echoed and reechoed in my work. *I felt that I had to in some way reconcile the two.* (cited in Translator's Preface to *Silence*, Endo, 1982 [1966]: 13, emphasis added; cf. Endō, 2006b: 190)[15]

Endō never did well in school, and was therefore not able to enter university immediately after high school. However, even when he was as young as eight, the precocious boy displayed his penchant for writing when his composition was published in the local newspaper in Dalian. When he finished high school, Endō decided to pursue a literary career. However, it was not merely for the sake of writing. Endō resolved to use literature as a means to develop a clearer understanding of how religious faith and culture are shaped by each other. Endō then moved from Kobe to live with his father in Tokyo where he hoped to acquire a university education. It was an emotionally difficult decision for Endō,

---

[15] Unless notated otherwise, all subsequent citations from *Silence* are taken from the 1982 English translation by William Johnston (Tokyo: Kōdansha), and are referenced as Endo (1982 [1966]).

especially since his father had remarried. Endō was never quite able to forgive his father for the pain that he had caused his mother by divorcing her.

Literary Studies in Tokyo (1941-50)

It was in Tokyo that the eighteen-year-old Endō published his first critical essay, *Keijijō teki kami, shūkyō teki kami* (*Metaphysical God, Religious God*) (Mase-Hasegawa, 2004: 171). Two years later, he enrolled and was accepted into the preparatory school of the Keio University to study literature. The decision caused him to be thrown out of the house by his father who had wanted him to study medicine.[16] This incident was to have a profound impact on Endō's works. Endō then moved into a dormitory under the mastership of the Catholic philosopher Yoshimitsu Yoshihiko who affirmed his literary gifts and encouraged him in his reading of Japanese literature.

In any case, Endō's studies at Keio were disrupted by the Pacific War. He was at first consigned to work in the munitions factory at Kawasaki. Then he developed pleurisy, which saved him from active military conscription. When the war ended, Endō was able to resume his studies. Around this time, he stumbled across a book at a second-hand bookstore that was to change his life. The book, *Furansu bungaku sobyō* (*A Sketch of French Literature*), was in fact written by Satō Saku, a professor of French Literature at Keio. The book captivated Endō, and he read it through in one sitting, and consequently decided to study French Literature under Satō at Keio. The twenty-two-year-old also bought a French grammar book and immersed himself in the language for a whole month.[17] When the school year started, Endō was disappointed to learn that Satō had gone on a year's medical leave from the university. Undeterred, Endō wrote a letter and asked if Satō would tutor him privately. To his delight, Satō agreed. "Professor Sato's residence became my university", writes a grateful Endō in retrospect (2006a: 119). Through Satō, Endō was inducted into the world of twentieth-century French Catholic literature. Endō graduated from Keio in 1948,[18] and over the next two years took up editorial work for two publishing houses.

Graduate Studies in France and Ensuing Illness (1950-1955)

Two years later, Endō was chosen by the Japanese government to receive a scholarship to study modern Catholic literature in France, becoming the first

[16] Although Endō moved back to his father's home after the war, the relationship between father and son was severely strained. It was not until 1989 when Endō's ninety-three-year-old father was dying that there was some measure of reconciliation. Endō's older brother had already died in 1977, and so the senior Endō was all alone.
[17] Endō had wanted to study French at a private school, but the only European language that was taught in Japan at that time was German.
[18] According to Mase-Hasegawa, Endō's graduation thesis is entitled *Neo-Thomism ni okeru shiron* (Poetic Theory in Neo-Thomism) (2004: 172).

Japanese to study abroad after the war.[19] With three other Japanese, the twenty-seven-year-old Endō set sail for France on June 4, 1950 on board the *Marseillaise*. It was on this ship where Endō first felt discriminated against (see Endō, 2000a/10: 376-91). The Japanese were relegated to a fourth-class cabin, and were not allowed to leave the ship at any port *en route*.

This is understandable since the war had only recently ended, and the four Japanese were on board the vessel of a former enemy nation. Yet, as Williams rightly notes,

> [T]he heat and the stench that these "pioneer" Japanese students were forced to endure in their fourth-class berth deep in the bowels of the *Marseille* [*sic*] represented a humiliating experience and one that was to reinforce the sense of distance between East and West that Endō and so many of his generation had come to experience as a result of events of the Pacific War and the ensuing Occupation. (1999: 59)

The arduous sea journey lasted more than a month. Endō then found himself in the academically enriching environment of the University of Lyons[20] where he was exposed to the best of French Catholic literature in a way that would never have been possible in his native Japan. He read extensively the works of François Mauriac, Julien Green, and George Bernanos. Yet, ironically, he became increasingly baffled by the inaccessibility of European culture to him as a foreigner. Being the only Japanese at Lyons further intensified his sense of loneliness. Moreover, Japan and France had still to conclude a peace treaty, and no Japanese embassy had yet been opened. Endo describes his experience in this way, "[T]he longer I stayed [in France] the more I felt I was bumping against a high wall. I lost all desire to enter the study room" (1974 [1973]: 180). Richard Durfee suggests, not unreasonably, that the source of Endō's frustration lay in the fact that Endō had gone to France "as a Christian going to a Christian country, with the assumption that he would find at least as much congruity for himself there as he did being a Christian in Japan – a non-Christian country" (1989: 44). It would not be hard to imagine how Endō must have been treated, given the anti-Japanese propaganda churned out continually by the Allies during the war so recently concluded. In any case, the antagonism and alienation that Endō experienced during his three years in France "greatly aggravated the intensity of his internal conflict over being a Japanese Christian" (Durfee, 1989: 44). The fresh realization that he was now in the land of a former enemy nation and practicing their religion must have affected him adversely. It would be hard

---

[19] One of the three other Japanese was Inoue Yōji, whom Endō would develop a lifelong friendship with. Inoue was to spend nearly eight years in a Carmelite monastery in France. He is today a well-established Catholic theologian in Japan. See p. 74, n. 72 above; see also p. 171 below.

[20] The city of Lyons is better known today as Lyon, and the university as the University of Lyon (Université de Lyon).

for any Japanese, let alone a Japanese Christian, not to feel like an outcast under these immediate post-war circumstances.

Not surprisingly, things came to a head when Endō went into depression. After two and a half years in Lyons, he moved to Paris. However, his health collapsed and he had to be hospitalized for a pleurisy relapse. Realizing that he was not in any position to continue his studies, Endō returned to Japan in early 1953. That whole year in Japan, he was either lying in bed at home or receiving treatment in the hospital. The following year, 1954, Endō recovered sufficiently to assume a lectureship at Bunka Gakuin, a fine arts college in Tokyo.

The Growth of a Theological Theme through Endō's Key Literary Works (1955-1994)

Endō's distinguished literary career began at the age of thirty-two with the publication of the widely-acclaimed *White Person, Yellow Person* shortly after he returned from France, and ended forty years later with the novel *Deep River*. Over the course of his literary development, one can discern the growth of a theological theme within it, which we shall explore in this section. This theme may simply be described as contextualization, to borrow the language from missiological literature. Within this theme, four chronological phases, each with its own theological emphasis, are distinguishable: (1) identifying Japan as a spiritual mudswamp, (2) exploring the possibility of salvation through the experience of unconditional love, (3) appropriating the concept of the eternal companionship of the suffering Christ, and (4) realizing the vision of a plural religious reality. In the next section, we will discuss these sub-themes by examining, albeit briefly, some of Endō's key works.

The "Mudswamp" of Japan
Shiroi hito, kiiroi hito 白い人、黄色い人 *(White Person, Yellow Person)*
(1955)
Umi to dokuyaku 海と毒薬 *(The Sea and Poison) (1958)*

While in Japan, Endō had experienced rejection by his fellow Japanese because he was practicing what was perceived to be not only a Western faith, but the very faith of their enemies; and in France, in what he thought was his "spiritual homeland", he experienced a second rejection.[21] Endō received another blow when his beloved mother suddenly died of cerebral apoplexy in 1954. She was only fifty-eight. Not surprisingly, Endō underwent a grave crisis of faith. Instead of causing him to give up his faith, his trials led him to ponder on two matters that would become the hallmark of his writings: the meaning of suffering and death, and how one could appropriate the Christian faith as a Japanese person.

---

[21] Endō's experiences in France would later be "hauntingly captured" in the autobiographical work *Foreign Studies*, published in 1965 (Brooker, 1999: 142).

Reflecting on his experiences in Lyons, Endō sieved out the cultural differences between Europeans and Japanese that made the former accept the Christian faith readily in a way that the latter could not. His initial conclusions were given literary expression through his two short stories, *Shiroi hito* 白い人 (*White Person*), and *Kiroii hito* 黄色い人 (*Yellow Person*), published in a single volume in 1955, two years after his return from France.

1955 proved to be a watershed year for Endō. Besides being awarded the Akutagawa Prize, Japan's most prestigious literary award, for *White Person*, Endō married Okada Junko, a lifelong Buddhist. It was a marriage arranged by the respective families when both Endō and Junko were still children. The following year, Endō's only son was born. Endō named his son Ryūnosuke after the famed novelist memorialized by the Akutagawa Prize, Akutagawa Ryūnosuke.[22]

These early works, *White Person* and *Yellow Person*, lay the foundation for all of Endo's subsequent writings. In *White Person*, Endō explores the innate sense of the transcendent God that is such an indelible part of the white person's psyche that even in the midst of the Nazi atrocities in wartime France, the victims could never quite renounce the existence of God although they might denounce him for allowing such radical evil to happen. Even the first-person protagonist who betrays his friends to the Nazis has to confess the awareness of a transcendent being as part of the human essence (*honshitsu* 本質), an awareness that does not fade even in the face of torture (Endō, 1955: 65). The companion novella *Yellow Person* centers on the interactions between a renegade French priest who is "not able to forget God for a single moment" (Endō, 1955: 136) and several "yellow characters," including Chiba the lapsed Christian, and Kimiko, the priest's illicit lover who wears "a countenance so completely devoid of God" (Endō, 1955: 119). Through the words of the unconscionable Chiba, Endō proposes that the psyche of the "yellow person" is insensitive to God, sin, and death (Endō, 1955: 91-94).

Interestingly, it is in *Yellow Person* that the concept of Japan as a swamp first appears. In his soliloquy, Father Durand refers to Japan as a "swamp country" (*shimetta kuni* 湿った国) in which the shoots of the gospel can hardly be planted (Endō, 1955: 152). In *Silence*, another renegade priest, the Portuguese Christovão Ferreira, is more explicit in his pronouncement of Japan as a mudswamp (*numachi* 沼地) in which the sapling of Christianity can only rot and wither away (Endō, 1966: 189).

In all probability, for Endō, the lack of sensitive consciousness of God, sin, and death on the part of the Japanese constitutes the cultural and psychological swamp that is Japan. This hypothesis is further explored in Endō's next major novel, *The Sea and Poison*, published in 1958.[23] The plot centers on the

---

[22] Endō Ryūnosuke is currently working as the Head of Publicity for Fuji Television.
[23] This novel was awarded the Shinchōsha Literary Prize and the Mainichi Shuppan Prize.

clandestine experiments in vivisection conducted by Japanese military doctors on American POWs at the hospital of Kyushu Imperial University during the Pacific War. The protagonist is a young, talented doctor, Suguro, for whom the existence of God is a complete non-issue (Endo, 1973 [1958]: 79).[24] Instead of feeling remorse for what is clearly a moral travesty in these death experiments, the surgeon could only feel "an inevitable and extreme sense of fatigue" (Endo, 1973: 157), very similar to what Chiba experiences in *Yellow Person* (Endō, 1955: 91). Of course, this does not mean that Suguro does not regard what he does as wrong; at one point he even thinks that he will receive retribution for his deeds (Endō, 1955: 125). Yet the numbing inability to respond to the promptings of his conscience, as dull as they might have become, and the sheer ease with which he rationalizes his actions in the light of present circumstances, serve only to expose the dark, swampy complexity of the human heart.[25]

The Potential of Salvation through the Experience of Unconditional Love
Obakasan おバカさん (Wonderful Fool) (1959)
Watakushi ga suteta onna 私が棄てた女 (The Girl I Left Behind) (1964)

The following year after the publication of *The Sea and Poison*, Endō published his first humorous novel, *Wonderful Fool*, in which he explores the possibility of salvation of those without a biblical consciousness of God, sin, and death. In this novel, redemption comes in the form of an ugly-looking, dull-witted Frenchman with a totally unattractive persona. Yet anyone who comes into contact with Gaston Bonaparte – a direct descendant of Napoleon Bonaparte – would be inexplicably touched and inspired by his meekness and his readiness, foolhardy at times, to help anyone in need, even animals. For he loves unconditionally, even though he is constantly abused by those he loves.[26]

Following the mysterious disappearance of Gaston near the end of the novel, Tomoe, who has only met Gaston a few weeks earlier, is moved to acknowledge, "[Gaston's] not a fool. He's not a fool. Or, if he is, he's a wonderful fool [...] a wonderful fool who will never allow the little light which he sheds along man's

---

[24] Unless notated otherwise, all subsequent citations from *The Sea and Poison* are taken from the 1973 English translation by Michael Gallagher (Tokyo: Tuttle), and are referenced as Endo (1973 [1958]).

[25] From time to time, one still hears a missionary misquoting Endō saying that the Japanese have *no* concept of God, sin, and death. The reality is more complex. Endō does not deny that Japanese people, like everyone else, have an understanding of God, sin, and death. But in a polytheistic culture informed by the Buddhist teaching on reincarnation and nirvana, and where relational harmony is highly prized, it is to be expected that its adherents will not share the clearly defined theological understanding of God, sin, and death as propagated by the West. In relation to the Western worldview, the swamp analogy therefore seems appropriate to Japan.

[26] Harold Netland notes that Endō's "wonderful fool" finds a Western precedent in Dostoevsky's "idiot" (personal communication). See Fyodor Dostoevsky, *The Idiot* (Oxford: Oxford University Press, 1992).

way to go out" (Endo, 1974 [1959]: 180).[27] Later, Tomoe's brother, Takamori, makes these telling remarks to her:

> Not all men are handsome and strong. There are some who are cowards from birth. There are even some who cry easily. But for such a man, a man both weak and cowardly, to bear the burden of this weakness and struggle valiantly to live a beautiful life – that's what I call great [...]. I feel more drawn to Gaston than I would to a splendid saint or hero. (Endo, 1974 [1959]: 187-88)[28]

Even the hardcore gangster and murderer Endō (curiously named after the author himself), who bullies and spites him whenever the occasion presents itself, cannot resist Gaston's genuine warm-heartedness and in the end finds himself transformed by the unwavering love of the Frenchman.

The climax of the novel takes place at the "Big Swamp," where Gaston, in his bid to save Endō's life, allows himself to receive the blows of Kobayashi and "finally, seriously injured, collapse[s] in the shallows of the swamp" (Endo, 1974 [1959]: 231). The motif of the swamp is significant, for here Endō is perhaps presenting an allusion that the answer to the spiritual mudswamp that is Japan is the sort of unconditional and self-sacrificial love displayed by Gaston, the most unexpected figure of Christ.

After the release of *Wonderful Fool* and *Kumo* (*Spiders*), an anthology of horror tales, in late 1959, Endō embarked on a two-month tour of Europe with his wife. However, soon after Endō returned to Japan in early 1960, he had a relapse of pleurisy and fell critically ill. He was in hospital for two and a half years, during which he survived three major operations. During this time, Endō's literary productivity was understandably curtailed, but he was still able to write shorter works. He spent a lot of time reading about the *kakure kirishitan* (hidden Christians) who practiced their faith secretly as a result of the persecutions during the Tokugawa period.[29] After he was discharged from hospital in July 1962, he and his family moved to Tamagawa Gakuen, a university town on the outskirts of Tokyo, for his rehabilitation. Endō started work on a full-length

---

[27] Unless notated otherwise, all subsequent citations from *Wonderful Fool* are taken from the 1974 English translation by Francis Mathy (Tokyo: Tuttle), and are referenced as Endo (1974 [1959]).

[28] Williams is right to suggest that Takamori's words serve "as a precursor of similar depictions by Endō of the 'weak' *Kakure* (Hidden) Christians" (1999: 87). In particular, the "cowards" anticipate the Judas-like figures that invariably appear in Endō's historical works, such as Kichijirō in *Silence* and Kisuke in *Saigo no junkyōsha* (*The Final Martyrs*). *The Final Martyrs*, a short story published around the same time as *Wonderful Fool*, is Endō's first work on the *kakure kirishitan*, the hidden Christians who practiced their faith secretly as a result of the Tokugawa persecutions. The English translation appears as the lead story in the 1993 anthology of the same title.

[29] As mentioned in the preceding footnote, the subject of the *kakure kirishitan* was not new to Endō. Indeed, Endō had always displayed a deep fascination with their faith and history.

novel to develop the Christ figure that he had created in Gaston, the Wonderful Fool.

Published in 1964, *The Girl I Left Behind* explores the suffering, maternal nature of Christ through the female protagonist. Mitsu is a country bumpkin who is jilted by the worldly Yoshioka; she possesses a selfless nature predisposed to sharing the suffering of those around her. Having been diagnosed with leprosy, the abject woman admits herself into a leprosarium. However, her condition is misdiagnosed; but even after she learns about the error, she finds herself unable to abandon her new friends, those *really* with leprosy. The problem of suffering is a difficult one for Mitsu to bear, and she is angry at "the God who inflicts leprosy on little children and who ultimately confronts them with nothing but death" (Endo, 1994 [1964]: 189).[30] Yet her childlikeness, strong sense of empathy, nurturing instincts, and enlarged capacity for personal suffering are strongly reminiscent of the image of the longsuffering Christ. Even the tragic death of Mitsu is no mere accident, for she willingly lays down her life in order to save those to whom she has come to extend her "hand of friendship" (Endo, 1994 [1964]: 158). It is not a wonder that in the end even the unscrupulous Yoshioka should discover the indelible influence that Mitsu has silently exerted on his life. In the Afterword of the English translation of the novel, Endō confesses that through this novel, he had hoped "to portray the drama of 'the Jesus I left behind'" (Endo, 1994 [1964]: 194). He adds, "Mitsu can be seen as modeled on Jesus, abandoned by his own disciples; she is modeled on the Jesus whom all Christians are guilty of abandoning on a daily basis in their everyday lives" (Endo, 1994 [1964]: 194).

In this novel too, we see the beginnings of the concept of the constant companionship of Christ, a key motif that Endō would develop in his next major novel *Silence* and a lesser known but nonetheless important work, *On the Shores of the Dead Sea*.

The Eternal Companionship of the Suffering Christ
Chinmoku 沈黙 *(Silence) (1966)*
Shikai no hotori 死海のほとり *(On the Shores of the Dead Sea) (1973)*

Soon after the publication of *The Girl I Left Behind*, Endō made his first trip to Nagasaki, the sixteenth-century "Rome of the East", to learn more about the Jesuit mission and the faith of the *kakure kirishitan*.[31] There, inside the *Jūrokubankan* (Historical Building No. 16, also the Tourist Information Center), Endō saw a *fumie* 踏絵 "enclosed in a small wooden frame that was covered with black marks apparently made by human toes" (Endo, 1974 [1973]: 180). It

---

[30] Unless notated otherwise, all subsequent citations from *The Girl I Left Behind* are taken from the 1994 English translation by Mark Williams (London: Peter Owen), and are referenced as Endo (1994 [1964]).

[31] For an overview of the Jesuit mission and the *kakure kirishitan*, see pp. 42ff above.

was an authentic artifact, a small bronze plaque bearing the image of Christ that was used by the Tokugawa authorities to determine whether one was a Christian by requiring the person to step on it. Those who refused would be tortured, even killed.

Endō describes the face of Christ on the *fumie* that he saw as "worn down" because it had been stepped on by so many people: "the formerly noble appearance, so solemn and strong, had changed into a tired, sad countenance" (Endo, 1974 [1973]: 181). The image of the pathetic Christ on the *fumie* lingered in Endō's mind for a long time even after he returned to Tokyo. Endō began to ponder over three nagging questions:

> First, if I had lived in that period of history, would I have stepped on the *fumie*? Second, those people whose black toe marks I saw – what feeling did they have when they stepped on the *fumie*? Third, what kind of people were they who stepped on it? (Endo, 1974 [1973]: 180)

Endō's desire to learn more about the Jesuit mission led him to enroll in a class on early Japanese Christian history at Sophia University. He was dissatisfied with the course because the lectures he attended and the books he read discussed only "those who held staunchly to their faith and died gloriously as martyrs" (Endo, 1974 [1973]: 181). Nothing was said about "the weaklings who compromised their convictions and trampled [the *fumie*] because they were forced to" (Endo, 1974 [1973]: 181). Endō decided to use the medium of the novel to bring back to life these "cowards" who were "buried in the ashes of silence" in order to hear what they had to say (Endo, 1974 [1973]: 181). Extrapolating from the earlier Christ figures that he had created in his previous novels, Endō was convinced that the emaciated face of Christ on the *fumie* "offered a matchless opportunity to fill in the gap between the Japanese and Christianity" (Endo, 1974 [1973]: 181). Within a year, *Silence* was born. This is a historical novel set in seventeenth-century Japan when the church was horrendously persecuted by the authorities.[32] It is a story of the unexpected spiritual journey of a Portuguese priest who secretly enters Japan to minister to the suffering faithful but ends up renouncing his faith in order to prevent further torture of the people he has come to serve. Yet at that very moment of his apostasy, the priest makes the transforming discovery of the presence of the suffering Christ who speaks to him as he steps on the *fumie*.

> You may trample. Your foot is in pain, isn't it? It must be suffering the same pain as all the feet that have until now stepped on my face. But that pain alone is enough. I share your pain and your suffering. It is for that reason that I am here. (Endō, 1966: 240)

---

[32] For a masterly summary of the plot of the novel, see Bosch (1994: 73-75).

Among the multiple levels of interpretation that one can make about the novel is a theological one which posits the unassuming but abiding companionship that Christ offers, without exception, to all who undergo deep suffering, including even the cowardly apostate Kichijirō into whose character all of Jesus' faithless apostles are taken up (Mathy, 1974: 217; Endō, 1966: 239-40). In this sense, the title of the novel, *Chinmoku* 沈黙 ("Silence"), ultimately, is not a reference to the silence of God in the midst of deep suffering even though it is often taken to be so. In his reply to Rodrigues' protest, "Lord, I resent your continual silence," Christ replied, "I was not silent. I suffered beside you" (Endō, 1966: 240). A more plausible interpretation for the title is the silence of the many apostates who faded away into historical oblivion and whose stories were never told.

Silence brings to fruition the major literary theme that has begun with *White Man*, namely, that the possibility of redemption for the denizens of the cultural and religious swamp that is Japan lies in the experience of being loved unconditionally by the suffering Christ. Although this theme would continue to evolve with Endō's later works, its core emphases would remain the same.

The runaway success of *Silence* inspired Endō to pursue the question, "[W]hat kind of Jesus is he that the Japanese can believe in and understand with genuine feeling?" (Endō, 1966: 182). Endō visited Palestine in 1966, the first of seven trips he would make over the next seven years. As he walked the Holy Land, Endō would read and reread his Bible. Endō adds, "While engaged in this reading, what spurred my spiritual development was not anything from the Catholics, but rather the books of Protestant scholars, particularly those of the form-criticism school – which began with Rudolf Bultmann – and the redaction and criticism scholars" (Endō, 1966: 182). To be sure, Endō did not accept uncritically everything he read, but he was undeniably attracted by their "approach and scholarly method" (Endō, 1966: 182).

Through his visits to Palestine, Endō was able to confirm and crystallize his view of Jesus as he had presented it in *Silence*, namely, that the whole of Jesus' life was *defined* by rejection. It also gradually dawned upon Endō that the key to resolving the conflicts he felt from being both Japanese and Christian is the incarnate companionship of Jesus, a man who experienced loneliness, weakness, and ultimately rejection. The love that Jesus offers embraces without discrimination social misfits, foreigners, outcasts, even apostates – characters that fill almost every story that Endō has written.

In sum, Endō was now more convinced than ever that just as his "Japaneseness" denied him entry into European culture (as evidenced from his negative experiences in France), conversely, the triumphant Constantinian faith of European Christianity could never take root in Japanese soil. Endō's encounter with the despised and rejected Jesus in his Palestinian sojourn would now launch him on a new quest to understand and convey that incarnate love which speaks to the marginalized and the lonely, a quest that he believed would make Christianity comprehensible to Japanese people. After collecting "data from seven years' research," Endō was ready to present his contextualized

Christology, through *On the Shores of the Dead Sea* (Endō, 1966). This work comprises two stories told in alternative chapters, the first about Jesus in his historical and geographical setting, and the second about a middle-aged Japanese novelist, in all aspects similar to Endō, visiting Palestine to find out the truth about Jesus. Both stories converge at the same conclusion: Jesus is a powerless man who could perform no miracle, but could only offer his constant companionship to the sick and suffering (1973b: 213, 247).

An Enlarging Religious Vision
Samurai 侍 *(The Samurai) (1980)*
Sukyandaru スキャンダル *(Scandal) (1986)*
Fukai kawa 深い川 *(Deep River) (1994)*

Around the late 1970s, Endō began to show signs of a move away from the uniqueness of Christ to a position where he considered all religions as equally legitimate means of salvation. The seeds of his new religious vision are first sown in the last few pages of his non-fictional *My Jesus* (Endō, 1976: 236-40), and allowed to germinate in another quasi-theological work, *What God Is to Me* (1983). Again, these ideas are explored and given expression through the medium of the novel.

Among the many works that Endō produced during the last fifteen years of his life, three novels merit special mention. The first, *The Samurai*, was published in 1980, and it developed the theme of the constant companionship of Christ with a deep intensity that had never been achieved before in Endō's preceding novels.[33] The protagonist, Hasekura Rokuemon, is a low-ranking samurai sent to Nueva España (today's Mexico) and España (Spain) as part of a trade mission in the early seventeenth century. Since it is expedient for the sake of the mission, the whole Japanese delegation receives baptism. On his part, Hasekura converts outwardly, but inwardly he has no intention whatsoever to change his allegiance from Buddhism to a foreign faith. The trade delegation includes Father Velasco, a Franciscan priest, who acts as the envoys' interpreter. Velasco is a pompous and arrogant man who harbors no small ambition to become the next bishop of Japan. The contrast between Velasco and Hasekura could not be greater.

Throughout the journey, however, the lowly samurai finds himself constantly perplexed by the image of a miserable, wretched man nailed on the cross, for he just cannot understand why this man, "whose arms were outstretched, and whose head drooped lifelessly" should be worshipped and addressed as Lord by

---

[33] *The Samurai*, which won the Noma Literary Prize, is in all probability the second most widely read of Endō's novels outside of Japan, after *Silence*.

Velasco and all the foreigners (Endo, 1982 [1980]: 83).[34] But as the story progresses, Hasekura begins to understand by degrees that even if he cares nothing about Jesus, "He is always beside us. He listens to our agony and our grief. He weeps with us" (Endo, 1982 [1980]: 243). As it later turns out, both Valesco and Hasekura are sentenced to death during the Tokugawa persecutions. Valesco faces his crucifixion with a renewed, tranquil faith. Hasekura by now has cultivated an emotional affinity with the powerless Christ with whom he can readily identify. During the last, climactic scene of the novel, as Hasekura is led away for execution, his retainer assures him of Christ's everlasting presence (Endo, 1982 [1980]: 262). The samurai simply nods silently. Mase-Hasegawa rightly notes, "[A]t that moment, [Hasekura] identifies his pain and suffering with Jesus. Christ became [*sic*] the God of the abandoned" (2004: 100). For the evangelical Christian, it might be unsatisfactory that Hasekura dies without a clear profession of faith. But as Williams observes, the characteristic restraint with which Endō depicts this scene opens up "boundless potential" (1999: 64). Here is perhaps a hint of Endō's initial openness to religious pluralism. Mase-Hasegawa picks up a similar thread of thought:

> [T]he samurai died for his lord as a Buddhist, yet he dies believing in the eternal attendance of Christ [...] In the novel, Endo's image of Christ as an everpresent companion provided new aspects of his belief: the universal significance of the atonement of Jesus Christ that expanded beyond religions. (2004: 100)[35]

The next novel, *Scandal*, published in 1986, is Endō's most profoundly psychological work as he explores the deep and murky workings of the human subconscious. The protagonist, Suguro, is a Catholic writer approaching the end of a distinguished literary career – very much like Endō himself. By all accounts, Suguro is the epitome of success; yet beneath the prim and proper public persona is a tormented soul who not only secretly struggles with his pedophilic urges but is also constantly frightened by the potential of his heart for unbridled perversion and evil. The duality of Suguro's character is brought out into greater relief through the complex mother-figure of Madame Naruse, a selfless volunteer nurse who cares for sick children in the pediatric ward of a hospital by day and a matron at a sadomasochistic sex club in the red-light district of Kabuki-chō in Shinjuku by night. The gentle nurse also derives strong sexual satisfaction fantasizing about innocent mothers and children being trapped in a burning house. The fragmented, inner world of a person is depicted by Madame Naruse's late husband in this rather unnerving way:

---

[34] Unless notated otherwise, all subsequent citations from *The Samurai* are taken from the 1982 English translation by Van C. Gessel (London; Peter Owen), and are referenced as Endo (1982 [1980]).

[35] Interestingly, Mase-Hasegawa calls *The Samurai* Endō's "inner autobiography" (2004: 179).

There are several rooms inside the human heart. The room at the lowest level is like the storeroom you have here in your home [...] [I]t has all kinds of things stored up in it. But late at night, the things you've locked up and forgotten in there begin to move. (Endo, 1988 [1986]: 118)[36]

Scandal is certainly a departure of sorts from Endō's previous novels. Yet this psychological drama, in a way reminiscent of the Twilight Zone, subverts the Christian's belief in "a single integrated world created by an omnipotent God" (Williams, 1999: 180). The novel reaches its climax when Suguro comes to the shocking realization that the foul and filthy imposter who has been stalking him up to now is actually Suguro himself. In the following scene, Suguro sees his double vanish, enveloped by "a profound light [...] filled with love and compassion, and with a maternal tenderness [...] The light increased in intensity and began to wrap itself around Suguro" (Endo, 1988 [1986]: 242). In desperation, Suguro cries out, "O Lord, have mercy [...] Have mercy on us whose minds are deranged" (Endo, 1988 [1986]: 243). This prayer constitutes the theological turning point of the novel. Suguro discovers that there is no deliverance from his divided self; rather, he begins a process of coming to terms with not only the mysterious reality of the human soul that presents more than meets the eye, but also the possibility of an open-ended God who subsumes both good and evil in his relation to the world. In the words of Hagiwara Takao, Endō's God in *Scandal* "is ready to embrace the world as it is" (1993: 58).

Scandal brings into question the nature of psychological and spiritual reality where good and evil dwell coexist. It also anticipates a theological openness that Endō would develop in his final novel *Deep River*. Interestingly, two years after *Scandal* was published, Endō wrote *What God Is to Me*. In the first chapter, Endō suggests that "it is perhaps better to think of God not as an object to relate to, but as someone who works in and through a person" (1983: 22). Endō's proposal, however, becomes a conviction by the end of the chapter.

It must necessarily be said that God's workings are present even in sin and evil. Indeed God's workings are to be found in all things. As I write my novels, it is gradually dawning upon me that God's workings are manifest in everything, in sickness, in one's desires, even in the act of embracing a woman. God is not a *being* (*sonzai* 存在), but a *working* (*hataraki* 働き). (Endō, 1983: 23, emphasis added)

This brings us to Endō's final novel, published just two years before his death. *Deep River* raises serious questions on theological reality as understood by orthodox Christians. The novel centers on a group of Japanese tourists visiting the Hindu holy city of Vārānasī by the River Ganges. Each person comes with a different set of personal agenda – which Endō skillfully explores – and

---

[36] Unless notated otherwise, all subsequent citations from *Scandal* are taken from the 1988 English translation by Van C. Gessel (London: Peter Owen), and are referenced as Endo (1988 [1986]).

each is unexpectedly brought to a profound experience of the workings of the divine through the rhetoric of the sacred river which symbolizes an all-encompassing spirituality. Interestingly, Mitsu, the protagonist in *The Girl I Left Behind*, is "reincarnated" in the person of Ōtsu, the main character of the novel (Endo, 1994 [1964]: 196). Madame Naruse, who disappears at the end of *Scandal*, has her role assumed by Mitsuko, the foil for Ōtsu.

Ōtsu is a fervent Christian, but utterly pathetic in demeanor. Moreover, he has to drop out of seminary because his heterodox faith constantly gets him into trouble with his ecclesiastical superiors. While earnestly seeking to emulate Christ in His weakness and suffering by serving others, Ōtsu also believes that "[the] many different religions [...] are merely various paths leading to the same place" (Endo, 1994 [1994]: 191).[37] Yet Ōtsu's love for Jesus is a passionate one. He would wake up at four every morning to spend time "in conversation with his Lord" (Endo, 1994 [1994]: 192). Indeed, it is Christ's eternal companionship that sustains him, and the selfless passion of Christ that inspires him to bear the agony of the outcasts of humanity (Endo, 1994 [1994]: 185). Before his final act of sacrifice, Ōtsu prays,

O Lord, [...] You carried the cross upon your back and climbed the hill to Golgotha. I now imitate that act. You carried the sorrows of all men on your back and climbed the hill to Golgotha. I now imitate that act. (Endo, 1994 [1994]: 193)

In sum, while the belief in the crucified Christ and the motif of Christ's eternal companionship are kept intact in this novel, they have become subsumed under an all-embracing vision of religious universalism. In this sense, *Deep River* is not only the culmination of a long and illustrious literary career, but also the realization of Endō's ultimate religious vision.

Endō's Final Years (1994-1996)

Toward the end of 1992, Endō suffered kidney failure and was admitted into hospital for a month. The following year, he underwent peritoneal dialysis but never fully recovered. The next three and a half years were spent in and out of hospital. Then in September 1995, Endō suffered cerebral hemorrhage which caused him to lose his ability to talk. On December 29, 1996, after experiencing breathing difficulties from pneumonia, Endō died. He is buried at the Catholic cemetery in Fuchū, together with his mother and brother.

Despite constant struggles with ill health and lengthy periods of hospitalization throughout his life, Endō led a very active life and made significant contributions to literature and the arts, not only in Japan but also

[37] Unless notated otherwise, all subsequent citations from *Deep River* are taken from the 1994 English translation by Van C. Gessel (New York: New Directions), and are referenced as Endo (1994 [1994]).

overseas. At various points of his life, he served as president of the Japan chapter of the Poets, Essayists and Novelists (P.E.N.) club, member of the Central Council of the Ministry of Education, screening member of the Akutagawa Prize committee, director of the Japan Artists Association, president of the Nikkatsu Visual Arts Academy, and was a founding member of the Japan Christian Art Center in Harajuku, Tokyo. It is noteworthy that Endō's explicitly theological or religious agenda did not cloud his impressive literary achievements. Besides being inducted into the prestigious Japan Arts Academy in 1981, he received numerous awards from other countries including the Vatican. He was also conferred hononary doctorates by a number of Jesuit universities, including America's Georgetown University, Santa Clara University, John Carroll University, and Taiwan's Fu Jen Catholic University. The year before his death, Endō was awarded the Order of Culture, a top national honor conferred on those with exceptional achievements in the fields of culture and academia

Having surveyed Endō's personal biography and the evolution of his literature, we shall now proceed to present his key theological ideas in relation to the nature of God and the person and ministry of Jesus. The three main sources used for our discussion here are Endō's principal non-fictional works on Jesus Christ, *Iesu no shōgai* イエスの生涯 (*A Life of Jesus*) (1973), *Watakushi no Iesu* 私のイエス (*My Jesus*) (1976), and *Kirisuto no tanjō* キリストの誕生 (*The Birth of Christ*) (1978). Of these three, only *A Life of Jesus* has been translated into English.[38]

Theological and Christological Perspectives of Endō

The Maternal God

Endō confesses that while *Silence* contains a multiplicity of themes, the one most meaningful for him is the transformation in the mind of the protagonist of the image of a majestic and powerful Christ into that of a weak and suffering Christ (Endo, 1974 [1973]: 181). Interestingly, Endō understands the latter in maternal terms.[39]

---

[38] Since the definite (or indefinite) article does not exist in the Japanese language, the title *Iesu no shōgai* could be translated as either "The Life of Jesus" or "A Life of Jesus." The former is certainly the more natural reading, and one can only guess that the use of the latter as the English title reflects the Jesuit translator's warning that the work is Endō's own interpretation of the four Gospels rather than official church teaching. Perhaps this could also explain why the sequel *The Birth of Christ* has not been translated.

[39] The use of the image of the mother is very common in modern Japanese literature, appearing frequently, for example, in the works of literary giants such as Izumi Kyōka, Dazai Osamu, Tanizaki Jun'ichirō, and Kawabata Yasunari, among others. Endō, however, is unique in the way that he transposes the image of the mother onto the Christian God. See Hagiwara Takao, "The Role of the Mother in Modern Japanese

Citing Erich Fromm, he categorizes religion into two kinds: father-religion and mother-religion (Endo, 1974 [1973]: 181). In father-religion, God is depicted as a fierce and harsh deity who gets angry easily. He judges and punishes humans for their sins. In stark contrast stands mother-religion, in which God is to humans what a mother is to her children. God forgives his children no matter how sinful they are, just as a mother forgives her children no matter how bad they are. More than that, the God of mother-religion is a suffering God who shares deeply in human suffering. The overarching theme of *Silence*, states Endō, is precisely "this revolution from paternal religion to maternal religion, the change from the father-religion Christ to the mother-religion Christ in the experience of the novel's hero" (Endo, 1974 [1973]: 181).

In *A Life of Jesus*, Endō suggests that the image of God that John the Baptist embraced was that of a wrathful father.

> It was the image of a grim, censorious deity, as he does appear under various circumstances in the Old Testament – a deity destroying whole cities for not submitting to him, or falling into a terrible rage at the sins of his own people, like a despotic father, punishing without mercy the perfidy of all human beings. John the Baptist, wearing camel's skin fastened at the waist with a leather strap, gave notice in advance concerning the wrath of this stern father-image of God: "You brood of vipers! Who warned you to flee from the wrath to come? Bear fruits that befit repentance." Such was God in the Old Testament, raging and punishing, against the backdrop of doomsday and the final judgment. (Endo, 1978 [1973]: 24 = Endō, 1973a: 29)[40]

It is not clear if Endō had read the writings of Marcion, the second-century heretic who made a distinction between the creator-judge God of the Old Testament and the redeemer God of love of the New Testament. For Endō does clearly make that distinction. In *My Jesus*, published three years after *A Life of Jesus*, Endō writes:

> The God of the Old Testament is fearsome, judging, and readily punishes sin [...]. In Japan, it is often said that the four most fearsome things in life are "earthquakes, thunder, fires, and fathers." For instance, the father of the Meiji period was extremely strict, and was always ready to hit his children when they misbehaved. He was always reprimanding or punishing them for the slightest wrong committed. This is indeed the image of the God of Judaism. However, the God of the New Testament is akin to an ideal mother who suffers together with her children, always in the end forgives their sin no matter how severe it might have been, and with her whole heart always comforts them in their sorrow. (1976: 61)

Literature: The Case of Shūsaku Endō," in *British Columbia Asian Review* 7, no. 1 (Winter 1993/94), pp. 55-63.
[40] References to the 1978 English translation of *A Life of Jesus* are notated as Endo (1978 [1973]). Whenever a citation is taken from the translated text, the equivalent reference to the 1973 Japanese text will be given alongside.

Endō believes that the maternal qualities of God were not only incarnated in Jesus, but that Jesus indeed came to correct the people's misconception of God (Endō, 1976: 192-93). According to Endō, Jesus himself had doubts at first if the father image of John the Baptist was the true image of God (1978: 24). In the lives of the ordinary folk living "in the poverty and squalor of his little town of Nazareth," Jesus knew that the last thing people needed was a God of wrath and judgment (Endo, 1978 [1973]: 24 = Endō, 1973a: 29-30). As he encountered the downtrodden and marginalized, he came to a growing understanding of a God which was increasingly divergent from that of established convention, and started preaching a "God of love who comes himself to experience the sorrows of humankind" (Endo, 1978 [1973]: 28 = Endō, 1973a: 36). Once Jesus had grasped the true nature of God, says Endō, the rest of his life became driven by a singular purpose: "to demonstrate the existence of the God of love and make it possible for other people to know the love of God" (Endo, 1978 [1973]: 44 = Endō, 1973a: 56-57).

This notwithstanding, laments Endō, orthodox Christianity continues to be characterized by "the European overemphasis on the paternal aspect of religion" (Endo, 1974 [1973]: 181). Endō goes on to claim that the father image of God has been propagated throughout the history of Christian mission, to the effect that "Christianity [seems] distant to us Japanese because the other aspect, maternal religion, [has] been grossly neglected" (Endo, 1974 [1973]: 181). In other words, even though Japanese people do understand the traditional image of strict father, they are drawn to the image of the kind mother.

In sum, Endō believes that the true biblical image of God, namely, his maternity, speaks deeply to the Japanese in a way that a paternal image is unable to. According to him, the most dominant feature of the spiritual psychology of the Japanese people is a responsiveness to a religion which offers comfort and compassion, rejecting any kind of transcendent being who sets unattainable moral standards only to punish those who fail to live by them (Endo, 1978 [1973]: 1). In fact, Endō believes this to be the reason why the Japanese accepted Buddhism readily when it first came to Japan (Endo, 1978 [1973]: 1). In sum, "the Japanese tend to seek in their gods and buddhas a warm-hearted mother rather than a stern father" (Endo, 1978 [1973]: 1). The traditional dogma of Christianity is too weighed down with the wrathful God of justice for it to survive the mudswamp of Japan. This is, however, not the case with the compassionate Buddha (Endō, 1976: 194). In Endō's reckoning then, what Japan needs is a "God of *amae*" (cf. Cohen, 1993: 115-17).[41]

---

[41] See p. 55 above, esp. n. 42. Doron Cohen defines *amae* (甘え) as "the feeling of normal infants toward the mother: dependence, the desire to be passively loved, and the unwillingness to be separated from the mother's protection and face the reality of the world" (1993: 115). According to psychiatrist Doi Takeo (1981), *amae* extends to adult life and shapes personal and social reality in Japan more than in any other culture.

Kitamori, in an essay on Endō, rebuts the latter's assertion that the Japanese can only accept Christianity in motherly terms as highly suspect (1991: 335-40). For one thing, culture is always changing, and it is doubtful that Japanese mentality has remained the same so many years after the war. Tongue in cheek, Kitamori claims from his observations that the images of the father and mother have been reversed in post-war Japan: "the indulgent father and the strict mother" (Kitamori, 1991: 340). Furthermore, the overly heavy involvement of the post-war Japanese mother in her children's education has earned her a rather uncomplimentary appellation, *kyōiku mamagon* (education mama-saurus). Endō did not offer any rebuttal, but if he did, one could expect him to say that Kitamori's argument does not in any way change his understanding of God as always kind and forgiving rather than stern and judging. In any case, Kitamori's comment raises the problem of representing divine realities given the inevitability of cultural change, therefore meaning that any metaphors are constantly shifting.

However, Kitamori is quite right to suggest that Endō rejected the image of the paternal God because of the hatred he felt toward his father, and in its place, created an idealized image of the maternal God while being influenced by his feelings toward his suffering mother (1991: 336).[42] Endō himself admits to the difficulties he had with his father:

> It had been that, as a youth, I had first tasted the bitterness of life, there that I had learnt to hate my father. I had experienced loneliness, and from the pained expression of my mother, I had come to know the countenance of an unhappy woman. Had I not had that experience I may well have rejected Christianity long ago. (cited in Noble, 1991: 28)

In sum, Endō understands God not as an all-powerful judge, but as one who suffers like a mother does, and therefore identifies with the suffering of his children. This motherly God reveals himself supremely, for Christians at least, in the incarnated life of Jesus.

The Jesus of History and the Christ of Faith

Endō understands the person of Jesus Christ as comprising two parts: the historical Jesus and the post-resurrection Christ, reminiscent of Martin Kähler's 1892 classic work *Der sogenannte historische Jesus und der geschichtliche, biblische Christus.* [43] This bipartite distinction, as reflected in Endō's

---

[42] Kitamori, however, is wrong when he says that "Endō lost his mother when he was fifteen or sixteen" (1991: 336). The fact is that Endō's mother died in 1954, when Endō was thirty-one years old.
[43] *Historische* means "historical", that is, relating to factual events. *Geschichtliche*, on the other hand, means "historic", that is, referring to an existential "history" that creates an impact on the believer. Kähler – the teacher of both Barth and Bultmann – never intended to divorce the two, but to suggest that while it is true that the

two-volume treatise *A Life of Jesus* and *The Birth of Christ*, does not, however, compromise the unity of the person of Jesus Christ. Endō consistently regards Jesus as the Christ, historically, but more significantly, at the theological level.[44] However, there is a fundamental and profound difference at the cognitive and affective level, a new apprehension mediated by the transfiguration of the historical Jesus into the metahistorical Christ. For Endō, it is the cataclysmic event of the Cross that is crucial in bringing about this new level of understanding and experience of the risen Christ.

Jesus the Ineffectual Man
In the preface to the American edition of *A Life of Jesus*, Endō sums up his theological intention:

> Jesus as I depict him is a person who lived for love and still more love, and yet he was put to death, for he chose to live without violent resistance […]. I wrote this book for the benefit of Japanese readers who have no Christian tradition of their own and who know almost nothing about Jesus. What is more, I was determined to highlight the particular aspect of love in his personality precisely in order to make Jesus understandable in terms of the religious psychology of my non-Christian countrymen and thus to demonstrate that Jesus is not alien to their religious sensibilities. (1978 [1973]: 1)

In this biography on Jesus, Endō attempts to construct a new *imago Christi*, one that fully expresses the mother image of God. As mentioned above, the fundamental presupposition underlying Endō's Christology is that the Jesus of historical fact is different from the fictive Christ of faith. In the *Birth of Christ*, Endō (1978) seeks to demonstrate how the latter actually originated in the kerygma of the early church. To begin, Endō employs Bultmann's program of demythologization and removes every trace of the supernatural, both from Jesus' personality and from his ministry. However, Endō operates from a different motivation. It is not that he does not believe that God can do miracles; it is just that miracles symbolize power, and that compromises the reality of human suffering.

> Jesus walked through the mountain coves and the gullies where these forsaken lepers were forced to live. He wanted to restore their healthy bodies. He wanted to

---

historical-scientific method may fail to uncover the historical Jesus, it does not compromise the historic, biblical Christ whose impact comes through the preaching of the Bible by the church. Endō seems to be adopting Kähler's approach, although his conclusions about both the historical Jesus and the Christ of faith are quite different from Kähler's.
[44] In contrast, there are scholars who attempt to effect a radical separation between the historical Jesus and the Christ of faith. See, for example, Alvar Ellegård, *Jesus: One Hundred Years Before Christ* (Woodstock, N.Y.: Peter Mayer, 1999).

restore to the blind the use of their eyes. He wanted to make the lame walk. He wanted to bring back a lost child to a bereaved mother.

But a look of sadness came to his eyes when he could not do it. He held the hand of a leper, or a lame man, and he pleaded earnestly his desire to take upon himself their misery and pain. He asked for a share in their suffering, a chance to be partners with them. (Endo, 1978 [1973]: 72 = Endō, 1973a: 96-97, emphasis added)

Jesus could not accomplish all the miracles the crowds pleaded for. In the towns by the lake he sat to wipe the sweat from a fever-wracked patient whom others had abandoned, and through the night he quietly held the hand of a mother who had lost her child, but miracles he could not do [...]. What they needed more than miraculous cures was love. Jesus knew the longing of human beings for changeless, enduring companionship. They needed a companion, the kind of mother who could share their wretched suffering and weep together with them. He believed that God by his nature was not in the image of a stern father, but was more like a mother who shares the suffering of her children and weeps with them; and in order to bear witness to the love which God bore for these men and women in their misfortunes, whenever Jesus met them near the Lake of Galilee he prayed that in God's kingdom they would arrive at his way of seeing things. (Endo, 1978 [1973]: 80 = Endō. 1973a: 107-8)

Endō describes Jesus emphatically as "essentially without power" (1978: 165).[45] Therefore, it is this Jesus who, by virtue of his utter powerlessness, had no capacity to heal, but only the ability to identify completely with the loneliness and hopelessness that inflict the sick and the poor. An *essentially* weak Jesus could give nothing that the people wanted, but he could offer the only gift that the people really needed: love.

For Jesus recognized that the greatest misfortune that could ever befall a human being is to be unloved (Endo, 1978 [1973]: 108). Since his heart was ablaze with God's love, Jesus sought to devote his whole life asserting the presence of God's love in the world, "to cast the fire of love into the world" (Endo, 1978 [1973]: 112). To achieve that, he aspired to become not just a companion to suffering people, but "the *eternal* companion of all people" (*hitobito no eien no dōhansha* 人々の永遠の同伴者) (Endo, 1978 [1973]: 118, emphasis added).

It needs to be noted that Endō implicitly assumes the divinity of Christ, but draws hardly any attention to it. This is understandable since doing so would only jeopardize his project of presenting a powerless Jesus. There is, therefore, nothing in Endō's writings that deals with the nature of Christ or the doctrine of the Trinity.

---

[45] This expression aptly translates *honshitsu teki ni muryoku* 本質的に無力) in the original text (Endō, 1973a: 232).

The Death of Jesus

Recalling the canticle of the Suffering Servant in Isaiah 52, Jesus came to the sobering realization that to become the eternal companion of all humanity requires no less than the ultimate sacrifice.

> In order to become man's eternal companion, in order to demonstrate the reality of the God of love, he [Jesus] himself had to meet death in its most harrowing form. He had to go through every misery and pain that men and women go through, because otherwise he could not truly share in the misery and pain of humankind, and because otherwise he couldn't face us to say: "Look, I am at your side. I have suffered like you. Your misery – I understand it; I went through it all myself." (Endo, 1978 [1973]: 125 = Endō, 1973a: 174, emphasis added)

According to Endō, Jesus had constantly rejected the title "Christ" or "Messiah" (1973a: 121). When the people realized that he could not fulfill their messianic expectations to overthrow the Romans who were occupying their land, they turned against him, resulting in his crucifixion. It was a pathetic death that Jesus died. Contrary to the Gospel records, Endō asserts, on the day Jesus died, there was no earthquake, no darkness spread across the land, the temple curtain was not torn, no rocks were split nor any grave opened, and the sky remained what it had been: "The fact is that nothing extraordinary happened at all" (Endō, 1973a: 215). On the cross, Jesus suffered the absolute silence of God but, in that suffering, displayed his profound love for the world of suffering humanity.

> Jesus displayed on the cross nothing but utter helplessness and weakness. Nowhere does the passion narrative depict Jesus except in this utterly powerless image. The reason is that love, in terms of this world's values, is forever vulnerable and helpless [...]. Jesus, powerless on the cross, is the symbol of love – nay the very incarnation of Love. (Endo, 1978 [1973a]: 147 = Endō, 1973a: 206)

Endō believes that the image of Jesus, who once participated in the very earthly conditions of human frailty and misery, failure, guilt and shame, but now hanging lifeless on the cross, speaks deeply to the Japanese in a way that the triumphant, risen Christ and the symbol of the empty cross do not. For instance, in *The Samurai*, it was "[the] man with the drooping head, that man scrawny as a pin, that man whose arms stretched out, nailed to the cross" that appeals to Hasekura the doubting samurai, "not the Christ whom the affluent priests preached in the cathedrals of Nueva España" (Endo, 1982 [1980]: 242-43).

As previously alluded to, Endo confesses that it is the transformation of the majestic Christ into a pathetic Jesus that he had intended to be *the* theme of *Silence* (1974 [1973]: 181). The protagonist, Father Rodrigues, believes in a powerful Christ, and brings this image with him to Japan. It is "from the strong face of Christ he gained courage to evangelize" (Endo, 1974 [1973]: 181). At last, however, he is apprehended and brought before the *fumie*, the bronze image of the suffering Christ on which he is to step.

> Standing there, he saw an image of Christ *he had never seen before*, an image shaped by Japanese hands. It was not the orderly, solemn face he had conceived as a European, but the worn-out face of a Christ suffering as we suffer. (1974 [1973]: 181, emphasis added)

As the priest agonizes at the prospect of renouncing his faith, he hears Jesus on the *fumie* saying, "Trample! Trample! [...] It was to be trampled on by men that I was born into this world. It was to share men's pain that I carried my cross" (Endo, 1982 [1966]: 271; also Endo, 1974 [1973]: 297). Some years after Endō's death, Father Inoue Yōji, Endō's lifelong friend, discovered that in the English translation of *Silence*, the verb "trample" is in the imperative mood, whereas in the original Japanese text, the expression is 踏むがいい (*fumu ga ii*), which is in the permissive mood, rather than 踏め (*fume*), which would be imperative (Endō Junko, 1999: 145; compare Endō, 1966: 219, 240 with Endo, 1982 [1966]: 271, 297). The permissive expression – translated, "You may trample on me" – certainly captures better the compassion of a non-coercive Jesus than the word "Trample!" in the command form. Eto Jun, a literary critic, comments, "The face of Jesus on the *fumie* is the mother's face in Japan" (cited in Endo, 1974 [1973]: 181). Endō agrees wholeheartedly with Eto's comment. Through the *fumie* scene, Endō intends the crucified Jesus to be the ultimate embodiment of the motherly nature of God.

To summarize Endō's position, the tragic death of Jesus is not to be interpreted in vicarious or penal substitutionary terms. Rather the cross, where Jesus experienced the absolute silence of God, becomes an emblem of identification in all human suffering (cf. Küster, 2001: 130-31). The existential human problem, for Endō, is not sin but suffering. Hence, instead of understanding Jesus as sin-bearer, Endō would have it that Jesus entered deeply into human suffering through his Passion. In other words, on the cross Jesus did not suffer *for* us; rather he suffered *like* us. In the process, he became transfigured into a sympathetic companion of all those who suffer, like Father Rodrigues in *Silence*. Endō's understanding of the death of Christ is hence closer to the moral influence theory, or more specifically, the contingent historical view.

The Historicity of the Resurrection
Since Endō has already demythologized away all the miracles from the Gospel records, it is understandable if he should also want to deny the historicity of the Resurrection. But this is not the case. It is true that he finds the account of the Resurrection "creepy" (*usukimiwarui* 薄気味悪い), and the absolute conviction of the apostles that Jesus rose from the dead perplexing (Endō, 1973a: 250). "Why did the disciples continue to insist on the factuality of anything so preposterous as the resurrection, an idea ridiculed even by the people of their

own times?" Endō asks (1978 [1973]: 176 = Endō 1973a: 250]. Yet, interestingly, he maintains the historicity of the Resurrection, claiming that "[t]he recent painstaking research by Campenhausen has corroborated the historical authenticity of the empty tomb" (Endo, 1978 [1973]: 177 = Endō, 1973a: 251). In fact, curiously, Endō considers it easier to argue that the miracles did not exist but were subsequently written into the Gospel accounts by the disciples than it is to argue that the Resurrection did not happen (1973a: 249). Later, in *My Jesus*, Endō makes the same claim that the Resurrection is "indeed an attestable historical event just as the Bible teaches that it is" (1976: 155). And in the *Birth of the Christ*, Endō again affirms that "the sudden disappearance of [Jesus'] body from the tomb is not a fanciful tale concocted in the Bible but a fact [...]. The Bible speaks of the 'empty tomb' as the result of Jesus' resurrection" (1978: 22).

However, it should be said that, after writing the *Birth of Christ*, Endō began distancing himself away from the historical veracity of the Resurrection. In the section "The Resurrection of Jesus" in *What God Is to Me* (1983: 84-87), Endō defines the resurrection of Christ *wholly* in spiritual terms: "When Jesus' central teaching remains in the disciples' hearts, he becomes alive in them. This is one manifestation of his resurrection" (Endō, 1983: 86).

Regardless, Endō has consistently deemed the historicity of the Resurrection as far less important than that which it is supposed to signify in relation to the remarkable life of Jesus before his crucifixion (Endō, 1976: 155). Endō is simply not convinced that the actual physical event of the Resurrection *alone* could bring about such a radical, earth-shaking change in the disciples. That being the case, he is presented with a real problem, especially in the light of his consistent depiction of a feckless and helpless Jesus stripped of all divinity: How is it that the cowardly disciples who fled during the capture of Jesus were suddenly transformed into fearless men so soon after the death of their teacher, men who went on to "turn the world upside down", and even build a church which has long outlasted them? Endō considers this as "one of the deepest mysteries we encounter in reading the Bible" (1973a: 221).

In all probability, "close on the time of Jesus' death there occurred something electrifying enough to make the hearts of the disciples do a somersault" (Endo, 1978 [1973]: 163 = Endō, 1973a: 230). Something amazing happened, something "different in kind yet of equal force in its electrifying intensity" such that it does not matter even if the Resurrection did not actually happen (Endo, 1978 [1973]: 177 = Endō, 1973a: 252). Endō elaborates,

> At least, logic impels us to conclude that, whatever it was that might have happened, it was enough to change the "powerless" Jesus in the hearts of the disciples into the "all-powerful" image of Jesus. And then we are constrained to suppose that this other event, whatever its nature, was enough to also persuade the disciples that the *resurrection* of Jesus was a *fact*. (Endo, 1978 [1973]: 177 = Endō, 1973a: 252 emphasis in text)

It is not a wonder that Endō should name the last chapter of his biography on Jesus *Nazo* 謎, which means riddle or puzzle. In the final analysis, the sudden, supernatural transformation of the disciples is a *nazo*. Endō (1973a: 240-46) offers a tentative hypothesis to explain what happened to transform the disciples so dramatically, which he would later expand and confirm in *My Jesus* (1976: 150-168) and *The Birth of Christ* (1978: 15-42). The answer hinges not so much on the physical event of the Resurrection, but on what transpired when Jesus was hanging on the cross. This is where the true significance of the Cross is to be found.

The True Significance of the Cross
According to Endō, the key to understanding the dramatic transformation of the disciples is found Jesus' last words, the three sets of utterances that he made from the cross amidst the silence of God:

"Father, forgive them, for they know not what they are doing."

"My God, my God, why have you forsaken me?"

"Father, into your hands I commit my spirit." (1973a: 241; 1976: 164; 1978: 18)

These cries from the cross "made their shattering impact on the disciples" (Endo, 1978 [1973]: 171 = Endō, 1973a: 241). To the disciples, it was inconceivable that a man could still love and forgive his enemies in the face of violent death, but Jesus did. Also, Endō argues that the words, "My God, my God, why hast thou forsaken me?" were not a cry of despair, but in the context of Psalm 22, they constituted a prayer of profound trust. These words were linked to the next utterance, "Into thy hands I commit my spirit," an expression of utter dependence on God despite God's stony silence. Jesus' supreme manifestation of love so moved the disciples, surmises Endō, that they became awakened to a true understanding of Jesus and of all that he had been teaching them before he died. The disciples now realized how they had misunderstood the mission of Jesus, and became emboldened to carry on Jesus' mission of actualizing God's love in the world. Having a true understanding of Jesus and his teaching, the disciples "began to feel that Jesus might still be close by their side. Their state of mind was like the feeling of a child bereaved of its mother, when the child can still feel how the mother, even after her death, always remains close by" (Endo, 1978 [1973]: 174 = Endō, 1973a: 246). In other words, the image of Jesus as *dōhansha* 同伴者 (companion) is being born in their hearts (Endō, 1973a: 246).

The Birth of Christ the Eternal Companion
It is telling that Endō's *A Life of Jesus* does not contain any birth narrative. The book begins with the chapter "Farewell to Nazareth." For Endō, the real birth narrative of Jesus is not the Bethlehem nativity – which, in any case "is not a fact" (1973a: 253) – but the birth of Christ in the hearts of men and women. Indeed, Endō understands this to be the true significance of the Resurrection:

Jesus died, but is risen as Christ in the hearts of his followers as their eternal companion (1976: 167-68; 1983: 86). This explains the *Birth of Christ* as a sequel to *A Life of Jesus*.

The birth of Christ, as it were, did not happen overnight. As mentioned above, the disciples were profoundly moved that Jesus, while hanging on the cross, did not express the slightest hint of anger, but continued to manifest love by asking God to forgive his enemies. According to Endō, the Roman centurion's exclamation, "Surely he was the Son of God" (Mt. 27:54), was not in response to the earthquake and the accompanying miraculous phenomena – for nothing of the sort happened – but to Jesus' expression of love, forgiveness, and faith through his unexpected three utterances from the cross (1973a: 242). And that exclamation takes up the exact sentiments of the disciples as they recalled Jesus' earthly mission and finally began to understand what his ministry as the Son of God was *really* about.

With his characteristic literary flair, Endō describes "the long and painful night" the disciples went through before the Resurrection (1978: 23-42). This was not an unfruitful night. Throughout the night, they replayed the last words of Jesus on the cross in their minds and pondered on their true significance. They recalled how when he was alive, Jesus, despite his utter powerlessness, served so selflessly among the people simply by being with them. He had nothing to give to the people but himself, and this he did supremely on the cross. The disciples now realized that here was the Suffering Servant prophesied in Isaiah 52 (Endō, 1978: 32-34). Through "the long and painful night", they came to a new understanding of Jesus the Son of Man, and created these teachings about him:

1. "The Son of Man must suffer many things, and be rejected by the elders, chief priests, and teachers of the law, and that he must be killed and after three days rise again (Mk. 8:31).
2. "The Son of Man is going to be betrayed into the hands of men. They will kill him, and after three days he will rise" (Mk. 9:31).
3. "The Son of Man will be betrayed to the chief priests and teachers of the law. They will condemn him to death and will hand him over to the Gentiles, who will mock him, spit on him, flog him and kill him. Three days later he will rise" (Mk. 10:33-34).
4. "The Son of Man must suffer much and be rejected" (Mk. 9:22).
5. "The Son of Man in his day will be like the lightning, which flashes and lights up the sky from one end to the other. But first he must suffer many things and be rejected by this generation" (Lk. 17:24-25).
6. "The Son of Man will go as it has been decreed" (Lk. 22:22).[46]

---

[46] It is interesting that Endō deliberately leaves out the second part of the verse, "but woe to that man who betrays him." Endō does not consider Judas' betrayal to be any more than the betrayal of the other disciples when Jesus was arrested (1973a: 177). On the contrary, Endō believes that by trying to return the thirty pieces of silver, Judas was expressing his faith in Jesus, and that when Jesus was sentenced to death, he felt too that

7. "The Son of Man did not come to be served, but to serve, and to give his life as a ransom for many" (Mk. 10:45). (Endō, 1978: 30-31)[47]

Endō claims that many scholars do not believe that these sayings were original to Jesus, but were made up by the disciples (1978: 31). For Endō, even if these sayings were not uttered by Jesus directly, they nonetheless express the very purpose of his life and ministry as his disciples understood it after his death (Endō, 1978: 31). More than anything else, these seven sayings about the Son of Man constitute the foundation of the Church which had already begun to come into being on the eve of the Resurrection. In other words, "even before the actual event of the Resurrection, the resurrection of Christ had already begun in the hearts of the disciples" (Endō, 1978: 22).

The resurrection of Christ is more than a cognitive experience for the disciples. Even as they began to understand the true significance of Jesus' earthly life, they would also come to experience his incarnational companionship in their hearts. This is borne out in the touching episode of the two disciples' encounter with the risen Christ on the Emmaus road. While not denying that these two might have actually met the risen Christ, Endō attaches far greater significance to their psychological state:

> Before the disciples knew what had happened, I am sure, the vivid feeling was born in them that Jesus, though he had died, was still very close to them. It was for them no act of abstract meditation; it was a non-metaphorical, tangible realization. Jesus wasn't dead. What is more, they came to sense that Jesus actually spoke to them. (Endo, 1978 [1973]: 174 = Endō, 1973a: 246)

In a word, the disciples were experiencing the birth of Christ in their hearts as their eternal companion.

The encounter with the risen Christ on the Emmaus road therefore becomes the archetypal experience of Christ's companionship for all of his followers. As with the first disciples, so it is in the hearts of all believers that the suffering Jesus is reborn as Christ the eternal companion. Elizabeth Willis observes that this is indeed the experience of Rodrigues in *Silence*, not only during the time of his apostasy but also later in his conversation with Jesus about Judas the betrayer: "It is the vivid reality of this presence which makes the meaning of

---

he had to die (Endō, 1973a: 177). Although betrayed by Judas, the condemnation of Jesus was only for the moment; in case of Judas, however, betrayed by Caiaphas, he suffered condemnation down through history (Endō, 1973a: 177). Endō writes, "Jesus understood the suffering of Judas. Even on the man who betrayed him, Jesus poured out his love" (Endō, 1973a: 177).

[47] Contrary to Endō's conjecture, the Gospel records show that the disciples did not come to any new understanding of Christ on the eve of his resurrection. Even after the Resurrection, it took a while for them to believe him and understand his mission (see Mk. 16:14; Lk. 24:36-49; Jn. 20:19-21:23).

Christ's past suffering on the cross so powerfully relevant to Rodriguez' predicament, transforming his faith" (1992: 99).

Interestingly too, Endō gives a personal example of his belief that Christ lived in his mother's heart when she was alive. Endō is certain that it was Christ who, through her mother's life, led him to become a Christian (1983: 80-81). The life of Christ in his mother as Endō understands it is the true meaning of the resurrection of Christ (Endō, 1983: 81).

The Working Power of the Holy Spirit

Endō is largely silent on the Holy Spirit in his writings, supposing it to be a subject "difficult for Japanese people to understand" (1983: 175). Instead of the person of the Holy Spirit, Endō prefers to talk about the working of the Spirit (*Seirei no hataraki* 聖霊の働き) (Endō, 1983: 176-77). It was this working of the Holy Spirit, explains Endō, that has empowered him and sustained his faith through the various trials he has encountered thus far in his Christian life (Endō, 1983: 176). In retrospect, Endō recognizes "the presence of an invisible power" (*me ni mienai aru chikara* 目に見えないある力) which provided the driving force for his literature, and identifies this invisible power as the working of the Spirit (Endō, 1983: 176). He even attributes the circumstances surrounding his illness over a three-year period in the early 1960s to the invisible working of the Holy Spirit, for he is convinced that had he not been taken seriously ill for such a long time, he would not have written *Silence*.

In addition, Endō argues that while the working of the Spirit is of the "same essence" (*honshitsu* 本質) in all instances, the shape (*katachi* 形) of its manifestation is different for each person.[48] Endō elaborates, "In the case of the apostles, the working of the Spirit brought about in them an awakened understanding of Jesus; in the case of Paul, the working of Spirit enabled him to transcend the law and receive Christ into his own life" (Endō, 1983: 177).[49] Curiously, he then gives the example of the power of the Buddha (*hotoke no chikara* 仏の力) derived from the embodiment of the dharma by a bodhisattva as a parallel to the working of the Spirit (Endō, 1983: 177). Just as a Buddhist experiences the power of the Buddha and is changed by it, so similarly the Christian experiences the working power of the Spirit and is transformed by it

---

[48] Endō does not, however, elaborate on what this "essence" might be other than describing it vaguely as an "invisible power" (1983: 176).

[49] In this passage, Endō uses the ordinary, intransitive verb *mesameru* 目覚める to describe the awakening of the disciples to the truth about Jesus. Elsewhere, he uses another intransitive verb *satoru* 悟る to describe the same experience (Endō, 1973a: 243; 1978: 20). This is also a common word, but can also be used to describe the Buddhist experience of enlightenment. Indeed, the noun *satori* 悟り means enlightenment in the religious, often Buddhist, sense. However, it is highly debatable whether Endō regards the disciples' awakening as similar to the enlightenment of the Buddha.

(Endō, 1983: 177). Beyond this, Endō has nothing more to say about the Holy Spirit.

It is clear that Endō makes a distinction between the working power of the Holy Spirit and the eternal companionship of Christ. It is through the former that the latter is experienced. The concept of the personal, indwelling Spirit of Christ in the believer is absent in Endō's pneumatology.

The Origins of the Church

A crucial point needs to be made about the formation of the Church. Other than the first two chapters which deal respectively with the death of Christ and the night before the Resurrection, the rest of *The Birth of Christ* is really an account of the beginnings of the Church based on the narratives of the Acts of the Apostles and church tradition. It is clear that for Endō, the birth of Christ is coterminous with the birth of the Church, the gathering of all believers in whose hearts is the common, eternal companionship of Christ. The early Church was characterized by intense persecutions under the Roman authorities, resulting in violent deaths, including the execution of James, Peter and Paul. According to Endō, through these persecutions, the Church encountered "a silent God", and as a result longed for the "the return of Christ" to restore Jerusalem as the city of God (Ps. 122:26-27) (1978: 231). However, God never seemed to break his silence, and Christ did not return as he had said that he would. For the early Christians, both the silence of God and the eschatological hope in Christ's return became another *nazo* (riddle), and they have remained so for all subsequent believers. A couple of observations can be made at this point. It is clear that Endō interprets the silence of God as the common felt experience of all believers who undergo prolonged and unrelieved suffering. One could say that Endō is perhaps overly presumptuous here. That notwithstanding, his concept of divine silence does raise real tensions in his thought, for he posits at the same time the eternal companionship of Christ in the hearts of all who suffer.

These tensions do not seem to bother Endō, however. The point he wants to make is that instead of giving in to an abject despondency, the suffering Church found the needed energy for her faith to grow in the dual mystery of the silence of God and the promised return of Christ, a faith sustained by the eternal companionship of Christ (Endō, 1978: 232). That energy fueled the passion of the early Christians to preach the gospel wherever they went. Matsuoka Fumitaka puts it this way,

> Endo's response to this question [of the silence of God] is the eschatological expectation of the coming of the triumphant Christ. God's silence meant hope and not "nihil." *Maranatha* was for the disciples the longing of a child for the mother who died. Thus the apostolic church was born out of the disciples' determination to face their own self-defeat squarely in the face of their rediscovery of the meaning of the person of Jesus. It was born out of their conviction that Jesus will return as the one who accompanies them in their struggle with the heavy burdens of guilt and

shame over their betrayal. Jesus is transformed into the Christ who is their eternal
companion in their inevitable sufferings and despair. (1982: 297)

With the establishment of the Church, the birth of Christ from the death of
Jesus is now complete. Endō cites Peter's declaration in Acts 2:36 to substantiate
his case: "God has made this Jesus, whom you crucified, both Lord and Christ"
(1978: 242). People of every age since, in their need for love, have constantly
sought an *eien no dōhansha* (eternal companion) (Endō, 1978: 250). Therefore,
despite the many sins committed by so-called Christians in the history of the
Church, the Christ of faith continues to be born afresh in the hearts of men and
women everywhere even today (Endō, 1978: 251; Endō, 1994: 350-51).

The Hermeneutical Key to Understanding Endō: Fact and Truth

One may rightly ask how Endō could cognitively maintain such an enduring
distance from the physical resurrection of Christ, especially since he does not
deny it, and focuses rather on its spiritual meaning instead. The key to
understanding this lies in the determined distinction that he makes between fact
(*jijitsu* 事実) and truth (*shinjitsu*真実) (e.g. Endō, 1973a: 52-54, 253-54). The
former is historical, but the latter transcends history. Using the example of the
Nativity, Endō remarks, "As all mankind has craved for the reality of Bethlehem,
so also did the authors of the New Testament crave it. The birth of Jesus in
Bethlehem may not have been a fact for them, but it was truth for their souls"
(Endo, 1978 [1973]: 179 = Endō, 1973a: 154). In other words, something can be
universally true even if it is not historically factual, for "the human condition is
not to be circumscribed by tangible facts" (Endō, 1973a: 154).[50] This radical
dichotomy between fact and truth is highly debatable, for it seems to imply that
truth can be conveyed through, even perhaps based on, a falsity. However, this
explains Endō's insistence that there is no need to accept the factuality of the
miracles as recorded in the Gospels – even of the Resurrection – in order to
appreciate the truth that they are intended to convey, namely, the truth about the
kingdom of God as "a universe of love based on the presence of a companion to
all mankind" (Endo, 1978 [1973]: 87 = Endō, 1973a: 121). On the contrary,
accepting these as facts may cause the truth to be obscured, even missed

---

[50] Endō, however, does not go as far as some who insist that truth can only be universal
if it is absolutely free from any historical conditioning. See, for instance, Book IV of
Immanuel Kant's *Religion within the Limits of Reason Alone* (1960 [1793]: 139-190),
where a "pure" religious faith predicated on a dehistoricized knowledge of God
becomes all but reduced to a universal moral code. See also Vinoth Ramachandra's
critique of Raimundo Panikkar's vision of an ahistorical transcendental mystery
(Ramachandra, 1996: 76-108).

completely. In sum, what finally matters is not the *fact* (*jijitsu*) of Jesus, but the *truth* (*shinjitsu*) of his life, death, and resurrection.[51]

In an essay published in 1980, entitled *Watakushi no bungaku to seisho* 私の文学と聖書 ("My Literature and the Bible"), Endō elaborates the distinction between fact and truth in literature:

> I have no intention of writing down facts (*jijitsu*). If I did, the result would no longer be a novel. Rather, to write a novel is to record truths (*shinjitsu*), not facts. Thus, having examined those around me, I analyse them [...] and gradually the character germinates [...]. The art of creating a novel is to use "truths" to reconstruct "facts": *real "facts" themselves are totally unimportant to the novelist.* (cited in Williams, 1999: 20, emphasis added)[52]

Endō's point is well taken, insofar as it is kept within the parameters of the novel. However, *A Life of Jesus* is not a novel, although one might argue that it is written with the genre style of the novel. When it comes to the Christian faith where divine revelation is historically mediated, the methodological validity of separating the kernel of truth from its husks of fact must be seriously questioned. Besides the ontological relationship between fact and truth which needs to be closely examined, the ethical issues involved in willfully separating the two have to be addressed as well.[53]

In any case, Endō's hermeneutical approach to reality sheds light on his tenacious belief that as the events of the first century recede from view, the Jesus of history must give way to the Christ of faith. Indeed, claims Endō, even in the conversion narrative of the apostle Paul, it is clear that the person Paul encountered on the Damascus road was the Christ of faith, not the Jesus of history whom he had never met (1978: 152). This again is highly questionable as

---

[51] Takayanagi Shun'ichi (1979: 612) correctly points out the choice of *jijitsu* 事実 and *shinjitsu* 真実 is intended to create a pun. The common word for truth is *shinri* 真理. The word *shinjitsu* is better translated as "truthfulness" or "faithfulness," and is used, for example in Romans 3:4 to describe God. Perhaps Endō is saying that while the New Testament traditions surrounding Jesus' life may not be *jijitsu*, they are *shinjitsu* in the sense of being a "symbol of God's faithfulness to humankind in the reality of Jesus" (Takayanagi, 1979: 613).

[52] This problem is, of course, not unique to Endō, but a central issue in literature. As Williams rightly points out, Endō's concern recalls the debate in the late nineteenth century between Mori Ōgai and Tsubouchi Shōyō on the distinction between "actuality" and "reality" in literary writings (1999: 20).

[53] This is one of the criticisms brought up against the movie *End of the Spear* (2006), based on the true story of the killing of five North American missionaries by a group of Waodani men in Ecuador in 1956. The question raised is this: In the name of conveying truth, how far is one allowed to change historical facts in the telling of a story? See Kathryn Long, "More Than Meets the Eye: An Historical Perspective on 'The End of the Spear'," presented at the Annual Meeting of the North Central Region of the Evangelical Missiological Society, Trinity Evangelical Divinity School, Deerfield, IL: 2006.

it is not clear if Paul ever made that distinction. After he was struck blind and fell to the ground, then Saul asked "Who are you, Lord?" To which the Lord replied, "I am Jesus, whom you are persecuting." Even more so than the Emmaus road narrative, Paul's encounter with Jesus is presented in a way which is completely grounded in real, historical circumstances. Indeed, Jesus did not even use his title Christ when identifying himself to Paul.

Nevertheless, Endō's marked distinction between fact and truth causes him to insist that like Paul, we should not to be fixated with the Jesus of history but experience the Christ of faith in our hearts. This point has already been well labored. Perhaps at this juncture, the words of Takahashi Takako, a fellow Catholic novelist of Endō's, would provide a fitting summary of what Endō considers to be "this most essential point":

> When I visited a certain convent, a sister said that she did not believe in a Christ who lived two thousand years ago, but that she believed in the risen Christ. I gasped and had the impression that now I had understood everything. Christ, not as a man, but whose presence as a man has come to an end, lives on another level which embraces the level of reality in which we live. (cited in Endō, 1977: 210)

Kitamori's Critique of Endō

In 1991, Kitamori published a book entitled, *Ureinaki kami: Seisho to bungaku* 愁いなき神一聖書と文学 (*Weeping God: The Bible and Literature*). This book consists of eleven chapters, each devoted to a discussion of a literary figure. The first three chapters discuss Tolstoy, Dostoevsky, and the French writer André Gide, while the last eight each cover a Japanese novelist. The common theme running through all the chapters is that of suffering. In this book, Kitamori basically provides an analysis of the writings of each of these figures and compares the portrayal of suffering in their works with his own understanding of divine pathos. The last chapter of the book, *Ashi no itami no bungaku* 足の痛みの文学 ("Literature of the Pain of the Foot"), is a discussion of Endō.[54] The chapter title, an obvious allusion to the pain that Father Rodrigues feels as he lifts his foot to step on the *fumie* in the climactic scene of *Silence*, is not original to Kitamori, but an expression concocted by one of Kitamori's friends to suggest its apparent affinity with Kitamori's *Kami no itami no shingaku* 神の痛みの神学, since both deal with the subject of pain. The linguistic similarities between the two expressions, phonetically and graphically, are not lost on the Japanese reader.

---

[54] It is not clear if Kitamori and Endō ever met or spoke with each other. It would not be surprising if they did, especially since Endō participated as a Catholic representative in the Christian Pavilion at the 1970 Osaka World Expo. Kitamori was the chairman of the committee that organized the Christian Pavilion. However, other than the critique of Endō in Kitamori's book, there is no record of any interaction between the two men.

For Kitamori, however, the similarities between Endō's *Ashi no itami no shingaku* and his *Kami no itami no shingaku* end at the pun (1991: 304). First, he clarifies that the pain of God in his theology is the result of "God loving and forgiving humans who have *betrayed* him" (Kitamori, 1991: 306, emphasis added). As we have seen, the key hamartiological concept in Kitamori's formulation is the betrayal of God's love by humans, for without this, it is impossible to understand the meaning of the pain of God. For Kitamori, the betrayal of God is an act of treason of the highest order, which can only arouse the wrath of God (Kitamori, 1991: 306). However, God still chooses to love and forgive sinners, the very ones who have betrayed him. This is no easy love, for in the process of it overcoming wrath, pain is necessarily generated (Kitamori, 1991: 306). Put another way, the pain of God is the "intertwining" (*karamiai* 絡 み合い) of God's love and his wrath caused by his betrayal at the hands of those he loves (Kitamori, 1991: 306). Turning his attention to the episode of Father Rodrigues' act of apostasy in *Silence*, Kitamori points out that, while on the surface the act of stepping on the *fumie* appears to be an act of betraying God, it actually is *not* since it is Christ who spoke from the *fumie* and encourages Rodrigues to step on it (Kitamori, 1991: 306-307).

Kitamori cites Romans 5:6 and 5:10 to further his argument (Kitamori, 1991: 308). He points out that in the first verse, Paul emphasizes that "while we were still *powerless*, Christ died for the ungodly" (emphasis added). In the second, the emphasis shifts to the fact that it was "when we were God's *enemies* [that] we were reconciled to him through the death of his Son" (emphasis added). Kitamori then makes the point that all humanity is simultaneously powerless and at enmity with God (Kitamori, 1991: 308). It is such humanity that Christ died for. Indeed, it is because of sinful humanity that Christ died. Kitamori notes that this dual theological identity of the human race is absent in Endō's literature (Kitamori, 1991: 309). Endō's focus is only on the weak and the powerless, the subjects of God's compassion and empathy. In so doing, Endō ignores the biblical fact that humans are *also* enemies and betrayers of God, and so does not view humans as the subject of God's wrath (Kitamori, 1991: 309).

Since humans in Endō's theological anthropology are understood as weaklings and not as God's enemies, their existential problem becomes understood as that of suffering and not sin. In other words, the principal tenet of Endō's anthropology is that of suffering humanity, not sinful humanity. Hence, in Endō's reckoning, Christ chose to suffer the cruelest form of death in order to be able to identify with and share in all the sufferings of all humanity (Kitamori, 1991: 329; cf. Endō, 1973a: 283). In this respect, it appears that Endō's thought is heavily colored by Buddhism, perhaps more than he cares to admit. In any case, the idea of Christ dying for the sins of humanity is absent in Endō. Kitamori puts it this way, "[In Endo] there is only the Christ who bore together with humanity their powerlessness, anguish, and suffering; the Christ who bore sin's judgment and divine wrath, humanity's just deserts, has completely vanished" (1991: 330). In Kitamori's assessment, and rightly so, Endō's understanding of the death of Christ is therefore defective because incomplete (Kitamori, 1991: 327-28).

Kitamori insists that the enmity between a holy God and sinful humanity is an essential factor that must be recovered in understanding the true significance of the Cross. Such an enmity cannot be resolved by divine compassion and empathy alone (Kitamori, 1991: 309). This is why the cross of Christ cannot be understood apart from God's love *and* God's wrath. For, on the cross, not only was divine love supremely displayed, but also divine wrath. Furthermore, it was on the cross, stresses Kitamori, that Christ bore fully the wrath of God, "the curse of God," so that humanity – powerless and at enmity with God – could be saved from it (Kitamori, 1991: 309).

Kitamori speculates that Endō's weak understanding of sin is likely inherited from Ruth Benedict's classic work *The Chrysanthemum and the Sword*, published in 1946, the same year that Kitamori's *Theology of the Pain of God* was released (Kitamori, 1991: 315-18). The Japanese translation of Benedict's book came out in 1948, and it aroused huge public interest. In any case, Kitamori charges Benedict with essentializing Japanese moral consciousness in terms of shame as opposed to guilt, and believes that Endō picked this up when he wrote *The Sea and Poison* (cf. Benedict, 1946: 222-27). Even though Endō does allude to sin as moral failure in his works such as *The Sea and Poison* and *Scandal*, he seems to think that his countrymen and women understand sin not in terms of the guilt that results from moral failure, but experientially through a vague but heavy sense of emotional fatigue (cf. Mathy, 1974: 214; Durfee, 1989: 49; Kitamori, 1991: 316-17). This sense of fatigue may never be fully extirpated; rather it is through the suffering that results from struggling with constant fatigue that existential meaning is derived. In any case, the connection that Kitamori makes between Benedict and Endō is certainly an interesting one – not verifiable but nonetheless plausible.[55] If Kitamori's hypothesis is indeed true, then one could surmise that the mudswamp in *Yellow Person* and *Silence* is not so much a cultural reality as it is a creation by Endō, imbued with his own understanding of God, sin, and death.

Without a biblical understanding of sin, there can be no concept of divine wrath. Hence, one may also say that Endō's God has no wrath. As in the case of the Buddha, Kitamori would argue that a god without wrath is a god who cannot experience pain *in and by himself* (cf. Kitamori, 1986: 37). Endō's God may indeed, in the name of love, presume to share in the pain of suffering men and women, and even experience *their* pain. But in the final analysis, he cannot know the pain of being betrayed – unlike Kitamori's God. The reason is that Endō's God has no ontological capacity to experience pain, only love.[56] One may, in

---

[55] It is extremely unlikely that Endō had not read the book given its popularity.
[56] One could further argue that in Kitamori's theology, the ontological relationship that exists between God and his creation means that when humans, created in the image of God, betray his love, God, without compromising his freedom, *necessarily* feels the pain

rebuttal, say that Christ did suffer pain in his Passion. That is certainly true, Kitamori would reply, but without divine wrath, the pain that Christ suffered is nothing more than a "sentimentalized pain" (1991: 339).

In sum, there is no divine pain in Endō, only human pain which God or Christ can experience only by partaking in it. This is evidently borne out in the two scenes of Rodrigues' apostasy in *Silence*.[57] In both scenes, the word "pain" appears eleven times altogether in the Japanese text – twice as an adjective (*itai* 痛い), three times as a verb (*itamu* 痛む and its grammatical conjugations), and the other six times as a noun (*itami* 痛み, or *itasa* 痛さ) (1966: 218-19, 240). It is noteworthy that ten out of these eleven instances refer to Rodrigues' emotional duress, the pain of those who step on the *fumie*, or the pain of suffering humanity. The eleventh instance refers to the pain that Judas felt in his heart when he betrayed Christ (Endō, 1966: 240). In other words, none of these words refers to the inherent pain of Christ or of God. The words of Christ from the *fumie* in the first scene are instructive: "You may trample on me. More than anyone else I know *the pain in your foot*. It was to be trampled on by you [plural] that I was born in into this world. It is *to share your [plural] pain* that I bore the cross" (Endō, 1966: 219, emphasis added).

According to Kitamori, because Endō accepts only the reality of divine love and rejects even the slightest possibility of divine wrath, he deliberately uses his writings to convert Christianity from a father-religion to a mother-religion (Kitamori, 1991: 335). However, for Kitamori, *both* paternal wrath and maternal love are evident on the Cross (Kitamori, 1991: 337).

As we have seen above, Kitamori is convinced that Endō's understanding of God is "strongly influenced by his personal experiences" (1991: 335). Richard Schuchert, the translator of *A Life of Jesus*, shares Kitamori's view, suggesting that Endō's belief that unless Christianity is changed, it cannot take root in Japanese soil, is really "an extrapolation of [Endō's] own interior conflict" (1978: 3).

Finally, Kitamori makes a comment on Endō's methodology which is worth pondering. He warns that unless the Bible is allowed to shed its light on literature, rather than allowing literature to define its message, we will end up, like Endō, misconstruing what the Bible is really saying (Kitamori, 1991:

---

of betrayal, just like the father in the Parable of the Prodigal Son in Luke 15:11-32. In contrast, there is no theology of creation underlying Endō's thought; consequently, the relationship between God and humans seems to be an arbitrary one, perhaps like the relationship between the Buddha and the rest of humanity as well. There is hence no possibility of any betrayal. God, like the Buddha then, is not compelled to experience pain as a result of human misbehavior.

[57] There are two scenes relating to Rodrigues' apostasy. The first scene is the actual scene of the apostasy (Endō, 1966: 218-19). The second scene takes place toward the end of the book (Endō, 1966: 240). Here, as he hears the confession of Kichijirō, Rodrigues plays back in his mind the vivid event of his apostasy and even carries on an extended conversation with Christ.

338-39). Kitamori's comment is relevant in the light of Endō's adamant insistence that there is no necessary connection between facts and truth. Endō would argue that the art of the novel lies in the author's skill in reconstructing historical "facts" from timeless truths, or to illustrate them (Williams, 1999: 20). The question that presents itself is whether it is methodologically valid to impose the literary framework and assumptions of the novel onto theology and biblical studies.

The Many Faces of God

Toward the end of his life, Endō became decidedly pluralist in his religious orientation. In this section, it is appropriate to take a brief look at his so-called ultimate religious vision. The two sources that yield the most helpful information on Endō's final thoughts on religion, and on Christ in particular, are his last novel *Deep River* and the journal in which he recorded the writing process and progress of *Deep River* from August 1990 to May 1993. The writing journal was published posthumously in 1997, and again in 2000.[58]

In a 1994 interview with the Jesuit William Johnston, Endō expresses his deep interest in inter-religious dialogue, especially the dialogue between Christianity and Buddhism (Johnston, 1994: 18).[59] Endō believes that "Buddhism and Christianity have in common the belief that what Buddhists call the Great Source of Life and what we call the Holy Spirit dwells within us and surrounds us" (Johnston, 1994: 19). At the same time, he acknowledges that there are "vast differences" between the two religions (Johnston, 1994: 18). In this regard, Endō finds the theme of love to be the most irreconcilable point of contention. Buddhism teaches that love is a form of attachment that needs to be removed along with all other attachments, while the central message of Christianity is love (Johnston, 1994: 18).[60] Nonetheless, Endō feels that Christianity, which emphasizes the external relationship between God and humans, has a lot to learn from Buddhism in the area of self-knowledge or human consciousness (Johnston, 1994: 19). Moreover, since Buddhism has

---

[58] The 1997 edition of the journal is out of print. The 2000 edition includes not only Endō's writing journal, but also an essay by Katō Munenari entitled *Shūkyō no konpon ni aru mono* ("The Fundamentals of Religion"), a transcription of a conversation between Miura Shumon and Kawai Hayao in 1997 concerning the journal, a commentary by Kisaki Satoko, and a chronology of Endō's life. It is this later edition that is referred to in this dissertation, and is referenced as Endō 2000b.

[59] *Deep River* and its English translation were both published in 1994. In the novel, Ōtsu, a devoted follower of Christ, sends a letter to Mitsuko in which he writes, "We live in a time when we must hold dialogue with other religions" (Endo, 1994 [1994]: 122).

[60] Since Endō radicalizes love as the supreme need of humankind, and *the* hallmark of Jesus' life and ministry, naturally he will not be able to accept the Buddhist attitude toward love (cf. Johnston, 1994: 18).

become so entrenched in Japanese culture, shaping it and being shaped by it, both Johnston and Endō are agreed that "there can be no inculturation of Christianity in Japan without dialogue with Buddhism" (Johnston, 1994: 19).

The vastly different beliefs and practices in the various religions notwithstanding, around the time he started writing *Deep River*, Endō had arrived at a position where he readily subscribed to John Hick's idea that the Ultimate Reality behind the religions is the same. The "central question" for Endō is: How does one address this Ultimate Reality? He asks, "Do we call it the Christ or the Buddha?" (Johnston, 1994: 20). The nature and naming of the Ultimate Reality is further explored in *Deep River*.

Endō's journal entry dated Thursday September 5, 1991 is extremely revealing of the decisive influence exerted by Hick on Endō's *Deep River*:

A few days ago, I was on the second floor of Taiseido Bookstore when I happened by chance to see [John Hick's] *Shūkyō tagen shugi* (*Problems of Religious Pluralism*) at the corner of the bookshelf. It seemed to have been left there by a store clerk or a customer, and forgotten. But more than a mere accident, it was as if my subconscious had summoned it. Since my encounter with Jung, which was quite a while ago, I had not had the same feeling of being stirred up in my heart until I read this book. Hick is a Christian theologian, but he believes that the different world religions are in fact seeking the same God, only through different paths, cultures, and symbols. He also criticizes Christianity for maintaining the tendency of subsuming the other religions within itself while at the same time claiming to dialogue with them following Vatican II. He also makes the daring claim that true religious pluralism has no place for a theology that proclaims Jesus as the Christ. In other words, the problems of Jesus' incarnation and the Trinity should be subject to the surgeon's knife. Since two days ago, I have been overwhelmed by this shocking book. And then so it happened that a staff member from Iwanami Publishing Company visited me and gave me the same author's *Kami wa ōku no na o motsu* (*God Has Many Names*). Now I am absorbed in reading the book. (Endō, 2000b: 23-24)[61]

Endō is clearly enthralled by the fact that the idea of religious pluralism could be espoused by a Western Christian who is not only his contemporary but a distinguished scholar.[62] As intimated earlier, Endō had actually asserted the validity of all religions as early as 1976. However, until his encounter with Hick, he apparently supposed that such a view was a distinctly non-Western view. Indeed, Endō's view of religion, which Morimoto refers to as "[a] Japanese reverberation of Hick's pluralism" (2003: 163), represents quite accurately the general attitude taken by many Japanese.

---

[61] The Japanese translation of Hick's *Problems of Religious Pluralism* is published in 1990, and that of *God Has Many Names* in 1986.

[62] Hick was only a year older than Endō.

> There are many ways to climb Mount Fuji. You can approach the ascent from the
> north, south, east, or west [...]. In the same way, if one person lives sincerely as a
> Buddhist, and another lives sincerely as a Christian, in the end they will both arrive
> at the same truth. In other words, they may travel on different roads, but I think they
> will reach the same destination. (Endō, 1976: 236)

Endō's religious relativity becomes fully articulated in *Deep River*, primarily
through Ōtsu who, on the one hand is branded as a heretic by the church, and on
the other finds it impossible to renounce his Catholic faith inherited from his
mother. There is no doubt that throughout the novel Ōtsu acts as Endō's
mouthpiece on matters of religious conviction. Concerning the religions, Ōtsu is
said to be "fond of these words" of Mahatma Gandhi:

> There are many religions, but they are merely various paths leading to the same
> place. What difference does it make which of those separate paths we walk, as long
> as they all arrive at the identical destination? (Endo, 1994 [1994]: 191)

Why then, one might ask, did Endō become a Christian, and not, say, a
Buddhist? Endō provides this reply, "The answer is simple. I happened to find
myself in the world of Christianity, not of any other religion" (1976: 236,
emphasis added).[63] As we have seen from the account of Endō's baptism, his
conversion to Catholicism was the result of circumstance rather than choice.
Again, we find Endō expressing the circumstantial nature of his inherited faith
through Ōtsu in *Deep River*, in which the latter tells the rector of his seminary
that it is only "natural" for him to be a Christian since he has been raised in a
Christian family, and that it would therefore not be right for him to revert to
being a Buddhist since he has never been one in the first place (Endō, 1994: 198).
But this does not mean that his faith is not a genuine one. Ōtsu also affirms that
another person being born and raised in a non-Christian family and naturally
becoming a believer of that family's religion is but a different manifestation of
divine grace (Endō, 1994: 195). Endō's conversion experience, as reflected in
Ōtsu's, is truly indicative of the tendency of many Japanese people to view
religion as a family matter and not merely a personal one.

This, of course, does not mean that one is not free to convert to another
religion. Endō, once again through his mirror character Ōtsu, likens conversion
to choosing a marriage partner (Endō, 1994: 195; Endō, 1983: 209). Although
Endō has never been able to give up his Christian faith, try as he might, he offers
this advice to the person seeking religious truth and fulfillment, "Why don't you
try one religion after another – Buddhism, Christianity, Islam – and then decide
which best suits your disposition and circumstances?" (Endō, 1994: 195).
Conflicting truth claims between the religions does not seem to be an issue for

---

[63] This is a point that John Hick makes as well. For a helpful account of Hick's
pluralism, see Netland (2001: 158-72).

Endō at all. This is, of course, hardly surprising given Endō's views on "fact" and "truth".

It is evident that while Endō started out seeking to present Christianity in a way that is culturally intelligible to his fellow countrymen and women, he gradually developed a religious vision which is pluralist and syncretistic. Three years after the publication of *The Samurai*, Endō wrote *What God Is to Me*, in which perhaps for the first time he moves beyond the mother imagery and describes God as an abstract, all-pervasive, unnamed force which one could arbitrarily choose to call X, or even "Onion" (*tamanegi*) (1983: 208). This theme is picked up in *Deep River* in the conversation between Ōtsu and his former college mate, the cynical Mitsuko, who cannot relate to the word *kami* 神 (God).

> "Sorry. If you don't like that word [*kami*], we can change it to another name. We can call him Tomato, or even Onion if you prefer."
>
> "All right, then, just what is this Onion to you? You said at school that you really didn't understand him very well when someone asked you whether God existed."
>
> "Sorry. To be honest, at that time I really didn't know. But now in my own way I do."
>
> "Tell me."
>
> "God is not so much an existence as a force. This Onion is an entity that performs the labours of love."
>
> "That's even more repulsive. How can you use unsettling words as 'love' with a straight face? And what do you mean by 'labours'?"
>
> "Well, for instance, the Onion found me abandoned in one place, and at some time he gave me life in a completely different location."
>
> Mitsuko chortled. "That hasn't got anything to do with the power of your Onion. Your feelings just sent you off in that direction."
>
> "No, that's not true. It was the work of the Onion transcending my own will." For the first time Ōtsu spoke decisively [...] (Endo, 1994 [1994]: 63-64)

Elsewhere in the novel, Jesus is identified with the Onion. Note this autobiographical sketch of Endō in the following letter that Ōtsu wrote to the spiritually-restless Mitsuko:

> My mother told me all about the person you call my Onion, and she taught me that this Onion was a vastly more powerful accumulation of this warmth – in other words, love itself. I lost my mother when I got older, and I realized then that what lay at the source of my mother's warmth was a portion of the love of my Onion. Ultimately what I have sought is nothing more than the love of that Onion, not any of the other innumerable doctrines mouthed by the various churches [...]
>
> My trust is in the life of the Onion, who endured genuine torment for the sake of love, who exhibited love on our behalf [...]. [W]hen I suffer alone, I can feel the

smiling presence of my Onion, who knows all my trials. And just as he told the travelers on the road to Emmaus when he walked beside them, he has said to me, "Come, follow me." (Endo, 1994 [1994]: 119)

At other times, the concept of the Onion-God borders on pantheism: "I don't think God is someone to be looked up to as a being separate from man [...] I think he is within man, and that he is a great life force that envelops man, envelops the trees, envelops the flowers and grasses" (Endo, 1994 [1994]: 118). In the same letter, Ōtsu encourages Mitsuko with these words, "But just as my Onion is always beside me, he is always within you and beside you, too. He is the only one who can understand your pain and your loneliness" (Endo, 1994 [1994]: 120).

Endō's move toward an increasingly syncretistic faith seems to have received a propulsive force after his numerous visits to India in the late 1980s and 1990s (Williams, 1999: 192). He was deeply impressed by the crowds of people, each carrying their own individual burdens, daily thronging to bathe, even die, in the Ganges River. These were people whose Hindu spirituality he could not doubt as inauthentic. At the holy city of Vārānasī, located at the confluence of the Ganges and the Yamunā rivers, Endō "detected a location rich in symbolism, an echo of the collective unconscious in which the lives of all mankind, regardless of background and life experiences, can be seen brought together into the flow of the great river" (Williams, 1999: 192). In India, Endō discovered the existence of another spiritual world which is different from any with which he was familiar. It was a world no less real; indeed it appealed deeply to his deepest religious sensibilities (Williams, 1999: 193).

It is interesting that despite his pluralist mindset, Endō's commitment to Jesus, albeit the Jesus of his own imagination, remains strong. William Johnston recalls hearing a Catholic priest in the United States saying that "the interesting thing about Endō is that he is fascinated with the person of Christ. He is always talking about Christ, struggling with Christ, trying to understand Christ, experiencing the presence of Christ" (1994: 18). Endō's response is that a Christian engaging in inter-religious dialogue must not flinch from "a firm commitment to Christ," for otherwise "something fundamental might be lost" (Johnston, 1994: 19). Evidently, the death of Jesus and the eternal companionship of Christ continue to be existentially significant for Endō, as seen in this testimony by Ōtsu:

When the Onion was killed [...] the disciples who remained finally understood his love and what it meant. Every one of them had stayed alive by abandoning him and running away. He continued to love them even though they had betrayed him. As a result, he was etched into each of their guilty hearts, and they were never able to forget him. The disciples set out for distant lands to tell others the story of his life

[…]. After that, he continued to live in the hearts of his disciples. He died, but he was restored to life in their hearts. (Endo, 1994 [1994]: 184-85)[64]

Williams describes this passage as providing "the most concerted attempt in Endō's entire corpus to encapsulate the essence of the *dōhansha* [i.e. companion]" (1999: 208). It is ironic that this unequivocal affirmation of Christ's abiding companionship should be found in the murky waters of *Deep River*. Obviously for Endō, Christological exclusivism is not a theological criterion at all for the appropriation of Christ's universal presence. In this regard, Harold Netland rightly observes that Endō's pluralist theology approximates the theocentric Christology of the Catholic scholar Paul Knitter, rather than Hick's reality-centered pluralism (personal communication). While Knitter agrees with Hick that the idea of Christological uniqueness in the sense of Christ being the *only* way to God "violates not only Christian revelation but [also] the revelation found in other faiths" (1985: 175), he does not go all the way with Hick by jettisoning Christ altogether. Rather, Knitter believes that "a theocentric, non-normative reinterpretation of the uniqueness of Christ" is more helpful in the light of the competing truth claims from other religions (Knitter, 1985: 200). In other words, rather than insisting on a soteriological uniqueness for Christ – a key tenet in evangelical theology – Knitter proposes what he calls a "relational uniqueness" as a new way to understand the person and work of Christ (Knitter, 1985: 171).[65] Here, we can see echoes of Knitter in Endō's conviction that Christ is but one of the many faces of God, although there is no clear evidence that Endō read Knitter.

In summary, Endō, on the one hand, insists that unless one believes the existence of God in all religions, there is no possibility of real dialogue; on the other, he highly values the significance of Christ, especially his death and ensuing companionship. The key to Endō's ability to maintain this paradox is his belief that "God has many different faces," an expression which appears, in varying forms, no less than three times in *Deep River* (1994: 196, 198, 201). This expression is, in all probability, inspired by John Hick's book *God Has Many Names* (1986 [1982]).

In other words, Endō resolves the almost unbearable tension between his personal faith in Christ and his religious pluralism by asserting that the man crucified on the cross is but one of the many faces of God. Or conversely, one

[64] Two brief points need to be made here. Firstly, although there was the act of betrayal on the part of the disciples, it did not provoke wrath in the betrayed Jesus. Kitamori would then argue that no real pain was inflicted on Jesus. Secondly, the word that Endō used that is translated "guilty" in this passage is *ushirometai*, a common and non-theological word describing the feeling of being reproached by one's conscience.
[65] For Knitter's understanding of Jesus in the context of the theology of religions, see his *No Other Name? A Critical Survey of Christian Attitudes Toward the World Religions* (Maryknoll, NY: Orbis, 1985), as well as his *Jesus and the Other Names: Christian Mission and Global Responsibility* (Maryknoll, NY: Orbis, 1996).

may also say that he is the God with many faces. This same God also dwells among Jews and Muslims, presumably putting on a different face for the benefit of different people. Clearly Endō in his assertion goes beyond the inclusivism of his own Catholic church. Indeed, in *Deep River*, Ōtsu explicitly rejects Karl Rahner's notion that "noble people of other faiths [are] actually Christians driving without a licence" because it does not lead to "a dialogue among equals" (Endō, 1994: 198).

Given such a radical interpretation of God and of Jesus Christ, it is not a wonder that Endō should reject words such as "heresy" (*itan* 異端) or "pagans" (*ikyōto* 異教徒) as "meaningless" (1976: 236; cf. Uchida, 1991: 26). Endō criticizes Christians who use these words against people of different religious persuasion as lacking sensitivity and imagination, and worse, as committing the sin of arrogance (1976: 237). There is certainly a point in Endō's harsh comment, but taken too far, it would become a case of the pot calling the kettle black.

Endō's wife of forty-three years, Junko, has this to say of her late husband's last novel *Deep River*, "Endo arrived at a view in which he saw every human being entering a flow of the great life symbolized by the River Ganges. In his view human life transcends the small boundaries set by various religions and is resurrected in the flow of the great life" (1999: 148). Indeed, through the spiritual soliloquy of his alter ego, Mitsuko, Endō himself hints that after a lifetime of pursuing Christ, he has reached his ultimate religious vision:

> I believe that the river embraces these people and carries them away. A river of
> humanity. The sorrows of this deep river of humanity. And I am a part of it. (Endo,
> 1994 [1994]: 211)

It is most telling that, at his death, in accordance to his last wishes, a copy each of *Silence* and *Deep River* were placed with his body in the coffin.

Western Influences on Endō

In the penultimate section of this chapter, we will consider very briefly some Western influences on Endō's works. This subject is beyond the scope of this study, but is, of course, worthy of extensive research in itself. To begin, Endō's exposure to modern French literature – first in Keio through Satō Saku, and then in Lyons – constitutes a significant factor in the shaping of his literary ideas. In particular, the influences of three French Roman Catholic writers, François Mauriac, Julien Green, and Georges Bernanos, are particularly discernible in Endō's works.[66] Endō's *A Life of Jesus* seems to have been inspired by

---

[66] For an introduction to these authors, see their most famous award-winning works: Mauriac's *Vipers' Tangle* (1932), translated by Gerard Hopkins (Chicago, IL: Loyola Press, 2005); Green's *The Dark Journey* (1929), translated by Vyvyan Holland (Dallas,

Mauriac's *Life of Jesus* (1936), if not in content then certainly in concept. Both works emphasize the suffering love of God in Christ. Also, the selfless and utterly devoted curate in Bernanos' *The Diary of a Country Priest* (1936) probably gave Endō his first inklings of what a Christ figure could look like in the twentieth century. Interestingly too, the religious struggles of Green as evidenced in his first conversion from Protestantism to Roman Catholicism in 1916, then to Buddhism shortly after, and then back to Catholicism in 1935, are in some way reflected in the tensions in Endō's uncomfortable identity as a Japanese Christian.

At the risk of over-simplification, the three French writers write on common themes relating to the unrelieved tensions and unresolved paradoxes of the spiritual life, and the struggle of the soul in search of salvation in the midst of spiritual darkness, within and without. At the same time, the vision of God and his provision of redemption through unexpected means and in unexpected places is never lost. In that sense, their works provide a bulwark against the spirit of naturalism that was characteristic of twentieth-century France. Although the principal theme in Endō's works is suffering, he deals with it by plumbing the depths of the human soul and shows the darkness therein. Redemption comes in Endō's works in unexpected ways, mainly through the encounter with a most unlikely person with an almost unnatural capacity to love. Unresolved tensions abound in Endō's novels as well. In the same way as his French predecessors, the religious themes in Endō's works provide a strong cultural alternative to the spirit of naturalism that infected Japan after the Second World War. It is not unreasonable to suppose that Endō's literary achievements have contributed to the usually rather large number of prominent writers in Japan who converted to Catholicism in their adult lives.

Endō's portrayal of the weak and suffering Christ is reminiscent of the paintings of the pathetically human Christ by the French Christian artist Georges Rouault (1871-1958). Rouault's many portrayals of the suffering – and sometimes clownish – Christ are a radical departure from those of earlier periods when the tendency was to convey a sense of divine dignity even in suffering. As William Dyrness (1971: 186) notes, "[In Rouault's art], Christ's presence is a presence of suffering in and with our sufferings". It is not clear if Endō had ever encountered these paintings, but it is highly conceivable that he did, especially given the fame and deep spiritual devotion of Rouault.

Endō readily acknowledges his indebtedness to Western precedent for many of his ideas (Williams, 1999: 248, f.n. 69). For example, the portrayal of some of his characters with multiple, divided selves – such as Suguro and Madame Naruse in *Scandal* – is derived, at least in part, from the precedent found in Graham Greene's character Francis Andrews in *The Man Within* (1929) and

---

TX: Texas Bookman, 1996); and Bernanos' *The Diary of a Country Priest* (1936), translated by Pamela Morris (New York: Carroll & Graf Publishers, 2002). Mauriac was awarded the Nobel Prize for Literature in 1952.

Dostoevsky's Golyadkin in *The Double* (1846) (Williams, 1999: 248, f.n. 69). Williams (1999: 179-88, 197-203) and Mase-Hasegawa (2004: 151-53) have also demonstrated the heavy influence of Jungian psychology in some of Endō's works, notably *Scandal* and *Deep River*.

Evaluative Summary

It must be remembered from the outset that Endō writes as a novelist and essayist rather than as an academic theologian. One must expect, therefore, that there are a number of theological loose ends in his thought that cannot be tied up neatly. Yet through his creative writing, one cannot help but recognize that Endō is indeed engaging in the task of doing contextual theology. The manner of his theologizing is neither discursive nor homiletic, but narrative, principally through the medium of the novel. Endō's perspective on the death of Christ is hence more accurately described as a literature of the Cross rather than a theology of the Cross.

Endō started out as a professed Catholic. For the most part of his life, he honestly struggled with the foreignness of his inherited faith. He did not believe that the Christian faith has to remain foreign, and so embarked on a lifework of constructing a cogent alternative to the prevailing image of the God of Western Christianity. Even though in the end he viewed Christianity as one of numerous equally legitimate paths to salvation – whatever the word "salvation" may mean – Endō had always believed in the possibility that Christianity could become a religion that the Japanese could identify as their very own. Like the protagonist Ōtsu in *Deep River*, Endō would spend a lifetime deconstructing traditional, Western Christianity, and recreating "a Christianity that fits the Japanese heart" (*Nihonjin no kokoro ni au kirisutokyō* 日本人の心にあう基督教) (Endō, 1994: 107).[67]

In contrast with Kitamori's focus on the pain of God, Endō's emphasis is on the suffering of humanity. Therefore, even though the common theme between Kitamori and Endō is pain, it is construed theocentrically for the former, and anthropocentrically for the latter. It is not a wonder then to find that Endō's Christology is fully circumscribed by the existential reality of human suffering. It is *completely* a Christology from below, with the kenotic principle applied to such an extreme that the Son of God is made to become a totally passive and ineffectual person in order that he might identify with all the suffering of humankind. In other words, the suffering of Christ is construed to mirror the suffering of humanity.

Indeed, Endō shares the view with Buddhism that the existential human problem is suffering, not sin. The ministry role of the Son of God becomes

---

[67] Endō also clarifies that it has never been his intention to use his writings as an evangelistic means to convert people to Christianity (1983: 203). He basically wants to present Christianity as one viable religious option, among several, for Japanese people.

defined as an empathetic participant in human suffering rather than the substitutionary bearer of human sin. Hence the reason why Jesus had to experience the most harrowing form of death then is not so that he can experience the full import of the wrath of God on behalf of humanity, but that he can truly share in the misery and pain of every human being. The death of Christ therefore has no saving efficacy in the traditional sense. That is, there is no atonement in Endō's theology of the cross. Undoubtedly the cross is the supreme manifestation of divine love, but it is not a love that redeems humans from their sin, but a love that identifies fully with humanity in their suffering. For on the cross, Jesus suffered not for us, but *like* us. In other words, the cross for Endō symbolizes identification but not redemption in the classical sense of being delivered from divine punishment. In fact, there is no punishment in the maternal religion which he has transformed Christianity into, because there is no divine wrath to speak of in the first place.

Indeed, the God of Endō has become radically domesticated such that not even sin can provoke him to anger. For Endō, love is the only divine identity. However, while it is true that the Bible teaches that "God is love" (1 John 4:16), it is quite a different thing from claiming that "love is God." One is reminded of C. S. Lewis' warning that "[l]ove, having become a god, becomes a demon" (1960: 83). In the case of Endō, the monism of divine love so characteristic of his literature ends up deconstructing the true meaning of the Cross.

Furthermore, when it comes to the Resurrection, Endō appropriates what he sees to be its true meaning not from its historicity – for that is irrelevant even if it is factually true – but from the idea that Jesus who paid the ultimate price of identification with humanity is now born into the hearts of men and women as Christ, their eternal companion. It is clear that Endō does not want personal Christian faith to rest on the triumph of Christ's resurrection, but on the suffering love of Jesus. Perhaps Endō believes that faith in the human and suffering Jesus, rather than the divine and victorious Christ, is more easily appropriated by the Japanese people. Colin Noble puts it this way,

> In refusing to desert those who betrayed his love, Endo's Jesus exhibited in death the comforting compassion which will perhaps appeal to the religious psyche of the Japanese. It is Endo's hope that the Japanese will, as he believes the disciples did, find in the love that transcends betrayal and death a Jesus in whom they will put their trust as an eternal companion. (1992: 10)

Yet, without Christ's powerful and decisive victory over sin and death, one can have all the love in the universe and still not make any sense of the pain and suffering to which Endō is so sensitive.

In conclusion, the two central themes underlying Endō's perspective on the death of Christ are Jesus' identification with human suffering, and the eternal companionship of Christ. These are important biblical themes, prone to be forgotten. In a very real sense, because of his suffering, Jesus is able to sympathize with every person who suffers (Heb. 4:14-5:10). It is curious that evangelical churches tend to "rush through" Good Friday in order to celebrate Easter Sunday. According to Marva Dawn, churches who consciously observe Good Friday tend to be more involved in mercy ministries than those who do not (personal communication). Moreover, the resurrection of Christ is more than a doctrine of orthodoxy; it is the experiential reality of his companionship mediated through the indwelling Spirit in the heart of the believer (cf. Mt. 28:20; 1 Cor. 6:19-20; Gal. 2:20).

However, these two themes of Jesus' suffering and Christ's companionship do not give us the whole meaning of the death of Christ. Indeed, in the canticle of the Suffering Servant, which Endō cites substantially both in *A Life of Jesus* (1973a: 113-15, 243) and *The Birth of Christ* (1978: 33-34), the Servant is portrayed not only as one who "took up our infirmities and carried our sorrows" (Is. 53:4), but also one who "was pierced for our transgressions, [and] crushed for our iniquities" (Is. 53:5). It is clear from Isaiah 53:10 that God caused Jesus to suffer so as to make him "a guilt offering" for the sin of humanity. This part of the verse, however, is left out in all three instances that Endō cites from the Song. The *principal* role of the Suffering Servant is that of sin bearer, not sympathizer of suffering.

Interestingly, Endō's understanding of the Cross recalls the contingent historical perspective of Elizabeth Johnson:

> The narrative memory of the life, death, and resurrection, and outpouring of the Spirit in Jesus the Christ traces the way of divine compassion in the midst of historical sin, death, and defeat. This living *anamnesis* of Jesus shows that instead of being absent, the gracious mystery of God is in the midst of historical suffering enabling resistance, bringing about healing, promising ultimate liberation. Instead of final failure, a future is promised to the defeated of history, who in the end are all of us. (1994: 18)

Although one wonders if Endō shares Johnson's vision of an "ultimate liberation." It seems that for Endō, the present companionship of Christ is all there is to comfort the sick and suffering. Existential meaning is to be found here and now in the very midst of suffering, not in the hope of some future deliverance. For that, the abiding presence of the suffering Christ seems to be enough.

In any case, Endō's Christological agenda leads him to write *A Life of Jesus* in such a way that the Gospels are selectively – and rather bizarrely – interpreted. Hagiwara points out that even the rather liberal New Testament scholar Tagawa Kenzō accuses Endō of disregarding proper biblical scholarship by choosing only those passages that serve his purpose of distilling the *shinjitsu no Iesu* (the true Jesus) from the *jijitsu no Iesu* (the factual Jesus) (1993: 60). In his work *Shūkyō to wa nanika* (*What is Religion?*), Tagawa presents historico-linguistic evidence to uncover what he disdainfully refers to as *Endō bushi* 遠藤節 (Endō tune) with its underlying *jakusha no ronri* 弱者の論理 (logic of the weak), asserting that it has "nothing to do with the teachings of Jesus" (cited in Kenzō, 1993: 55). It is clear that in *A Life of Jesus*, "the total fact of Christ" is not presented (so Newbigin, in Hunsberger, 1998: 195). The message that Jesus preached cannot simply be reducible to the singular attribute of love; it encompasses a more comprehensive vision of the reign of God. Catholic missiologist Stephen Bevans helpfully defines Jesus' vision of God's reign as *shalom*, "that rich Hebrew word that means justice with peace and peace with justice" (2002: 130).

In his book *Models of Contextual Theology*, Bevans classifies Endō as someone who practices what he calls the "transcendental model" of contextual theology (Bevans, 2002: 107). In this model, the starting point is "one's own religious experience and one's own experience with oneself" (Bevans, 2002: 104).[68] Bevans is right, of course. Earlier, Schuchert (1978: 3) and Kitamori (1991: 336) have already pointed out that Endō's ideas of God and Christ are derived from his personal experiences, particularly his failed relationship with his father, than from Scripture. One can hence see why Endō rejects the father image of God which connotes severity, discipline, judgment, and little else.[69] It is a pity that Endō did not allow his defective idea of fatherhood to be corrected by Scripture's portrayal of the true fatherhood of God but jettisoned the idea altogether.[70] In its place, he recreated God in the image of his mother. Such a

---

[68] It is interesting to note that Karl Rahner's theology is also associated with the transcendental method. One of Rahner's theological presuppositions is that the "experience of grace from within [every human being] [...] is the most original and most important root of all Christian piety and holiness" (cited in Kress, 1982: 26). See Kress, 1982: 24-32 for an exposition on Rahner's theological methodology.

[69] By contrast, the novels and theological works of the Scottish novelist George MacDonald (1824-1905) are consistently governed by theme of the fatherhood of God. MacDonald understands fatherhood as "the last height of the human stair whence our understandings can see him afar off, and where our hearts can first know that he is nigh" (1867: 21). MacDonald's experience of his father stands in stark contrast with Endō's: "In my own childhood and boyhood my father was the refuge from all the ills of life, even sharp pain itself" (1885: 48).

[70] MacDonald offers this piece of advice to those with a poor view of fatherhood: "'You must interpret the word by all that you have missed in life. Every time a man might have been to you a refuge from the wind, a covert from the tempest, the shadow of a great rock in a weary land, that was a time when a father might have been a father indeed. Happy you are yet, if you have found man or woman such a refuge; so far have you known a shadow of the perfect, seen the back of the only man, the perfect Son of the perfect Father. All that human tenderness can give or desire in the nearness and readiness of love, all and infinitely more must be true of the perfect Father – of the maker of fatherhood, the Father of all the fathers of the earth, specially the Father of those who have specially shown a father-heart.' This Father would make to himself sons and daughters indeed – that is, such sons and daughters as shall be his sons and daughters not merely by having come from his heart, but by having returned thither – children in virtue of being such as whence they came, such as choose to be what he is.

theological presentation of God, besides being inherently flawed, has no claim to universality (cf. Bevans, 2002: 109). The same argument applies as well to his Christological construction. The ineffectual Jesus is the result of overstretching the biblical portrayal of a meek and lowly Jesus, and viewing him *only* through the lens of suffering.

It is a biting irony that Endō should reject what he perceives to be a triumphalist, Western Christology only to embrace the negative assumptions that underlie the historical criticism of modern Western scholarship (cf. Endō, 1973a: 53-54). His Enlightenment mindset is also evident in the way he distinguishes between truth and fact (Endō, 1973a: 52-54). Endō insists that one does not have to accept the factuality of the miracles as recorded in the Gospels in order to appreciate the truth that they are intended to convey, namely, the truth about the "kingdom of God as a universe of love based on the presence of a companion to all humankind" (Endō, 1973a: 120).

On the subject of fact and truth, a brief excursus is in order here. It appears that many Japanese people are not concerned about historicity as long as truth is preserved or conveyed. This topic came up at a conversation that took place in June 1960 between Paul Tillich and some Buddhist scholars and students of Ōtani University, the Pure Land Sect Buddhist university in Kyoto. (Tillich was visiting Japan at that time.) A couple of important points were made in relation to the historicity of the Buddha. Firstly, Buddhists have always assumed the Buddha's historicity since no historian had ever said otherwise (Wood, 1961: 49). However, the eternal nature of the *dharma kaya*[71] does not depend upon the historicity of the Buddha (Wood, 1961: 50). It is clear that the Buddhist position on the Buddha is diametrically opposite of the Christian position on Christ and the Word of God.

When Koyama was working in Thailand as a missionary, he learned that the Thai outlook of life, especially its understanding of history, is very much influenced by Buddhism (1972: 42-50). The same can surely be said of Japanese culture. For example, very few Japanese would in fact regard the events recorded in the two ancient texts of the *Kojiki* (*Record of Ancient Matters*) and *Nihonshoki* (*Chronicles of Japan*) to be historically authentic, yet these two texts are considered to constitute the spiritual and moral foundation of Japanese culture and nationality. To be sure, there are historical events recorded in the *Nihonshoki*, but much of this text, and virtually everything in the *Kojiki*, are a

---

He will have them share in his being and nature – strong wherein he cares for strength; tender and gracious as he is tender and gracious; angry where and as he is angry" (1885: 48-49). Later, of course, Karl Barth would make a similar argument that one does not decide on the meaning of God's fatherhood by observing human fathers, but rather one understands the potential of human fatherhood by observing God the Father (1975: 389).

[71] The *dharma kaya* or *hōshin* 法身 in Japanese, is a key concept in Mahayana Buddhism. It literally means Truth-Body, and refers to the unmanifested principle of the Buddha out of which all phenomena arise, and return upon dissolution.

telling of the mythological exploits and follies of the deities. But the stories are crafted in such a way so as to present a particular "truth" about the genesis of Japan and the Japanese people, and it is from this "truth" that the values of Japanese culture come into being. Many Western Christians find the Japanese indifference to history hard to comprehend, for biblical revelation assumes an intrinsic relationship between truth and history.[72] Koyama calls the Japanese perspective the "cosmological" view of history, contrasting it with the "eschatological" view of history as taught in the Bible (1999: 20-21). He has much to say about the fundamental importance of history and historicity. The relationship between fact and truth is an important missiological issue, and we will pick up this discussion again in the next chapter.

Some may argue that a miracle needs not be factual in order for it to be true, since what is important is the meaning behind it rather than what actually happened. Even so, it is not hard to see the problems that occur when historicity and truth become so radically separated as in the case of Endō, where he unwittingly placed himself on the slippery slope of syncretism. It is really not surprising that in the end Endō's religious vision should become pluralist and syncretistic. Endō might have started out seeking to commend to his fellow countrymen and women a Japanese expression of Christianity, but ended up with no credible message since there is now no compelling reason why one should become a Christian if all religions, notwithstanding their different historical accidents, indeed lead to the same timeless truth.

Despite his professed allegiance to Christ, the contents of Endō's religious pluralism in his later life are uncannily similar to John Hick's. This is hardly surprising considering the acknowledged influence Hick has on Endō. The reader is directed to Harold Netland (2001: 221-46) who has most ably provided a critique of Hick's model of religious pluralism, a critique which equally applies to Endō's (see also Morimoto, 2003). The point to note here is that, in the case of Endō's quest for religious and cultural authenticity, the biblical integrity of the message is unfortunately sacrificed.

It is indeed a positive thing to pursue with passion an authentic expression of one's religious and cultural identity. The problem arises when personal experience and one's social location are used uncritically as *the* locus of revelation at the expense of Scripture. Furthermore, while Endō's overriding concern for taking seriously the cultural psychology of the Japanese is commendable, an inherent danger lies in the fact that given the inevitability of

---

[72] Many Asians who suffered under the Japanese during the war continue to be bewildered and perplexed by the persistent efforts on the part of many Japanese government leaders and historians to deny that there was ever a Nanjing Massacre or that women were forced to work in frontline war brothels despite overwhelming evidence produced by third party historians. See Yoshida Reiji, "Sex slave history erased from texts; '93 apology next?" in the online edition of *The Japan Times*, http://search.japantimes.co.jp/ cgi-bin/nn20070311f1.html, Mar 11, 2007 (accessed Apr 9, 2007).

social and cultural change, the gospel message needs to be constantly adapted. The question is: How do we decide on the parameters of adaptation? How do we ensure that the gospel does not metamorphose into something unrecognizably Christian? We will pick up the discussion in chapter 7. Until then, we will now turn our attention to Koyama Kōsuke.

6. Koyama Kōsuke and the Crucified Mind

The third and final Japanese subject of our study is Koyama Kōsuke 小山晃佑 (1929-), arguably the most well-known Japanese theologian in the world of ecumenical Christianity. Although younger than Kitamori by thirteen years, and Endō by six, Koyama can still be said to belong together to the same generation as these two men, for they were all born in the intervening years between the two world wars. But unlike Kitamori and Endō, Koyama has lived outside Japan for most of his adult life: seven years in the US as a theological student at Drew and Princeton, eight years as a missionary teaching at the Thailand Theological Seminary in Chiangmai, six years in Singapore as an educational administrator for two theological consortiums, five years in New Zealand lecturing at the University of Otago, and the last twenty-five years back in the US, mostly teaching at the Union Theological Seminary in New York.

In a personal tribute to Koyama on the occasion of his retirement, Donald Shriver, Jr., President Emeritus of New York City's Union Theological Seminary, praises his colleague as "one of [the twentieth] century's great biblical theologians", and suggests that "[e]very student of biblical hermeneutics has something to learn from his writings" (1996: 228). Shriver's compliment is not an isolated one, and is echoed even by Roman Catholics. In October 2001, Seattle University, a Jesuit institution, honored Koyama by naming him Visiting Ecumenical Theologian for the fall quarter of that school year. In the news announcement to the university, Father Patrick Howell, the then dean of the university's School of Theology and Ministry, described Koyama as "one of the greatest theologians of this century."[1]

Koyama came into the international limelight in 1974 as a result of the runaway success of his *Waterbuffalo Theology*. While the book led many to regard Koyama as "a representative Japanese theologian" (Furuya, 1997: 146), it is extremely ironic that he is still a virtual nonentity within the theological community in Japan. Edmond Tang puts it well when he calls Koyama "the most famous theologian in diaspora, disowned by academic theologians in Japan" (2004: 95). The primary reason for this curious state of affairs, in all probability,

---

[1] See web article, "Renowned Theologian Kosuke Koyama Named Visiting Ecumenical Theologian at Seattle University," posted on the Seattle University homepage, http://www.seattleu.edu/home/news_events/news/news_detail.asp?elYear=2001&elID=5212002111820 (accessed April 12, 2007).

is that Koyama has done virtually all his theological work outside his native country. He has published more than one hundred journal articles and book chapters, but they are mostly in English. Of the twenty-one books he has authored, nine are in English,[2] including his most important works *Waterbuffalo Theology* (1974)[3] and *Mount Fuji and Mount Sinai* (1984).[4] Five of his books are in Thai;[5] and the remaining seven are lesser-known works in Japanese, written for the general Christian readership rather than for the theological academy.[6] It is a pity that of his eight English titles, only *Three Mile an Hour God* has been translated into Japanese, and even then, only selected passages from the original work have been translated.[7]

Furuya Yasuo offers another reason why Koyama is relatively unknown among theologians in Japan.[8] According to Furuya, Japanese theologians have, until recently, only been interested in doing theology *in* the Japanese context rather than working on a theology *of* Japan (1997: 146). By theology of Japan, Furuya means "making Japan an object of theology" (Furuya, 1997: 146). In the case of Koyama, even though his contribution to theology in Japan is virtually nil, his theological writings reveal a consistent and objective engagement with Japan (Furuya, 1997: 146).[9] This explains why Koyama, for example, is able to deliver such a sustained and stinging theological critique of the Japanese imperial system that led Japan into the disastrous war of the last century, in a

---

[2] One of the English works is a monograph co-authored with Esther Stine, entitled *"Where Are You?" God asked: Reflections on a Mosaic of Biblical Images of Mission* (New York: United Presbyterian Church in the USA, 1980).

[3] As mentioned earlier in the dissertation, the word "waterbuffalo" appears as two words in the title of the twenty-fifth anniversary edition of the book: *Water Buffalo Theology* (Maryknoll, NY: Orbis, 1999). For the purposes of this dissertation, both editions of the book are used.

[4] The original 1984 edition of the book was published in London by SCM Press. The edition used in this dissertation is the American edition published in 1985 by Orbis, and is hence referenced as Koyama (1985).

[5] The five Thai titles, all published in 1966, are essentially a reorganization into book form of Koyama's notes from his lectures at the Thailand Theological Seminary.

[6] All his Japanese works are published by Dōshinsha 同信社. One of the titles, *Josanfu wa kami o osoreteita node* (*For the Midwives Feared God*) (Tokyo: Dōshinsha, 1988), is co-authored with Hara Michiko.

[7] The Japanese title is *Jisoku go kiro no kami* (*Five Kilometer an Hour God*) (Tokyo: Dōshinsha, 1982). It is curious to note that Koyama's magnum opus, *Water Buffalo Theology*, is not translated into Japanese.

[8] Koyama receives a mention only in a single paragraph on the last page of Furuya's book *A History of Japanese Theology* (1997: 146). However, the friendship between the two men goes back to TUTS days just after the war. Furuya was Koyama's senior schoolmate.

[9] Furuya may well be right. However, it appears that the primary reason why Koyama is unknown in Japanese theological circles appears to be that the only non-Japanese works read by most Japanese theologians are those written by Westerners. As a missionary working outside Japan, it is not surprising that Koyama attracted little attention in Japan.

way that theologians inside Japan are not (see Koyama, 1985: 17-56). Furuya is hopeful that as the newer generation of Japanese theologians turn their attention to Japan as a theological object of study, they will begin to take notice of Koyama's work (1997: 146).[10]

Through his years of ministry as a theological educator, Koyama was always actively involved in ecumenical work, especially with the Christian Conference of Asia and the World Council of Churches. His East Asian cultural background coupled with his training in Western Reformed theology certainly stood him in good stead when it came to the complex task of cross-cultural theologizing. Ever popular as a speaker, he gave many keynote addresses at theological and missiological conferences all over the world, including one delivered in Edinburgh in 1985 on the occasion of the seventy-fifth anniversary of the 1910 International Missionary Conference. Koyama is a strong proponent of inter-religious dialogue, and has worked with scholars from other faiths in many commissions and study groups. Because of his cultural background, Koyama takes a special interest in Buddhism.

Most, if not all, of Koyama's extensive writings touch on the interface between theology and lived human realities in the realms of history, culture, economics, and politics. He is not a systematic theologian as such, but rather adopts a distinctive style of moving dialectically to and from the biblical text and pertinent social concerns. Koyama's writings are creative and engaging, and touch on a whole plethora of social issues such as violence, poverty, the AIDS crisis, racial discrimination, social injustice, military armament, ecological damage, religious intolerance, and such like. Jaecheon Lee rightly describes the breathtaking array of Koyama's writings as a "kaleidoscope of Asian theology" (2002: 8). Yet, when one sieves through the corpus of his works, one can discern a singular underlying theological purpose, namely, to bring the Church to the realization that "[t]he goal of Christian mission is to create a humanity whose form is conformed to the 'form of Christ' (Gal. 4:19)" (Koyama, 1993b: 59). For Koyama, this "transfiguration of humanity in the form of Christ" (1993c: 214; cf. Mk. 9:2-3) – as he often calls it – will never happen unless it is based on a right theological understanding of the death of Christ. Moreover, Koyama declares unequivocally that his theology is built on nothing less than the crucified Christ, and that the death of Christ constantly informs his spirituality and reminds him to cultivate an epistemological attitude of a "crucified mind" in all his theological endeavors (1994a: 203).

---

[10] Iwahashi Tsunehisa, a pastor-theologian, translated ten articles that Koyama wrote between 1974 and 1995 on the themes of the world, culture, and Christ, and compiled them into a reader entitled, *Sakareta kami no sugata* (*The Shape of a Broken God*) (Tokyo: United Church of Christ in Japan Press, 1996). Also, Morimoto Anri, a theologian at the International Christian University in Tokyo, devoted a chapter to Koyama in his book *Ajia shingaku kōgi* (*Lectures in Asian Theology*) (Tokyo: Sōbunsha, 2004), pp. 107-39, focusing particularly on the contents of Koyama's 1984 work *Mount Fuji and Mount Sinai*.

Koyama sees the incarnation, crucifixion, and resurrection of Jesus Christ as belonging together in Christological unity. He does not admit the slightest possibility of a theological controversy here. "What I do understand is that there is one Jesus Christ who was born, crucified and risen," declares Koyama (1980b: 25). At the same time, pointing to Paul's great Christological confession in 1 Corinthians 2:2 and Galatians 6:14, Koyama believes firmly that the "most powerful summary of the whole ministry of Jesus Christ" is to be found in the Cross (Koyama, 1980b: 25).

> Crucifixion is the ultimate depth of incarnation [...] and resurrection is the "therefore" of crucifixion [...] The story of Jesus Christ which we find in the New Testament gospels gives us the impression that the event of the cross of Christ illuminates, by the grace of God, the meaning of his life and death and resurrection. (Koyama, 1980b: 25)

The passionately Christocentric and cruciform orientation of Koyama's theology certainly brings to mind the theology of his teacher Kitamori Kazō. In the spirit of his predecessor, Koyama affirms that "[t]he theology of the cross is not just one kind of theology as distinct from others. It is the foundation of all theological thoughts" (1994b: 12).

Believing that the crucified Christ stands "at the foundation of our life", Koyama proceeds to develop his vision of a renewed and transfigured humanity from his hermeneutics of the Cross (Koyama, 1994b: 12). As "the supreme act of self-giving love", the death of Christ becomes the "central event of the world's history" through which "humanity is personally, communally and cosmically recreated" (Koyama, 1993b: 59). Koyama firmly believes that "the mystery of the transformation of humanity begins in Christ's self-emptying (*kenosis*)" (Koyama, 1993b: 59). Therefore, the work of transforming humanity through self-emptying service is nothing more than the high calling of the Church.

The theology of the Cross must therefore shape the self-consciousness of the apostolic Church so that the Church understands herself to be "the Church of the Cross" for the sake of the world (Koyama, 1994b: 2-5). In a word, the theology of the Cross is to be understood as constituting the very source and reason for the Church's missiological mandate "to bring forth the wholesomeness of abundant life to all upon the earth" (Koyama, 1997b: 59). This mandate is larger than the so-called evangelistic mandate of helping people procure "individual salvation or a blessed eternity after death" (Koyama, 1997b: 59), which, when it becomes the be-all and end-all of the gospel, can only render the Christian faith myopic and irrelevant.

It should be evident by now that Koyama is less interested in the theological details of how the Cross saves humanity than he is in its missiological significance. For this reason, it would be more accurate to describe the subject of Koyama's writings as a *missiologia crucis* rather than a *theologia crucis*. As a matter of fact, Koyama himself coins the phrase "missiology of *theologia crucis"* to define his understanding of the mission of the church from the perspective of the "central event" of the Cross (Koyama, 1997b: 59; 1993a: 165). Koyama's missiology of the Cross is the subject of our study for this chapter.

As it is with Kitamori and Endō, the theological ideas that Koyama has of God and Jesus Christ are very much shaped by his personal experiences as well as the socio-historical contexts that he finds himself in. It is therefore important to look at his life so as to discern the key events that have contributed significantly to his theological understanding. Like Kitamori and Endō, Koyama was a precocious boy. Even from his early teens, he displayed a keen sensitivity to the Word of God and to the world around him. Admittedly, when one reads Koyama's recollection of his early years, it is not always easy to discern whether his theological reflections on events were his original thoughts around the time when these events happened or whether they are the product of a much later period. However, two things are certain. The events from an earlier period that Koyama often talks about as an adult are significant in that they provided him definitely with the context and contents for his theologizing. It would also be a mistake to treat Koyama's reflections as a finished theological product. The truth is that he often recalls and reflects on the past. It would not therefore be unreasonable to assume that even as a young boy, Koyama, especially with his sensitive nature, would have already begun the process of seeking to understand more deeply the spiritual significance of unfolding historical occurrences.

Following the biographical sketch in the next section, we will look at Koyama's perspectives on God and Christ, especially in relation to the Cross, and discuss the implications of his theological perspectives on his vision of the Church's mission in transforming humanity.

Koyama's Theological Pilgrimage[11]

A Christian Heritage (1929-1939)

Koyama was born into a devout Protestant family in Tokyo on December 10, 1929, six years after the Great Kanto Earthquake, the third of four children.[12] Unlike many of the Christian families around that time, the Koyama clan was not of samurai descent. His grandfather on his father's side was the first in the family to convert to Christianity through the witness of a young British man by the

---

[11] This biographical section draws mainly from Koyama's testimony article "My Pilgrimage in Mission," in *International Bulletin of Missionary Research* 21(2), pp. 55-59, the first chapter of his book *Mount Fuji and Mount Sinai* (Maryknoll, NY: Orbis, 1985), pp. 3-16, and my telephone interview with him on March 26, 2007. "My Pilgrimage in Mission" is reproduced as the Epilogue of the twenty-fifth anniversary edition of *Water Buffalo Theology* (Maryknoll, NY: Orbis, 1999), pp. 171-79.

[12] Koyama's two older brothers live in Tokyo, and his younger sister in Los Angeles.

name of Herbert George Brand. At that time, the senior Koyama was still single, and after his conversion, sought and married a Christian woman. Almost nothing is known about Brand except that he graduated from Cambridge University in 1887 and then came to Japan the following year – on his own without joining a mission board – and worked in Japan and Korea as a lay missionary for the next thirty-three years. The simple and unassuming manner in which Brand led the elder Koyama to faith in Christ left a deep impression on Koyama:

> The gospel of Christ which my grandfather heard was presented in broken Japanese with a heavy English accent. What a moment of inspiration to hear the gospel in a broken language! One of the few things I heard and I still remember from my grandfather about his conversion to Christianity from Buddhism was that he was impressed by this man who was able to say that Jesus Christ is Lord without ever making derogatory comments upon Japanese culture or Buddhism. "This made me [want] to follow Christ!" he told me. (Koyama, 1985: 15-16)

So profoundly grateful was Koyama to Brand that he dedicated his book *Mount Fuji and Mount Sinai* "[t]o the memory of Herbert G. Brand (1865-1942), an English gentleman, through whose preaching, in broken Japanese, my grandfather was converted to Jesus Christ."[13]

Koyama's father had been a successful businessman, but his whole estate was wiped out by the devastating earthquake of 1923.[14] When Koyama was only five years old, his father contracted acute pneumonia. Apparently because of the financial straits the family was in, he was admitted into a benevolent Buddhist hospital. However, he died shortly after. Koyama describes the circumstances of his father's death with particular poignancy:

> [My father] breathed his last in the name of Christ on a bed provided by the generosity of Japanese Buddhists. I am grateful for the help he received from this hospital. My mother wrapped the body in a blanket and brought him home in a taxi. For the driver it must have been inauspicious to carry a dead body which would pollute his cab. I am always grateful to this unknown taxi driver who helped the

---

[13] Presumably, Koyama never met Brand since the latter returned to the UK before Koyama was born. Brand died in 1942, the year when the twelve-year-old Koyama was baptized.

[14] Koyama's grandfather on his mother's side, described by Koyama as a "Meiji humanist," was a businessman who traded in charcoal (personal communication). His financial success was also ruined by the Great Kanto Earthquake, but he managed to recover from the disaster. He was one of the owners of Tokyo's first skyscraper, the fabled twelve-story *Ryōunkaku* 凌雲閣 in Asakusa. The building was, however, destroyed in the earthquake.

poor widow. My father died a Christian accepting the kindness of the Buddhists. (Koyama, 1985: 15)[15]

Although Koyama lost his father at a young age, his paternal grandfather stepped in and provided an environment conducive for spiritual growth for the whole family. Through the godly influence of his grandfather, Koyama cultivated a love for the Bible, and understood that "the Bible is the Word of God not because it is so defined by the church, but because it speaks to us urgently and deeply" (Koyama, 1997b: 55). Years later, after entering Christian ministry, Koyama would learn from his mother that his grandfather had been praying for one of his grandchildren to become an evangelist (Koyama, 1997b: 55). It is evident that Koyama's solid Christian upbringing through his formative years stood him in good stead at the difficult and confusing time when Japan's fascist leaders were leading the country down a path of destruction. For it was a time when the small Christian population was regarded with increasing distrust by the government.

Three Life-Changing Events (1939-1942)

Three events in the early years leading up to the Pacific War cast a lifelong imprint on Koyama's view of the Christian faith. The first was an encounter with what Koyama refers to as his "first theological book" (1997b: 55), when he was about ten years old: *Tenro rekitei*, the Japanese translation of John Bunyan's *The Pilgrim's Progress*. He found himself totally enthralled by the sheer devotion and determination of the main character Christian to overcome every obstacle in order to reach the cross of Christ. Even though the young Koyama could not fully understand the meaning of the story at that time, it left in his heart an indelible impression that has stayed with him all his life. He was deeply fascinated by the rich symbolism in *The Pilgrim's Progress*, and that would later inspire him to articulate his faith not in propositional terms but by using familiar images from everyday life (cf. Morse, 1991: 16). The theological significance of Bunyan's story was not lost on the young boy, for it initiated him into a Christian understanding of history as linear progression. Reminiscing on his encounter with *The Pilgrim's Progress*, Koyama writes:

> Our lives, and even the great panorama of human history, have beginnings and ends that contain the movement (i.e., the pilgrim's progress) toward God. This understanding of life and of history gives a fundamental orientation for the Christian understanding of mission. (1997b: 55)

Such an understanding is, of course, completely different from the cyclical view of history that is part and parcel of Buddhist and Shinto thought. But

---

[15] In Shinto belief, death is a polluting event, and anyone who comes in contact – not necessarily physically – with the dead has to undergo purification rites.

perhaps because of his tender age, Koyama's mind was malleable enough to accommodate a view somewhat alien to indigenous Japanese culture.

Japan's involvement in the Second World War drew international attention after the bombing of Pearl Harbor on December 7, 1941. A few months later, as the war was escalating, Koyama, barely thirteen, decided to confess his Christian faith in public by being baptized. It was "an unusual occurrence", as Koyama later puts it, that "a young Japanese boy, born to a Christian family but moulded by the Japanese imperial cult in the schools, [should be] baptized into the religion of the enemy" (1985: 5). Indeed, his friends and neighbors interpreted his baptism as "an act of betrayal" to the country (Koyama, 1995: 271). But for the young boy, the act of baptism was not so much a public admission of personal sinfulness, but it was intended as a personal testimony to what he perceived as the impending destruction of Japan because of the national idolatry of emperor worship (Koyama, 1997b: 55). The baptismal experience as such "provoked a radical appraisal" of his cultural and religious heritage (Koyama, 1985: 7). Despite his less than spiritual intention, Koyama was struck when the minister baptizing him made the pronouncement that "the God of the Bible is concerned about the well-being of all nations, even including Japan and America" (Koyama, 1985: 7). For the startled Koyama, it was his "first ecumenical lesson" (Koyama, 1985: 7), as he grappled with the idea that what baptism signifies "can transcend even the divisions of humanity brought about by war" (1995: 272). And so, even as he confessed in public that Jesus Christ is "the Lamb of God who takes away the sin of the world" (Jn. 1:29) (Koyama, 1985: 6), Koyama discovered that his baptismal experience took on added significance with the affirmation of the "universality of the gospel" in the context of a violent international conflict: "the message of forgiveness" (1995: 272).

The third transforming event happened on April 18, 1942, the day that the United States staged their first air raid on Tokyo, five months after the start of the Pacific War. Koyama remembers that very day well, for he had learned a profound lesson from the Bible even as he experienced for the first time the frightening fury of the B29 bombers. He happened to be reading the story in Genesis 13:1-12 of how Abram gave Lot the first choice of the land. The young Koyama felt strangely at ease with Abram's attitude of non-insistence: "I still feel, as I felt then, that Abram fits into the image of the 'religious person' in the Asian tradition which portrays renunciation as a central symbol for religious life" (Koyama, 1985: 6). In the flow of biblical narrative, it turns out in the end that though initially exploited, Abram, by virtue of his meekness, would finally be the one – and not Lot – who would "inherit the earth" (Koyama, 1985: 6). Koyama states that a posture of non-insistence testifies to a way of life which is "expectant of an open future" (Koyama, 1985: 5).

The War Years (1942-1945)

The encounter with Bunyan's *The Pilgrim's Progress*, with Abram in the Genesis account, and the profound experience of his baptism, provided Koyama with the spiritual resources to cope with the almost nightly air raids over the next three years. He held on quietly to the thin hope that God would bring the war to an end, and that good would come out of it, even as he struggled increasingly with the experience of "utter confusion, violence, and destruction [...] as night after night the bombs rained down [on Tokyo]" (Koyama, 1997b: 55).

Although spared from the unspeakable horrors of an atomic holocaust that would later annihilate Hiroshima and Nagasaki, Tokyo suffered complete incineration through an air campaign of concentrated firebombing that began in March 1945. Koyama would later speak repeatedly of the trauma of the bombings that he had experienced as a teenager.

Bombs rained incessantly over Japan from the bellies of the American B29s. In the night of 10 March 1945, 88,000 perished in Tokyo in two hours twenty-two minutes of bombings. From 13 to 15 April Tokyo was devastated by 4069 tons of fire bombs. The job of destruction was complete in May (23rd to 25th) when American planes dropped 6908 tons of fire bombs on the already charred city. The night of the 25th [of] May began with an ominous silence, but by midnight our section of Tokyo became a sea of fire as the fire bombs rained upon it. (Koyama, 1985: 23)

Needless to say, Koyama's house was burnt to the ground (Koyama, 1980b: 108).

The raids continued until early morning. I was alone, running from one shelter to another. I heard the screech of a bomb coming towards me. In a panic, I ran as fast as I could in what proved to be the wrong direction. Had I run a little faster my head would have been crushed by the impact of a huge bomb which landed in front of me and by some chance did not explode. It disappeared into the ground, I jumped over it and ran towards another shelter where I hoped to find the other members of my family. (Koyama, 1980b: 108)

The morning came as though nothing had happened. I knew the morning came because I saw the sun rising over the wilderness that had been Tokyo. I saw the sun [...] but it was a sun I did not know. The sun I knew did not come up *that* morning. It was a different, strange sun that came up over the wilderness. Overnight Tokyo was changed. I felt homeless. I felt misplaced and lost. I felt an intolerable loneliness encircling me. Tokyo was a forsaken city and I a forsaken person. I was orphaned. I felt as though I had been deserted by time ... as though submerged into lifeless timelessness ... I do not want to experience 25 May 1945 again. (Koyama, 1980b: 108-109)

Less than three months after the firebombing of Tokyo, on August 6, 1945, the Enola Gay dropped an atomic bomb on Hiroshima, the first nuclear weapon ever to be used in the history of warfare. Three days later, another American B29 bomber named Bockscar dropped the second atomic bomb on Nagasaki – the famed center of the Jesuit mission three hundred years earlier. 200,000 perished in Hiroshima and Nagasaki. Within a week, on August 15, ordinary Japanese people heard the "Diamond Voice" of their demigod emperor for the very first time when he announced over the radio Japan's unconditional surrender to the Allied Forces. The war was over. As Koyama puts it in a matter-of-fact way, "Counting from the date of the Japanese victory over China in 1895, the Japanese Empire was annihilated exactly in her fiftieth year" (1985: 23).

> With five hundred other high school students who had been mobilized to work in a military factory, I listened to the broadcast, standing at attention in a badly bombed compound. I went home [...] to a small hovel in which our family had taken shelter after our house had been destroyed. Physically and mentally exhausted from the lack of food and sleep and from fear of death by the constant air raids, I stood like a ghost and once again saw Tokyo. As far as my eyes could survey Tokyo had become a wilderness. (Koyama, 1985: 25-26)

> All familiar sights had vanished: schools, hospitals, railroad stations, rice shops, bean-curd shops, bicycle repair shops, public bath-houses, my friends' homes [...] As everything around me sank in desolation, the basic human sense of orientation, both physical and spiritual, departed from me. For a moment my soul glimpsed the awesome power of desolation. (Koyama, 1995: 270)

The sight of carnage and destruction all around was so traumatic that Koyama could only pray, "Lord, have mercy!" (Koyama, 1997b: 56). Yet it was in the midst of this very crisis of utter despair and disorientation that the boy strangely came to appreciate what it means to be sustained by divine grace. He likens the experience to being "found by Someone" (Koyama, 1995: 270). The Parable of the Prodigal Son became all the more meaningful for Koyama. Since then, Koyama confesses, his life has always found sustenance from the words of the father of the prodigal son, "He was lost and is found!" (Lk. 15:24) (Koyama, 1995: 270). Even long after the war, Koyama admits that he "cannot read the story of the prodigal son without thinking of that time in 1945" (1985: 30). While Koyama never explained what actually happened that him to feel personally that he was "found", he seemed to have a spiritual awakening of sorts that helped him understand the all-out defeat of his country (Koyama, 1985: 31).

More precisely, the devastation of Japan at the hands of the Americans revealed to Koyama three theological realities that would inform much of his work later. First, the historical consequences of sin often are visited upon those who committed it. Even as a sixteen-year-old, Koyama understood that the destruction that had come upon Japan with such fury was indeed her retributive punishment for the terrible crimes she had committed against humanity (Koyama, 1985: 26-27). Later, he would develop a more nuanced theological perspective on this point.

By their own standards the Japanese had created chaos in Asia. The ancient Japanese definition of sin (*tsumi*) is said to be breaking down the ridges (between rice paddies), covering irrigation ditches, opening the sluices (causing flood), double planting (sowing other seeds between the rows of rice), setting up stakes (denoting false ownership), skinning alive, flaying (an animal) backwards, and defecation in the wrong place. *Tsumi* disturbs social organization in an agricultural community. It brings chaos into ordered society. Japan broke down the ridges between the Southeast Asian nations for her own advantage, opened the sluices and damaged the welfare of other peoples, setting up stakes and occupying the territories of other nations, murdering Koreans and Chinese by skinning [them] alive, defecating in the sacred places of other peoples. We did not know that we were doing to other peoples would come home to us. Chaos did come to us, extensively and profoundly. *I had become aware of the boomerang effect in history.* I have seen "waste and void" [Gen. 1:2] concretely and personally in history. It descended upon Tokyo. (Koyama, 1985: 26, emphasis added)

It is now easy to understand why Koyama holds so firmly to the conviction that Japan needs to express contrition and apologize unreservedly for the violence she has committed against her neighbors (cf. Koyama, 1985: 27-30; 1995: 270-75).[16]

The second theological reality for Koyama is that even in the bleakest hour of abject desolation, the surprising grace of God can still be found.

In desolate Tokyo all things that had cluttered our lives vanished. Baptized by the all-cleansing fire bomb, our lives were radically simplified and denuded. Silence came over us. We whispered. We sat on the ground. Our hands were empty. Our eyes gazed toward heaven. Even the summer sun failed to warm us. We were brought down to our knees by the victors. "To put one's mouth to the dust, there may yet be hope" (Lam. 3:29). Unexpectedly, the unconditional surrender was a moment of national purification. *It was a special gift of God.* I was there to experience the blessed denudedness. At that moment no one said that "the Japanese people are the best people in the whole world." (Koyama, 1995: 271, emphasis added)

In the wilderness that was Tokyo, Koyama began to ponder anew on the meaning of the baptismal grace which he had partaken in only a few years earlier. He would later record his reflections in this way:

---

[16] Koyama laments that until now the Japanese church has still not engaged in a sustained theological reflection on the war, especially on the 1937 Massacre of Nanjing. He attributes this to the prevailing Eurocentric orientation of theological education in Japan. However, he notices that more and more students at TUTS are now writing their graduating theses in biblical theology rather than on Western theologians or theological themes, and believes that if this trend continues, sooner or later, Japanese theologians will be led to reflect on Nanjing and Hiroshima (personal communication).

In my Christian experience the image of baptism and that of [the] wilderness became inexpressibly united. Baptism, the renewal of life, has meant to me, all these years, an experience of spiritual purification [...]. In my mind an outer event, the destruction of proud, violent Japan, and an inner event, my baptismal death in the hope of new life in the risen Christ, coincided. What happened in 1945 to Japan has become part of my Christian identity. (Koyama, 1985: 31)

In sum, Koyama saw that by the grace of God, the historical experience of being reduced to nothing can be transformed into "a strangely creative moment" (Koyama, 1985: 30), out of which shines "the light of hope" (1995: 272).

The third theological reality is derived from the atomic bombing of Hiroshima and Nagasaki, and it was a lesson that Koyama drew over time rather than learned there and then. By degrees, Koyama came to see the nuclear destruction of Hiroshima and Nagasaki as a moral tragedy of obscene proportions that not only proves the sinful depravity of all humankind – Christians and non-Christians – but also rightly places Western culture and Christianity on the same level as all other cultures and religions.

Significantly it was not the atheistic Soviet Union but the "Christian" United States, sender of missionaries, which dropped two nuclear bombs on fully inhabited cities. The annihilation of Hiroshima, which climaxed the destructiveness of two world wars in this century, closed the books on the presumed moral superiority of Western Christendom. The world saw that all humanity stands on the same moral plane. *No culture can claim superiority.*

Life in Christian culture is as violent as that in any other culture. Christians are as self-centered as Hindus, Buddhists and Muslims. Sexism, racism and economic exploitation are as rampant in Christian nations as anywhere else. Hiroshima has done a rough job of leveling all to the same plane. None higher. None lower. "There is no one who is righteous, not even one" (Rom. 3:10). As Reinhold Niebuhr said, "The original sin is equally distributed among humanity."

In its annihilation Hiroshima emancipated humanity from any illusion that one culture or religion is morally superior to others. *The traditions of the great world religions, such as Buddhism, Hinduism, Christianity and Islam, are thus placed on the same level.*

Hiroshima also demolished the idea that human history can be interpreted from an exclusively Western perspective. The main player of the history of India is the Indian people. A Western interpretation of the culture and history of Asia or of Africa is only one interpretation among many. This is a great blow to the West's historic confidence in its intellectual superiority. Hiroshima set off a tsunami of critique of historical Christianity. In my view it is good that this happened to Christianity. Over the centuries Christianity had armed itself excessively, both spiritually and intellectually. It needed to be disarmed. Only the disarmed can disarm others. Only the repentant can lead people to repentance. Only the forgiven can forgive. (Koyama, 1995: 273, emphasis added)

Koyama rightly observes that religious studies in the Japanese universities and seminaries suddenly became very popular after 1945, and attributes that to the belief on the part of many Japanese (and Asian) people that Hiroshima has relativized the moral and spiritual authority of Western Christianity (Koyama, 1995: 273). He may well be right. Perhaps this is why Western missionaries have not had much success evangelizing Buddhists in East Asia.[17]

Returning to our discussion on Koyama, one can say that his view of history as a linear outworking of concrete events under the grace of God, his unfailing hope that humanity can indeed be transformed, and his belief in what he understands as the truth of cultural (and religious) relativity, all have their origin in his vivid and life-changing experiences of war in the 1940s. Indeed, these specific ideas would later inform Koyama's writings in a foundational way.

Theological Studies in Tokyo (1946-1952)

With his astute theological mind and keen sensitivity to spiritual realities, it is little wonder that Koyama would want to pursue theological studies after high school. This he did, enrolling in the preparatory school of the Tokyo Union Theological Seminary (TUTS) the year after the war ended. It was later that same year that Kitamori made his mark on the Japanese theological scene with the publication of his *Theology of the Pain of God*. In a 1980 interview with Koyama, Merrill Morse learned that initially there were two reasons for Koyama's decision to study theology (1991: 17). First, the seventeen-year-old wanted a theological environment for him to work out the meaning and implications of the war. His "Christian sentiment" told him that the humiliating defeat that Japan suffered was the result of the sin of national idolatry of worshipping a mere human being rather than the true God, but he was surprised to hear the strong objections expressed by many of his friends to the national campaign of repentance launched by Prime Minister Higashikuni Naruhiko. Many ordinary Japanese felt that they themselves were victims, not perpetrators, of the hideous crimes committed by their fascist leaders, and that therefore the government, not the people, should repent. Koyama learned "[t]he brutal truth about human community [...] that the majority of the people can be hostaged [*sic*] by a tiny section of the community" (1985: 27). It was "his first experience with the complexity of history" (Koyama, 1985: 27), which he wanted to understand better within a biblical framework. The second reason for Koyama's decision to enter seminary is simply that he wanted to serve as a minister in post-war Japan.

---

[17] The loss of moral authority on the part of America, the "Christian" nation, because of Hiroshima may also explain diplomatic impotence in defusing the current nuclear tensions in North Korea and Iran. The blunting of America's moral edge is, however, compensated by her increasing military might. This in turn creates serious repercussions for Western missions.

Koyama's six years at TUTS, however, proved not totally satisfying. First, the war, although so recently concluded, was hardly talked about in school, and when it was, it raised more disturbing questions. Koyama told of a particular chapel service when Kuwada Hidenobu,[18] the president of the seminary, spoke from 2 Kings 25:6-7 and commented that American President Harry Truman treated Emperor Hirohito far more mercifully than the Babylonian king Nebuchadnezzar had treated Zedekiah, the king of Judah (1995: 55). On the one hand, Koyama was moved by the attitude of the Americans, yet on the other, he could not make sense of the death sentence passed by the International Military Tribunal for the Far East – commonly known as Tokyo Trial – on seven Japanese leaders convicted of Class A war crimes, including "the newly minted crime of engaging in conspiracy to wage war" (Gordon, 2003: 230). Koyama thought, "[H]ad Japan won the war, they would surely not have been hanged" (1997b: 55).[19] In summary, at TUTS, he found no satisfying theological response to the war and the attendant issue of war guilt.

Next, Koyama felt that the curriculum at TUTS on the whole did not and could not relate to the present critical situation that the country was in. At that time, he could not figure out why that was so. In any case, he did not think that the training he received at TUTS prepared him adequately for parish work, and so decided instead to pursue further theological studies in the United States after his time at TUTS. It was only years later that he realized the reason for his restlessness at TUTS: the curriculum then was just too Western, hence irrelevant to the Japanese context.

Koyama's time at TUTS, however, cannot be said to be a totally negative one. He was delighted to study under Kitamori, whom he fondly refers to as "my revered teacher" (1974b: 116).[20] He remembers how one afternoon his teacher sent him to deliver part of the final manuscript of his *Theology of the Pain of God* to the publisher, and for the errand rewarded him with a "middle-sized pumpkin" that fed his hungry stomach (Koyama, 1974b: 116). Koyama reminisces, "Since then the sight of pumpkin has become a reminder to me of the truth of 'communion in pain' which Dr Kitamori shares with us in his lucid exposition of the Pain of God" (Koyama, 1974b: 116). It was from Kitamori that Koyama came to understand that God refuses to give up on humanity, hence centrality of the cross of Christ. Koyama further recalls how his teacher "often illustrated the

[18] Kuwada was a systematic theologian credited together with Kumano Yoshitaka for introducing dialectical theology to Japan in the early 1930s. Kitamori was much influenced by Kuwada's work *Dialectical Theology* (1933).
[19] The Americans convicted and executed nearly one thousand Japanese military personnel for Class B and Class C war crimes, mostly related to prison abuses (Gordon, 2003: 230). It is only recently coming to light that up to one-third of those executed were ethnic Taiwanese and Koreans who served as low-ranking guards in the camps that housed many American POWs.
[20] Even during our telephone interview, Koyama refers himself as Kitamori's "disciple."

pain of God, in his classroom informal talks, as a piece of fine silk cloth wrapping heavy sharp augers" (Koyama, 1999: 84). This image impressed Koyama as "superbly Japanese" (Koyama, 1999: 84), and convinced him that the motif of divine pain can be appropriately utilized as an indigenous hermeneutical concept by which the gospel could be "re-rooted" in the cultural milieu of Japan (see Koyama, 1999: 84-89).

Koyama graduated from TUTS in 1952 with a thesis on Francis of Assisi. He summarizes what he learned from this academic exercise in this way:

> In my mind St. Francis's ability to converse with a wild wolf was united with his mystical reception of the holy stigmata of Christ. I concluded that the lifestyle of the stigmata overcame all barriers to communication, even between the animal and human worlds. I seemed to detect an Oriental (India, China) element of saintliness in Francis. (Koyama, 1997b: 55)[21]

After graduation, the twenty-three-year-old Koyama enrolled in the undergraduate program in theology at Drew University in Madison, New Jersey. Until the war, most Japanese theological students would do their overseas studies in Germany. However, since Germany suffered the same ignominious fate as Japan, the decision to study in the land of the victors was an easy one to make.

A Time of Cultural and Theological "Floating" (1952-1959)

Koyama excelled at Drew, and upon receiving his bachelor's degree proceeded to graduate studies at Princeton Theological Seminary. There, he completed his master's degree in 1955 with a thesis on Augustine,[22] and four years later earned his Ph.D. degree after defending his dissertation on Luther's exegesis on the psalms.[23] It is important to note that Koyama's doctoral work on Luther was instrumental in inculcating in his theology and spirituality the central significance of the Cross.[24]

---

[21] Koyama calls Francis an "ecological saint" whom Japanese could appreciate because of his love for nature (personal communication).

[22] Koyama's M.A. thesis is entitled "St. Augustine's View of the Inner Structure of Sinful Man Examined in the Light of His Conception of Order" (1955). Koyama finds that Augustine's conception of order resonates with Japanese aesthetics, especially that of Zen Buddhism (personal communication).

[23] The title of Koyama's doctoral dissertation is "What Does It Mean to Have a God? According to Luther's Second Commentary on the First Twenty-Two Psalms (*Operationes in Psalmos, 1519-1521*): A Study of the Theology of Faith and the Theology of Immediacy" (1959). Koyama's research focus was motivated by his interest in Luther's *theologia crucis* which he first learned from Kitamori at TUTS (personal communication).

[24] See Koyama (1985, 245-48) for a very good summary of Luther's *theologia crucis* as it relates to the psalms. The material is taken from Koyama's dissertation.

Koyama altogether spent seven years as a student in the US, and received a solid education in Western theology. Given that these years constituted his first significant cross-cultural experience overseas, it is interesting that Koyama does not say very much about this period of his life in his writings. He does refer, however, to these seven years as "a time of cultural and theological floating" (Koyama, 1997b: 55).[25]

> During those years I was convinced that whatever my professors taught me was universally valid, since, after all, Christian theology had been developed in the West. Almost intentionally, I ignored my own culture and language, deciding that they were worthless [...]. I was able to obtain the doctoral degree in theology [...] without bringing what I learned in New Jersey to dialogue with my own spiritual and cultural roots. Vaguely, however, I was aware of the need for integration. (Koyama, 1997b: 55)

While at Princeton, Koyama met and married the love of his life, a fellow American student by the name of Lois Rozendaal.[26] After completing his theological studies in the US, Koyama was deliberating about returning to Japan when he received an invitation from the United Church of Christ in Japan (Kyōdan) to serve as a missionary teacher at a seminary in northern Thailand. Thinking that it would be "deadly" for his young wife to struggle with learning a language that he had absolutely no problem with, Koyama chose Thailand over Japan since they would then both be learning a new language together (Koyama, 1971a: 132-33).

The Beginnings of Water Buffalo Theology *(1960-1968)*

After spending some months in Japan as missionary candidates, the Koyamas and their newborn son arrived in Bangkok in August 1960. They were officially Kyōdan missionaries, but received most of their financial support from the US. Thailand was a watershed in Koyama's life in more ways than one. To begin, it inaugurated a lifetime ministry of teaching and writing.

Before moving up to Chiangmai to assume his teaching position, Koyama and Lois spent a year in Bangkok learning Thai. Koyama describes language learning as an experience humiliating, and calls it his "second spiritual baptism, a baptism into the unfamiliar sounds and symbols of a different culture and religion" (1997b: 56). Yet, it was this very experience that provided the grounding for the last few years of his "rootless floating" (Koyama, 1997b: 56). Koyama also began to see the importance of doing theology in the vernacular

---

[25] In all probability, Koyama has in his mind the Japanese word *uiteiru* 浮いている, which, while literally meaning "floating", connotes an unsettled state of mind.

[26] Rozendaal graduated in 1958, a year earlier than Koyama, with a Master of Religious Education degree. She wrote a thesis entitled "Philosophy of Education for Lay Leaders in the Church School." The same year, Koyama and Rozendaal married, and a year later, their oldest son was born.

tongue, and later even suggests that "anyone who wants to understand multiculturalism or religious pluralism would first have to endure this linguistic baptism" (Koyama, 1997b: 56).

Koyama started teaching at the Thailand Theological Seminary from his second year in Thailand. His years in Chiangmai were profoundly transformational. First, he grew to appreciate the Theravada Buddhism that is so ingrained in Thai culture, and in the process began to discover the indelible stamp of his own Buddhist heritage on his very being. Koyama would later put it this way, "No matter what I do, 'Prince Shotoku' is within me, just as Moses is found in every Jew" (1985: 6).[27] Before long, he found himself confronted with the question of the relevance of Luther's theology on his religious heritage. It gradually dawned upon him that the years of "theological and cultural floating" had not helped him define his cultural and theological identity.

In relation to his teaching practice, Koyama discovered the "vast differences in religion, culture, and language" that existed between north Thailand and New Jersey, and wondered how he could bridge the yawning gap (1997b: 56). As he taught Luther's theology in the classroom, he could not help but question what "the connection between Chiangmai and Wittenberg" was (Koyama, 1997b: 56). For him, "[t]his simple question of relevance was [like] Elijah's hand-sized cloud that became, in a short time, a storm." For the first time, he realized the inadequacy of Western theology, and discovered the need to "come to some kind of meaningful integration of [his] theological thought that would express itself in Japanese, English, and Thai" (Koyama, 1997b: 56). His confidence in Western theology greatly shaken, Koyama could only allow "the intense wartime experience of *Kyrie eleison* reclaim the center of [his] theological thinking" (Koyama, 1997b: 56). He decided then that he would do theology using, not foreign materials, but the very raw materials from the soil of the land where he had been called to serve. It was a simple decision, but one that was to change the entire course of his theological career. It marked the beginnings of his water buffalo theology. In the preface to the first edition of *Waterbuffalo Theology*, Koyama expresses his sentiments in a most memorable way:

> On my way to the country church, I never fail to see a herd of waterbuffaloes grazing in the muddy paddy field. This sight is an inspiring moment for me. Why? Because it reminds me that the people to whom I am to bring the gospel of Christ spend most their time with these waterbuffaloes on the rice field. The waterbuffaloes tell me that I must preach to these farmers in the simplest sentence structure and thought-development. They remind me to discard all abstract ideas, and to use exclusive objects that are immediately tangible. "Sticky rice", "banana", "pepper", "dog", "cat", "bicycle", "rainy season", "leaking house", "fishing", "cock-fighting", "lottery", "stomach-ache" – these are meaningful words for them. "This morning," I say to myself, "I will try to bring the gospel of Christ through the medium of cock-fighting." (1974b: vii-viii)

---

[27] See p. 134, n. 81 for a brief word on Prince Shōtoku.

In a word, Koyama decided from then on "to subordinate great theological thoughts, like those of Thomas Aquinas and Karl Barth, to the intellectual and spiritual needs of the farmers" (Koyama, 1974b: viii).

Thailand Theological Seminary serves the educational needs of the Church of Christ in Thailand, a Protestant denomination with ecumenical affiliations. Naturally, Koyama found himself drawn into the world of Asian ecumenism. There, he "experienced firsthand the reality of the community of faith spread throughout Asia" (Koyama, 1997b: 56). At the same time, he made the sobering discovery that many of his Asian colleagues experienced the war as he did, yet differently, for they were "victims of Japanese imperialism" (Koyama, 1997b: 56). This timely realization expanded the "local" emphasis of his new theological orientation, for it helped him to see the importance of ecumenism "because it affects the destiny of nations" (Koyama, 1997b: 56). Koyama decided that part of his theological project would be to explore the question of how the Church can "affirm the ecumenical Gospel in the face of global violence" (Koyama, 1997b: 56). While in Thailand, Koyama also read Abraham Heschel's newly-translated work, *The Prophets*. The book left a profound impression on Koyama, indeed it marks for him "the beginning of a departure from Anselm" (personal communication).

In Thailand, two more children were added to the Koyama family, a girl born in Bangkok, and the youngest son born in Chiangmai.

The Decolonization of Theology (1968-1974)

The Second World War left virtually every country in Southeast Asia in social and economic shambles. Theological education came to a complete standstill during the war years and, as the Church in Southeast Asia made its slow recovery from the ruins of war, it faced the daunting task of building up theological education again. A conference was convened in 1952 in Bandung, Indonesia to assess the state of theological education in the region. This was followed up four years later by a second conference in Bangkok. The 1956 Bangkok consultation turned out to be historic, for it led to the formation of the Association of Theological Schools and Colleges in South East Asia the following year.[28] The association originally comprised sixteen schools, and had the following aim:

> [T]o establish standards for theological education in the region, to promote mutual understanding, and to advise and assist in the solving of problems in theological education, *with special reference to the sociopolitical issues unique to doing theology in South East Asia.* (Yeow, 2004: 26, emphasis added)

---

[28] The group changed its name to Association for Theological Education in South East Asia (ATESEA) in 1981. Today, it has more than ninety member institutions in fourteen countries.

The rationale for this last aim was recorded in the minutes of the consultation by way of the following elaboration:

> The teaching of systematic theology must be relevant to the environment. It must, on the one hand, be grounded in the Bible; on the other, related to the actual situation [...] The Christian faith should be presented in relation to the totality of questions raised by the local situation, and it should not be assumed that certain questions are relevant to all times and situations. (cited in Koyama, 1997b: 56)

One of the principal outcomes of the Bangkok conference is the formation of the South East Asia Graduate School of Theology (SEAGST) in 1966, with the following three objectives: "to counter a brain drain problem, to save money, and to develop contextual theology" (Koyama, 1997b: 27).[29] Headquartered in Singapore, SEAGST was actually organized as a "cluster system" in five countries, SEAGST provided library and faculty resources through the participating theological institutions.[30] The rationale for the "cluster system" is the so-called "Critical Asia Principle", which encouraged theological education to be done in specific cultural contexts (Koyama, 1997b: 27). For example, "Thailand provided Buddhist studies, while Indonesia and Malaysia were responsible for the study of Islam. Hong Kong and Taiwan presented Confucian studies" (Koyama, 1997b: 27). Students were even allowed to use their own Asian languages, if they so desired, to write their theses.

Scottish missionary John Fleming (1910-1999) was named founding dean of SEAGST. When Fleming returned to Scotland two years later, Koyama was asked to take up the deanery. The invitation could not have come at a better time since Koyama was defining his new theological vision as a result of his experiences in Thailand. Without hesitation, he took up the appointment, and moved to Singapore in 1968. There, he also agreed to serve as the Executive Director of the Association of Theological Schools and Colleges in South East Asia under which aegis SEAGST was formed – a fully sensible decision since it would give a larger platform to work out his agenda of doing theology in context. Together with his colleagues, Koyama set in motion "the process of the decolonization of theology" with the "selfhood of the Asian church" in mind (Koyama, 1997b: 58). It is obvious that he enjoyed his years in Singapore as theological teacher and administrator.

> When I was the dean [of SEAGST], some eighty Ph.D.s constituted the federated faculty of professors who taught in the theological schools in several countries of

---

[29] The churches in Southeast Asia noted that many of the brightest students who left for the West for graduate theological work in the 1950s and 1960s did not return home after their studies. Those who did experienced severe reentry problems, especially because of the rapid post-war development in many Southeast Asian countries. Also, the costs of theological education in the West were – and still are – prohibitive for many Asians.

[30] Today, twenty-six theological schools from eight countries participate in SEAGST.

Southeast Asia. The degrees of all of these professors, including my own, were earned from theological schools in the West. All of the professors were people of two cultures ("fork and chopsticks"), committed to the direction of theological education expressed at the Bangkok conference of 1956. In our Senate discussions we explored together the nature and limits of cultural accommodation of the Gospel not from the North Atlantic theological perspective but from the contexts of diverse local cultures in Asia. A marked absence of paternalism and imperialism among these multicultured [sic] faculty members nurtured the healthy growth of the school. (Koyama, 1997b: 58)

Koyama's work required him to travel most of the time. It was through his many visits to the different Southeast Asian countries that Koyama was exposed to the multifarious cultural and religious contexts of Asia. While on one hand, he affirmed that there is "one Gospel and many cultures" (Koyama, 1997b: 56), he saw the pressing need to dialogue with the non-Christian religions and develop a theology of religious pluralism.

At the same time, Koyama saw the ambiguous nature of culture. In his mind, the male-dominated culture of China and the caste system of India were examples of a violent oppression of certain groups of people in the name of culture and tradition. An Asian theology of the Cross, Koyama came to understand, must realistically bring together not only "Christ and culture," but also "Christ and liberation" (Koyama, 1997b: 56). It must be a theology in which "love, becoming completely vulnerable to violence, conquers violence" (Koyama, 1997b: 56).

From his reflections on the complexity of human and historical realities and the saving act of God in history, Koyama came to the conclusion that the identity of the missionary must be rooted in self-denial as exemplified by Christ. Koyama put these ideas together in a paper which he read at a mission's consultation in 1971 in Kuala Lumpur, Malaysia. It was in this paper, "What Makes a Missionary?" that the creative expression "crucified mind" made its first appearance (Koyama, 1971b: 66-75), and over time, it metamorphosed to become the central theme of Koyama's writings.[31]

From his capacity as theological educator, Koyama could now understand clearly the reason for his restless dissatisfaction as a student at TUTS, namely, that the curriculum at TUTS was too Western, hence largely irrelevant to the critical situation that Japan was in at that time. He came to the full conclusion that while Western theology is an indispensable tradition that must be addressed in theological education, it is only "one of several main spiritual and intellectual experiences of humanity. It cannot and must not claim universality" (Koyama, 1993e: 94).

---

[31] The consultation was organized by the Asia Methodist Advisory Committee in partnership with the East Asia Christian Conference. The theme of the consultation is "Missionary Service in Asia."

Under the leadership of Koyama, SEAGST became an important center of ecumenical theological discussion in Asia. One of the most effective means which Koyama used to stimulate discussion on the contextual relationship between Christianity and culture and on inter-religious dialogue is the *South East Asia Journal of Theology*, which he edited during his years in Singapore. Over the years, it developed into what Volker Küster calls "the most important theological journal in Asia" (2001: 121).[32]

Ministry in Writing (1974-1979)

In 1974, Koyama, with his wife and three children, left Asia and accepted an invitation from the University of Otago in Dunedin, New Zealand, to become Senior Lecturer in the Phenomenology of Religion. This assumedly was a welcome change for him and his family from the hectic ministry of the past six years. At Otago, Koyama could settle down to full-time teaching and writing. Finally, he was able to put in print the many theological ideas which had been developing in his mind since the beginning of his missionary sojourn in Thailand. In terms of his theological output, these five years in New Zealand are perhaps his most productive. In addition to many articles, Koyama published some of his most important works: *Waterbuffalo Theology* (1974),[33] *Theology in Contact* (1975), *50 Meditations* (1975),[34] *No Handle on the Cross* (1976), and *Three Mile an Hour God* (1979).[35] These books launched Koyama to international fame.

Toward a Theology of the Cross (1980-1996)

In 1980, Koyama received a telephone call from Donald Shriver, the then president of the Union Theological Seminary in New York City, to become Professor of Ecumenics and World Christianity. Koyama gladly accepted the invitation. It was in New York that Koyama sought to develop a full-orbed theological understanding of the death of Christ as the basis for the transformation of humanity into the image of Christ.

It was in New York that Koyama, for the first time in his life, encountered two ethnic groups with which he had no historical connections: Jewish Americans and African Americans. As he learned about their respective histories, he

---

[32] The journal merged with the *North East Asia Journal of Theology* in 1983. Today, it is known as the *Asia Journal of Theology*.

[33] Although it must be said that *Waterbuffalo Theology* is actually a collection of articles mostly published when Koyama was in Singapore. In fact, a number of his books consist of individual essays put together around a common theme.

[34] The original 1975 edition of the book was published in Belfast by Christian Journals Limited. The edition used in this dissertation is the American edition published in 1979 by Orbis, and is hence referenced as Koyama (1979a).

[35] The original 1979 edition of the book was published in London by SCM Press. The edition used in this dissertation is the American edition published in 1980 by Orbis, and is hence referenced as Koyama (1980).

realized that "their critical appraisal of [the] Christian faith derives from their historical experience of violence" (1997b: 58). Recalling the violence that he and many others had suffered during the war, Koyama became disturbed by the problem of violence, which he came to identify as the hallmark of the twentieth century. The very presence of black and Jewish people in New York "raises the ultimate question of violence in human civilization" (Koyama 1997b, 58). Sadly, in their case, "Christian theology and the church have participated" in the perpetration of the violence they had suffered. "Why should Christian civilization be so especially violent?" Koyama asked, in a moment of self-critique (Koyama 1997b, 59).

Koyama is adamant that a theology of the Cross must respond missiologically "to the fact of enormous violence" in the world (Koyama, 1997b: 58).

> I believe we can speak forcefully and intelligently about [the] Christian faith only when we are engaged in the common battle against violence. Christian speech on the uniqueness of Christianity would speak to the world if the world had been impressed by Christian work toward the elimination of violence. (Koyama 1997b, 59)

Koyama, however, is not advocating an unbridled activism. For him, it is of vital importance to think and live theologically under the Cross and by the grace of God.

> The primary duty of *theologia crucis* is to confront violence and destroy it. Grace is global. Violence is also global. My New York *theologia crucis* began to have the two themes simultaneously: grace and violence. I came to understand that grace is the grace of God, but it must become our inner power to resist and eradicate violence as personally demonstrated by Martin Luther King, Jr. In this empowerment the grace of God becomes real. (Koyama 1997b, 59)

In summary, Koyama believes that the transfiguration of humanity after the image of the crucified Christ begins with the work to eliminate violence. Here, we see an example of the appropriation of the crucified mind as the primary motif in Koyama's theological project.

Retirement (1996 to present)

Turning seventy-eight this year, Koyama now lives in retirement in Minneapolis, Minnesota. However, he continues to be active at the House of Hope Presbyterian Church in the twin city of St. Paul, a church affiliated with the Presbyterian Church (USA) denomination. Besides teaching occasionally in the local church, Koyama still engaged in writing for publication during his retirement. He passed away in 2009, followed by his wife two years later.

Having examined at length the personal history of Koyama, we should now be able to appreciate the centrality of context – historical and socio-political – in the work of theologizing. For the remainder of this chapter, we shall look at

Koyama's theological method, his understanding of the death of Christ, and what he believes the Cross must mean for the Church in her witness and presence in the world today.

Koyama's Theological Method

The Meaning of Theology

Koyama understands theology first and foremost to be "a gift from God" (1975a: 52). It has to be simply because God is the one who takes the initiative to come to humans and speak to humans. If God kept silent, then there can be no possibility of knowing God and knowing about God; we could do no more than speculate about divine realities. Therefore, the true basis of theology, according to Koyama, is John's Prologue: "In the beginning was the Word, and the Word was with God, and the Word was God" (Koyama, 1975a: 79).

In spite of God having revealed himself, it is not possible for humans to apprehend that revelation in a cool, detached and objective way as they would study, say, a fish (Koyama, 1975a: 54). The reason is not only human finitude – true as that is – but also that the nature of the theological process is such that God interacts and is deeply involved with humans. In other words, theology as an exercise of humans understanding God is predicated on the divine reality of God understanding humans. For this reason, Koyama describes theology suggestively as "anthropology by God" (Koyama, 1975a: 54).

> It is as a child understands his mother only by way of his mother's far more intense and profound understanding of the child. Theology does not and cannot speak about God apart from man. Theology is then, "God-man-ology." (Koyama, 1975a: 54)

Joseph Martin summarizes Koyama's thought as follows:

> Theology has one starting point, but two poles. The starting point is God, who takes the initiative to establish [a] relationship with people and who continues to speak to them. But theology is not monistic, as though God carried on a soliloquy about Himself. It is a dialogue, a deep involvement of God and people in which there is a real response to God's initiative, because this initiative is taken by One who is aware of the ability of the other party to respond. It is God's self-revelation in the light of what He understands about people, as their Creator. (1981: 102)

Theology begins with God's revelation to and involvement with humankind. As a consequence, it is impossible to study God with the human element factored out of the process. Here, we find parallels between the academic discipline of theology and the science of quantum mechanics with its observer's paradox (cf. Kitamori, 1981: 261). Moreover, unlike the hard sciences, the nature of theology is such that it demands an existential response on the part of the student. Koyama says it well,

> The "logy" of theo-logy […] is not a "logy" that comes from "observing" God. It is a "logy" that develops within our heart, soul, and mind (Mt. 22:37) when we obey, repent, hope, love, believe, worship God. It is a "logy" of obedience, repentance, creation, hope, judgment, love, faith, worship and eternal life. It is an unusual "logy" indeed! (1999: 134)

The Historical Dimension of Theology

The prolegomenal principle of theology is that it is derived from divine revelation, not human speculation. Next, Koyama shows from the biblical narrative the fundamental historical character of God's revelation (1975a: 52). The Old Testament writings – laws, stories, poetry – are all placed in specific, verifiable historical settings. The New Testament opens with the event of the Incarnation, and that too took place in a definite place at a definite time. In other words, God never speaks abstractly or idealistically outside a specific context; rather divine revelation is always given, hence grounded in, concrete human situations. Unlike Endō, Koyama understands the historical dimension as one of the distinctive markers separating Christianity from the great religions of China and India, which, if compromised, would transform the Christian faith into something totally unrecognizable (1999: 31).

Koyama clarifies, however, that it is not only Western civilization or the Christian religion that has a sense of history (1993b: 73). Indeed, every culture and religion has its own particular understanding of history. Here, Koyama identifies two main types of historical orientation: cosmological and eschatological (1984b: 438-40). The cosmological worldview is characteristic of many East Asian cultures, and is derived from the cyclical movements of nature and from the influence of Buddhism (Koyama, 1972: 44-45). The seasons come and go with predictable regularity, giving people the impression that Mother Nature "does not forget them and that she is, in all that she does, dependent and benevolent" (Koyama, 1999: 23). Indeed, in the spiritual tradition of Asia, nature is often personified as "the benevolent mother" (Koyama, 1999: 24). Despite the presence of surd evil, for example, natural disasters, nature is basically "non-argumentative" (Koyama, 1999: 24). The cycles of nature are never broken by earthquakes or floods.

Within the cyclical orientation of nature, human life is organized in circular movements as well. This is most evident in agricultural societies where sowing and harvesting follow the rhythms of nature. Within the cosmological view of reality, history is marked by unbroken regularity and endless repetition. To its adherents, it brings a fatalistic sense of familiarity and tranquility (Koyama, 1999: 23). For them, history is therefore "nothing but a story of *karma* for the present" (Koyama, 1975b: 50). And *karma* does not admit any strange or unexpected work (Koyama, 1975b: 50). Koyama remarks that, in such an orientation, "[t]here are always second, third, fourth, fifth [...] chances for people and nature to accomplish what they intend to do" (1999: 23). This explains why the Asian cosmological with its *"apatheia* ideal" obscures the wrath of God and embraces all people indiscriminately (Koyama, 1972: 42; 1985: 251).

In contrast to cosmological history, the biblical view of history is eschatological. It is first of all linear, with a beginning and an end defined by Jesus Christ (Rev. 22:13) (Koyama, 1993b: 72). By the mercy of God, history becomes purposeful, hence eschatological (Koyama, 1993b: 72). In this sense, the concept of biblical eschatology is not so much temporal, but rather "salvational" (Koyama, 1984b: 440). There is an unexpected, "strange," decisive, "once-for-all" aspect to it (Koyama, 1999: 23). For the Christian, that unpredictable aspect is the anti-karmic act of God breaking into history to bring hope and judgment. According to Koyama, this is why, unlike the Asian cosmological mind, the Western eschatological mind, founded on Judeo-Christian worldview, tends to confront rather than embrace (1985: 250).

In sum, the biblical view of history is not circular but linear, not cosmological but eschatological. But since God is the one who creates and rules over both nature and history, circular nature has a "proper place *within* linear history [...] [where] it finds its purpose" (Koyama, 1999: 31, emphasis in text).

For this reason, theology can also be defined as "an intelligent and spiritual reflection on history in its fundamental relationship [...] to the Word of God" (Koyama, 1999: 76). It is an intelligent reflection because it requires "committed thinking" (Koyama, 1975a: 52); and it is spiritual because it is "inspired by the Holy Spirit of God, [...] not an ahistorical Spirit, but a Spirit concerned and involved in history" (Koyama, 1999: 76).

On the distinction that Endō makes between fact and truth, Koyama suggests that it is more helpful to understand history in terms of "events" (*dekigoto* 出来事) rather than "facts" (personal communication). Events imply historical verifiability. A historical event may have different layers of "truth" to it, but the point Koyama wants to emphasize is the inseparability of event and truth. For example, the "truth" of a woman acquiring a new identity of a mother presupposes the necessary "event" of her giving birth (Koyama, personal communication). In the same way, our identity as Christians is necessarily predicated on the historical events of Christ's death and resurrection.

Doing Theology in Context

God's involvement with humanity by virtue of his revelation in human history carries a profound implication for the theological task. As necessarily creatures of time and space, we must therefore do our theology by paying attention to people and taking seriously the various concrete situations they are in. This is the only "responsible" way of responding to God and his revelation.

Theology is responsible talk. It is responsible talk to one's neighbors. Theology is talk that takes one's neighbors seriously. "Love your neighbor as yourself" (Lk. 10:27). Theology is deeply "neighbor-logical." Jesus Christ is a "neighbor-logical" man. "His name shall be called Emmanuel (which means, God with us)" (Mt. 1:23). (Koyama, 1975a: 52, 53)

Koyama calls this approach doing "theology from below" (1974b: viii).[36] It begins "not with the great thoughts developed in *Summa Theologiae* and *Church Dogmatics*" but with the needs of the people (Koyama 1974b, viii). Indeed, Koyama disparages theology which is not rooted in the aspirations and frustrations of the people by calling it "docetic" (1976: 34). It does not deal with vague generalities but with contextual specifics. It starts with a real human situation but it does not end there. Rather it "call[s] God" into it (Koyama, 1974b: viii). Because there is a whole range of human situations, theology cannot be rigid but must be dynamic (Koyama, 1979a: 53). This does not mean, however, that the great Christian systems of Augustine or Barth are to be discarded. It simply means that there must be a "[t]heological re-rooting [...]" from one cultural zone to another, one period to another period, one history-consciousness to another history-consciousness" (Koyama, 1999: 82). In modern missiological language, one would describe theology as necessarily contextual in character.

Nature of Theological Discourse

Because of the way Koyama frames the theological task, one can expect the language of his theology to be reflective and dialogical rather than propositional. We have seen that Koyama made a deliberate move in this direction from his first contact with the farmers in northern Thailand. While he does not nullify the importance of systematic theology, Koyama sees it as a contextualized Western theology which has contributed important theological insights to the universal Church (Koyama, 1993e: 90-94). However, as theology interacts with real, and often messy, human situations, it is hard to imagine how it can speak to these situations in a well-defined, systematic mode. Yet, as David Ford rightly observes, "A lively engagement with the Bible runs through all of Koyama's theology" (1989: 227).

Martin captures the manner of Koyama's theological discourse accurately and succinctly as follows:

> Koyama exemplifies the reflective aspect of theology. He is not a dogmatist, keen on convincing people of the correctness of his position. What one sees in reading his works is not expression or defense of positions adopted a priori, but rather his

---

[36] This is not to be confused with the methodological distinction that is made between "Christology from above" and "Christology from below." For a helpful discussion on this problem of orientation of Christology, see Erickson (1998: 682-89).

musings on Biblical themes or human situations. He raises issues more often than he answers them. At times he fixes his attention on a Biblical event, allowing his fertile imagination to wrestle with what that event could say to a specific modern context. At other times he paraphrases a passage from the Scriptures so that its message is given in terms of modern society and its concerns. At still other times he fixes his attention on a specific modern issue or problem, sometimes so specific that it refers to a given situation in a given city, and reflects on what the Bible says to that situation. His theology is self-consciously contextual, in the sense that he seeks to reconstruct the Biblical context as well as interpret the Bible in terms of specific contemporary contexts.

Because Koyama's reflections are deeply rooted in the concrete context of life in the world, his language is earthly and unusual for a theologian. He uses images from daily life that smell of market places and subway stations rather than musty books and libraries. (1981: 99)

Irvin and Akinade describe Koyama's distinctive style aptly as "imagistic and aphoristic" (1996: x). This is clearly evident just from the titles of Koyama's books, such as *Water Buffalo Theology*; *No Handle on the Cross*; *Three Mile an Hour God*; and *Mount Fuji and Mount Sinai*. Hence, it is not unexpected that his theological reflections should often be so open-ended and fraught with paradoxes. Indeed, Koyama is not afraid of ambiguity, recognizing that life is itself full of unresolved tensions. On the contrary, he often problematizes issues, and exposes the simplistic answers that theology sometimes dispenses hurriedly to complex problems.

An emphasis that Koyama makes in relation to theological discourse is the use of the vernacular. There are two related points here. Firstly, the gospel needs to be conveyed through the vernacular. This point is simple enough, although its implications are often not well thought through. As an illustration, Koyama tells of a conversation which took place in Thailand between a missionary and a woman suffering from cancer (1999: 64-65). The woman, who had difficulty in understanding the missionary's standard (Bangkok) Thai, asked him if he could speak to her in her northern Thai dialect, and expressed sore disappointment when he could not. She told him bluntly, "You missionaries are always trying to teach people while you really do not understand the people. The Buddhist monks are much better than you missionaries. [They] can speak my own language" (Koyama, 1999: 64-65). Koyama's point, of course, is not language proficiency per se, but that the failure to use the language of the people often conveys the impression that the missionary is relating to them on the missionary's own terms, not theirs (Koyama, 1999: 64-65). People often then become suspicious that that they are nothing more than "[objects of the missionary's] religious conquest" (Koyama, 1999: 64-65).

Secondly, for the gospel to be truly received and understood, it needs "indigenous appropriation" by the "indigenous intuition" of the people (Koyama, 1994a: 205). Otherwise the theology that often results from the indigenous church is nothing more than a weakened strain of an imported –

usually Western – theology. As a remedy, Koyama advocates what he calls "mother-tongue theology" (Koyama, 1994a: 204). Koyama's proposal of the vernacular principle is, of course, echoed by Lamin Sanneh (1989), Kwame Bediako (1995: 59-74), and Andrew Walls (1996: 26-42).

Koyama's method of theology does raise questions – questions relating to how theology can or should be done in a way that profits not just the local church but the also the universal Church; who decides on how theology is to be done; the relationship(s) between text and context, history and truth; among others. These questions will be explored in the next chapter. We now proceed to examine Koyama's key concepts of God, and from these discuss his understanding of the meaning of the Cross. This next section on the subject of God in Koyama's thought may appear belabored, but it is an important one, for as we shall see, Koyama's views on the death of Christ are intrinsically bound up with his ideas of God.

Because Koyama does not write in a systematic way, it is admittedly difficult, if not somewhat artificial, to present his ideas in a linear, propositional manner. Nevertheless, the common principal themes of his theology and Christology are clearly discernible from his extensive writings, and they are invariably conveyed through particular word images. We shall explicate these themes by fleshing out their corresponding word images. The findings are presented in an organized way, but the reader needs to bear in mind that in the original contexts of Koyama's writings, these themes are intentionally embedded within a discursive rhetoric. Also, because Koyama uses language in such a creative and vivid way, it is helpful to hear him in his original words. We shall hence let him speak directly as much as possible.

Four Principal Images of God

As is expected, Koyama does not write about the metaphysical nature of God. While affirming the reality and mystery of the Trinity, he does not offer any theological treatise on the doctrine. Rather, in the presentation of God in his writings, Koyama always talks about God in relation to his creation and human history. The multiple word images that Koyama uses to describe the God of the Bible include the embracing God (1984b: 443), the periphery God (1984b: 445), the holy God (1985: 37), the angry God (1985: 55), the God of relatedness (1987: 4), the self-giving God (1987: 4), the eschatological God (1987: 5), the broken, healing God (1987: 6), the homeless God (1992a: 38), the ecumenical God (1992a: 38), the indiscriminate God (1993d: 158), and the vulnerable God (1994b: 7). All these metaphors, however, can be subsumed under four principal images: the impassioned God, the suffering God, the slow God, and the discontinuous God. Although there remains much semantic overlap in the content of these images, we shall look at these divine metaphors one by one.

The Discontinuous God

The first image of "the discontinuous God" is of fundamental importance, especially in a setting such as Asia where Christianity is constantly challenged by the ubiquitous presence of the Eastern religions. Having witnessed the utter destruction of his country brought about by an ideology that divinizes the emperor, Koyama is only too well aware of the blurring of the boundary between divinity and humanity in many Eastern spiritual traditions. In contrast, there exists a radical discontinuity between the God of the Bible and the rest of humanity whom he has created (Koyama, 1984b: 441).

> A telling illustration of the discontinuity of God to humanity in the biblical tradition is the non-sexual nature of the biblical God. In all other religions and cultural traditions gods are sexually engaged. They are presented in male and female pairs. Only in the biblical tradition God is not thus presented. The God of the Bible is the creator of sexuality, and thus understands the meaning of sexuality, yet this God is not engaged in sexual acts. Here is an intriguing expression of the discontinuity between humanity and divinity. Gods who engage in sexual acts are continuous with humanity. (Koyama, 1984b: 441)

Koyama observes rightly that this striking image of the non-sexual God is unique to Judaism, Christianity, and Islam (Koyama, 1984b: 441). Interestingly, it is only these religions that teach *creatio ex nihilo*. Koyama explores the theological implications of this idea as follows:

> God who does not create through sexual union is the God who creates all things out of nothing. This God comes from the "beyond." This God is not a part of any human system (economic, military, political, religious, cultural, biological, racial, ethnic) and refuses to be domesticated by any of these powerful systems. *God's relationship with these systems creates judgment and hope in the human world.* (Koyama, 1984b: 441, emphasis added)

Alluding to Martin Buber's relational concept of *Ich und Du*, Koyama suggests that the genuine discontinuity between God and humanity creates the possibility of humanity addressing God as the genuine "Thou" (Koyama, 1984b: 442). The presence of a transcendent God as the ultimate "Thou" in relation to humanity means that he can come to humanity in judgment *and* hope. This, according to Koyama, is the "biblical meaning of eschatology" (Koyama, 1984b: 442). Biblical eschatology stands in stark contrast with the cosmological worldview of Eastern religiosity where humans and gods are placed on the same existential continuum; there is no possibility of a final, authoritative word from "beyond," neither of judgment nor of hope.

The two ideas of the "absolute God" by virtue of his discontinuity with humanity and his coming to humanity in judgment and hope must be held in a single dialectic. Koyama issues a dire warning against Christians who stress one at the expense of the other. There are those, for instance, who (mis)use the concept of divine absoluteness in order "to assert human control over the absolute," and in the process produce a "destructive idolatry" (Koyama, 1984b: 442). Koyama does not mince his words when he points out how it was the "Christian Empire," with her sense of Manifest Destiny, which developed the atomic bomb "and actually dropped it upon two inhabited cities" (Koyama, 1984b: 442). Koyama's insightful critique can be applied to both Christian and Islamic fundamentalism today, where the theology of divine absoluteness is hijacked and converted into an unforgiving and cruel ideology.

The Impassioned God

One of Koyama's favorite texts on the subject of God is the second part of Hosea 11:8, which he always cites from the Anchor Bible translation: "My mind is turning over inside me. My emotions are agitated all together" (Koyama, 1987: 4; cf. 1985: 212, 241).[37] That God should experience agitated emotions within himself, according to Koyama (1985: 212), "is one of the most disturbing pieces of information on the 'psychology of God'." Relating the Hosea text to the part in Exodus 20:5 which reads "For I the Lord your God am an impassioned God" in the translation of the Jewish Publication Society of America,[38] Koyama asserts that "[t]he Bible speaks of a God who is not *without passion*. God is not an *apatheia* God" (1999: 108, emphasis in text). Rather, God is a "God of pathos," to use the words of the Jewish rabbi Abraham Heschel (2001: 288) to whom Koyama acknowledges as having a seminal influence on his theology.

The theological thesis of the impassioned God may be scandalous to some, but from the biblical evidence, it is one which is hard to dispute. For instance, in Isaiah 49:15, God exposes his heart as a passionate lover: "Can a mother forget the baby at her breast and have no compassion on the child she has borne? Though she may forget, I will not forget you!" In the tumultuous context between Isaiah 48 and 50, alternating between Israel's sin and the obedience of the Suffering Servant, it does not take much imagination to catch a glimpse in this verse of the "agitated mind of God" (Koyama, 1985: 221).

Again, in the Parable of the Prodigal Son, possibly Koyama's favorite of Jesus' stories, there is the description of "the deep emotion of the father"

---

[37] In the NIV, Hosea 11:8b reads, "My heart is changed within me; all my compassion is aroused." Koyama does not offer an exegesis of this text, but looking at the Hebrew text, it seems that a good case can be made for the Anchor Bible translation. Koyama's citation of Hosea 11:8 brings to mind Jeremiah 31:20, the verse central to Kitamori's theology of the pain of God.

[38] In the NIV, this part of Exodus 20:5 reads, "[F]or I, the LORD your God, is a jealous God." Again, Koyama chooses a translation that serves his case without defending it on exegetical grounds. According to The Brown-Driver-Briggs Hebrew and English Lexicon (BibleWorks: 7), the lexical form *anq*, from which *aN"q;* is derived and translated as "jealous" in the NIV, refers to a condition of "becom[ing] intensely red, or black." A case can indeed be made to show that besides meaning "jealous," *aN"q;* can also mean "zealous," "envious," "ardent," or "ready to be filled with rage."

(Koyama, 1987: 4). Jesus is not simply teaching about the undeserved gift of forgiveness that the prodigal received, but he is showing us what God is really like: "[a] father [...] waiting in anxiety intensified by his love for [his children]" (Koyama, 1987: 4).

Koyama believes that the biblical record is unambiguous in its presentation of an impassioned God who is personally, patiently, and intimately involved in the experience of human history (1985: 212). Much of history is, as Cecil Hargreaves puts it, "untidy, agonizing, [and] tragic" (1972: 10). One may argue that the pathos of God is nothing more than an anthropomorphism, but then the Bible does not provide a "better", or indeed, any other, alternative for us to understand God in his relation to his creation (cf. Koyama, 1999: 108). Heschel is indeed right in his description of the God of Israel as "a God Who loves, a God Who is known to, and concerned with, man" (2001: 289).

> He not only rules the world in the majesty of His might and wisdom, but reacts intimately to the events of history. He does not judge men's deeds impassively and with aloofness; His judgment is imbued with the attitude of One to Whom those actions are of the most intimate and profound concern [...] He is personally involved in, even stirred by, the conduct and fate of man. (Koyama, 2001: 289)

With characteristic eloquence, Heschel goes on to elaborate on the meaning of divine pathos:

> Pathos denotes, not an idea of goodness, but a living care; not an immutable example, but an ongoing challenge, a dynamic relation between God and man; not mere feeling or passive affection, but an act or attitude composed of various spiritual elements; no mere contemplative survey of the world, but a passionate summons. (Koyama, 2001: 289)

Koyama could not agree more. Explaining the impassioned and jealous God as portrayed in the Second Commandment (Ex. 20:4-6), he writes:

> The reason for God's jealousy is that God has entered into a covenant relationship with Israel. God and Israel are to live in a specially close "attachment." If, therefore, Israel breaks this relationship and shows his love to anyone else, God becomes jealous. There is a covenant relationship (attachment); *therefore* there is jealousy. The strong covenant-awareness of God produces a strong emotion, jealousy! A weak covenant-awareness will produce only the weak emotion of indifference. (1999: 108, emphasis in text)

Compared with the "cool" enlightened *arhat* in Buddhism,[39] the God of the Bible is a "hot" God (Koyama, 1999: 96). The *arhat* is detached from the world, but God is attached to it, historically through the covenantal acts of creation and

---

[39] An *arhat* is the ideal, worthy person who has attained Enlightenment by virtue of his thoroughgoing detachment from all worldly involvements.

redemption (Koyama, 1999: 105-109). Such a history-oriented, emotionally-agitated God would have no place in a cosmologically-oriented, *nirvana*-seeking culture. But all is not lost, for "[t]he hot God does not reject the cool person" but is able to draw them into a covenantal relationship, and in so doing "heat up" the cool Buddhist ideals of *dukka* (suffering), *anicca* (impermanence), and *anatta* (renunciation) (Koyama, 1999: 108, 112). Missiologically, Koyama suggests that the way to appropriate these Buddhist values into Christianity is to theologize them "by placing them in the context of specific historical urgency" (Koyama, 1999: 117).[40]

The idea of the impassioned God inspires Koyama to make a slight modification to the linear view of history. While affirming the purposefulness of history and retaining the poles of the beginning and the end, Koyama suggests that a "zigzag" view of history describes the work of the impassioned God better than a linear view.

> [The pathos of] God cannot behave "smoothly" and "efficiently" since it bears [the] infirmities and diseases of others [...]. It works its way painfully through frustrations. "They made kings, but not through me. They set up princes, but without my knowledge" (Hos. 8:4). It engages in debates. "The Lord has a controversy with the inhabitants of the land" (Hos. 4:1) [...]. God even "repents"! "God repented of the evil which he had said he would do to them" (Ex. 32:14). (1987: 4)

A zigzag view of history provides a safeguard against the "chronological eschatology" that often makes the Church "arrogant and imperialistic" and causes theology to "degenerate into a Manifest Destiny ideology" (Koyama, 1984: 5). The eschatology of the impassioned God is quite a different thing altogether.

The Suffering God

The impassioned God is a God capable of experiencing and expressing wrath and love. Indeed, he intervenes in human history in two ways, confronting sinful humans with his wrath and embracing them with his love. It is God who, in his agitation, confronts and "judges all forms of idolatries", as he confronted and judged Baal worship during the time of Elijah (Koyama, 1999: 220). It is also the same agitated God who embraces sinful humanity to himself as he repeatedly embraced disobedient Israel (Koyama, 1984b: 444). Koyama notes that embrace is originally a cosmological concept, and confrontation an eschatological one (Koyama, 1984b: 444). However, through the death of Christ – "the eucharistic truth of history" – the impassioned God is now not only able to confront, but also to embrace eschatologically (Koyama, 1984b: 445). Koyama explains, "When

---

[40] See Koyama (1999: 112-16) on how he does this creatively using the example of God's faithful dealings with Israel in the Old Testament.

the cosmological embraces us there would be no judgment implied. But when the eschatological embraces, there is judgment" (1985: 251).

In other words, the divine acts of confrontation and embrace are not mutually exclusive. For justice and love belong inseparably in God. Indeed, it is through the death of Christ that sinful humanity is confronted with divine judgment; paradoxically, it is also through the death of Christ that sinful humanity is embraced with divine love. Koyama states, "This is the moment of eschatology in which salvation is achieved through the embrace of the broken Christ" (1984b: 444).

The important point to note here is that the simultaneous divine acts of confronting and embracing imply divine suffering. This is why Koyama (1985: 241) understands Hosea 11:8 as describing "the painful inner life of God" (1985: 241). The impassioned God is a God who "is willing to suffer for the sake of others" (Koyama, 1987: 5). In the same vein, Heschel affirms that "God does not stand outside the range of human suffering and sorrow" (2001: 289).

One can certainly detect more than a hint of Kitamori in Koyama. The language may be different, but Koyama's concepts of confrontation and embrace certainly correspond to Kitamori's concepts of wrath and love. In the same way that divine wrath and divine love produce divine pain when brought together in Kitamori, divine confrontation and divine embrace together produce divine suffering in the case of Koyama. Drawing from his teacher's formulation, Koyama exclaims, "This is the surprise! God who is not supposed to embrace sinner [*sic*] is embracing sinner [*sic*]! This is the paradox of the grace of God" (1985: 251).

Although Koyama does not make any comment on Endō, it is clear from his theological schema that he would judge the monism of love in Endō as an example of indiscriminate cosmological embrace with no eschatological significance. Therefore, even though Koyama suggests that the theme of Christian theology may be stated as "God who suffers for our salvation" (1987: 5), unlike Endō, he does not interpret the suffering vulnerability of God as a sign of ineffectual weakness. "The divine paradox," states Koyama, "is that the vulnerable God is a truly strong God. In the same vein, an invulnerable God who is 'absolute' would be weak" (cf. 1 Cor. 1:25) (Koyama, 1987: 5). Indeed, "the idea of the suffering God who is in truth 'stronger than men'" subverts the world's understanding of power. The evidence is nowhere clearer than on the Cross where the suffering, vulnerable God "disarmed the powers and authorities [... and] made a public spectacle of them, triumphing over them" (Col. 2:15). Koyama states succinctly, "The strength of the vulnerable God exposes the weakness of the invulnerable empires" (1987: 5). Koyama's view of the vulnerable, strong God is far removed from the vulnerable but utterly weak Christ of Endō. The reason is clear: Koyama's God both confronts and embraces; Endō's maternal God can only embrace but has no capacity to confront.

The Slow God

The fourth word picture that Koyama uses often is a very interesting one, that of "the slow God" who adapts to human beings at their walking speed of "three miles an hour" (1980b: 5, 7). Koyama developed this image as he pondered over why God willingly spent forty years in the wilderness with the fledging nation of Israel just to teach them the single lesson that "man does not live on bread alone but on every word that comes from the mouth of the LORD" (Dt. 8:3) (Koyama, 1980b: 3). In his reflection, Koyama discovered "[God's] basic educational philosophy" (1980b: 7). According to him, God chooses to work in history "inefficiently" because enduring spiritual truths and values cannot be imparted with "technological efficiency" (Koyama, 1999: 46-48).

Koyama points out that this slowness is inherent to a God of love who works patiently with his children in order to effect their growth.

> God walks "slowly" because he is love. If he is not love he would have gone faster. Love has its speed. It is an inner speed. It is a spiritual speed. It is a different kind of speed from the technological speed to which we are accustomed. It is "slow" yet it is lord over all other speeds since it is the speed of love. It goes on in the depth of our life, whether we notice it or not, whether we are currently hit by storm or not, at three miles an hour. It is the speed we walk and therefore it is the speed the love of God walks. (Koyama, 1980b: 7)

Of course, the slowness of God is not a quantitative concept but a qualitative one (Koyama, 1974a: 234). It is the hallmark reflection of God's intensively personal and historical involvement with people. Such is the divine *modus operandi* consistently portrayed in Scripture.

The slowness of God hence speaks against the modern temptation of short-circuiting ministry processes in order to attain instant results. It is an indictment against the depersonalizing effects of "running" the church like a business in the name of speed and efficiency, where the bottom-line values are number of converts and financial power. The slowness of God retards all "spiritual drive towards deification of technology" (Koyama, 1974a: 235), and calls people to pay attention to the mysterious movements of divine grace. Furthermore, God's slow work of salvation is often hidden from those who live life at supersonic speeds. This is why God often leads his children into the desert, for it is here that humans are forced to slow down until gradually they come to their *natural* walking speed: three miles an hour (Koyama, 1980b: 5).

Lest one be mistaken, Koyama is not advocating dispensing with technology altogether. He recognizes that technology may – and indeed does, often unintentionally – lead a person to behold the holy; his point is that technology must not usurp the place which is rightfully God's (Koyama, 1974a: 235). Rather technology must be brought decisively under the lordship of the crucified Christ. Contrasting technological efficiency with what he calls "crucified efficiency", Koyama writes:

Going through a most inefficient process, God proved Godself to be the most efficient One. God's efficiency is not, however, an ordinary efficiency. It is the efficiency in a great paradox, the efficiency of the Crucified One! [...] "Crucified efficiency" teaches us, whether we are lumbering along the inhospitable country road on an ox-cart, or penetrating the depth of awesome space, that technological efficiency needs to be enlightened by the sense of the "efficiency" of the Crucified One.

[A]part from the understanding of the "efficiency" of the Crucified One, universal technological civilization may be eventually occupied by demonic efficiency. (1999: 48-49)

It is no accident that these four images of God – as impassioned, suffering, slow, and discontinuous with humanity – should constitute the central pillars of Koyama's *theologia crucis*. Christ, as the divine Son of God, images God the Father in his deep compassion, profound suffering, and inexhaustible patience. Of course, one can also argue the converse, that Koyama understands the nature of God through the revelation of Jesus Christ. There is a dynamic relationship between God the Father and God the Son. There is, of course, the Old Testament revelation of God, which finds its supreme fulfilment in Christ.

In the next section, we shall explore Koyama's theological understanding of the death of Christ in some depth. As in his writings of God, Koyama does not present a systematic theology of the cross in the way that Kitamori does. However, there are key themes that surface repeatedly in his writings that we can examine.

The Death of Christ in Koyama's Theology

Christian theology is unequivocal in its teaching that Jesus Christ died for sinners (Rom. 5:8). Koyama affirms the teaching of the Apostle Paul that on the cross "God made him who had no sin to be sin for us" (2 Cor. 5:21) (1999: 131). It is hence fitting to begin our discussion of Koyama's theology of the Cross by considering his view of sin.

The Problem of Sin

To be sure, Koyama does not have a sustained hamartiology; it has never been his intention to develop one. In fact, other than quoting from the Bible, he does not use the word "sin" very much in his writings. Rather, he employs multiple images to describe the phenomenon of sin. By paying attention to the emphases that he makes repeatedly in his writings, one can safely infer that in Koyama's mind sin is made up of three components: idolatry, dehumanization, and ecological damage. These components are in many ways interrelated, the first often leading to the second and third.

Idolatry

The theme of idolatry is given extensive treatment in the 278-page *Mount Fuji and Mount Sinai*, explicitly subtitled, "A Critique of Idols." In the fourth chapter of the book entitled "The Holy God Repudiates Idolatry," Koyama defines idols as "false gods," neither holy nor impassioned, which humans use to domesticate the true God and rob him of his proper honor (1984a: 37-52). These false gods may not only be material entities. As long as one ascribes absolute value to that which is relative, idolatry arises (Koyama, 1985: 38; 1992a: 42). Here, Koyama cites Paul Tillich's helpful definition of idolatry as "the elevation of a preliminary concern to ultimacy" (1985: 3). It is a phenomenon that comes about when "[s]omething essentially conditioned is taken as unconditional, something essentially partial is boosted into universality, and something essentially finite is given infinite significance" (Tillich, cited in Koyama, 1985).[41] So, for instance, idols can be made of money, and even one's own ethnicity and gender. Even theology can become idolatrous if it is made into an ideology. This happens when theology "loses the dimension of the strange paradox and makes a claim that it is at the center, thus pushing aside the living God" (Koyama, 1985: 100; cf. 1993: 228).

Koyama firmly believes that "idolatry is harmful to human welfare" (1985: 49). As can be seen in the examples of the idolatry of Baal worship in the Old Testament and the political ideology that divinizes the emperor in pre-war Japan, human dignity is tragically compromised.

Dehumanization

Dehumanization happens when people (mis)use their God-given freedom to oppress, exploit, and discriminate against others so as to relegate them to the realm of subhuman or inhuman existence (Koyama, 1975a: 41). Of course, the acts of oppression, exploitation and discrimination are in and of themselves subhuman and inhuman (Koyama, 1975a: 41). Political oppression, economic exploitation, religious persecution, racial discrimination, and the like, lead to the abominable evils of slavery, human trafficking, the torture of political and religious dissidents, debilitating poverty, ethnic cleansing, and all-out war. At the more mundane level, Koyama warns against dehumanizing consequences that can easily be multiplied as result of modern technology (1999: 44-49).[42]

---

[41] Tillich's original definition of idolatry is found in the first volume of his *Systematic Theology* (1953: 16).

[42] Giving the example of a church midnight run to feed homeless people in Lower Manhattan, New York City, Koyama comments, "It takes four hundred sandwiches to ease the hunger of four hundred homeless people. God is doing something through these sandwiches that the American B2 bomber, with a pricetag [*sic*] of eight hundred and fifty million dollars, cannot do. (The bomber is appropriately called a 'stealth' bomber, which literally means 'thievery.') Who can eat the bomber and satisfy his or her hunger? A ten dollar blanket can keep a person under Brooklyn Bridge warm. That is more than any atomic submarine can do" (1992a: 40).

Here, Koyama makes the insightful observation that among all created beings, only humans can be inhuman (1975a: 40). This paradox is rooted in the mystery of freedom, the unique gift which God confers on humanity. The "perplexing problem," as Koyama puts it, is that human freedom consists of "[the] freedom to misuse [this] freedom" (1974b: 208). This is what Reinhold Niebuhr means when he says that "Man has always been his most vexing problem" (cited in Koyama, 1974b: 208). The misuse of freedom is sin because it violates the human being as well as the integrity of the created order.

Ecological Damage

The misuse of freedom in the destruction of the environment is sin because it blatantly ignores that "[t]he earth is the LORD's, and everything in it" (Ps. 24:1a) (Koyama, 1993c: 216). Moreover, when humans forget that everything in the created order is "delicately webbed" and they abuse the environment, they are destroying not only that which belongs to God but are also destroying themselves (Koyama, 1993b: 67; cf. Koyama, 1992b: 85).

> The earth is the only ark in which all living things are aboard. We are all earth-bound (Gen. 3:19). If we are to go to space, we must take earth's environment along with us. If the ark is destroyed, all in it will be destroyed. When humanity disappears, God will "disappear." When there is no human being, obviously no one will say *kyrie eleison*. Where there is no human being, theology will disappear as well. This points to the awesome reality of ecological reality. (Koyama, 1993b: 66)

For Koyama, the widespread prevalence of suffering and violence in this world is the result of the sins of idolatry, dehumanization, and ecological damage (cf. Koyama, 1985: 53-56; 1992b: 86-90). This is to be expected since sin has caused a breach in relationships at all levels, with God, with one another, and with creation.

The Meaning and Means of Salvation

In its simplest terms, salvation is the reversal of the process and consequences of sin. Koyama refers to salvation as "the redemption of humanity in Jesus Christ" (1992b: 81), and uses two principal images to explore the idea: reconciliation and transfiguration. The gospel is indeed a message of reconciliation, between sinful humanity and a holy God, and between humans themselves (Koyama, 1999: 133). Salvation results when idolatry is judged under the cross of Christ, and humans acknowledge the true God (Koyama, 1985: 49, 260-61). Salvation also results in the renewal of community life, "the basic form [of life] in which humanity can find its fulfillment" (Koyama, 1993b: 68). It is expressed in the formation of the "universal church" where all dividing walls of, say, racism and denominationalism, are broken down (Koyama, 1994b: 10).

The next image that Koyama uses for salvation is the transfiguration of all creation after the image of Christ (1993b; 1993c). By this he means the transformation of every aspect of human existence, including culture and the environment. Here, Koyama emphasizes the this-worldly aspect of salvation, which he sees to be fundamental to the understanding of the gospel. Contrasting with the Buddhist teaching of salvation as leaving this world and entering *nirvana*, Koyama states unequivocally,

> The image of salvation as "getting out" of the situation is not applicable to the ecological crisis. "Exit-Egypt" is possible, but "Exit-Earth" is not [...]. There is no other place in which we should expect the appearance of the kingdom of God but in this ecologically devastated world of ours. (1993b: 66-67)[43]

Because sin is fundamentally a historical reality, Koyama believes that the means of salvation must be located in the arena of human history as well (1999: 73). This is where the story of Jesus Christ comes in. Christ as the Incarnate Son of God brings to humanity salvation, not from a mythical deity, but from God "the Maker of heaven and earth" (Ps. 121:2) (cf. Koyama, 1993b: 66). Koyama's position recalls the similar point that Kitamori makes, namely, that since sin is a real and historical phenomenon, its punishment must necessarily be borne by a real and historical person (1986: 51-52).

The Biblical Theology of the Cross

Koyama sees the whole mission of Jesus Christ as summarized in his death and resurrection (1999: 132). He subscribes fully to the teaching of the Apostle Paul that Christ died for sinners and was raised for their justification (Rom. 4:25; 5:8) (Koyama, 1999: 132). Indeed, the Cross and the Resurrection are to be treated as belonging inseparably together in a single complex event.

> The cross is the moment of God's supreme love (*agape*) revelation. The resurrection is the confirmation of God given to the reality of *agape* that "Christ loved us and gave himself for us" (Eph. 5:1) [...]. With the resurrection, the new age has come! (Koyama, 1999: 132)

The effect of Christ's death and resurrection is reconciliation between God and humanity. For this reason, Koyama also refers to the Cross-Resurrection as the "reconciliation-event of Jesus Christ" (1999: 133). This, in a nutshell, is "the biblical theology of the cross" (Koyama, 1994b: 4).

Koyama acknowledges the limitations of human language in elucidating the divine mystery of the Cross. He notes that Paul uses a whole range of images to describe the "inexpressible gift" of God in Christ (2 Cor. 9:15): "expiation, atoning sacrifice, paying the price, service, vicarious suffering, representative penalty" (Koyama, 1999: 133). Even Luther has his own metaphor: *Selige Tausch* (blessed exchange) (Koyama, 1999: 133). Each of these images points to

---

[43] This is why Koyama insists that the welfare of God's created order should also be a missiological concern (1993b: 65).

an aspect of the Cross, but even when put together, they will always lack explanatory adequacy (Koyama, 1999: 133). "Theology," says Koyama, "can only *stammer* about the person and work of Jesus Christ" (Koyama, 1999: 134, emphasis added).[44] In all probability this is why Koyama never shows any real interest in discussing the details of the nature of the Atonement. Rather, by focusing his attention on the demeanor of the crucified Christ, Koyama is suggesting an alternative whereby we can appropriate the death of Christ in a more concrete way. Like Kitamori, Koyama displays a greater inclination to reflect on the Cross in order to learn about God's character rather than to speculate on how the Cross saves sinful humanity. One can say that the focus of Koyama's *theologia crucis*, like Kitamori's, is theocentric rather than anthropocentric.

The Crucified Mind of the Divine Christ

A proper theology of the Cross hence begins with who Jesus Christ really is. Here, Koyama, following Paul, is careful to affirm the divinity of the pre-incarnate Christ.

> The Lord Jesus Christ was "in the form of God" (Phil. 2:6). "He is the image of the invisible God, the first-born of all creation" (Col. 1:15; 1 Cor. 8:6). He was the Word in the beginning with God (Jn. 1:1f.). This is the *richness* of "our Lord Jesus Christ." (1999: 132, emphasis added)

Having acknowledged the pre-eminence of Christ, Koyama then turns his attention to Paul's words in 2 Cor. 8:9, and suggests that these words provide a summary of "the place of the cross of Christ in the divine career of the Son" (Koyama, 1999: 131):

> For you know the grace of our Lord Jesus Christ, that though he was rich, yet for your sakes he became poor, so that you through his poverty might become rich.

Koyama calls this "the story of the 'rich Lord' becoming the 'poor Lord'" (Koyama, 1999: 132). The Lord became poor by becoming flesh and dwelling among humans (Jn. 1:14). Citing C. K. Barrett, Koyama understands "flesh" (*sa,rx*) in John 1:14 to mean "human nature as distinct from God" (Koyama, 1999: 132). The image calls to mind that of the discontinuous God. In coming from beyond into earthly humanity, the discontinuous God became what he was not. He assumed continuity with humanity. This is what Paul means when he says that Christ became poor for our sakes so that we might become rich.

Poverty consists not only of the Lord laying aside his divine splendor and assuming human finitude, but also in his rejection (Jn. 1:10) and his ultimate,

---

[44] This brings to mind Father Neuhaus' comment that it is "unspeakably presumptuous" to explain what happened on Good Friday (2000: x).

disgraceful death. For Koyama, the divine act of "going out" and the consequence of "being rejected" constitute "the structure of the 'word of the cross'" (1999: 134). This is why Koyama consistently uses the term "crucified mind" as the principal leitmotif in his *theologia crucis* to understand and express the divine demeanor of the rich Lord who became poor for the sake of humanity. For the purpose of this work, we shall look at three specific concepts that Koyama developed to explore the "crucified mind" of Christ.

The Peripherized Christ[45]
First, Koyama understands Christ's "going out" of the triune Godhead and "coming into" human history as a movement "towards the periphery," from a place of prestige, privilege, and honor to a place without. In moving to the periphery, Christ subverts the "center-symbolism" of the world by challenging its ideas of power and lordship (Koyama, 1993d: 153; cf. Mt. 20:25-28).

Beginning with his lowly birth in a manger "because there was no room [...] in the inn" (Lk. 2:7), "the periphery image continues throughout the life of Christ" (Koyama, 1987: 6). The peripheral experience of homelessness is not only confined to the Nativity scene, but extends itself even into Christ's adult life: "Foxes have holes and birds of the air have nests, but the Son of Man has no place to lay his head" (Mt. 8:20). The Son of God venturing into the desert to be tempted by the devil is another astounding example of what it means to go to the periphery (Mt. 4:1). In his public ministry, the peripherized Christ deliberately sought out "sinners, tax collectors, and prostitutes" (Mt. 9:10; 21:31) and, in so doing, revealed the crucified mind of God who is concerned with people on the margins (Koyama, 1993d: 153). Indeed, Jesus keeps moving outward peripherally, until he reaches the cross, the place of "utter periphery" (Koyama, 1993d: 154). The site of the crucifixion "outside the city gate" of Jerusalem (Heb. 13:12) is symbolic of this extreme periphery. As Koyama insightfully notes, "No one is beyond the point of periphery at which Christ was crucified" (1997a: 494; cf. Ps. 139:7-12).

Here we encounter a divine paradox. It is by constantly breaking boundaries and going to the periphery that Christ, "the center of all peoples and all things" (Jn. 1:2-3), establishes his centrality. Koyama explains:

Jesus Christ, the Lord of all, affirms his lordship by being crucified. Here the new concept[s] of center and [of] lordship have come to humanity. In this paradox both the center and the periphery have received a new meaning. In the systems of paganism the center person (for instance, the emperor) stays at the center and says that he is at the center. There is no dynamic salvational movement between the center and [the] periphery, the center remains at the center, and periphery at

45 The word "peripherized" is made up by Koyama to describe the attitude of one who constantly moves toward the periphery (1997a: 494). Although the word was coined rather late, the theme of Christ going to the periphery was already established in Koyama's writings as early as 1984 (See Koyama, 1984b: 445-46).

periphery. Periphery becomes an object to be devoured by the center. Here ethics becomes an imperial ethics of devouring others for one's own glory. In contrast, Christianity presents a far more dialectical view of the center. It intends to relocate the glory from the center to the periphery, and thus it really enhances the prestige of the center, and in doing so, enhances the prestige of periphery, as well. (1984b: 445-46)

In summary, with the presence of the center at the periphery, the periphery no longer becomes insignificant. Rather, it becomes dynamic, having now the authority of Christ bestowed on it (Koyama, 1993d: 155). Indeed, it is from the uttermost periphery of the cross that Christ establishes his authority over all things. This is what is meant by the words of Mary's *Magnificat*, "He has brought down rulers from their thrones but has lifted up the humble" (Lk. 1:52). The peripherized Christ now "stands at the center of a new life" (Koyama, 1987: 6).

Intrinsic to the concept of Christ's constant movement toward the periphery is the divine virtue of self-denial (Phil. 2-6-11; Koyama, 1985: 254; 1999: 132). Koyama seems to imply that the "strange logic" of self-denial is one that is deeply appreciated in Eastern spiritual tradition (1980b: 79; cf. 1976: 38).

That which can be loudest can become quietest. That which can be strongest can become weakest. That which can be wisest can become most foolish. The quality of quietude, weakness and foolishness here is different from the ordinary concept of quietude, weakness and foolishness. They are extraordinary. They suggest "self-limitation" and "self-denial." (Koyama, 1980b: 79)

However, Koyama is quick to point out that there are two kinds of self-denial: self-denial for the sake of oneself, and self-denial for the sake of others. He goes on to explain, "Egocentric self-denial is sickly. Other-centered self-denial is creative" (Koyama, 1980b: 79). The latter form of self-denial is supremely exemplified by Christ. Because he gives himself "for the sake of others," even unto death, Christ becomes "the person of utter self-denial" (Koyama, 1980b: 79; Koyama 1985, 243). And Christ's self-sacrifice is creative because it strengthens the weak, makes wise the foolish and lovable the unlovable, justifies the unrighteous, and imparts eternal life (Koyama, 1980b: 80). Indeed "[t]he whole gospel radiate[s] from the self-denial of Jesus Christ" (Koyama, 1976: 42). The theology of the cross can therefore be understood in its simplest terms as "the radical self-giving of God in Christ" (Koyama, 1993e: 87).

There is another interesting aspect to Christ's self-denial which Koyama develops creatively from Martin Luther's commentary on the first twenty-two psalms. In Luther's *theologia crucis*, the God who is revealed through the cross is the hidden God (*Deus absconditus*). Koyama interprets this rightly to mean that God is "hidden in contradictions".

Thus Luther asserts that when God visits us in his secret operation "man is savingly killed (*salubiterque occiduntur*). *God kills man* (strange work – *opus alienum*) in order to save him (proper work – *opus proprium*)." (Koyama, 1985: 246, emphasis in text; cf. Luther, 1962: 288-89)

In other words, no one can come to the God who saves without first meeting the God who kills. The encounter with the "contradictory" God demands a profound faith. Here, Luther, in his commentary on the twenty-second psalm, shows that in making the desolate cry of Ps. 22:1 his own when forsaken by God, Christ demonstrated at that very moment that he deeply trusted in God.

A strong faith! Which can speak to an angry God, call to him when persecuting you, flee unto him when driving you back, praise him as your helper, your glory, and the lifter up of your head, when you feel him deserting, confounding, and oppressing you. (Luther, cited in Koyama, 1985: 247)[46]

This is a profound theological paradox. The content of the ultimate faith displayed by Christ is "to flee to God against God" (*ad Deum contra Deum confugere*).[47] The unwavering trust in the forsaking God, believing that he is true and good, especially in the time of his utmost need, is evidence of Christ's radical self-denial (Koyama, 1985: 247). Koyama suggests that such self-denial is "the character of the Christian faith" (Koyama, 1985: 247).

Luther's *theologia crucis* tells us that it is not "fleeing to God," but "fleeing to God against God" that we affirm our faith in God. "Fleeing to God" is an easy theology which will eventually end up [...] [taking] "the name of the Lord in vain." Those who "flee God against God" dethrone the idols." (Koyama, 1985: 247)

In sum, Koyama interprets the peripherized life of Christ, marked by such utter self-denial, as nothing less than an impassioned life (1997a: 494). The radical nature of Christ's life could not have been possible without divine pathos. It truly expresses the crucified mind of the impassioned God. Indeed, the first peripheral event of the Incarnation could not have happened at all if not for the crucified pathos of God.

The Broken Christ
The crucified mind of Christ also reveals itself clearly through the intense pain that he suffered on the cross (Koyama, 1994a: 200-201). Koyama points out that

---

[46] Koyama also notes that Uemura Masahisa, the Protestant statesman from an earlier generation and founder of TUTS, once preached that the cry of Christ from the cross was not only that of pain, but of trust, for he called upon God even though "he felt a chilling distance between God and himself" (1981: 102). Like Kitamori, Koyama is also very much influenced by Uemura.

[47] Years before, Bonhoeffer had expressed a similar idea from his meditation on Mark 15:34. In a letter written to Eberhard Bethge from his cell in a Nazi prison, Bonhoeffer writes, "The God who is with us is the God who forsakes us" (1971: 360).

the pain of Christ is powerfully symbolized by the broken Christ, the image of which has been perpetually preserved for the Church through the sacrament of the Eucharist (1984b: 443; 1985: 243). In other words, Christ's pain is the pain of brokenness which he experiences through his death as he confronts and embraces humanity simultaneously.

> This broken Christ, indeed, confronts us. But he goes further than that. By being broken he indicates to us the new possibility of embracing others [...]. This is the moment of eschatology in which salvation is achieved through the embrace of the broken Christ. This brokenness is creative. And this creativity is called eschatological since it brings to us unexpected salvation. (Koyama, 1984b: 444)

Koyama goes on to reflect on the meaning of "sacred space" and "sacred time" created by Christ's brokenness in the sacramental event of the Eucharist:

> When the bread is broken, there is created a space between the two pieces of the bread. This space is sacred. This eucharistic space is the space in which the divine embracing of sinful humanity takes place. (Koyama, 1984b: 444)

> This special space is charged with the suffering love of Christ [...]. All other space must receive its meaning from this sacred – sacramental – space. (Koyama, 1985: 243)

> "Space" is usually considered to be more a cosmological than an eschatological concept. I am suggesting here that [the] "space" created by the breaking of the bread – the image of the broken Christ – is eschatological as much as the time indicated by these fateful words: "[...] on the night he was betrayed." The new concept of space has come to us since that night, that is, an eschatological concept of space. (Koyama, 1994a: 444)

> Christian understanding of the sacred goes back, thus, to the image of the broken bread at the Last Supper. [And] it was not only sacred space that was created there, but also sacred time. [As] it has been pointed out, the event of love took place [on] the night [...] he was betrayed. (Koyama, 1985: 243)

In sum, the highly symbolic re-enactment in the Holy Eucharist of the historical ("space-time") self-sacrifice of Christ conveys the divine message that through the broken Christ, ordinary space and time find redemption and are now charged with sacramental and eschatological significance.

Returning to the theme of confrontation and embrace, Koyama writes, "Christ comes to embrace sinners. He cannot do that unless he is broken. And this 'coming' is 'embracing' and not just 'confronting'" (1984b: 444). This explains the expression "the 'painful' embrace of humanity" which Koyama creates to describe how God comes to humanity eschatologically, "in the ultimate fashion" (Koyama, 1984b: 443). In another place, Koyama calls the divine embrace of humanity a "confrontation of embrace" (1985: 248), for it involves divine judgment:

But he was pierced for our transgressions,
he was crushed for our iniquities;
the punishment that brought us peace was upon him,
and by his wounds we are healed (Is. 53:5).

The images of divine embrace and divine confrontation recall Kitamori's images of divine love and divine wrath. In both cases, the juxtaposition of the two poles – embrace and confrontation for Koyama, love and wrath for Kitamori – results in pain. The indelible influence of Kitamori on his student is unmistakable (cf. Koyama, 1994a: 201-203). Recalling how the publication of *Theology of the Pain of God* was "a tremendous event" in Japan, Koyama asserts that "[the] concept of pain is a very important concept," theologically and missiologically (Koyama, 1994a: 201). Indeed, in his discussion on "the confrontation of embrace," Koyama recalls his teacher's definition of "the love of God revealed through Jesus Christ as the love that embraces us who are 'not worthy to be embraced'" (1985: 251).

Although Koyama talks about the pain of Christ rather than the pain of God, it is clear that for him, Christ's pain reflects unambiguously the suffering of God. The image of the broken Christ in pain is not only a direct correlation to Kitamori's idea of the suffering God, but also a powerful symbol of the crucified mind.

The Immobilized Christ
In the same way that the peripherized Christ reflects the impassioned God, and the broken Christ the suffering God, Koyama uses the image of the immobilized Christ to explore the motif of the slow God. The impassioned Christ moves constantly toward the periphery, but it was at the cross – the place of utter periphery – that he finally comes to a full stop.

[Jesus Christ] lost his mobility. He was nailed down! He is not even at three miles an hour as we walk. He is not moving. "Full stop!" What can be slower than "full stop" – "nailed down"? At this point of "full stop," the apostolic church proclaims that the love of God to man is ultimately and fully revealed. (Koyama, 1980b: 7)

The immobilized Christ is hence symbolic of the "maximum slowness" of God (Koyama, 1999: 4). This symbolism is often captured in the crucifix, but insufficiently reflected upon. In a clever use of alternating tenses between his description of the bronze sculpture of the crucified Christ that he saw outside the Newman College Chapel in Melbourne, Australia, and his interpretation of its deeper symbolism, Koyama muses,

[Christ] is *wide open*, because He was nailed down like this. Obviously He was in pain, and He is open, and He was immobilized; it is in openness-in-pain that He invites everybody to come to Him. As it were at the moment of greatest defeat, immobilized, in form of a crucifixion He comes to us and He invites us. (1994a: 200, emphasis in text)

Koyama is careful to say that the pierced hands of the immobilized Christ are *not* indiscriminately open. He compares the defenseless, nail-pierced hands of Jesus with the confident ideological fist of Lenin, and the merciful, webbed hands of the Buddha (Koyama, 1976: 25). Unlike Lenin's hands which are discriminately closed against the bourgeoisie and the Buddha's hands which are indiscriminately open to everyone, Jesus' crucified hands are painfully neither open nor closed, for they are the expression of both God's truth (*tm,a/*) and God's gracious love (*ds,x,*) (Koyama, 1976: 26). Koyama sees in the hands of the crucified Christ "a theologically striking intersection (cross)" of truth and grace (Koyama, 1976: 26). Koyama adds:

> All forms of hands – the hands of welcome, the hands of rejection, the hands of hope, the hands of despair, the hands of determination, the hands of love, the hands of understanding [...] must be related to the crucified hands because the crucified hands are painfully neither open nor closed. The crucified hands are the hands of ultimate love and respect for our history. They are the hands of divine invitation. The mind that contemplates the crucified hands, neither open nor closed, is the crucified mind. The crucified mind is perceptive about the varieties of forms of hands and their relationship to the crucified hands. (Koyama, 1976: 26)

In sum, contrasting with Lenin's defiant hands that only inflict pain on others, and the Buddha's hands that know no pain, only the nailed-down hands of Christ can draw all people to himself (Jn. 12:32), for they are the hands of unconditional love.

At this point, it is important to note that Koyama sees the gracious, steadfast love of God (*ds,x*), not sacrifice, as central to the cross of Christ. Koyama confesses that since the crucified Christ "cuts an extremely violent image," he is afraid that it "may inadvertently exalt violence" (1992b: 81). He does not deny the motif of sacrifice, but insists that it "must be subordinated to the ultimate reality of *hesed*" (Koyama, 1994b: 4). If the unfailing love of God is made subordinate to sacrifice, then the result is magic (Koyama, 1994b: 4). And Koyama caustically remarks, "There is no need of discipleship in magic" (Koyama, 1994b: 4).

Indeed, Koyama understands the Songs of the Servant in Isaiah 52 and 53 as an expression of God's loving kindness rather than sacrifice. Moreover, argues Koyama, "[th]e religious practice of sacrifice-making tends to become mechanistic and distanced from the inner spiritual experience. It is the impassioned *hesed* that can speak critically against the perils of [the] human spirit (Hos. 11:8, 9)" (Koyama, 1994b: 4). In another article written shortly afterwards, Koyama picks up again his point on the centrality of love over sacrifice:

> The sacrifice Christ made is not to satisfy a vengeful God. God is not vengeful. God is generous. The sacrifice is not required to placate the divine sense of justice. It is, on the contrary, a demonstration of the overflowing and overwhelming fullness of

love of God towards all creation, including humanity. A sacrifice which is not an outpouring of love is neurotic. Jesus is not neurotic. He is enemy to none because he loves the enemy with his free mind, soul and spirit (Mt. 5:44). He "extends hospitality to strangers" (Rom. 12:13) completely and perfectly. That was the reason – how strange! – why he was crucified (Jn. 13:1). This strange event is the heart of the gospel (1 Cor. 2:9). As we look at him, we come to know who we are as sinners forgiven.

God's eagerness to forgive derives from God's love. It is the nature of the loving God to forgive. God loves and forgives us in spite of the injustice and violence that characterize our community. In the fathomless depth of divine forgiveness, love and justice are united and holiness is revealed. This is certainly an extraordinary holiness. The forgiveness that comes from the holy God bestows hope on the repentant. Forgiveness invites mutuality, transforming our community life. Forgiven by God, we are enabled to forgive one another. The vertical intersects with the horizontal. Justice meets forgiveness in this intersection. (1995: 268-69)

In his strong assertion that sacrifice in itself is "tragedy" (Koyama, 1997b: 59), one wonders if Koyama has come dangerously close to rejecting the satisfaction theory of the Atonement in favor of the moral influence theory as espoused by Peter Abelard. The development of Koyama's thought on the subject from 1992 to 1997 is instructive. As mentioned above, Koyama expresses discomfort with the violent image of the Atonement in an article published in 1992 (1992b: 81). Two years later, he insists that if the Cross is to be understood in terms of sacrifice, then its sacrificial meaning must be grounded in the larger context of divine love and compassion (Koyama, 1994b: 4). A year later, Koyama does away with the idea of satisfaction originally inherent in the meaning of sacrifice, and redefines sacrifice as the supreme display of God's love (1995: 268). Although it must be said this new definition is rather devoid of content, for it does no more than explain the effect of Christ's sacrifice. Two years later, in his crowning piece, "My Pilgrimage in Mission", published in the *International Bulletin of Missionary Research*, Koyama comes to a firm conviction that "*theologia crucis* is a doctrine of love, not of sacrifice" (1997b: 59). Reading the statement in its context, it is clear, however, that Koyama is unwilling to debunk the idea of sacrifice altogether from his understanding of the Atonement. He is deeply concerned that the self-sacrifice of Jesus must not be interpreted to mean that Christians too should sacrifice because they believe there is an inherent value in sacrifice-making (Koyama, 1997b: 59). From his contact with Jews and African Americans in New York City, Koyama comes to perceive, rightly, the possible relationship between sacrifice and violence. As he puts it, "Sacrifice is often another name for self-protection and even for self-righteousness" (Koyama, 1997b: 59). This is plainly illustrated by the theology of sacrifice that inspires the suicide bombers in Palestine and Iraq.

In this regard, it is true that God makes clear his desire for mercy and not sacrifice (Hos. 6:6). Koyama's point that the supreme sacrifice of Christ on the cross is a demonstration of "the ultimate intensity of God's *agape* for humanity" (1987: 6) is hence well taken. In other words, while true love invariably leads to sacrifice, the act of sacrifice does not necessarily imply true love. In this sense, Koyama's emphasis on the centrality of divine love in his *theologia crucis* does not negate the biblical teaching that there is saving efficacy in Christ's once-for-all sacrifice for the sins of humankind (Heb. 7:27; cf. Mouw, 2001; Boersma, 2003). It is a sacrifice based on God's gracious love. Indeed, Koyama understands the Cross first and foremost as expressing the love of God, but that also it is "a love that takes the form of sacrifice" (personal communication). This is why he regards Anselm's satisfaction theory of the Atonement as "helpful but inadequate," for ultimately Christianity is a "love religion," not "sacrifice religion" (personal communication). Interestingly too, Koyama's understanding of the primacy of love over sacrifice in his theology of the Cross brings to mind Kitamori's classification of the love of God as an *opus proprium* and the wrath of God as *opus alienum Dei*.

Koyama also suggests that the Cross as "the ultimate symbol of immobility" provides us with a theological criterion to distinguish between the true God and all false gods (1999: 4). Most ironically, this criterion is found in the cruel and mocking words of the chief priests and the teachers of the law: "He saved others, but he cannot save himself" (Mt. 27:42; Mk. 15:31) (Koyama, 1985: 260). Koyama (1985: 260) comments, "This 'Christ who saved others [but] did not save himself' reveals the fundamental character of the true God. False gods save themselves; they do not save others." Put another way, the content of the theology of the cross can be understood as confrontation by the one who saved others but not himself (Koyama, 1985: 250).

In sum, we see in Koyama's *theologia crucis* a theological isomorphism between the impassioned God, the suffering God, and the slow God, and the peripherized Christ, the broken Christ, and the immobilized Christ. For Koyama, the heart of the Cross is located in the divine demeanor – the way the impassioned God experiences human history in Christ, in suffering and in love. Christ journeying to the periphery, his painful brokenness, and his immobility that keeps him from saving himself, belong properly to the theology of the cross, as opposed to the theology of glory. Consequently, the theology of the Cross is, for Koyama, the theology of the crucified mind.

The Risen Christ

Koyama affirms the resurrection of the crucified Christ as foundational to the kerygma of the Church (1976: 110).

> The apostolic preaching proclaims that Jesus Christ crucified is the victor! The risen Christ means the vindication of his life which culminated as he carried the [...] cross and was nailed to it. He suffered for us. (Koyama, 1976: 119)

Unlike Endō, Koyama attaches great historical significance to the Resurrection.

> The crucified Lord was timed. "It was now about *the sixth hour* […]. Then Jesus, crying with a loud voice, said, 'Father, into thy hands I commit my spirit'! And having said this he breathed his last' (Lk. 23:44-46). He suffered under Pontius Pilate. 'On *the third day*' he rose from the dead. This is the day on which the ultimate mystery of the covenant God took place. (Koyama, 1976: 111-12, emphases added)

Yet at the same time, the Resurrection, being the "ultimate mystery" that it is, marks an eschatological disruption in the flow of time. As Koyama puts it, "Chronology cannot contain the event of the resurrection as paper cannot contain fire" (Koyama, 1976: 111).

> Time must stop, since it does not know how to behave at this great mystery [of the Resurrection]. When time stopped, the whole creation stopped. That is to say that the whole creation was brought into crisis in order to exist on the new quality of time henceforth. The risen Lord means, then, the coming of the new time, the new order, the new covenant and the new humanity. (Koyama, 1976: 112)

In sum, with Christ's resurrection, "the old has gone, the new has come" (2 Cor. 5:17). History continues, but now takes on an eschatological character. The *kairos* of Jesus Christ has graced *chronos* by giving it a new meaning (Koyama, 1980b: 109). On his disciples Christ confers the gift of the "risen mind" so that they can discern "the presence of the new quality of time within this history of ours" (Koyama, 1976: 112).

With characteristic insight, Koyama also observes that the events of the Crucifixion and the Resurrection are framed on both ends by the breaking of the bread (Koyama, 1976: 111). On the night he was betrayed, Christ broke bread with the disciples. On the very evening after he rose from the dead, Christ *again* broke bread with two disciples in Emmaus. Here, Koyama sees the significance of the Eucharist as joining the Cross and the Resurrection into "*one* saving story" (Koyama, 1976: 111). Citing Karl Barth, Koyama declares that there is no Easter without Good Friday, and equally, there is no Good Friday without Easter (Koyama, 1976: 112). Drawing from the theological unity of the Cross and the Resurrection, Koyama proceeds to elaborate on the nature of the risen mind.

First, Koyama reminds us that the "risen mind" on its own is awkward in expression and unintelligible in meaning. The risen mind needs to be defined with qualification, as "the crucified mind which looks up to the risen Lord" (Koyama, 1976: 110). It is a mind trained twice at the table of the Lord; hence, it is characterized by *both* renunciation *and* faith (Koyama, 1976: 115). The crucified mind lives in perpetual self-denial and death, and the risen mind lives in the promise of the ultimate victory over death (Koyama, 1976: 112). In other words, without the Resurrection, the crucified mind remains a defeatist mind;

but without the Cross, the risen mind degenerates into a triumphalist mind. Forgetting one or the other, the mind of the Christian becomes theologically schizophrenic, spiritually diseased, and missiologically ineffective.

> The risen mind is […] [therefore] the crucified mind, the crucified mind is the risen mind […]. It is the Good-Friday-Easter mind. It is the Easter-Good-Friday mind […].
>
> The risen mind is not a quietist mind. It is not an activist mind. It is "always abounding in the work of the Lord" because it is guided by the experience gained at the two tables of the Lord. It is "steadfast, immovable" in the way the crucified and risen Lord is. (Koyama, 1976: 113)

Missiology of the Cross

Human language is ultimately "powerless" when it comes to fully elucidating the divine mystery of the death of Christ (Koyama, 1999: 133). There will always be gaps in our understanding. In this regard, Koyama (Koyama, 1999: 133) notes that Paul's oral profession of "Jesus Christ and him crucified" is necessarily complemented by his experience of living out the word of the Cross, and suggests that the apostle's testimony contained in 1 Corinthians 4:9-13 and 2 Corinthians 11:22-28 actually expresses more powerfully and more eloquently the meaning of the Cross than the finest oratory on the subject. For Koyama, the missiological practice of the Cross is hence more important than its theological articulation.

Cultivating a Crucified Mind

The missiology of the cross demands that each Christian live their life in *imitatio Christi* (Koyama, 1997a: 494). This essentially means cultivating within oneself the crucified mind of Christ, the Christological attitude of foregoing prestige and honor and living the peripherized life, willing to be broken in order to embrace others, especially the poor and lowly. Commenting on the injunction that Jesus gave to his disciples to participate in his crucified life, Koyama interprets the mind portrayed by Matthew 16:24 as a "crucified mind."

> [The crucified mind] is the mind of Christ. It is not a neurotic mind. It is not a morbid mind. It does not have a persecution complex. It is a positive mind. It is a healthy mind. It is the mind which is ready to deny the self […] for the sake of building up a community. This mind is a theological mind. It is a free mind. And it is the missionary mind in contrast to the "crusading mind." This mind does not live by itself. It lives by constantly creating the life that practices such a mind. It lives with constant frustration and a sense of failure. Yet, it is joyous. It is resourceful. (1999: 18)

In the previous section, we discussed Koyama's concept of the risen mind. Although Koyama sees the risen mind as synonymous with the crucified mind, he uses the latter term more often than the former. The reason is that he does not see defeatism as a missiological problem; rather he perceives triumphalism as an ever-present danger that needs to be checked constantly. It is not a wonder that Koyama often criticizes what he calls the crusading mindset of many missionaries, and instead, calls on them repeatedly to develop instead a crucified mind (1976: 119; 1999: 150-59). The crusading mind is a manipulative mind: it seeks to "handle" people and history (Koyama, 1976: 2-3). It forgets that the cross that the Lord calls his disciples to bear has no handle, and so it creates one so that it can be carried around like the way a businessman carries his briefcase (Koyama, 1976: 7). The crusading mind is therefore a technological mind, for it is "handle-minded" (Koyama, 1976: 3). The crucified mind, on the other hand, is truly a theological mind: it is "non-handle-minded," for it "refuse[s] to handle the saving power of God" (Koyama, 1976: 3). Rather than "handling" history, it respects it (Koyama, 1976: 113). In other words, the crucified mind participates in history through self-denial, recognizing that there is no other way of preaching the gospel of the crucified Lord.

Koyama, however, does not reject the crusading mind completely, although he finds the word "crusade" (or "crusading") "replete with the memory of tragic human limitation of vision, self-righteousness and arrogance," hence problematic (Koyama, 1976: 119). His point is that while it is crucial not to display any sense of triumphalism in one's service, it is important to understand that the risen Christ has given the Church a triumphant hope that should motivate her service to the world. The crusading mind must therefore "be placed in the light of the crucified mind" so that as it is shaped by the death and resurrection of Christ, it becomes the risen mind (Koyama, 1976: 5).[48] The "crusade" staged by the renewed mind is one that, instead of bulldozing others, "accepts humiliation in order to save others from humiliation" (Koyama, 1993d: 161). In the place of the self-generating resourcefulness of the crusading mind, the risen mind receives its resourcefulness from Christ himself. Koyama calls the resourcefulness of the risen mind "crucified-and-risen resourcefulness" (1976: 113). It is the resourcefulness of the triumvirate Christian virtues of faith, hope, and love (Koyama, 1976: 113).

Neighborology

The crucified mind is not a pathological condition because it is "*love* seeking the benefit of others" (Koyama, 1995: 159, emphasis in text). The other-centered nature of the crucified mind is elucidated in Koyama's concept of neighborology. In its simplest terms, neighborological practice means refraining from looking at others as "inanimate objects", that is, as merely evangelistic

---

[48] Koyama sometimes uses the expression "crucified crusading mind" (e.g. 1976: 119), but only sparingly.

targets, but acknowledging their "reality" as people created in the image of the living God (Koyama, 1999: 64-66, 150).

> Our sense of the presence of God will be distorted if we fail to see God's reality in terms of our neighbor's reality. And our sense of our neighbor's reality will be disfigured unless seen in terms of God's reality. (Koyama, 1999: 65)

Koyama then defines the missionary as a person "sandwiched between Christ's saving reality and his neighbor's 'other-than-myself' reality" (Koyama, 1999: 65). In preaching the gospel, it is hence incumbent upon the missionary to exegete both the Word of God and the life and culture of the neighbors among whom the missionary lives (Koyama, 1999: 65). Citing 1 John 4:20, Koyama notes that the beloved apostle does not say, "He who does not love God whom he has not seen cannot love his brother whom he has seen," but rather the reverse. In other words, the order is "neighbor-God" (Koyama, 1999: 66). Koyama finds this significant because people often "are not concerned with our christology, but they show, from time to time, their interest in our neighborology" (Koyama, 1999: 66). According to Koyama, neighborology is hence "the best vessel to convey Christ" (Koyama, 1999: 67). He also reminds missionaries to present the gospel not with theological jargon, but with neighborological language (Koyama, 1999: 67).

Neighborology also compels the Church to obey Paul's injunction in Romans 12:13 to "extend hospitality to strangers." Indeed, for Christian theology to maintain its authenticity, it "must be constantly challenged, disturbed, and stirred up by the presence of strangers" (Koyama, 1993a: 165). Strangers must include people who are culturally and religiously different. Koyama believes that since the eucharistic *koinonia* that Christ is creating through his death and resurrection is a community of faith that transcends all boundaries, "Christ's way of extending hospitality must [therefore] be the way for the whole world" (Koyama, 1993a: 169).

> In the *koinonia* of the self-giving Christ there is no struggle between unity and diversity. Both unity and diversity are signs of the blessing of God as manifested in the Body of Christ [1 Cor. 10:17]. The missiology of *theologia crucis* aims to create the *koinonia* of the whole creation. (Koyama, 1993a: 169)

In practical terms, this means, more than anything else, placing a high premium on personal encounters, recognizing that every person is a "staggering anthropological, sociological, and historical complexity," "a *full* person" indeed (Koyama, 1999: 150, emphasis in text). The Lord commands his disciples to love *people*, not the "anthropological, sociological, theological 'formulations'" that are used to define them (Koyama, 1999: 151; cf. the Parable of the Good Samaritan in Luke 10:30-37). It does not mean that these formulations are completely unimportant. It means, for instance, valuing the Buddhist more than his Buddhism. Indeed, Koyama understands inter-religious dialogue as therefore, first and foremost, a dialogue "between Buddhists and Christians, not between Buddhism and Christianity" (Koyama, 1993a: 173). Koyama insists that it is only with a crucified and neighborological mind that missionaries can shed their "centuries-old 'teacher's complex'" and proclaim the gospel with the true spirit of *metanoia* (Koyama, 1993a: 173-74).

In sum, the theology of the Cross, according to Koyama, is essentially about the demeanor of the incarnate Christ as he seeks to reconcile the world to God and to transform it after his image. The content of *theologia crucis* is the crucified mind. Koyama states, "At this point, theology becomes missiology, and missiology becomes theology" (Koyama, 1993a: 135).

Sources of Koyama's Theology of the Cross

There are four principal sources of Koyama's theology: Kitamori's theology of the pain of God, Luther's *theologia crucis*, Heschel's notion of divine pathos, and Koyama's own experiences as a Christian and as a missionary. First, the influence of his teacher Kitamori on his theology is unmistakably obvious. Echoing his teacher, Koyama affirms that the Cross is "the foundation of all theological thoughts" (1994b: 12; cf. Kitamori, 1986: 74). In fact, Koyama has a whole chapter in *Water Buffalo Theology* in which he not only summarizes Kitamori's theology of the pain of God but also shows how Kitamori's theology is in essence a "re-root[ing of] the gospel of Christ for the Japanese mind" (1999: 86).[49] As the conclusion of the chapter, Koyama gives his positive evaluation of Kitamori's theology:

> Is not this theology of the analogy of suffering a most comprehensive accommodational principle? Wherever and whenever human pain exists, a person who is involved in pain is, repentant or not, embraced by the *tsurai* [painful] love of God. Does the God of Kitamori embrace too much? Yes, it does. But it does so *christologically*, that is, in the light of the Son who was crucified *outside* the city! (Koyama, 1999: 89, emphasis in text)

Much of the Kitamori's theological structure is reflected in Koyama's own *theologia crucis*, notably, the tension between divine confrontation and divine embrace. However, unlike his teacher, Koyama does not go as far as to absolutize divine suffering. He does not speculate on the status of suffering in relation to divine ontology, but only asserts that God has the capacity to suffer by virtue of his impassioned nature.

While it is an overstatement to say that Koyama's theology of the Cross is Lutheran, it is certainly not an exaggeration to say that it draws much of its

---

[49] Kitamori's theology is summarized in chapter 10 of Koyama's *Water Buffalo Theology* (1999: 82-89). The title of the chapter is "Theological Re-Rooting in the Theology of the Pain of God."

theological material and inspiration from Luther. This is hardly surprising since Koyama wrote his doctoral dissertation on Luther's theology. The centrality of the Cross in Koyama's writings is reminiscent of Luther's *theologia crucis*. The gospel, according to Koyama, is *"essentially* 'the word of the cross'" (1999: 131, emphasis in text). Indeed, he would go so far as to say that "all theologies must be theology of the cross" (Koyama, 1999: 131). Koyama is also clearly influenced by the distinction Luther makes between the theology of glory and the theology of the cross. Koyama explicitly rejects the former, calling it "a theology that controls God by reason which is not crucified with Christ" (1985: 256). Rather, following Luther, Koyama (1994b: 3) understands the theology of the cross as mediating the knowledge of God to us "through the humiliation and suffering of Christ" (1994b: 3). It calls for nothing less than a theological and missiological commitment to "the broken Christ embracing the broken world."

Heschel's influence on Koyama has already been mentioned above. Through Heschel, Koyama saw clearly how the Old Testament portrayed the God of Israel not only as the sovereign Lord, but also as an impassioned lover. In Heschel, Koyama found the corrective to Anselm's satisfaction theory of the Atonement.

The large extent to which Koyama's understanding of the death of Christ is shaped by his biography has already been demonstrated. Only one more point needs to be made here. From his missionary experience, Koyama has come to make a clear distinction between Christ and Christianity (1980b: 51). Christ is the eternal Son of God, while Christianity, like all religions, is a historically-determined religion. As such, Christianity stands under the judgment of the Cross, together with every human system and institution (Koyama, 1980b: 52; 1993a: 174).[50]

Koyama's understanding of the historical conditioning of Christianity could also have been influenced by Paul Tillich, who had earlier taken issue with Hegel's labeling of Christianity as an absolute religion, insisting that "Christianity is characterized in each historical period by the predominance of different elements out of the whole of elements and polarities which constitute the religious realm" (Tillich, 1964: 56). Tillich's influence on Koyama is more directly evident in the former's definition of idolatry and his application of that definition on the "salvation-myth" of Nazi nationalism (Tillich, 1964: 17; Tillich, 1953: 16). In Part I of *Mount Fuji and Mount Sinai*, Koyama clearly adopts Tillich's method in his harsh critique of the Shintoist imperial ideology of pre-war Japan (1985: 3-56).

Koyama also mentions the influence of Uchimura Kanzō on his theology. Uchimura's courageous refusal to bow to the Imperial Rescript in the so-called Irreverence Incident in January 1891 inspires Koyama, prompting him to comment that "Mount Sinai entered the land of Mount Fuji at this moment"

---

[50] Koyama mentions Barth to support his case, presumably referring to Barth's treatise on "Real Religion" in the second part of *Church Dogmatics* I (Barth, 1956b: 325-61).

(Koyama, 1980b: 105). Koyama also appreciates Uchimura for "combin[ing] cultural sensitivity for Japanese history with the study of the Bible" (1989b: 772). Indeed, paying attention to cultural and historical situations while bringing the Bible to bear on these situations would become Koyama's lifelong theological method.

Both Morse (1991: 59-60) and Lee (2002: 124-127) suggest striking parallels between Koyama's theology and Kagawa Toyohiko's understanding of the death of Christ. While it is true that both men are Christocentric and cruciform in their theological understanding, there is little evidence of any substantial influence of Kagawa on Koyama. Koyama rightly perceives redemptive love as the central theme of Kagawa's writings, but does not quite share the social reformer's liberal optimism that a perfect social order can be fully established on earth through an absolute ethic of love (1989a: 397; cf. Germany, 1965: 39; Kagawa, 1934: 113). Although Koyama talks about the transfiguration of humanity as the mission of the Church, he is sufficiently aware of the prevalent reality of sin to admit the dialectic of the "already-not yet" in his eschatology. That tension seems to be missing in Kagawa. Interestingly, when he was interviewed by Morse in 1981, Koyama expressed that he felt strong affinities between his theology of the cross and that of Jürgen Moltmann (Morse, 1991: 67).

Evaluative Summary

Like Kitamori, Koyama understands the Cross as "the center for the Church's theological existence" (1999: 136). Koyama's unique contribution to the theology of the Cross is the strong missiological dimension which he brings. This is not unexpected given his cross-cultural experiences, first as a missionary in Thailand, and then as a theological educator in Singapore, New Zealand, and most recently in the US. Very much like Kitamori – and unlike Endō whose theological ideas evolved over a lifetime – Koyama's theology has remained rather stable since his watershed experiences in Thailand. His writings focus on the singular theme of the crucified mind of Christ, as he seeks to exhort Christ's followers to imitate Christ in his service and self-denial.

Many Western theologians approach the Atonement by deliberating on its nature, necessity, and extent. Koyama approaches it differently. He does not deny the value of understanding the Atonement as an objective reality as it relates to the redemption of humankind, but sees the saving death of Christ as ultimately a divine mystery. Rather, he opts to appropriate the Atonement by examining Christ's demeanor as revealed through the way he lived and died. The Incarnation, according to Koyama, reveals an impassioned God who is deeply involved with history, who suffers for and alongside human beings, and whose dealings with them are painstakingly patient.

The historical component is extremely important to Koyama. Human history is the very stage on which the work of God takes place. Koyama's critique of the cyclical understanding of history conditioned by a cosmological worldview in which Mother Nature embraces everything indiscriminately is totally applicable to Endō's view of history and his concept of an all-embracing maternal God. Since God is God of both nature and human history, Koyama posits a linear, eschatological view of history within which is contained both the natural rhythms of life and the real events that take place in space and time. In such a view of history, God comes to humanity, eschatologically, to confront and embrace.

The coming of God to humanity is fully expressed through the Incarnation. Christ, as "the image of the invisible God" (Col. 1:15), models God by living the impassioned life in the midst of created humanity (Koyama, 1999: 132). Despite his preeminent status as "the firstborn of all creation" (1 Cor. 8:6), Christ took the path of poverty, and in that choice, reveals the divine *modus operandi* of moving toward the periphery in the divine scheme of redeeming and transforming humanity (Koyama, 1999: 132). The peripherized life, as Koyama calls it, is marked by self-denial. Indeed, if pain is the cardinal experience of God in Kitamori's *theologia crucis*, then self-denial can be interpreted as the fundamental divine virtue in Koyama's theological understanding. Koyama would even go as far as to suggest that self-denial, as exemplified in the Cross, becomes "the criterion of the symbols of all religions" (1993a: 174). By this, he is implying that all religions should be judged by the "crucified criterion [...] of radical-self denial" (Koyama, 1993a :174).

According to Koyama, Christ allows himself to be broken on the cross so that through his death he can confront *and* embrace sinful humanity at the same time. The structure of Koyama's thought finds parallel in Kitamori's dyadic framework where divine wrath and divine love meet at the cross, generating divine pain as a consequence. Koyama does not use the expression "the pain of God," but the content of "the suffering God" in his writings is similar. However, Koyama does not absolutize this idea in the way Kitamori does. He is simply satisfied with highlighting what for him is the reality of divine pathos that makes it possible for God to suffer.

Unlike Endō who sees Christ's suffering on the cross as a means of suffering "like us", Koyama, following Kitamori, takes a more traditional interpretation of Christ's suffering "*for* us" (1976: 119, emphasis added). However, he does not elaborate what he means by the preposition "for", whether he is referring to substitution, representation, or vicarious suffering. He is simply not interested in discussing this further. This does not mean, however, that the idea of Christ identifying with humanity in his suffering is absent in Koyama. Indeed, he sees human suffering, especially violent suffering, as a huge problem that needs to be addressed by the Church. However, unlike Endō, Koyama understands suffering to be the result of human sin, especially the sin of idolatry. The theology of the Cross then, before becoming the answer to the existential problem of suffering, must first confront the deeper problem of idolatry.

Koyama describes God as a God who "walks 'slowly' because he is love" (1980b: 7). As the symbol of "maximum slowness", the Cross is therefore a proclamation of the supreme love of God (Koyama, 1999: 4). In this regard, Koyama believes that the Cross is primarily about love, not sacrifice. While not denying the sacrifice motif in the New Testament, Koyama insists that it must be made subservient to the more important motif of love. Koyama's heavy emphasis on love, while entirely different from Endō's monism of love, may cause some evangelical theologians to be concerned that the objective, saving efficacy of Christ's sacrifice may be compromised. Koyama's position does not necessarily lead to such compromise of doctrine, although the concern is not an illegitimate one.

The theology of the Cross, according to Koyama, must lead to a missiological imperative. Affirming the universality of the gospel, Koyama insists that such universality is incomprehensible to the world unless it is made demonstrable in self-denying servanthood. The true universality of the gospel, asserts Koyama, is a "crucified universality" (1992b: 84). The lordship that the Church ascribes to Christ is a "crucified Lordship" (Hargreaves, 1972: 10). In following their Lord, Christians everywhere are to serve their neighbors and extend hospitality to strangers. Theology must therefore not only be Christological but also intensely neighborological. Alluding to the Parable of the Good Samaritan, Koyama describes theology that "passed by on the other side" as a theology that "denies the neighbor himself, Jesus Christ" (1980a: 13). In sum, Koyama's understanding of the death of Christ can indeed be more appropriately described as a missiology of the Cross.

7. Theological and Methodological Evaluation

Having examined in depth the perspectives on the death of Christ held by Kitamori, Endō, and Koyama, we now proceed in this chapter with a discussion of some pertinent theological and methodological issues related to this study. We begin by answering the research questions that were formulated in the first chapter. Although many of the issues that these questions were designed to address have already been discussed at length in the course of our presentation on each of Kitamori, Endō, and Koyama, it is helpful to summarize the key points in an organized manner. After working through the research questions, we will address three interrelated theological concerns that have surfaced from this research study. The first relates to the theological problem of divine impassibility. The reason for this discussion is that the idea that God can suffer is implicitly assumed by Kitamori, Endō, and Koyama – and not only by them, but by many, if not most, non-Western Christians. Next, we will also examine, albeit briefly, the alleged relationship between the sacrifice motif in the Cross and perpetuation of violence in the world, a concern which is raised by Koyama, and perhaps also one which is implicit in Endō. The third issue is the problem of eternal damnation – a stumbling block for many Japanese people. Following these discussions, we will then raise some pertinent questions from our research on the important subject of theological methodology. The chapter ends with a consideration of some principles for doing theology in a cross-cultural context.

Research Questions Revisited

RQ 1. What is the nature and significance of the death of Christ in the writings of Kitamori, Endō, and Koyama? What are the similarities and differences between the three views?

Kitamori and Koyama stand in the historic tradition of the Church, and particularly that of the Reformation, in their affirmation of the death and resurrection of Jesus Christ as the defining centrality of the Christian faith. Endō, despite his lifelong ambivalence toward the Catholic faith which he felt compelled to believe in because of his mother, could still be interpreted as viewing the Cross as an important symbol of Christianity. However, he locates its significance not in the theological sense of its efficacy in redeeming sinful humanity from sin and eternal punishment, but rather in what he believes to be the supreme display of Christ's full identification with suffering humanity. In this sense, Endō can still be located within Christian tradition. However, it is noted that he does not attach any importance to the historicity of the Resurrection, for he believes that its true meaning lies symbolically in the experience of the abiding companionship of the crucified Christ in the hearts of his disciples. Kitamori and Koyama, on the other hand, subscribe to the teaching that the Cross is God's historic and historical means of redeeming fallen humanity and reconciling men and women to himself. In any case, all three thinkers show less interest in *how* the Cross actually saves – for that is ultimately unknowable – than in what it reveals about God's nature. Such theological posture brings to mind Takakura Tokutarō, a Japanese theologian of an earlier generation, who said that "we are not saved by an atonement theory [… but] only by Christ's Cross" (cited in Jennings, 2005: 334).[1]

For Kitamori, the Cross reveals a God who experiences intense pain as he puts to death his own Son in order to save sinful humanity. Divine pain, according to Kitamori, is generated when God, in his intentional embrace of those who have become his enemies because of their betrayal of his love, overcomes his wrath against them with his love for them. Indeed, the brutal death of the Son of God on the Cross is indicative of the pain of the Father as he embraces sinful humanity. In other words, God's love is a suffering love. In sum, Christ suffered *because of* sinful humanity, hence the pain of God; and he suffered *for* sinful men and women, thereby reconciling them to God.

Koyama adopts an essentially similar perspective, positing a suffering God who embraces and confronts sinful humanity through the death of Christ. However, Koyama does not make pain a divine attribute, and hence finds himself free from all the theological knots that entangle Kitamori. Divine pain, for Koyama, is neither an ontological nor a cosmological concept, but an intensely historical one. That being said, Koyama's overriding concern is really not so much with the theology of the Cross – important as that is – but with its ethical and missiological implications. For him, the Cross reveals an impassioned God who continually moves toward the periphery in search of that one lost sheep. The Church therefore must do the same, putting on the crucified mind of Christ as she ministers to transform the world into the image of Christ.

In contrast to Kitamori's God who acts in wrath and in love, and Koyama's God who confronts and embraces at the same time, Endō's God knows no wrath and hence does not confront. God, according to Endō, is like a suffering mother who only knows how to love and embrace completely.

---

[1] The great Scottish novelist George MacDonald similarly insists that Christians must place their faith in the atoning Christ and not in any theory of the Atonement (1885: 91). Takakura could have been influenced by MacDonald, having spent about nine months at New College, Edinburgh, from June 1921.

This fundamental difference between Kitamori and Koyama on one side and Endō on the other can be explained by their views on sin and suffering. While the former commit to the teaching that Christ suffered for the sins of the world, Endō takes the view that Christ suffered in order to share in the world's sufferings. Indeed, Endō would go so far as to project onto Christ all human suffering, making the Incarnation, and particularly the Passion narrative, the paschal mirror of the sufferings of the world. It is clear that, for Endō, the existential human problem addressed by the Cross is suffering, whereas for Kitamori and Koyama, it is sin. While sin is defined by Kitamori primarily as the betrayal of God's love, and by Koyama concretely as idolatry, dehumanization, and ecological damage, the idea is vague, almost absent, in Endō. Indeed, whatever little he has to say about sin is discussed in terms of moral failure. The lack of theological understanding of sin in Endō explains why he sees the death of Christ as exemplary suffering rather than as atonement.

In Endō's reckoning, the problem of suffering is not resolved by its removal; that would be impossible since suffering is an integral part of human experience. Rather, it is through suffering that one experiences the love of Christ, the eternal companion who understands suffering since he has participated in it. In other words, Christ suffered *like* all suffering humans. It is this experience of love that gives human life its existential meaning. Indeed, Koyama appreciates Endō's perspective for what he calls the "Immanuel factor" (personal communication).

Kitamori, on the other hand, is largely silent about human suffering, not unexpectedly since his full occupation is with the pain of God. He does talk about human pain, but sees it as fulfilling the singular function of serving or testifying to the pain of God. Koyama's view is the most balanced of the three. He views suffering as an inevitable consequence of sin. The sins of idolatry (against God), dehumanization (against one's fellow human beings), and ecological damage (against God's creation) create boomerang effects of suffering. In this sense, Koyama may be thought of as being a bridge between Kitamori and Endō. The Cross, for Koyama then, not only pronounces God's decisive judgment against sin, but also addresses the problem of suffering through the suffering of Christ.

In sum, we see that Kitamori, Endō, and Koyama are less interested in the classical debates in Western theology on the Atonement with regard to its nature, extent, and necessity. It is not that they see these as unimportant, but they focus their primary interest not on abstract theories but on the divine demeanor revealed through the incarnated life and ultimately the death of Christ. Although the theological details are different, the three men share a common understanding of the death of Christ as the supreme demonstration of the suffering love of God. It is this suffering love of the impassioned God that makes the Cross existentially meaningful for all humanity.

RQ 2. To what extent do the views of Kitamori, Endō, and Koyama reflect the
perspectives on the Cross in Scripture?

Kitamori and Koyama are to be commended for their unflinching commitment to the whole biblical text as the Word of God. Their writings are permeated with Scriptural quotations. Their love for the Old Testament is especially evident. Both men believe that the Bible speaks of a God of pathos, a God who is intensely involved in the experiences of human history. The revelation of God as he is first known through the pages of the Old Testament reaches its fullness in Jesus Christ, the incarnated Son of God. Endō, in contrast, has little use of the Old Testament, believing that it paints a wrathful deity completely different from the God described in the Gospels. He hardly ventures into the rest of the New Testament beyond the four Gospels, preferring to set his focus singularly on the nature of God as he is revealed through the life and death of Christ. For his interpretation of the Gospels, Endō employs Bultmann's hermeneutic of demythologization, and comes to the conclusion that many, if not most of, Jesus' sayings were concocted by the disciples after the event of the Cross in order to present what they had come to understand as the "truth" about Christ as the eternal companion of suffering people everywhere. Needless to say, the miracles are also weeded out altogether, not because they are thought to be incompatible with modern science, but because they do not contribute to Endō's preconceived image of Jesus as a person who is ultimately ineffectual.

Of course, Endō's view of the Cross as the supreme symbol of identification with suffering humanity and his portrayal of the "risen" Christ as eternal companion cannot be said to be unbiblical. On the contrary, these are powerful biblical themes. The problem, however, arises when these are the *only* themes that define Endō's theology of the Cross. The idea that the Cross truly and objectively achieves the redemption of sinful humanity is completely absent. Any theory which contains some truths and yet asserts itself as complete could often be more theologically dangerous than a theory which is completely wrong.

Kitamori and Koyama acknowledge the multiple images that the Bible uses in its presentation of the atoning event of the Cross. They are also aware of the fact that the Bible does not contain any Atonement theory: it simply states that Jesus died for sinful humanity without saying exactly how. Kitamori and Koyama therefore do not develop any of the images directly related to the mechanics of the Cross. As mentioned earlier, their focus is on divine pathos, a theme that both men developed first from the Old Testament, Jeremiah 31:20 for Kitamori, and Hosea 11:8 for Koyama. According to Kitamori, the impassioned God possesses the capacity to experience pain, and he did experience that pain when he saw his Son die on the Cross. Koyama understands that the earth-shaking event of the Cross provides nothing less than an irrefutable testimony of an impassioned God who suffers for humanity. Interestingly, both men cite the Parable of the Prodigal Son to prove their point about the impassioned Father.

If there is one biblical theme that is shared commonly by Kitamori, Koyama, and Endō in their perspectives on the death of Christ, it must be that of divine love. All three affirm that it is the principal attribute of love that compels God to willingly choose the path of great suffering for the sake of all humanity. According to Kitamori, divine love generates pain within God because, as God, he is also deeply committed to justice. But divine love triumphs over divine wrath because, while both are part of God's nature, the former is his primary attribute while the latter is understood as secondary to his nature. Koyama shares a somewhat similar view, maintaining that the meaning of Christ's sacrifice must be understood in the larger contextual reality of God's love.

RQ 3. To what extent do the views of Kitamori, Endō, and Koyama reflect the perspectives on the Cross within classical Christian theology?

It is hard to compare the views of Kitamori, Endō, and Koyama with classical theories of the Atonement since it was never the intention of any of these three men to construct a theory to explain how the Cross saves people. Kitamori, as we have seen, judges all Atonement theories which do not take into account God's pathos as deficient. He subscribes to the view of the magisterial Reformers that the death of Christ is both penal and substitutionary, believing that, since this theory possesses the intensity of divine passion, it best represents the biblical account of the Cross. We have also suggested that despite Kitamori's theological confession, it is more accurate to describe his *theologia crucis* as a *Dolor Dei* "model" of the Atonement, comprising the objective dimension of penal substitution and the subjective element of divine pain when God, within himself, struggles to overcome wrath with love. The triumph of God's love at the Cross recalls God's triumph over his enemies in Aulén's theory – only in the case of Kitamori, it is the triumph of divine love over divine wrath. This battle is certainly no less intense in Kitamori than it is in Aulén.

Koyama does not align himself with a particular Atonement theory. However, he derives theological validation from Luther's parallel concepts of *opus alienum* and *opus proprium* to suggest that God confronts sinful humans on the cross in order to embrace them. The Christian's faith then must be modeled after Christ whose cry of dereliction using the lament of Psalms 22:1 is a demonstration of ultimate faith, *ad Deum contra Deum confugere*. In this sense, Koyama relates the divine demeanor of Christ on the cross to the First Commandment, the message of which is "[t]o believe in, to hope in, to love and to fear God (*credere, sperare, diligere, timere deum*) at all times" (1985: 246; so Luther). The firm understanding that Koyama has of the confrontation of God as *opus alienum* and the embrace of God as *opus proprium* leads him to conclude that divine wrath as a motif of the Atonement is subservient to that of divine love, and that therefore the sacrifice of Christ is not to be interpreted as a means to placate God's wrath or satisfy God's justice (1995: 268).

Two points are in order here. First, Koyama appropriates Luther's *opus alienum* and *opus proprium* with a nuance that is different from Luther's original intention. Let us recall that Luther first introduces the concepts in his explanation of the sixteenth thesis of the Heidelberg Disputation:

> [W]hen sin is recognized grace is sought and obtained. Thus to those who are humble after this fashion God gives grace, and he who is humbled is exalted. The law humbles us, grace exalts us. The law works fear and wrath, grace works hope and mercy. Through the law comes knowledge of sin. Through the knowledge of sin comes humility, and through humility grace is acquired. In this way, when God makes a man a sinner that he may make him righteous, God is bringing in his strange work [*opus alienum*] that he may in the end bring in his proper work [*opus proprium*]. (Luther, 1962b: 289)

Alister McGrath interprets *opus alienum* in the last line of Luther's explanation either "as *passiones Christi* or human *Anfechtung*," and suggests that whichever it is, Luther understands its ultimate source to be God (1990: 151). Horst Beintker understands *opus alienum* as the latter; it is a "strange work" because "God assaults man in order to break him down and thus to justify him" (McGrath, 1990: 151).[2] In either case, the point is that God uses a totally unexpected means to bring about his desired ends, namely, the salvation of sinners. This is why the Cross is "foolishness" to the wise (cf. 1 Cor. 1:18).

The second point relates to Koyama's comment in his later life that the theology of the Cross is "a doctrine of love, not of sacrifice" (1997b: 59). While it is undeniable that God's mercy lies latent beneath his wrath, it is presumptuous to dismiss sacrifice as an important soteriological theme. Luther's bifurcation of the work of God into *opus proprium* and *opus alienum* does not in any way compromise the sacrificial element in the Atonement. On the contrary it presupposes that Christ bore divine punishment (*opus alienum*) on the cross, and through his sacrificial death secured forgiveness for humankind (*opus proprium*). If Christ's sacrifice does not in effect satisfy God's wrath, there can no objective possibility of forgiveness even if it is a full demonstration of love. Moreover, Luther's dictum *ad Deum contra Deum confugere* makes sense only in the context where divine love and divine wrath are simultaneously operative, even if the latter is considered penultimate to the former. Indeed, as we have seen in chapter 2, the apostle Paul consistently treats the death of Christ as propitiatory, that is, it appeases God's wrath against sin (cf. Rom. 3:25; 5:9; Eph. 1:7; 2:13; Col. 1:20). Therefore, instead of driving a wedge between love and sacrifice, one could say that, on the Cross, God demonstrated his *real* love through a *real* sacrifice. In this sense, Kitamori is closer to the biblical witness

---

[2] McGrath also points out that, similarly, Luther understands the devil as "God's instrument, who performs the *opus alienum Dei* on his behalf in order that the *opus proprium* may be realized" (1990: 151).

when he posits the Cross as the site where divine love and divine wrath are united.

Endō's understanding that Christ died in order to share his love with humans by identifying with their sufferings comes close to Abelard's moral influence theory. Just as Christ's first disciples were profoundly moved and transformed by his utter selflessness and embracing love, and in the process experienced his eternal companionship in their hearts, so would men and women today should they come into encounter with him in their religious circumstances, in the way that Endō did. As we have seen, Endō in his later life believes that God will reveal himself differently, but no less truly, in other religions and through other religious experiences. This is, of course, a radical departure from classical Christian doctrine.

RQ 4. To what extent do the views of Kitamori, Endō, and Koyama reflect themes and values generally identified with Japanese culture and religion?

Anyone who expects to read exotic theology from Kitamori, Endō, and Koyama will be sorely disappointed. While it is true that their writings are a function of their particular understanding of Scripture mediated through their socio-cultural settings and personal life experiences, the premise of anthropological universality and the common text of the Bible do in effect set the parameters for their theological reflection so that their perspectives are never so novel to the extent of being completely unintelligible to a person from another society or culture. Yet culture does exert a profound influence on the way one interprets the Bible, so much so that in order to engage in the theological task, one need to understand language, cultural symbols and their meanings. Conversely, one can therefore expect theological insights to be nuanced differently from culture to culture. The writings of Kitamori, Endō, and Koyama do indeed reflect some common values that can be identified with Japanese culture and religion. We will now examine three common themes that have surfaced from their works: self-negation, suffering, and universal embrace.

The concept of self-negation is inherent in the religious consciousness of people in South and East Asia where the cultural worldview[3] is shaped by monism (e.g. Hinduism) or pantheism (e.g. Taoism and Shinto). It is not that there is no sense of the existence of the individual self among these people; rather the self constantly and instinctively negates all individualizing tendencies and submerges itself in what Indologist Nakamura Hajime calls the "Universal Self" (1964: 99).[4] The influence of Buddhism on China and Japan is, of course,

---

[3] The worldview concept is, admittedly, not an unproblematic one. For the purpose of our discussion, however, we use Paul Hiebert's definition of worldview as "the fundamental cognitive, affective, and evaluative assumptions and frameworks a people make about the nature of reality which they use to order their lives" (2003: 15).

[4] Although Nakamura uses the term "Universal Self" to refer specifically to the Indian view of life, the idea is applicable to Chinese and Japanese cultures as well.

seminal, and the Buddhist teaching of *nirvana* as the ultimate negation of the self finds a ready reception in these two cultures. The meontological approach to philosophy characteristic of the Eastern sages testifies to the centrality of the principle of negation.

In Japan, the philosophical idea of self-negation finds concrete expression in such cultural values as harmony (*wa* 和) and modesty (*kenkyo* 謙虚), and in the aesthetic qualities of simplicity and austerity (*wabi-sabi* 侘び 寂び). So, for instance, self-effacement is highly regarded as good moral behavior. Young children are taught that the description *iiko* ("good boy" or "good girl") is very often modified by the adjective *sunao na*, which means "gentle, mild, meek, obedient, submissive, docile, compliant, yielding" (Davies and Ikeno, 2002: 147). Hence, to be called *sunao na iiko* 素直な良い子 is extremely complimentary for any child. In the arts, there is the classic example of the *haiku*, the traditional form of Japanese poetry that makes use of only seventeen syllables. Japanese people find beauty in the "artistic asceticism" of the *haiku* (Takenaka, 1986: 76). Of course, in *bushidō* 武士道, the code of the samurai, the ultimate honorable act of self-negation is to commit ritual suicide.

The principle of self-negation is evident in the writings of Kitamori, Endō, and Koyama. For Kitamori, the pain of God is the result of divine negation. For Endō, it is the ineffectual and powerless Christ who models self-negation. And Koyama locates divine negation in the self-denial of Christ which ultimately leads him to the cross. The crucified mind of Christ and the "painful helplessness" of God in human history reflect "the depth of biblical grace and ethics" (Koyama, 1985: 125). The self-negating character of God is revealed through this Christ who saved others but refused to save himself (Koyama, 1985: 260; cf. Mk. 15, 31). In sum, all three men, because of their cultural disposition, find themselves completely amenable to the idea of the kenotic Christ. This is why Kitamori and Koyama find such strong affinity with Luther's rejection of the theology of glory in favor of a theology of the Cross which always stands on the "outside," in the periphery (Kitamori, 1986: 12; Koyama, 1985: 255). Endō, unfortunately, stretches the idea of the kenosis to the extreme, such that Christ is completely devoid of his divine power.

Second, we find suffering presenting itself as a key theme in all three's writings. In all probability this has to do with the Buddhist understanding of suffering as the existential human reality. The suffering mentality of the Japanese has led to the cultivation of the virtues of endurance (*gaman* 我慢) and perseverance (*gambari* 頑張り). In other words, rather than fleeing suffering, Japanese people are schooled to face it with fortitude, either by waiting it out patiently, or if possible, by working determinedly to overcome it.[5]

---

[5] It is no exaggeration to say that it is the spirit of *gaman* and *gambari* that motivated Japan to overcome suffering and transform the country from the ashes of war into a modern economic powerhouse within a single generation.

In the writings of Kitamori, Endō, and Koyama, we see the motif of patient suffering projected onto God. In other words, they all assume without qualification that God can suffer, hence the emphasis on the pain of God in Kitamori and the suffering love of God in the writings of the other two. That God can suffer poses no theological difficulty to them. Endō and Koyama are also concerned about human suffering, but find salvation possible because of the capacity of God to suffer for and with humanity. Kitamori acknowledges the reality of human pain, but suggests that its resolution is to be found in its willingness to be used to witness to divine pain. Since some Christians find offensive the idea that God can suffer, we shall discuss the theological problem of the impassibility of God in the next section.

The third common theme in the writings of Kitamori, Endō, and Koyama that appears to be culturally motivated is the idea of a universal embrace. This idea is related to the Buddhist spirit of benevolence. Nakamura, in his magisterial *Ways of Thinking of Eastern Peoples*, explains:

> The Japanese lay special emphasis upon the love of others. Banzan Kumazawa (1619-1691), a famous Confucianist of the Tokugawa period, calls Japan "The land of benevolence." The love of others in its purified form is named "benevolence." [...] This idea was introduced into Japan with the advent of Buddhism. Among many sects of Japanese Buddhism, the Pure Land Buddhism (Jōdo sect), a religion which typically emphasizes benevolence, enjoys great popularity. The Pure Land Buddhism preaches the benevolence of Amitābha Buddha who saves the bad man as well as the ordinary man. (1964: 381)

It is no coincidence that many Japanese see the parallel between the mercy of Amitābha Buddha and the grace of the Christian God. This may explain the fond use of the word "embrace" to describe the saving act of God. Kitamori, for instance, employs the words *daku* 抱く (embrace) and *tsutsumu* 包む (enfold) frequently to describe God's love in action toward his enemies.[6] Koyama too describes the cross as the site where God not only confronts sinners but ultimately embraces them. Moreover, he juxtaposes the image of the self-negating God with the metaphor of divine embrace when he suggests that the crucified Christ embraces humanity by choosing not to save himself (1985: 260). And of course, the Jesus that Endō portrays is full of love and embraces all whom he encounters, especially those who suffer at the margins of society. Toward the end of *Deep River*, Endō expresses his pluralist religious vision through the words of Mitsuko about a "deep river of humanity" which "embraces" (*daku* 抱く) people and carries them away (1994: 342). As mentioned earlier, Endō's religion does not confront but only embraces.

---

[6] The metaphor of "embrace" is used by Miroslav Volf for his work *Exclusion and Embrace: A Theological Exploration of Identity, Otherness, and Reconciliation* (Nashville, TN: Abingdon, 1996). Volf readily admits that the metaphor is a culturally conditioned one, that is, it will work in some cultures but not others (Volf, 1996: 29).

Even though Kitamori and Koyama talk about divine confrontation besides divine embrace, it is clear that for them, the latter is the ultimate divine act that subsumes the former. Moreover, it seems that all three men seem to posit the idea of a universal embrace. In other words, no one is excluded from the embrace of God. It is clear that Endō believed in universal salvation, especially toward the end of his life, but it is harder to conclude the same for Kitamori and Koyama. One could imagine them professing agnosticism on whether all people will be finally saved. However, even if they do not believe in universal salvation, one can certainly make a case to say that they understand Christ's death provides universal redemption.[7]

It is instructive to note that all three writers are silent on the subject of hell. It is a difficult subject, to be sure, but one which is important to Christian doctrine. While one needs to exercise caution not to draw any definitive conclusion by arguing from silence, one could perhaps say that the cultural sensibilities of these three men cause them to steer clear from this topic. Nakamura, citing Anezaki Masaharu, calls the Christian teaching on hell "the outstanding line of demarcation between Christianity and Buddhism" (1964: 384).

> For the Japanese, full of the spirit of tolerance, *eternal damnation* is absolutely inconceivable. A Catholic priest, who forsook Christianity under the persecution of the Tokugawa Government, condemned the idea of eternal damnation preached in Christianity. He said, regarding reward and punishment in the other world, if God be the Lord of Benevolence, he ought to condemn Himself rather than condemn and punish His creatures for their sins. Among the doctrines of Christianity the idea of eternal damnation was especially hard for the Japanese to understand. This also reveals one of the characteristic ideas long held by the Japanese.
>
> The idea of "being beyond deliverance forever" was also hard for the Japanese to comprehend [...]. The idea of discriminating predispositions to salvation, like the idea of eternal damnation, was not generally accepted by the Japanese Buddhists. Generally accepted, instead, was the view, "All men are predisposed to become Buddhists." (Nakamura, 1964: 384-85, emphasis in text)[8]

The difficulty on the part of the Japanese to comprehend eternal condemnation is in all probability related to the fact that they find the idea of exclusion repugnant. Perhaps this is not surprising in a highly communitarian

---

[7] Universal salvation presupposes universal redemption, but the converse relationship is not a necessary one. That is, Christ died for *all* humanity, but this does not mean that all will be saved. In classical Reformed teaching, however, the argument is made that since nothing that the sovereign God wills to do can fail to actualize, Christ could not possibly have died for all because the biblical record is clear that there will be some who will not be saved. Five-point Calvinism therefore affirms limited atonement. See Murray (1962: 27-31); Packer (1974: 37-39); and of course, John Owen's 1648 classic treatise *The Death of Death in the Death of Christ*, especially Chapters I-III of Book III (1959: 124-49).

[8] I am indebted to Dr. Harold Netland for directing me to this reference.

society like Japan where the experience of being excluded from one's group is highly stressful and distressing. In such a cultural context, one can see why Koyama's notion of the cosmological embrace is so appealing. In any case, Nakamura's comment above sheds light on Endō's conception of the maternal God who neither confronts nor condemns but embraces indiscriminately, and perhaps even on the silence on the part of Kitamori and Koyama on matters concerning the eternal destiny of human beings.

In any case, the point is clear: the subject of hell poses a huge challenge to evangelizing a people who are conditioned to believe in an all-embracing benevolence, and hence would reject the idea of hell as fundamentally repulsive. The church in Japan needs to grapple with the issue of divine exclusion, as she takes on the huge challenge of communicating the reality of divine judgment as part of the gospel message. We will pick up the discussion later when we examine the relationship between the Cross and violence later.

RQ 5. To what extent are the views of Kitamori, Endō, and Koyama shaped by their respective biographies?

It should be clear by now that biography plays a hugely significant role in shaping the respective theological perspectives of Kitamori, Endō, and Koyama. Interestingly, all three men possess a penchant for introspection. They all cultivated a love for reading from a young age. Perhaps the social turbulence of the pre-war years and the absence of modern entertainment caused them in their teenage years to turn inward and reflect deeply on their reading in the light of what was happening around them.

In the case of Kitamori, the gift of spiritual sensitivity cultivated in him a sort of Christian mysticism that predisposed him to apprehend biblical truths by intuition (*chokkan* 直感; 1960: 12). The vision he had of the crucified Christ, the numerous close encounters with the deaths of different people in his youth, and his frequent emotional struggles with his own sinfulness recall the experiences of the mystical saints in times past. Kitamori's intuitive nature may also explain his attraction to the philosophy of Nishida, especially the theory of pure experience. Also, the fact that Kitamori never married but devoted his whole life to theological and pastoral work is but a reflection of his singular, monastic-like desire to witness to the pain of God to the Church and to his fellow countrymen and women.

Unlike Kitamori, Endō and Koyama inherited their faith from their families. In the case of Endō, it was an unlikely conversion experience through his baptism which he reluctantly agreed to receive just to please his mother and assuage the pain of her recent divorce. However, he discovered that the sacramental imprint of his baptism on his life was a permanent one; he found it uncomfortable to his cultural identity, yet he could never erase it. Endō's difficult years as a student in France, his recurring illnesses, and his fascination with the turbulent history of the Catholic Church in his own country all contributed significantly to the shaping of his particular understanding of human religiosity, namely, the quest for love in the midst of suffering.

Koyama's theological understanding is largely shaped by his horrific experiences of the war and his years of overseas service as a missionary and theological educator. The untold suffering caused by the war experienced by both the Japanese as well as the many Asians whom he came into contact with as a result of his ministry in Thailand and Singapore, and the experience of what he perceived to be Western theological imperialism led Koyama to be extremely wary of the evils of a triumphalist ideology in whatever realm, whether in politics, theology, or mission. This is why Koyama finds Abraham's posture of non-insistence in Genesis 13 and the supreme example of Christ's self-denial powerfully illustrative of who God is, and by extension, what Christians should be, living and serving in a world wracked with so much violence and suffering. It is not a wonder that Koyama should always insist that theology must bear fruit through sound ethical and missiological practice.

American novelist and former missionary to Japan, Katherine Paterson, recalls C. S. Lewis when she says "a book cannot be what a writer is not. Who you are informs what you write on a very deep level" (Chattaway, 2007: 65). Our study certainly validates Paterson's comment. The influence of biography on theology is significant, yet one which is not sufficiently acknowledged. The typical scholar working on a particular theologian is often content to provide cursory biographical information as "background" to the "real" discussion of ideas of that theologian, not realizing the full extent of the relationship between one's personal experiences and the way one thinks about the larger issues of life and faith. The autobiographical nature of theology is a subject that certainly merits further examination.[9]

Having surveyed the five research questions pertinent to this discussion, we now move on to the next section where we will discuss the theological problems of divine impassibility, of violence, and of eternal damnation.

Three Theological Concerns

The Problem of Divine Impassibility

It is beyond the scope of this work to engage in an in-depth discussion on the theological problem of divine impassibility (*apatheia tou theou*). Nevertheless, it certainly warrants at least a brief treatment since Kitamori, Endō, and Koyama all assume the suffering of God without qualification. We begin by noting that for the major part of the history of the Church, the notion of divine impassibility was taken so much for granted that, until the last half century, it was never really critically examined at all in Western theological circles. In all probability,

---

[9] Once again, I am grateful to Dr. Harold Netland for this insight.

impassibilitas Dei as a divine attribute came to be accepted as theologically axiomatic after a string of debates over the relations between Father, Son, and Holy Spirit within the divine Godhead in the third century (cf. McWilliams, 1980: 35). Fiercely-committed monotheists such as Praxeas, Epigonus, and Noetus sought to refute the potential heresy of tritheism by emphasizing the identity of the Son with the Father. Such teaching, however, is problematic for its failure to maintain a clear distinction between the persons of the Trinity, and its necessary implication that God the Father suffered and died in the crucifixion of Christ. This view, known as patripassianism, was rigorously refuted by Hippolytus and Tertullian. In their total rejection of patripassianism – and later, theopaschitism, the notion that the whole Godhead suffered on the Cross – some of the early Church Fathers unwittingly applied the Stoic ideal of the human person as one who is in full mastery of one's emotions onto divine personhood. In other words, the divine ideal, postulated as unchanging and unchangeable, was logically extended to include the inability to experience any pain or suffering. [10] The Council of Chalcedon (A.D. 451) condemned as "vain babblings" the idea that God could be subject to suffering (Ngien, 1997: 38). However, because of the Council's primary affirmation of the unity of two natures of Christ "without confusion or change, without division or separation," some have argued that its adoption of the *theotokos* formula amounts to an implicit admission of divine suffering (Nnamani, 1995: 89).[11]

The concept of divine impassibility as we have it today was actually shaped by Thomas Aquinas. Although Thomas rejected the idea that God can be defined, he utilized the Aristotelian metaphysical understanding of God as the "Unmoved Mover" – the pure being with pure actuality and no potentiality that "moves" all things from a state of potentiality to actuality – to posit a necessary being as the uncaused cause of all things, hence the cosmological argument for the existence of God (see Erickson, 1998: 182-83). Clearly in Thomas' mind, divine immutability implies divine passibility. God's impassability as such is hence understood to mean that God cannot be acted upon or affected emotionally

---

[10] The biblical passages that have been used to support divine impassability, such as Numbers 23:19; 1 Samuel 15:29; Psalms 110:4; and Jeremiah 4:28, are therefore the same passages that are used to teach divine immutability. The notions of divine immutability and its doctrinal cousin, divine impassibility (and the later idea of divine simplicity that consequently developed), are in all probability the legacy of neo-Platonism. Netland calls this "another case of culture or the intellectual *zeitgeist* shaping theology" (personal communication). See Feinberg (2001: 233-337) for a masterful critique on the classical understanding of these and other non-moral attributes of God.

[11] There appears to be considerable latitude in the way the Church Fathers understand divine impassibility; there is indeed no uniform consensus among them. For a detailed study, see Amuluche Gregory Nnamani, *The Paradox of a Suffering God: On the Classical, Modern-Western, and Third World Struggles to Harmonise the Incompatible Attributes of the Trinitarian God* (Frankfurt: Peter Lang, 1995), pp. 59-99.

by anything in creation.[12] After Thomas, that God is impassible was simply assumed to be true; and even right through the first half of the twentieth century, theologians by and large maintained a stony silence on the subject (Lee, 1974: 1).[13]

The notion that God cannot suffer, however, has come to be seriously challenged, especially in the last sixty years following the end of the Second World War.[14] The Jewish Holocaust and the atomic catastrophes of Hiroshima and Nagasaki provided disturbing material for theological reconsideration of the infinite opposition (of the early Barth) between God and humans. Christian philosopher Charles Hartshorne fired the first salvo in the theological debate by critiquing Anselm's portrayal of God as a deity who "can give us everything, everything except the right to believe that there is one who, with infinitely subtle and appropriate sensitivity, rejoices in all our joys and sorrows in all our sorrows" (1948: 54).[15] In essence, Hartshorne is asking the question if God could *really* be intelligible to humans if he were "a totally impassive, nonreceptive [*sic*], non-relative being" (Hartshorne, 1948: 54). The metaphysical challenge to divine impassibility was so potent that Daniel Day Williams (1967: 172) could claim that it led to a "structural shift in the Christian mind." It is interesting to note that the groundbreaking work on the Old Testament prophets by the Jewish scholar Abraham Heschel in 1962 probably did more than any other book in helping Christians re-evaluate the notion of the impassible God. In the 1970s, a fresh wave of critiques was launched against the notion of divine impassibility, this time by theologians such as Jürgen Moltmann

---

[12] J. I. Packer describes the impassable God as a God locked in a "frozen pose" (personal communication).

[13] There are, of course, notable exceptions such as Brasnett (1928) and Robinson (1939).

[14] It was revealed after the war with the publication of his prison letters and papers that Dietrich Bonhoeffer firmly believed in the idea that God suffers. Commenting on what he sees to be the "decisive difference between Christianity and all religions," Bonhoeffer writes, "Man's religiosity makes him look in his distress to the power of God in the world. God is the *deus ex machine*. The Bible directs us to God's powerlessness and suffering; only the suffering God can help" (1971: 361). Bonhoeffer also composes a moving poem entitled *Christen und Heiden* (translated as "Christians and Others" by Conway, 2006: 6), the second stanza of which conveys the same idea with raw potency:
All men go to God in His distress,
find Him poor, reviled, without shelter or bread,
watch Him tormented by sin, weakness and death.
Christians stand by God in His hour of grieving. (translated by Conway, 2006)
Bonhoeffer received his inspiration for this poem from Matthew 26:40. Recalling the point made above on the influence of biography on theology, it would be almost impossible to imagine Bonhoeffer holding fast to the idea of divine impassibility in the context of what he was going through.

[15] See chapter VIII of Anselm's *Proslogium*, in *Saint Anselm: Basic Writings*, trans. S. N. Deane, 2d ed., (La Salle, Ill.: Open Court, 1962), pp. 13-14

(1974), James Cone (1975), and Geddes McGregor (1975). Their point was simple: If we believe that God is actively engaged with humankind, why should we not believe that in his compassion he does indeed share in human suffering?

It appears that the debate whether God can suffer is largely confined within the Western church. Asian Christians, for instance, have always thought the notion of divine impassibility unintuitive and strange (see Lee, 1974; Kwok, 1984). Of course, as we have seen, Kitamori's *Theology of the Pain of God* is one of the earliest and most provocative analyses on the suffering God to come out after the war. Kitamori himself confesses that his goal in publishing the book is to "convert a villainous theology which teaches that God has no pain" (1986: 29). Another seminal work on the subject is that of Korean theologian Jung Young Lee. In a theological *tour de force*, Lee demonstrates from Romans 5:6-10 how the death of Christ is indeed an expression of "the depth of divine empathy," and therefore that the reality of the Cross cannot but nullify the concept of divine impassibility (1974: 57-63). Lee asserts, "The impassible God cannot bear the sins of the world" (Lee, 1961).

Western theologians are more open today to the idea that God can suffer. The seminal writings of Oxford theologian Paul Fiddes in recent years, such as *The Creative Suffering of God* (1998) and *Participating in God* (2000), have made an enormous contribution by clarifying the theological meaning and meaningfulness of divine suffering. Nowadays, it is not uncommon to hear or see in print the expression "God's suffering love" without any qualification (e.g. Volf, 2004: 201). Interestingly, the March theme for "Reflections: Quotations to Stir Heart and Mind," a regular column in *Christianity Today*, is "Suffering God" (Kauffman, 2007: 71). Also, in the brochure entitled *10 Reasons To Believe In A God Who Allows Suffering* published by the theologically-conservative RBC Ministries, the eighth reason cited is that "God suffers with us in our suffering."

> No one has suffered more than our Father in heaven. No one has paid more dearly for the allowance of sin into the world. No one has so continuously grieved over the pain of a race gone bad. No one has suffered like the One who paid for our sin in the crucified body of His own Son.

By all accounts, the evidence is that the idea that God can suffer does not pose a huge theological challenge today than it did, say, a generation ago. It remains a theological paradox, especially when the idea is placed in the context of the traditional teaching of God's moral and metaphysical perfection. The Nigerian theologian, Nnamani, argues that the motif of kenosis often used to interpret the idea of divine suffering only makes sense within the framework of a relational ontology that defines the Trinity (1995: 369-403). Thomas Weinandy, a Catholic theologian at Oxford, argues from the presupposition of God as *actus purus* that because God is "immune to suffering" (2000: 154), he suffers only through the humanity of the incarnate Son (Weinandy, 2000: 172-226). Paul Gayrilyuk, another Catholic theologian teaching at the University of St. Thomas in St. Paul, Minnesota, debunks the common idea that patristic theology limited the suffering of God to the human nature of the Son as a mistaken one, and suggests that the Church Fathers used the notion of divine impassibility in a restricted and nuanced sense "as an *apophatic qualifier* of all divine emotions [...] to rule out those passions and experiences that were unbecoming of the divine nature," while admitting qualified divine passibility of the Son of God within the framework of the Incarnation without compromising "the irreducible divinity of God" (2004: 16, emphasis in text). According to Gavrilyuk, the way that the Fathers understood divine (im)passibility proved to be effective in countering the Christological heresies of docetism, patripassianism, Arianism, and Nestorianism (Gavrilyuk, 2004: 64-174).

As we can see, the last word on the subject is yet to be spoken. Perhaps this wondrous paradox that "the impassible God suffers" can never be resolved (cf. Weinandy, 2000: 172). That notwithstanding, the suffering love of God has proved to be a helpful concept in pastoral counseling. The reason precisely why we can receive the very real comfort of God in our suffering is that on the cross, God has shown that he does not only understand suffering but that he has experienced the worst of it. We leave this section now, and turn our attention to addressing Koyama's fear that the motif of sacrifice in the Cross could legitimize the use of violence in a world already wracked by so much violence-induced suffering.

The Cross and Violence

Koyama is not the only one who has expressed reservations about the relationship between the Cross and the (mis)use of violence. In the last fifteen years or so, there have been a growing number of voices decrying the traditional understanding of the Atonement as too gory (e.g. Brown, 1992; Winter, 1995; den Heyer, 1998; Bartlett, 2001; Weaver, 2001). The question has been ably tackled by Mouw (2001), Boersma (2003), and Volf (2004), so that a couple of pertinent points will suffice here. Volf rightly points out that a proper understanding of the Cross "gives no warrant for [any] perpetration of violence" (2004: 20; cf. 1 Pet. 2:21-24). Recounting the violence that Christians had historically committed against Jews and Muslims, Volf laments:

> Whenever violence was perpetrated in the name of the cross, the cross was depleted of its "thick" meaning within the larger story of Jesus Christ and "thinned" down to a symbol of religious belonging and power – and the blood of those who did not belong flowed as Christians transmuted themselves from would-be followers of the Crucified to imitators of those who crucified him. (2004: 21)

Volf suggests that the cure against violence "is not less religion, but in a carefully qualified sense, *more* religion" (2004: 17). By this, he means practicing "a stronger and more intelligent commitment to the faith as faith" (Volf, 2004:

17), as Christ's followers imitate the trinitarian God whose life "is characterized by mutually uncoerced and welcomed generosity" (Volf, 2004: 18).

Yet, it is undeniable that the Bible contains violent images that often accompany the salvation narrative. Isaiah 63:1-6, for instance, describes a righteous God "mighty to save," but who accomplishes salvation by trampling his enemies with such wrath that their blood is splattered on his garments. This imagery reminds us of Christ, the conquering Son who dons "a robe dipped in blood" (Rev. 19:3). How are we to make sense of these disturbing images? For a start, these images subvert our domesticated image of God, and remind us that the God of love is also the God of wrath. The Bible is hence unequivocal in its teaching that divine judgment on sin *is* indeed a necessary condition for salvation. This is where the good news comes in. The judgment that is due to sinful humanity is assumed by Christ on the cross. In the eloquent words of Karl Barth, "the Judge delivers Himself to be judged" (1956: 251; cf. 1960: 49). And he does this "for us," that is, "in our place" (Barth, 1956: 251). This is "the good news of Good Friday" (Barth, 1956: 251).

In relation to the thought that Christ died in our place on the cross, John Stott warns against two theological pitfalls. The first is to construe our substitute as Christ *alone*, for that would make him an independent third party intervening between God and humanity; and the second is to speak *only* of God suffering and dying, for that would negate the historical Incarnation and necessary mediation of the Son (Stott, 1986: 156). The right approach is to understand our substitute as "*God in Christ*, who was truly and fully both God and man, and who on that account was uniquely qualified to represent both God and man and to mediate between them" (Stott, 1986: 156). When we think in these terms, we will realize that "[t]he Father did not lay on the Son an ordeal he was reluctant to bear, nor did the Son extract from the Father a salvation he was reluctant to bestow" (Stott, 1986: 151). In other words, although the Cross is a violent event, the Father and the Son are not warring against each other in a divine conflict. On the contrary, as Stott rightly observes, "their wills coincided in the perfect self-sacrifice of love" (Stott, 1986: 152). Indeed, it is hard to justify the use of violence from the Cross when one understands that "[t]he biblical gospel of atonement is of *God satisfying himself by substituting himself for us*" (Stott, 1986: 159-60, emphasis added).

Richard Mouw continues the same line of thought:

> The very same God who pours out the divine wrath is the One who experiences the wrathful forsakenness of divine abandonment. God, in the unity of the divine being, is both the violated One and the One who counts that violatedness as satisfying the demands of eternal justice.
>
> In the death on the Cross, God also took our violent impulses upon himself, mysteriously absorbing them into his very being in order to transform them into the power of reconciling love; and then offers that love back to us as a gift of sovereign grace. (2001: 17)

Such is the unfathomable mystery of the Atonement.

"When atonement theories carve out a place for judgement and punishment, do they really legitimate unjust violence?" Hans Boersma asks rhetorically, and then suggests that the opposite might indeed be the case.

> By ignoring the judicial meaning of the cross, we convey to victims of violence that their pains and concerns are irrelevant, that they need to "get over it and get on with it." When punishment has no place at all in our thinking about the cross, sin and evil receive a legitimate and permanent place as an intrinsic part of a world that forever remains out of joint. (2003: 34)

Rather, as Moltmann puts it, on the cross, Christ "identifies God with the victims of violence," and at the same time identifies "the victim with God, so that they are put under God's protection and with him are given the rights of which they have been deprived" (1992: 131).

In other words, rather than lending legitimacy to the use of violence, the violence of the Cross is in effect the redemptive last word on violence, for it is the divinely-ordained means of abolishing all the violence and bloodshed in the world (Chua, 2006b: 24). That is, the nature of the violence of the Cross is redemptive, not vindictive. Even so, the use of redemptive violence is solely a divine prerogative. Volf puts it well, "Though imitating God is the height of human holiness, there are things which only God may do. One of them is to deploy violence" (2004: 21). Commenting on the violence that permeates John's Apocalypse, Volf suggests that in the context of the whole biblical revelation, it is best understood as a "symbolic portrayal of the final exclusion of everything that refuses to be redeemed by God's suffering love" (Volf, 2004: 21). Volf therefore warns Christians against arrogating for themselves what God has reserved only for himself, to transpose the divine action from the end-time to a time in which God explicitly refrains from deploying violence in order to make repentance possible, and, finally, to transmute a possibility of violence into an actuality (Volf, 2004: 21)

Koyama's fears are perfectly understandable, but ultimately unfounded. It is true that as a historically-determined religion, Christianity has been extremely violent. Indeed, so-called Christian nations have not been known to exercise the restraint of violence on the global scene. In the light of the gospel of Jesus Christ, who willingly gave his life for the sake of the world's welfare, it is indeed extremely difficult to justify any use of violence.

The Problem of Hell

Volf makes the insightful observation that the insistence on human non-violence and the divine "prerogative of exercising violence against 'false prophets' and 'beasts' if they refuse to be redeemed by the wounds they inflicted on the Crucified" (1996: 30) creates "an asymmetrical dialectic" between the divine grace and divine justice (Volf, 1996: 29). What this means is that "even if the *will* to embrace is indiscriminate, the *embrace* itself is conditional" (Volf, 1996: 29). In other words, the "eschatological confrontation" of the cross, to use Koyama's words, really leads to eternal punishment.[16] But this is also precisely why the death of Christ as penal and substitutionary is truly such good news.

According to Wolfhart Pannenberg, Luther was likely the first since the apostle Paul to apprehend the death of Christ as vicarious penal suffering (1968: 279). Pannenberg might well be right, for Luther in his commentary on Galatians 3:13 makes this exuberant oration of how Christ bore fully the divine punishment for human sin:

> [O]ur most merciful Father, seeing us to be oppressed and overwhelmed with the curse of the law, and so to be holden [*sic*] under the same, that we could never be delivered from it of our own power, sent His Only Son into the world, and laid upon Him all the sins of men, saying, be Thou Peter that denier; Paul that persecuter [*sic*], and cruel oppressor; David that adulterer; that sinner who did eat the fruit in Eden; that thief who hanged upon the cross, and briefly, be Thou that person who hath committed the sins of all men: see therefore that thou [*sic*] pay and satisfy for them. Here cometh the law and saith: I find Him a sinner, and such a one as hath taken upon Him the sins of all men, and I see no sins else but in Him: therefore let Him die upon the cross: and so it setteth upon Him and killeth Him. By this means the whole world is purged and cleansed from sin, and so delivered from death and all evils. Now sin being vanquished and death abolished by this one man, God would see nothing else in the whole world, if it did believe it, but a mere cleansing and righteousness. And if any remnants of sin should remain, yet for the great glory that is in Christ, God would not see them. (1979: 167-68)

In sum, because of the nature of the penal-substitutionary death of Christ, no human being needs to fear the threat of eternal damnation. By the mercy of God, sinners do not need to receive what they deserve, for Christ has fully received on himself their due punishment. By the grace of God, not only are sinners acquitted in Christ, they now receive what they do not deserve, namely, the gifts of eternal, abundant life and reconciliation with their Creator God. In other words, the Cross *is* the answer to the problem of eternal damnation. Within the biblical message of judgment there is always the offer of grace. For "[b]y divine grace, the violence that we, as God's enemies, ought to have suffered, was borne for us by our Savior. The divine hospitality extended to us comes at the cost of divine violence suffered on our behalf" (Chua, 2006b: 24).

What about the eternal destiny of those who, through no fault of their own, die without the gospel? Here, we need to take the path of theological agnosticism. Perhaps Barth can help us here. He suggests that while we must not presume on

---

[16] Other than asserting that eternal punishment involves the complete absence of God, it is beyond the scope of this dissertation to debate the nature of hell, especially in relation to the theories of annihilationism and conditionalism. See Erickson (1998: 1242-48) for a helpful discussion and critique on these theories.

God's grace and assume "eternal patience" on his part, we could also be open "to the possibility that in the reality of God and man in Jesus Christ there is contained much more than we might expect and therefore the supremely unexpected withdrawal of that final threat" (Barth, 1961: 477-78). In other words, instead of affirming or denying universal salvation, "we can only hope" in the sovereign compassion of God while not neglecting the work of calling people to repentance in Christ (Barth, 1961: 477). That is quite possibly the theological posture as well adopted by Kitamori and Koyama.

The gospel therefore is not to be preached in negative terms, that is, using the threat of eternal damnation as a means to coerce belief. Such conversion motivated by fear is not likely to last. Rather, the gospel is good news, not bad news. It is the glorious message that God is *for us* (*Deus pro nobis*; cf. Jn. 3:17). The focus of the preaching of the gospel then should be on the demeanor of God's suffering love, and what God has done through the painful death of Christ in order to redeem us from the judgment of sin and death, and reconcile us to himself. For indeed it is true, as Kitamori and Koyama point out – in accordance with Luther and Barth – that God's dealing with humankind is ultimately defined by his love rather than his wrath.

Methodological Concerns

An important question that arises from this research is the nature of theology, and the attendant problem of theological language. In this section, we will discuss these two issues, paying particular attention to the works of Kitamori and Koyama. Reference is made to Endō from the sidelines since the genre of most of his works fall under literature rather than theology.

The Nature and Modes of Theology

Kitamori is regarded in Japan as a systematic theologian, even though his work on the pain of God has never quite been accepted as an important idea in the discipline. In the case of Koyama, while it is undeniable that he works within the theological guild, one would be hard-pressed to classify his works under the rubric of systematic theology. As David Ford rightly observes, Koyama's theology

> is not concerned to develop lengthy analyses and arguments, it subverts or explodes positions that seem to him [Koyama] too neatly systematic and coherent, and it points in many ways to the complexity, variety, and ambiguity of reality. There are few confident overviews in this theology. Rather there is a constant questioning, ethical, and imaginative engagement with particular issues and situations, and the attempt to open them up to a better understanding and future. The approach is dialogical and practical. It proceeds usually in short bursts and in a staccato style which provokes the reader and creates new perceptions and connections. It is a combination of prophetic and wisdom literature suited to the perplexing, agonizing

and exciting meeting of ancient and modern, Buddhist and Christian, East and West, rich and poor. (1989: 226-27)

Despite the differences between Kitamori and Koyama in their theological orientation and content, it is interesting to note that in contrast with the emphasis on right doctrines about God, which is implicit to the traditional Western understanding of theology as "the queen of sciences", both men would, in all probability, view theology as an art whose primary function is that of a servant impressing upon the Church and expressing to the world the mysterious ways of God.

First of all, Kitamori is right to insist that theology must be based on divine revelation and not human speculation (1986: 34). The source of divine revelation is the Bible, which Kitamori likens to the walls of a Japanese castle, perfect and dependable (2000: 170). Koyama similarly subscribes to the fundamental importance of the Word of God as the proper basis of all theology (1999: 76).[17] In other words, both men define theological prolegomena by the primacy of the revealed Word of God. Since the Word of God contains mysterious divine realities that God has chosen so graciously to reveal to humankind, theology must hence inculcate within the believer a profound sense of awe and wonder (Kitamori, 1986: 70). Consequently, Koyama regards the Atonement not as a theological problem to be solved but as a mystery to be marveled at (1985: 256).[18] In this regard, Kitamori laments that much of the theology of the Church "has lost its wonder" (Kitamori, 1986).

As with all mystery, divinity cannot be mastered and neatly systematized. The mystery of faith can only be apprehended through thoughtful participation, by reflecting on it and ultimately living it out. Here, we see the positive contribution that the Japanese cultural disposition can make to the theological enterprise, for it lends to the formation of thought forms which are more amenable to intuitive comprehension rather than to the organization of dogmatic details. It is hardly surprising that the writings of Kitamori and Koyama are commonly characterized by linguistic elements relating to the aesthetic, the intuitive, and the emotional – the primacy of which traits is often stressed in Japanese culture (cf. Nakamura, 1964: 551-57; Spae, 1971: 171-206).

The literary nature of the writings of Kitamori, Endō, and Koyama indeed confirms Frederick Ferre's observation that theological discourse is

---

[17] Koyama understands the Word of God not as a static entity divorced from historical reality, but as the prophetic divine Word illumined and enlivened by the Holy Spirit in a specific socio-historical context (1999: 76-77; cf. John 14:26).

[18] The French philosopher Gabriel Marcel makes the classic distinction between a problem and a mystery. A problem is one that seeks a solution, while a mystery calls for different levels of understanding. See Marcel, *The Mystery of Being: 1. Reflection and Mystery* (Chicago: Henry Regnery, 1950), pp. 197-219. I am indebted to Dr. Kevin Vanhoozer for directing me to Marcel. See also Gallagher (1962: 30-49) for a discussion on Marcel's distinction.

multifunctional, hence multimodal (1961: 93). Each type of theological speech carries with it specific and distinguishing linguistic features. Broadly speaking, theological language can be divided into two kinds: statements *about* religion and statements *in* religion. The first type is largely conceptual and propositional in form, and it is the linguistic vehicle for the study and understanding of religion. The study of systematic theology would utilize language of this sort. The second type is predominantly expressive and symbolic in form, its main terms being images, and its function being the direct expression of personal religious expression. Here, language is used to experience and express a spiritual sense of wonder. It does seem evident that Japanese theological writings fall under the latter category.

Paradox as a Theological Device

From the writings of Kitamori and Koyama, we see the turn to the aesthetic as one of the principal means to recover or maintain the sense of wonder when reflecting on divine realities. For them, theological aestheticism is expressed primarily through the device of the paradox. Indeed, their writings are fraught with dialectical tensions. However, unlike the dialectical theology of the neo-orthodox theologians which propositionalizes the relationship between thesis and antithesis by holding them together in tandem, Kitamori and Koyama seem to focus on the antithesis, or the "lesser idea," thereby straining the effect of the paradox. For instance, while traditional doctrine may simply explain the Incarnation as God becoming human, Kitamori and Koyama would emphasize the distinctive message of the Incarnation as revealing the "smallness" of God in contrast to the common idea of the greatness of God. Hence, we see, for example, Kitamori's particular accent placed on the pain of God. Koyama, of course, revels in the divine paradox that the omnipotent, omnipresent, and omniscient God who creates the universe is indeed the God who walks at the speed of three miles an hour, constantly moves toward the periphery in search of the one lost sheep, embraces impassionedly with his crucified mind, and who gives of himself in suffering for the redemption of others. To the Japanese mind, there is an austere beauty to these ideas.

The ready acceptance of paradox on the part of Kitamori and Koyama is certainly reflective of their Japanese cultural sensibilities, and this seems to move them away from the propositional theologizing that is so highly valued in the Western academy. [19] Their works, in contrast to Western theological writings, clearly conform to the Eastern tradition of wisdom where truth is often – and more powerfully – conveyed through paradox than through proposition.

---

[19] The linguistic fact that in the Japanese language, the same word is used for paradox and contradiction, namely, *mujun* 矛盾, for example, hints at the Japanese difficulty of systematizing ideas in a rational and logical fashion.

The use of the paradox as a methodological device is one that Kitamori intentionally and repeatedly uses in his theologizing (2000: 162). For instance, he insists that the meaning of Immanuel in Matthew 1:23-25 cannot be fully understood except in its paradoxical relationship with the meaning of Christ's cry of dereliction from the cross in Matthew 27:45 (Kitamori, 2000: 7-21). In this case, the paradox, or the "wondrous truth" (*zetsumyō no shinr* 絶妙の真理) as Kitamori calls it, is that our experience of "God with us" is made possible by his desertion of Immanuel on the cross. Here is another example. In order to avoid theological distortion, says Kitamori, the Parable of Workers in the Vineyard (Mt. 20:1-16) must be read in tandem with the Parable of the Talents (Mt. 25:14-30) (2000: 155-63). The paradox here is the relationship between grace and responsibility. Takenaka Masao applies the same technique when he employs the aesthetic motif of *wabi* 侘び in his presentation on the life of Christ, "the Son of the living God" – a life characterized, paradoxically, by the *wabi* of solitariness, poverty, simplicity, emptiness, and humility (1986: 78-82).

By all accounts, the supreme divine paradox is the death of Christ. We have already seen how Kitamori and Koyama expound on this through the respective motifs of the pain of God and the crucified mind. The paradox of the death of the God-man in Christ on the cross for the salvation of humankind is shared by Lee, for whom "the meaning of the Cross as the depth of divine empathy implies paradoxically the unconditional penetration of divine love into the ultimate negativities of human existence" (1974: 58). It is an unfathomable mystery that we should "die with [Christ's] death to sin and live with His resurrection to God" (Lee, 1974: 58).

The Problem of Theological Language

The tendency toward the intuitive rather than the rational in the writings of Kitamori, Endō, and Koyama is due in part to the fact that Japanese linguistic forms "are more oriented to sensitive and emotive nuances than directed toward logical exactness" (Nakamura, 1964: 531).[20] Here, we see the intrinsic and intricate relationship between culture and language. Indeed, the intuitive

---

[20] When I was Dr. J. I. Packer's teaching assistant at Regent College, I always found great difficulty grading the examination essays of many international students from East Asia. One day, an elderly Japanese pastor, who was then taking a sabbatical year at Regent, came up to me after the systematic theology finals and said, "We Japanese are very bad in systematic theology. We don't think like that." This example is, of course, purely anecdotal, and it would be absolutely wrong to conclude that Japanese people do not think logically. The international reputation of Japanese students in the mathematical sciences attests to their ability in the use of rigorous analytical logic. The point maintained here is the "non-rationalistic tendencies" that Japanese people display when it comes to the existential issues of life and faith (Nakamura, 1964: 531). (Note that "non-rationalistic" does not mean "irrational.") One reason for this is that the Japanese language does not facilitate precise, careful definitions when it comes to matters of the heart.

orientation of the Japanese mind is often mirrored in the language, and it is not uncommon to hear Westerners complaining about the vagueness of Japanese linguistic expressions. We note, for instance, that Kitamori's use of the word *itami* 痛み (pain) is very broad and not always consistent, referring at various times to Christ's passion, divine sorrow as a result of human sin, and the conflict between divine love and divine wrath. Also, the distinction he makes between *jittai* 実体 (substance) and *honshitsu* 本質 (essence) is logically murky, and leaves unanswered the nagging question as to whether he understands the pain of God as a divine ontology of substance or of relation? Kitamori is obviously unperturbed by the problem, if he ever thought that there was one.

The nature of the theological impasse for the English reader in this case is both semantic and cognitive. The point to be borne in mind is that there is no exact conceptual equivalence between Japanese and English – or for that matter, any two languages – and this has to do with the relationship between language and thought. Subsequent research following the pioneering work of American linguist Edward Sapir and his student Benjamin Lee Whorf in the 1930s has shown that language does exert a substantial – although not total – influence in predisposing speakers of that language toward adopting a particular way of thinking.[21]

The relationship between language and thought bears profound implications for the theological task. With regard to this, the perception on the part of the non-Western Church of the imperialism of Western theology purveyed through the linguistic juggernaut of English cannot be summarily dismissed. Along with the current movement of the center of gravity of the Church to the southern hemisphere comes the growing inevitable reality of a preferred option for the vernacular in the apprehension of biblical revelation (cf. Sanneh, 1989; Bediako, 1995; Walls, 1996; Jenkins, 2002; Phan, 2003). This will have significant repercussions on the theology of the Church in view of the growth of world Christianity. Indeed, the first Pentecost on which people gathered from different nations and praised God *together* in their respective languages, hence signaling a reversal of the Tower of Babel, is now interpreted to provide fresh motivation for what Harold Netland calls "globalizing theology" (2006: 30).[22] Interestingly, the Pentecostal reversal of Babel is not total in that there was never a divine impulse

---

[21] For an excellent summary of the Sapir-Whorf Hypothesis, see Trudgill (1983: 24-27). See also Whorf (2001: 363-81) on his work among the Hopi Indians showing how their interpretation of experience is directly affected by the structure of the Hopi language.

[22] Netland provides a "preliminary definition" of globalizing theology as "theological reflection rooted in God's self-revelation in Scripture and informed by the historical legacy of the Christian community through the ages, the current realities of the world, and the diverse perspectives of Christian communities throughout the world, with a view to greater holiness in living and faithfulness in fulfilling God's mission in all the world through the church" (2006: 30).

toward a common language; rather it confers theological and missiological justification on the vernacular principle (cf. Rev. 5:9; 7:9).

For a long time now, non-Western Christians who want to study theology in the academy need to learn the European languages. Many of these students, ironically, experience the cognitive constraints imposed by the Western languages such that it becomes difficult for them to theologize in their original contexts.[23] There must come a time – if it has not already come – for Western theologians to take up the challenge of learning non-Western languages so that they can pay closer attention both to *how* non-Western Christians do theology and to *what* they are saying. In the words of Kenyan theologian John Mbiti, "[W]e have eaten theology with you [...] will you eat theology with us?" (cited in Bediako, 1995: 167). Theological idioms from another culture can only enrich one's own understanding of faith. Conversely, the Church can only become theologically impoverished if the barrier of language is allowed to maintain the mutually-indifferent bifurcation between Western theology and non-Western theology.

There is another problem relating to theological language – a philosophical one. Originally, the debate was about the possibility of using language to talk about God, but the concern has now moved to the meaning and meaningfulness of God-talk, as it is called.[24] The possibility of God-talk is predicated on two factors, one linguistic and the other theological. First, the symbolic nature of human language makes it possible *in some way* to talk about God and matters of ultimate concern (see Chua, 2007).[25] Besides this linguistic fact, there is the

---

[23] This is another instance of the Sapir-Whorf Hypothesis. Koyama is, of course, a fine exception. He circumvents the problem of linguistic constraint by creating new words and expressions (e.g. "neighborology," "the peripherized Christ, etc.).

[24] See William Alston, *Divine Nature and Human Language: Essays in Philosophical Theology* (Ithaca, NY: Cornell University Press, 1989) for a sustained discussion on the subject from the perspective of modern analytical philosophy. I am indebted to Harold Netland for this reference.

[25] Language as a uniquely human phenomenon is distinguished by three properties: arbitrariness, displacement, and creativity. By arbitrariness is meant the absence of a necessary relation between a linguistic form and the meaning it carries. For example, other than conventional agreement, there is no compelling reason why English speakers should call a canine animal *dog*, rather than, say, *kog*. Next, displacement allows language users to symbolize objects, events and concepts which are not immediately present in time and space. Thus, we can talk about things outside our immediate environment or even things that have only an imaginary existence. Displacement enables humans to handle generalizations and abstractions, and manipulate concepts such as truth, infinity, multiplication, etc. Third, creativity, or productivity, is evidenced by the fact that human speakers can, without conscious effort, generate and understand an infinite number of grammatically well-formed utterances from a finite set of linguistic symbols. This is why there are word dictionaries but not sentence dictionaries. In the realm of human cognitive endeavour, linguistic creativity enables humans to bridge the common and the extraordinary, the familiar and the extremely unfamiliar. For example, although there are no ready-made words for all the discoveries and inventions

theological assertion that God always speaks in human terms – through his word and through the historical event of the Incarnation (so Irenaeus; cf. Behr, 2000: 89-90). However, any discourse about God must respect his uniqueness and mystery. There indeed exists a linguistic form of divine transcendence which necessitates "speaking at the edges of language and straining its limits" (van Buren, 1972: 115). The implication then is that *all* language about God is in some sense metaphorical (cf. Boersma, 2003: 33).[26] In other words, although as humans we cannot comprehend the essence of God, divine revelation is such that we use trust human language to speak properly about God (Boersma, 2005: 4). Through the Thomist device of analogical predication, circumscribed by biblical revelation, divine realities can be described by reflecting on human experience.

The Bible certainly speaks of God acting and feeling like a human being. Therefore, the objection voiced by proponents of divine impassibility against the use of linguistic expressions such as "the pain of God" and "divine pathos" on the grounds that such language is purely anthropomorphic or anthropopathic is, of course, rhetorical, since descriptions of divine impassibility are *also* couched in anthropomorphic or anthropopathic language, albeit negatively (e.g. Num. 23:19). In a similar vein, Boersma points out the inconsistency of people who understand God's wrath metaphorically while applying a literal interpretation to his love (2003: 33). In conjunction with this, Boersma also warns against the common fallacy that metaphors are "somehow less real" because they are perceived as "*just* metaphors" (Boersma, 2003: 33, emphasis in text). Quoting the late Colin Gunton, Boersma insists that the contrary is true, that metaphors plumb the depth of reality by facilitating "a new way of thinking about and living in the world" (Gunton, 1989: 51-52, cited in Boersma, 2003: 33). The various metaphors in the New Testament describing the death of Christ, for example, are precisely employed in order to show the *reality* of the Atonement. The Church's understanding of the death of Christ becomes amplified.

This, of course, does not grant us the license to impose our cultural categories onto God uncritically and unilaterally. As Boersma cogently points out, "[W]e cannot simply exchange [metaphors] for others without also affecting the contents of what we are saying. *We need to ask what is lost in the shift from one metaphor or model to another*" (Boersma, 2003: 33, emphasis added). In other words, if a new metaphor compromises or excludes the existing meaning conveyed by other biblical metaphors rather than enlarging it, then that is a good indication that it is an unsuitable metaphor. Using this test to evaluate the

---

of cyber technology, we are able to use the linguistic resources at our disposal in novel ways, and we do so successfully. The linguistic properties of arbitrariness, displacement and creativity are intrinsically tied up with the symbolic nature of language. See Chua 2007.

[26] This, of course, begs the question on the meaning of "metaphorical" and "literal," or of "analogical" and "univocal." See Alston (1989: 39-63) for a helpful discussion on this vexing issue.

plethora of metaphors in the writings of Kitamori and Koyama, one can safely say that they enrich biblical revelation rather than detract from it. On the other hand, Endō's metaphor of the maternal God is not a good metaphor if it insists on the exclusion of God's paternal characteristics. In any case, the point is well taken that theologians need to constantly wrestle with the nature and limits of God-talk so as to check the ever-lurking danger of humans creating God through their culturally-formed and embedded images.

The Place of Western Theology in Contextualization

The cause of Christ would be gravely jeopardized if in the name of the vernacular principle, Western theology and non-Western theology are pitted against each other. On this matter, Kitamori and Koyama offer some helpful thoughts. First, we need to acknowledge "[t]he impressive quality and scope of Western scholarship in all areas of theological studies" (Koyama, 1993e: 90). There are historical reasons for this, and they are not accidental. Theological education throughout the world is therefore, in a real sense, indebted to Western theological achievements (Koyama, 1993e: 90). It would be wrong to reject Western theology outright, not only on philosophical grounds but also for practical reasons.

> [I]t is simplistic to call for the complete elimination of the influence of Western theological thought, for instance, from Asia. It would require the resignation of nearly all theological professors and church leaders from their positions. Nearly all books on every shelf of the theological libraries throughout Asia would be declared worthless. (Koyama, 1993e: 93)

Instead of mutual antagonism, Koyama advocates a posture of "mutual correction" between Western theology and indigenous theologies (Koyama, 1993e: 94). While non-Western Christians should continue to be open to learn from the West, Western Christians should exercise humility to seriously listen to and learn from the rest of the world as well.[27] As Clifford Geertz would say, "Monologues are of little value here" (1973: 29). Geertz' comment, though made in an entirely different context, is totally applicable to theological reflection and missiological practice. This point has already been belabored above.[28] One needs to note, of course, that theological division is not a problem that exists solely between the West and the non-West; it will indeed become an increasing challenge even between non-Western cultures as "new centres of

---

[27] At the moment, many Western theology textbooks simply relegate non-Western theologians to a line or two in the footnotes, hence not presenting an accurate picture of them. For example, Erickson's magisterial work contains a single reference to Kitamori in a footnote (1998: 295 n), and a one-liner on Koyama (Erickson, 1998: 80).

[28] This dissertation hopes to set a good example of what cross-cultural theological interaction could look like.

Christianity's universality" sprout all over the world (Mbiti, cited in Bediako, 1995: 163). Koyama's call for an attitude of openness and humility is relevant for all instances. In sum, cross-cultural or globalizing theologizing is best done not by confrontation between the different contexts, nor by mutual indifference, but through respectful conversation.

Kitamori offers a similar, but slightly nuanced, take on the issue of Western theology. First and foremost, he asserts that theology must seek to be concretely universal even though it must be mediated by the particular (2005: 7-8). Indeed, he acknowledges that much of the orthodox dogma of the Church that had historically grown out of Greek theology could claim universal validity despite the particularity of Greek thought (Kitamori, 2005: 8). Theologizing today from the Japanese perspective – for that matter, any cultural perspective – involves a tension between two poles. On the one hand, Kitamori sees the need for Japanese theology to be freed from what Harvie Conn calls a "Constantinian cultural captivity" (1978: 41); on the other, given the long and venerable tradition of Western theology, he believes that any non-Western theology must necessarily be mediated through the established entity of Western theology as it seeks to approach the Bible from a fresh point of view and renew the tradition of orthodox Western dogma (Kitamori, 1978: 8). Kitamori's approach certainly brings to mind the "indigenizing principle" and the "pilgrim principle" that Andrew Walls posits to prevent contextual theology from becoming either syncretistic or provincial (1996: 7-9). Kitamori is exemplary in this regard. Unashamedly Lutheran by confession, he exercises great facility in interacting with Western thought as well as with Japanese cultural ideas. Although he writes in Japanese, he constructs his theology with the welfare of the whole Church in mind.

Distinctives of an Evangelical Approach to Cross-Cultural Theologizing

In an interesting article entitled, "Is 'Japanese Theology' Possible?" (1969), Kitamori explores the tension between cultural relevance and syncretism in the discussion on indigenization. Rather than pitting "theology from above" against "theology from below," Kitamori advocates a third way of doing theology, namely, "from above *to below*" (Kitamori, 1969: 81, emphasis in text). The universal gospel has to be particularized in context. Kitamori elaborates, "Universality which is not mediated through particularities is a mere result of imagination and it does not exist anywhere in reality" (Kitamori, 1969: 83).

In a similar vein, Stephen Bevans states in the opening line of his book *Models of Contextual Theology* that "[t]here is no such thing as 'theology'; there is only *contextual* theology" (2002: 3, emphasis in text). The fact that biblical revelation – in both the Old and the New Testament – is given to humankind in concrete socio-cultural contexts implies that the subsequent task of theology cannot be anything less than "an attempt to understand Christian faith in terms of a particular context" (Bevans, 2002: 3). Indeed, the cultural contextualization of theology is not only a missiological possibility, but a "theological imperative" (Bevans, 2002: 3). In this final section of the chapter, we draw from our research on Kitamori, Endō, and Koyama, and propose three distinctives that can serve as parameters for an evangelical approach to doing theology in a cross-cultural context.

The Incarnation as Theological Model

Koyama suggests rightly that the first requirement for doing theology is not reason, but faith, that is, "a total personal commitment" to the revelation of God (1975a: 52). Such faith leads to an understanding of the supreme revelation of God through the incarnation of Jesus Christ in history as the locus of what Koyama calls "authentic contextualization" (1999: 15). For the Incarnation is not only a historical event, but a theological one in that it mediates God's self-disclosure under culture-specific conditions (Koyama, 1999: 17). In other words, Christ did not simply become human: he became a *particular* person "in a particular locality and in a particular ethnic group, at a particular place and time" (Walls, 1996: 27). Walls develops further the idea of the Incarnation as "translation":

> Christ can become visible within the very things which constitute nationality. The first divine act of translation into humanity thus gives rise to a constant succession of new translations. Christian diversity is the necessary product of the Incarnation. (1996: 27-28)

In sum, theological contextualization is possible because of the Incarnation which affirms the "infinite translatability of the Christian faith" (Walls, 1996: 22). Biblical revelation can indeed be contextualized and embedded in any culture. Besides providing a philosophical basis for the possibility of theology, Koyama also sees the Incarnation, through the example of suffering of the incarnated Christ, as constituting a practical model for living as well as for doing theology. Koyama recalls Luther's famous words to substantiate his point, "Not reading books or speculating but living, dying and being damned make a theologian" (Walls, 1996: 22).

Using the kenotic example of Christ, Koyama believes that theology must be done with a "self-emptying" attitude (1974b: viii). Minimally, this means that the language of certainty and superiority must give way to the language of self-denial and interrelatedness.

> Superiority is a cultural concept. To say that Christianity is superior to Buddhism, or vice versa, is empty talk. The Gospel is not called to be superior. It calls us to bear "good fruits" (Mt. 7:17). The "no other name" theology (Act. 4:12) signifies an exclusiveness whose character is "full of grace and truth" (Jn. 1:14). Unlike the ordinary cultural concept of exclusiveness, this Christological exclusiveness, drawing its life from love of unfathomable depth (1 Cor. 13:13), goes far beyond

any comparative discussion of superiority or inferiority of religions. (Koyama, 1997b: 58)

Epistemic Humility as Theological Virtue

Koyama goes even further than saying that theology has to be incarnate: it has to be crucified just as Jesus was crucified. He then asserts, "It is the crucified mind that can meaningfully participate in authentic contextualization" (1999: 18).

> [The crucified mind] is accommodational and prophetic. It knows that only by the grace of God can it be, and remain, accommodational and prophetic at all [...]. The mission of the church begins with the nurture of the crucified mind, the mind of Christ in the context of theological raw situations. (Koyama, 1999: 18)

Doing theology with a crucified mind implies first and foremost cultivating an attitude of humility. True theological insights are by nature "*humble* theological insights," for "[t]hey are *servants*, not masters, to the 'inexpressible gift' of God in Christ (2 Cor. 9:15)" (Koyama, 1999: 142, emphases in text). Indeed, all theologies are but "*humble* theological attempts to express some fragment of the fullness of God's glory in Christ (Isa. 6:1-8);" even put together, they "cannot exhaust and prove the depth of God's purpose in Christ (Rom. 11:33-35)" (Koyama, 1999: 142, emphasis in text). For this reason, Koyama is extremely critical of the theological structure of denominationalism which he lambastes as "sick," "deadly," and "demonic" (Koyama, 1999: 143). For denominationalism causes "humble theological insights to be puffed up" and seeks "[to] monopolize Christ theologically" (Koyama, 1999: 143).[29] In the final analysis, in casting aside the crucified mind of Christ, denominationalism betrays faith, for it turns from its total commitment to divine revelation to a relentless quest for power and control (cf. Koyama, 1975a: 52). In a word, without putting on the crucified mind, theology can only become "the force for 'tearing apart' and 'rending'" rather than what it is supposed to be: a healing balm for a suffering world (Koyama, 1999: 143).

Koyama's emphasis on humility is echoed by Hans Boersma. Responding to Richard Neuhaus' comment that "all theories of atonement are but probings into mystery, the mystery of a love that did not have to be but was, and is," Boersma issues a call to all theologians to exercise "epistemic humility" in their work, because "love cannot, in the final analysis, be grasped and explained" (2004: 13). This, of course, does not mean abdicating all theological responsibility and

---

[29] It is important to note the vital distinction that Koyama makes between denomination and denominationalism. Denominations are "valuable products of the history of the Christian church [with] serious *theological* beginnings" (Koyama, 1999: 141). Denominationalism happens when non-theological factors – often relating to power and money – hijack and essentialize the theological understanding of denomination (Koyama, 1999: 143).

surrendering the use of reason. What it means is the acknowledgement that when it comes to divine realities, our understanding can only be partial even if it is clear.[30] The opposite attitude is "epistemic arrogance," the insistence that there is such a thing as "the pure theology" which represents the whole truth and only the truth, and the consequent condemnation of every idea that does not conform to it. Koyama finds the idea of pure theology repulsive and perceives that it contains in it "more danger to human welfare [...] than in syncretism" (1993c: 228). Such theology is ideological, because "it loses the dimension of the strange paradox and makes a claim that it is at the center, thus pushing aside the living God" (Koyama, 1985: 100). The result is theological imperialism which, in its idolatrous confusion between Christological uniqueness and ideational exclusivism, does not tolerate contextualization of any sort. The threat is more often than not an insidious one, and missionaries, especially theological educators in another culture, therefore need to be constantly self-critical of their theological assumptions and posture. In missionary practice then, while we must not lose our message, we must also not lose our manners (Robert Solomon, personal communication). Dean Gilliland's wise words are instructive, "Contextualization is, ultimately, a matter of attitude, translated into ministry" (1989: 28).

Canonicity and Catholicity as Theological Principles

Granted that no one has monopoly on theological truth, how then does one guard against interpretive relativism? This question is especially crucial to evangelicals, defined by their commitment to the Bible as the inspired and authoritative Word of God. The answer is twofold: recognizing that the Bible is "overdetermined in meaning" (Vanhoozer, 1999: 27), and understanding the Church, the Body of Christ – historically and globally – as the ultimate hermeneutical community. The former means that divine revelation is much larger and richer than the capacity of any finite culture to contain it. Steve Strauss has rightly observed that every context will increase awareness of some aspects of the biblical text while *at the same time* decreasing awareness of other aspects of the text (2006: 110-113). Even though there is a single meaning in the biblical text, it is such an "abundant" meaning that multiple insights from different individuals and cultures are needed *together* in order to explicate it fully. Vanhoozer suggests that "[t]he single correct meaning may only come to light through multicultural interpretation" (1999: 27). Koyama is therefore correct in his assertion that there can be no private theology (1999: 77). Criteria for theological assessment must be drawn from two sources: the biblical canon and the global ecclesiastical community. In sum, all theological construction

---

[30] This is indeed the presupposition behind the critical realist epistemology, "that the world is orderly and that that order can be apprehended, *in some measure*, by human reason" (Hiebert, 1999: 71, emphasis added).

must pass the rigorous tests of canonicity and catholicity (see Vanhoozer, 2005: 115-237; 2006: 62-64; Chua, 2007).

Conclusion

The works of Kitamori, Endō, and Koyama certainly provide us with rich fodder for reflection, not only on the meaning of the Cross but also on the nature of theology. Although Endō departs considerably from the Bible by focusing only on divine love and ignoring divine judgment altogether, he helps us understand Japanese proclivities for abiding companionship and an embracing inclusiveness, and challenges us to think more deeply and creatively about the nature of the divine confrontation that Christ experienced on behalf of humankind on the cross. Concerning the relationship between divine love and divine wrath – or between divine embrace and divine confrontation – Kitamori's motif of divine pain and Koyama's reflections on the crucified mind of the suffering God can prove missiologically useful in redirecting our attention from the mystery of eternal damnation to the divine demeanor of impassioned love and abject humiliation displayed on the cross for the sake of sinful and suffering humanity.

As we have seen in this chapter, the writings of Kitamori, Endō, and Koyama have raised numerous questions regarding theological methodology. Minimally, it calls into question whether it is necessary for theology to be predicated on a *particular* method or framework. Who then gets to set the criteria for "right" methodology? Is it legitimate to think of the possibility of theology being expressed in different culturally-conditioned modes? What about the use of literature as a theological medium? In relation to this last question, one may consider the theological intent and implications of Endō's religiously-motivated novels. What is the difference between, say, Endō's *Silence* and John Bunyan's *The Pilgrim's Progress*? These are important questions. Obviously, they are beyond the scope of this present work, but suffice it to say, for our purposes, that Kitamori, Endō, and Koyama have shown us that theology as an activity of reflecting on the mystery of God as revealed through his Word, through history, and ultimately through the Incarnation of Jesus Christ, is truly a multifaceted discipline. These Japanese Christians have reminded us that there are paradoxical and parabolic modes of doing theology, that truths about God are not only cognitive but also affective, and that they can therefore be presented in a creative and aesthetic manner.

Indeed, theology begins with wonder, but it also should end with it. In the words of J. I. Packer, "theology must always lead to doxology" (personal communication). It is truly my experience that this study on the death of Christ from the perspectives of Kitamori, Endō, and Koyama has certainly led me to a deeper and more profound appreciation of the wondrous mystery of God's suffering love and his saving work for the sake of the world. For on the cross, the

Son of God not only suffered because of sinful humanity, he suffered like sinful humanity; and most of all, he died for sinful humanity.

Epilogue: Some Missiological Reflections

Emil Brunner calls the Cross "the shortest summary of the whole life of Jesus" (1952: 282). The centrality of the Cross to the Christian faith is indisputable. There are some Christians like Mase-Hasegawa who do not see the Cross as essential to Christianity insofar as it "represents 'the West' and 'Western Christianity'," and therefore argue that it "should not be placed in another culture" (Mase-Hasegawa, 2004: 165). Their points are well taken. However, rather than dispensing with the symbol altogether, we should strive to recover the *true* meaning of the Cross, and to show that its message of redemptive love is radically different from the religious triumphalism that it has unfortunately come to connote. This study affirms that the Cross is not only a place of redemption, but also a place of deep suffering and selfless sacrifice.

The motif of suffering seems to resonate more immediately with Japanese people than other motifs such as guilt and sin. The impassioned God who identifies with the suffering of the people seems to speak more readily to Japanese culture than the sovereign God who judges them. This is, of course, not an either-or matter; and many evangelical missionaries especially need to rid themselves of this unhealthy mindset of seeing things in strictly binary terms. The uniqueness of Christ as the *only* Lord and Savior, and the scandalous nature of the Cross, cannot be "contextualized" such that these become compromised (so Schnabel). The point here is that the truth of the Atonement is far deeper and larger than even the most theologically-astute missionary can grasp. Japanese Christians teach us that, on the Cross, the Son of God not only suffered *because of* us, and *for* us, but that in a deeply profound way he also suffered *like* us (so Endō). They help us to understand that neither grace without suffering nor suffering without grace is redemptive. The redemption that God brings to us in Christ is both suffering in grace and grace in suffering. In the pain of God, grace is obtained for us. And in all our suffering, sustaining and redemptive grace is available to us through the knowledge of God in Christ.

Let me suggest four ways in which we can appropriate missiologically some of the lessons on suffering that Kitamori, Endō, and Koyama teach us from their perspectives on the death of Christ.[1] First, we must acknowledge that suffering

---

[1] This section is adapted from my paper presented at the 2006 Annual Meeting of the Evangelical Missiological Society in Orlando, Florida. The title of the paper is "Divine Violence and Divine Grace: A Missiological Interpretation of Kitamori Kazō."

is an inescapable part of human experience. While Christians should work to alleviate pain and suffering, we must realize that suffering can never be fully eliminated this side of heaven. However, it can be illuminated, so that we can experience more deeply and participate more fully in the work of divine grace through our suffering. For suffering is not a uniquely human experience; it is also a divine experience. One of the wondrous implications of the Incarnation is that in the person of the God-man Jesus we see the unity of divine pain and human pain. This means that God knows our pain and suffering. For not only is the Son the object of God's pain, but through the Son all human beings have become objects of God's pain as well (Kitamori, 1986: 91). Kitamori would even go so far as to say that since God is the Father of humankind, He also experiences pain when we suffer (Kitamori, 1986: 91).

To illustrate this point, Kitamori tells the following true story of Orikuchi Shinobu (1883-1953), a well-known folklorist and Shinto scholar (2000: 29). Orikuchi never married but adopted a son. However, his son died fighting in the Battle of Iwo Jima during the Second World War. Overcome with grief, Orikuchi wrote this poem:

ningen o fukaku aisuru kami arite
moshi mono o iwaba ware no gotokemu
(人間を深く愛する神ありて
もし物を言わば我の如けむ)

This poem is translated as such, "If indeed there is a god who loves humanity profoundly, and if indeed such a god speaks, he would speak like me." In essence, Orikuchi was lamenting that there is no divine being among the eight million Shinto gods who could ever understand the excruciating pain of losing a son. Kitamori comments that while this may be true of the Shinto pantheon, the God and Father of Jesus Christ *did* suffer profoundly when his only Son died on the cross (Kitamori, 2000: 29). Kitamori adds that it is only through the suffering of God that our suffering can be truly redeemed and our wounds healed (Kitamori, 2000: 29). Such is the "wondrous truth" of the gospel (*zetsumyō no shinri* 絶妙の真理) (Kitamori, 2000).

Secondly, suffering is not only an inescapable part of human experience; it is a necessary component in missionary service. We learn from Kitamori the missiological purpose of the pain that God experienced in embracing the world, the enemy of God, in love. In the same way, when missionaries live incarnationally among a people who have no knowledge of God, or worse, who are overtly antagonistic to the gospel, they should not be surprised when they encounter pain and suffering as if something strange were happening. Indeed, if God had to suffer in order to save the world, it would be presumptuous of us to think that we can be exempt from suffering when we preach the gospel.

The apostolic life is an impassioned life. And the impassioned life is a life of suffering. This is what Paul means when he says that he bears in his body the stigmata of Christ (Gal. 6:15, 17). These are scars of suffering, "a symbol of communion between Paul and the crucified Christ" (Koyama, 1993d: 159-60). By extension, the missionary identity as "sent ones" is a "stigmatized" identity (cf. Koyama, 1976: 33). Indeed, a life marked by self-denial is a "stigmatized" life, *imitatio Christi*, but it is through the stigmata that the message of the Cross is authenticated. In sum, the missionary in their willingness to suffer demonstrates the presence of the crucified mind. Koyama suspects that the gospel preached in Asia often lacks convicting power simply because many missionaries who proclaim the message of the Cross refuse to suffer; hence, they do not carry the stigmata of Christ (Koyama, 1976).[2] On the contrary, the huge temptation in Christian ministry today is the temptation "to make a career out of the Crucified" (James Houston, personal communication).

Third, an integral part of the missionary vocation is to enter into the lives and sufferings of the people we serve. We do this by adopting the posture of the "anti-hero" (Boberg, 1979: 416). David Bosch similarly suggests that in the process of communicating the gospel, it is "victim-missionaries, in contrast to exemplar-missionaries [who] lead people to freedom and community" (1994: 81). Such a "radical" missionary attitude entails acknowledging, first and foremost, one's lack of self-sufficiency. Minimally, this means cultivating an attitude to learn from others by being willing to listen and to give an understanding context to the other (cf. Thomas, 2006: 10). Listening is an act of incarnation because, by it, one enters into the world of the other. Houston puts it this way:

> The purpose of listening is more than healing, for it is also to enjoy a measure of self-transcendence. The exercise of kindness, in "giving space for the other to be" and in the desire to free the hearts of others, is a sign we are moving forward into the realm of beneficence, where love is being radiated selflessly. (2002: 121).

It is hard to be humble if one adopts a posture of omniscience, presuming to know what people need, and professing to have all the answers to life's problems. Even the Son of God asked on numerous occasions: "What do you want me to do for you?" (Mt. 20:32; Mk. 19:36, 51; Lk. 18:41).

> "What do you want me to do for you?" "Give me a drink." "Which of these proved a neighbor?" "Take this cup away from me." These are not the words and actions of one who lords it over others. Nor do they point to one who undertakes so-called

---

[2] The unwillingness on the part of Christians to suffer is an age-old problem. In a letter to the people of Thibaris, Cyprian (200-254), bishop of Carthage, reflects on the Roman persecutions: "How serious a cause it is then, for a Christian to be unwilling to suffer since our Lord has first suffered, or indeed, to be unwilling to suffer for our sins, since the One who had no sin, first suffered for us! The Son of God suffered that he might make us sons of God, and yet the children of men do not want to suffer in becoming a child of God! (cited in Houston, 2006: 64).

dialogue from a position of strength, unwilling to modify or react to the other person. These are the words – and the whole life of Jesus bears them out – of one who came looking for faith, who was moved by the faith he found, and was surprised by some of the persons and places where he found it.

Jesus is the model for a ministry of risk and trust, an example of the mutually liberating effects of dialogue. Mission in reverse is nothing if not mission undertaken in the spirit of Jesus. It is predicated on true mutuality. Jesus was constantly criticized for this palpable mutuality, for eating and consorting with "sinners": prostitutes, lepers, unclean people, outcasts, tax collectors, and the rest. Furthermore, he did not simply patronize them; they *were* his mission and ministry. They contributed to his transformation in mission, as he encouraged and marveled at theirs [...]. *[All] had their say and were heard.* (Gittins, 1993: 62, emphasis added)

In a similar vein, missionaries must avoid what Koyama calls a "passive answer-theology," which simply announces that "Jesus is the Answer" without bothering to find out what people are asking (1976: 71). Rather, we should practice a "lively invitation-theology," meeting people on their own terms, entering into the reality of their lived experiences, and inviting them to come and walk with Jesus, so that they can "taste and see that the Lord is good" (Ps. 34:8; Koyama, 1976: 71).

The attitude of listening to and learning from others becomes all the more important in the light of the huge role biography plays in influencing faith, as we have seen from this study. We do well to listen to people's stories, and perhaps even point to the hitherto invisible work of God at different points of their lives. Tim Dearborn suggests that missionaries working in Japan should do what Buddhist monks do, namely, helping people make spiritual sense of their life experiences (personal communication). This obviously requires godly cultural wisdom. Missionaries are encouraged to cultivate such wisdom by reading and appreciating indigenous theology.

The last– although not the least – point relates to the ministry of the church. It is in the person of Jesus where we see the unity of divine pain and human pain. Kitamori sees the Church, being the extension of the life and ministry of Jesus Christ, as now tasked with the responsibility of bearing the pain of God in the world and relating human reality to divine pain (1986: 179). In other words, a theology of pain must service an ecclesiological appropriation of pain and suffering, so vital in the mission of the church. Next, if we truly believe, as Kitamori does, that "the answer to every human problem lies in the gospel" (1986: 256), then our theology must engage lived human realities. The task of preaching the gospel must therefore include an active engagement with the universal existential human realities of pain and suffering, violence and death. In practical terms, it means that, in order to relieve the suffering of the world, the Church must be involved in its suffering.

We now come to a conclusion. Hopefully, through the study of the creative work of these three Japanese Christians, Kitamori, Endō, and Koyama, we can be reminded that the mystery of who God is and what he has done for us is far deeper than we can ever fathom. Here is a God who not only loves us passionately, but who chooses to share profoundly in our pain and suffering.

Let me conclude with an anecdote from Kitamori relating to Japanese Buddhism. More than half of Japanese Buddhists belong to the True Pure Land Buddhist Sect. Like Christianity, True Pure Land Buddhism teaches salvation by grace through faith. Only the object of faith is different. In Pure Land, one is saved by the grace of the Amida Buddha, by putting one's faith in him. Kitamori observes that while the doctrinal structure of salvation between Christianity and Pure Land is similar, the fundamental difference is that in Pure Land there is no cross (1986: 36-37). In other words, the Buddha knows and feels no pain. Enlightenment for the Buddha is freedom from pain, but for the Christian God, the existential reality is one of pain. For that reason, ultimately, only the suffering God, not the passionless Buddha, is able to love, embrace, and redeem sinners through the death of his Son.

But God demonstrates his own love for us in this: While we were still sinners, Christ died for us. (Rom. 5:8)

しかし私たちがまた罪人であったとき、キリストが私たちのために死んでくださったことにより、神は私たちに対するご自身の愛を明らかにしておられます。（ローマ書五章八節）

Bibliography

10 reasons to believe in a God who allows suffering. 1996. Grand Rapids, MI: RBC
    Ministries.
Abramsky, Sasha. 2007. 'Defining the indefinable West'. *The Chronicle Review, Section
    B of The Chronicle of Higher Education* 53(29), (Mar 23, 2007): B6-B8
Akutagawa, Ryūnosuke 芥川龍之介. 1922. *Ogin* おぎん (*Ogin*). Tokyo: Chūōkōron.
    _____. 1922. *Kamigami no bishō* 神神の微笑 (*The faint smiles of the gods*).
    Tokyo: Shinshōsetu.
    _____. 1923. *Oshino* おしの (*Oshino*). Tokyo: Chūōkōron.
    _____. 1927. *Yūwaku* 誘惑 (*Seduction*). Tokyo: Kaizō.
Alexander, Delroy, and Margaret Ramirez. 2006. 'Rev. Moon and the black clergy:
    Taking down the cross (and taking trips) part of an unlikely alliance with local
    pastors'. *The Chicago Tribune*, Nov 5, 2006.
Alston, William P. 1989. *Divine nature and human language: Essays in philosophical
    theology*. Ithaca, NY: Cornell University Press.
Anselm of Canterbury. 1962a [1077-78]. 'Proslogium'. In *Saint Anselm: Basic writings*,
    2d ed. Trans. S. N. Deane. La Salle, IL: Open Court, pp. 1-34.
    _____. 1962b [1098]. 'Cur Deus Homo'. In *Saint Anselm: Basic writings*, 2d ed.
    Trans. S. N. Deane. La Salle, IL: Open Court, pp. 177-288.
Asakawa, Toru. 2003. 'Kitamori Kazō: Theologian of the pain of God'. Ph.D. thesis.
    McGill University.
Atkinson, James, ed. and trans. 1962. *Luther: Early theological works*. Philadelphia,
    PA: Westminster.
Aulén, Gustaf. 1931. *Christus Victor: A historical study of the three main types of the
    idea of the Atonement*. Trans. A. G. Herbert. London: SPCK.
Baillie, John. 1996 [1949]. *A diary of private prayer*. New York: Fireside.
Baker, Mark D., ed. 2006. *Proclaiming the scandal of the Cross: Contemporary images
    of the Atonement*. Grand Rapids, MI: Baker.
Ballhatchet, Helen J. 2003. 'The modern missionary movement in Japan: Roman
    Catholic, Protestant, Orthodox'. In *Handbook of Christianity in Japan*, ed. Mark R.
    Mullins, Leiden: Brill, pp. 45-68.
Barth, Karl. 1932-67. *Die kirkliche dogmatik*. Zürich: Evangelischer Verlag A. G. Zollikon.
    _____. 1956a [1953]. *Church dogmatics*, vol. IV/1: *The doctrine of
    reconciliation*. Trans. G. W. Bromiley. Edinburgh: T. & T. Clark.
    _____. 1956b [1955]. *Church dogmatics*, vol. I/2: *The doctrine of God
    (Prolegomena to church dogmatics)*. Trans. G. T. Thomson and Harold Knight.
    Edinburgh: T. & T. Clark.
    _____. 1957 [1942]. *Church dogmatics*, vol. II/2: *The doctrine of God*. Trans.
    G. W. Bromiley, J. C. Campbell, Iain Wilson, J. Strathearn, Harold Knight, and R. A.
    Stewart. Edinburgh: T. & T. Clark.

_____. 1960. *The humanity of God.* Trans. John Newton Thomas and Thomas Wieser. Atlanta, GA: John Knox Press.

_____. 1961 [1959]. *Church dogmatics,* vol. IV/3, first half: *The doctrine of reconciliation.* Trans. G. W. Bromiley. Edinburgh: T. & T. Clark.

_____. 1975 [1932]. *Church dogmatics,* vol. I/1: *The doctrine of the word of God (Prolegomena to church dogmatics).* Trans. G. W. Bromiley and T. F. Torrance. Edinburgh: T. & T. Clark.

Bartlett, Anthony. 2001. *Cross Purposes: The violent grammar of Christian atonement.* Philadelphia, PA: Trinity Press International.

Baynes, Simon. 1980. 'The Japanese and the Cross'. *Japan Christian Quarterly* 46(3), (Summer), 146-50.

Bediako, Kwame. 1995. *Christianity in Africa: The renewal of a non-Western religion.* Maryknoll, NY: Orbis.

Behr, John. 2000. *Asceticism and anthropology in Irenaeus and Clement.* Oxford: Oxford University Press.

Beilby, James, and Paul R. Eddy, eds. 2006. *The nature of the Atonement: Four views.* Downers Grove, IL: InterVarsity Press.

Beintker, Horst. 1954. *Die überwindung der anfechtung bei Luther: Eine studie zu seiner theologie nach den Operationes in Psalmos 1519-21.* Berlin: Evangelische Verlagsanstalt.

Benedict, Ruth. 1946. *The chrysanthemum and the sword: Patterns of Japanese culture.* Boston, MA: Houghton Mifflin Co.

Benedict, Ruth ルース・ベネディクト. 1948 [1946]. *Kiku to katana: Nihon bunka no kata* 菊と刀ー日本文化の型 (*The chrysanthemum and the sword: Patterns of Japanese culture*). Trans. Hasegawa Shōji 長谷川松治. Tokyo: Research Institute of Social Thought.

Bernanos, Georges. 2002 [1936]. *The diary of a country priest.* Trans. Pamela Morris. New York: Carroll & Graf.

Bernard, H. Russell. 2002. *Research methods in anthropology: Qualitative and quantitative approaches.* 3^d ed. Walnut Creek, CA: AltaMira Press.

Bevans, Stephen B. 2002. *Models of contextual theology.* Rev. ed. Maryknoll, NY: Orbis.

Bevans, Stephen B., and Roger P. Schroeder. 2004. *Constants in context: A theology of mission for today.* Maryknoll, NY: Orbis.

Birdsall, Judd. 2007. Ich bin ein Lausanner. Lausanne Committee for World Evangelization: www.lausanne.org/gatherings/ylg/younger-leaders-gathering-2006-2 [accessed September 12, 2020].

Black, Matthew. 1973. 'Romans'. *New Century Bible.* London: Oliphants.

Boberg, John T. 1979. 'The missionary as anti-hero'. *Missiology: An International Review* 7(4), (Oct), 411-21.

Boersma, Hans. 2003. 'The Disappearance of Punishment: Metaphors, models, and the meaning of the atonement'. *Books & Culture* 9(2), (Mar/Apr), 32-34.

_____. 2004. *Violence, hospitality, and the cross: Reappropriating the atonement tradition.* Grand Rapids, MI: Baker.

_____. 2005. 'Accommodation to what? Univocity of being, pure nature and the anthropology of Irenaeus'. *CRUX* 41(3), (Fall), 2-13.

Bonhoeffer, Dietrich, 1995 [1937]. *The cost of discipleship.* Trans. R. H. Fuller and Irmgard Booth. New York: Touchstone.

_____. 1971 [1951]. *Letters and papers from prison.* Enl. ed. Trans. and ed. Eberhard Bethge. New York: Macmillan.

Bosch, David J. 1991. *Transforming mission: Paradigm shifts in theology of mission.* Maryknoll, NY: Orbis.
_____. 1994 [1992]. 'The vulnerability of mission'. In *New directions in mission and evangelization 2: Theological foundations*, eds. James A. Scherer and Stephen B. Bevans. Maryknoll, NY: Orbis, pp. 73-86.
_____. 2000 [1979]. *A spirituality of the road.* Eugene, OR: Wipf & Stock.
Boxer, C. R. 1967. *The Christian century in Japan 1549 – 1650.* 2ᵈ printing, corrected. Berkeley, CA: University of California Press.
Brasnett, Bertrand R. 1928. *The suffering of the impassible God.* London: SPCK.
Brooker, Jewel Spears. 1999. 'In memoriam: Shusaku Endo'. *Christianity and Literature* 48(2), (Winter), 141-44.
Brown, Joanne Carlson. 1992. 'Divine child abuse'. *Daughters of Sarah* 18(3), (Summer), 24-28.
Brown, F., S. Driver, and C. Briggs. *The Brown-Driver-Briggs Hebrew and English lexicon.* In BibleWorks 7. Norfolk, VA: BibleWorks. CD-ROM.
Brunner, Emil. 1952. *The Christian doctrine of creation and redemption: Dogmatics*, vol. II. Trans. Olive Wyon. Philadelphia, PA: Westminster.
Buber, Martin. 1970 [1923]. *I and Thou.* Trans. Walter Kaufmann. New York: Simon & Schuster.
Bunyan, John ジョン・バンヤン 1926 [1678]. *Tenro rekitei* 天路歴程 (*The Pilgrim's Progress*). Trans. Matsumoto Ryōshū 松本霊舟. Tokyo: Keiseisha.
Burkman, Thomas W. 1994. 'The historical novels of Endo Shusaku: Alien Christianity in the "mud-swamp" of Japan'. *Fides et historica* 26(1), (Spring), 99-111.
Buss, Siegfried A. 1974. 'A comparative study of Andres' *Wir sind Utopia* and Endo's *Silence*'. *Japan Christian Quarterly* 40(4), (Fall), 221-26.
Bussie, Jacqueline Aileen. 2003. 'Laughter, language, and hope: Risibility as resistance in Elie Wiesel's "Gates of the Forest," Shusaku Endo's "Silence," and Toni Morrison's "Beloved."' Ph.D. thesis. University of Virginia.
Calvin, John. 1960 [1536]. *Calvin: Institutes of the Christian religion*, vol. I, ed. John T. McNeill. Trans. Ford Lewis Battles. Philadelphia, PA: Westminster.
Chattaway, Peter T. 2007. 'Deeper into Terabitha. (An interview with Katherine Paterson)'. *Christianity Today* 51(3), (Mar), 64-66.
Chiyozaki, Hideo 千代崎秀雄, ed. 1990. *Tennōsei no kenshō: Nihon senkyō ni okeru fukahi no kadai* 天皇制の検証ー日本宣教のおける不可避の課題 (*The Japanese emperor system: The inescapable missiological issue*). Tokyo: Tokyo Mission Research Institute.
Chinmoku 沈黙 (*Silence*). 1971. Dir. 篠田正浩 Shinoda Masahiro. Tokyo: Tōhō. DVD.
Chua, How Chuang. 2005. 'Reinterpreting Endō Shūsaku's swamp motif in the light of the historical Jesuit mission to Japan'. Paper presented to the 54ᵗʰ Midwest Conference on Asian Affairs, Michigan State University.
_____. 2006a. 'Divine violence and divine grace: A missiological interpretation of Kitamori Kazō'. Paper presented to the Annual Meeting of the Evangelical Missiological Society, Orlando, FL.
_____. 2006b. 'Violence and grace'. In *The cradle and the crown: A Regent College advent reader*, eds. G. Richard Thompson and Susan M. Fisher, 24. Vancouver, B.C.: Regent College Publishing.
_____. 2007. 'Language/Linguistics/Translation'. In *Dictionary of mission theology*, ed. John Corrie. Nottingham: Inter-Varsity Press.
Clark, D. S., Jr. 1991. 'Introduction to Nishitani Keiji', *Nishida Kitarō.* Berkeley, CA:

University of California Press, pp. vii-xxii,

Coe, Shoki. 1973. 'In search of renewal in theological education'. *Theological Education* (Summer), 233-43.

_____. 1976. 'Contextualizing theology'. In *Third world theologies*, ed. Gerald H. Anderson and Thomas F. Stransky, New York: Paulist Press, pp. 19-24.

Cohen, Doron B. 1993. 'The God of *amae*: Endo's *Silence* reconsidered'. *Japanese Religions* 19(1 and 2), 106-21.

Cone, James H. 1975. *The God of the Oppressed*. New York; Seabury Press.

Conn, Harvie M. 1978. 'Contextualization: A new dimension for cross-cultural hermeneutics'. *Evangelical Missions Quarterly* 14(1), (Jan), 39-46.

Conway, John. 2006. 'Bonhoeffer's last writings from prison'. *CRUX* 42(3), (Fall), 2-9.

Dale, Kenneth J. 1998. 'Why the slow growth of the Japanese church?' *Missiology: An International Review* 26(3), (Jul), 275-88.

Davies, Roger J. and Ikeno Osamu, eds. 2002. *The Japanese mind: Understanding contemporary Japanese culture*. Boston, MA: Tuttle Publishing.

Davis, Bret W. 2006. 'The Kyoto School'. *Stanford Encyclopedia of Philosophy*: http://plato.stanford.edu/entries/kyoto-school/ [accessed Sep 29, 2020].

den Heyer, C. J. 1998. *Jesus and the doctrine of the Atonement: Biblical notes on a controversial topic*. Trans. John Bowden. Harrisburg, PA: Trinity Press International.

Dever, Mark. 2006. 'Nothing but the blood'. *Christianity Today* 50(5), (May), 29-33.

Dodd, C. H. 1935. *The Bible and the Greeks*. London: Hodder & Stoughton.

Dohi, Akio. 1997. 'The first generation: Christian leaders in the first period'. In *A History of Japanese theology*, ed. Furuya Yasuo. Grand Rapids, MI.: Eerdmans, pp. 11-42.

Doi, Takeo. 1981. *The anatomy of dependence*. Trans. John Bester. Rev. ed. Tokyo: Kōdansha.

Doi, Takeo 土居健郎. 1965. *Amae no kōzō* 甘えの構造 (*The anatomy of dependence*). Tokyo: Kōbundō.

Dostoevsky, Fyodor. 1992 [1869]. *The Idiot*. Trans. Alan Myers. Oxford: Oxford University Press.

_____. 2004 [1846]. *The Double*. Trans. Hugh Aplin. Chicago: Trafalgar Square Publishing.

Drummond, Richard H. 1971. *A History of Christianity in Japan*. Grand Rapids, MI: Eerdmans.

_____. 1994. 'Missiological lessons – From events new and old'. *Missiology: An International Review* 22(1), (Jan), 19-42.

Dunn, James D. G. 1998. *The theology of Paul the apostle*. Grand Rapids, MI: Eerdmans.

Durfee, Richard E., Jr. 1989. 'Portrait of an unknowingly ordinary man: Endō Shūsaku, Christianity, and Japanese historical consciousness'. *Japanese Journal of Religious Studies* 16(1), 41-62.

Durgin, Russell L. 1953. 'Christianity in postwar Japan'. *Far Eastern Survey* 22(2), 13-18. American Institute of Pacific Relations.

Dyrness, William A. 1971. *Rouault: A vision of suffering and salvation*. Grand Rapids, MI: Eerdmans.

_____. 1990. *Learning about theology from the Third World*. Grand Rapids, MI: Baker.

Earhart, H. Byron. 1974. *Japanese Religion: Unity and diversity*. 2d ed. Belmont, CA: Wadsworth.

Ebisawa, Arimichi 海老沢有道. 1981. *Nihon no seisho: Seisho no waku no rekishi* 日

本の聖書―聖書の和訳の歴史 (*The Japanese Bible: History of the Japanese translation of the Bible*). Rev. ed. Tokyo: United Church of Christ in Japan Press.

Elision, George. 1973. *Deus Destroyed: The image of Christianity in early modern Japan*. Cambridge, MA: Harvard University Press.

Ellegård, Alvar. 1999. *Jesus: One hundred years before Christ*. Woodstock, NY: Peter Mayer.

End of the spear. 2006. Dir. Jim Hansen. Los Angeles: 20th Century Fox. DVD.

Endo, Shusaku. 1973 [1958]. *The Sea and Poison*. Trans. Michael Gallagher. Tokyo: Tuttle.

_____. 1974 [1959]. *Wonderful Fool*. Trans. Francis Mathy. Tokyo: Tuttle.

_____. 1974 [1969]. 'Mothers'. Trans. Francis Mathy from *Haha naru mono* 母なるもの. *The Japanese Christian Quarterly* 40(4), 186-204.

_____. 1974 [1972]. 'Mine'. Trans. Peter Schumacher from *Watakushi no mono* 私のもの. *The Japanese Christian Quarterly* 40(4), (Fall), 205-13.

_____. 1974 [1973]. 'The Anguish of an Alien'. Trans. Calvin Parker from *Ihōjin no kunō* 異邦人の苦悩. *The Japanese Christian Quarterly* 40(4), (Fall), 179-85.

_____. 1977. 'At the baptism of one Friend after another …' Trans. F. Uyttendaele. *Japan Christian Quarterly* 43(4), (Fall), 208-10.

_____. 1978 [1960]. *Volcano*. Trans. Richard Schuchert. New York: Taplinger.

_____. 1978 [1973]. *A Life of Jesus*. Trans. Richard Schuchert. New York: Paulist Press.

_____. 1979 [1974]. *When I Whistle*. Trans. Van C. Gessel. Tokyo: Kōdansha.

_____. 1982 [1966]. *Silence*. Trans. William Johnston. Tokyo: Kōdansha.

_____. 1982 [1980]. *The Samurai*. Trans. Van C. Gessel. London: Peter Owen.

_____. 1988 [1986]. *Scandal*. Trans. Van C. Gessel. Tokyo: Shinchōsha.

_____. 1989 [1965]. *Foreign Studies*. Trans. Mark Williams. London: Peter Owen.

_____. 1993 [1959]. 'The Final Martyrs'. Trans. Van C. Gessel from *Saigo no junkyōsha* 最後の殉教者. In *The Final Martyrs*. London: Peter Owen, pp. 9-27.

_____. 1993 [1968]. 'Shadows'. Trans. Van C. Gessel from *Kagebōshi* 影法師. In *The Final Martyrs*, London: Peter Owen, pp. 28-57.

_____. 1993 [1976]. 'A fifty-year-old man'. Trans. Van C. Gessel from *Gojussai no otoko* 五十歳の男. In *The Final Martyrs*, London: Peter Owen, pp. 58-73.

_____. 1993 [1983]. 'A sixty-year-old man'. Trans. Van C. Gessel from *Rokujussai no otoko* 六十歳の男. In *The Final Martyrs*, London: Peter Owen, pp. 128-46.

_____. 1994 [1964]. *The Girl I Left Behind*. Trans. Mark Williams. London: Peter Owen.

_____. 1994 [1994]. *Deep River*. Trans. Van C. Gessel. New York: New Directions.

Endō, Junko. 1999. 'Reflections on Shusaku Endo and *Silence*'. *Christianity and Literature* 48(2), (Winter), 145-48.

Endō, Shūsaku 遠藤周作. 1955. *Shiroi hito, kiiroi hito* 白い人・黄色人 (*White man, yellow man*). Tokyo: Kōdansha.

_____. 1958. *Umi to dokuyaku* 海と毒薬 (*The sea and poison*). Tokyo: Shinchōsha.

_____. 1959a. *Obakasan* おバカさん (*Wonderful fool*). Tokyo: Chūō kōronsha.

_____. 1959b. *Kumo: Endō Shūsaku kyofutan* 蜘蛛一遠藤周作恐怖譚 (*Spiders: The horror stories of Endō Shūsaku*). Tokyo: Shinchōsha.

_____. 1960. *Kazan* 火山 (*Volcano*). Tokyo: Bungei shunshū shinsha.

_____. 1964. *Watashi ga suteta onna* わたしが棄てた女 (*The girl I left behind*). Tokyo: Kōdansha.

_____. 1965. *Ryūgaku* 留学 (*Foreign Studies*). Tokyo: Shinchōsha.

_____. 1966. *Chinmoku* 沈黙 (*Silence*). Tokyo: Shinchōsha.

_____. 1973a. *Iesu no shōgai* イエスの生涯 (*A Life of Jesus*). Tokyo: Shinchōsha.

_____. 1973b. *Shikai no hotori* 死海のほとり (*By the Dead Sea*). Tokyo: Shinchōsha.

_____. 1974. *Kuchibue o fuku toki* 口笛を吹く時 (*When I Whistle*). Tokyo: Kōdansha.

_____. 1976. *Watakushi no Iesu* 私のイエス (*My Jesus*). Tokyo: Shōdensha.

_____. 1977. *Nihonjin wa kirisutokyō o shinjirareru ka* 日本人はキリスト教を信じられるか (*Can the Japanese believe in Christianity?*). Tokyo: Kōdansha.

_____. 1978. *Kirisuto no tanjō* キリストの誕生 (*The Birth of Christ*). Tokyo: Shinchōsha.

_____. 1980a. *Samurai* 侍 (*The samurai*). Tokyo: Shinchōsha.

_____. 1980b. *Watashi no bungaku to seisho* 私の文学と聖書 (My literature and the Bible). In *Kirisutokyō bunka kenkyūjo kenkyū nenpō* 基督教文化研究所研究年報 (Annual report of the Research Center for the Study of the Culture of Christianity), 12, 1-21.

_____. 1983. *Watakushi ni totte kami to wa* 私にとって神とは (*What is God to me?*). Tokyo: Kōbunsha.

_____. 1986. *Sukyandaru* スキャンダル (*Scandal*). Tokyo: Shinchōsha.

_____. 1994. *Fukai kawa* 深い河 (*Deep River*). Tokyo: Kōdansha.

_____. 2000a. *Endō Shūsaku bungaku zenshū (jūgokan)* 遠藤周作文学全集（十五巻）(*The Complete Works of Endō Shūsaku, 15 vols*). Tokyo: Shinchōsha.

_____. 2000b. *"Fukai kawa" sōsaku nikki* 「深い川」創作日記 (*Diary of the making of Deep River*). Tokyo: Kōdansha.

_____. 2006a. *Korian kōyūroku* 狐狸庵交遊録 (*Records of Korian and Associates*). Tokyo: Kawade shobō shinsha.

_____. 2006b. *Endō Shūsaku essei senshū I hito to kokoro: kanari, umaku, ikita* 遠藤周作エッセイ選集 I　人と心一かなり、うまく、生きた (*Selected essays of Endō Shūsaku, vol. I: Man and spirit: I lived fairly well*). Tokyo: Kōbunsha.

England, John C., Jose Kuttianimattathil, John Mansford Prior, Lily A. Quintos, David Suh Kwang-sun, and Janice Wickeri, eds. 2004. *Asian Christian theologies: A research guide to authors, movements, sources*, vol. 3: *Northeast Asia*. Delhi: ISPCK.

Enns, Robert. 2001. '"Making all things new"? Remembering the ancestors in a Japanese Protestant family'. *Japanese Religions* 26(1), 55-84.

Erickson, Millard J. 1998. *Christian Theology*. 2d ed. Grand Rapids, MI: Baker.

The Evangelical Free Church of America. 2003. 'Doctrine: Statement of faith of The Evangelical Free Church of America': http://www.efca.org/about/doctrine/ [Updated 2019], [accessed September 29, 2020].

Faure, Bernard. 1993. *Chan insights and oversights: An epistemological critique of the*

Chan tradition. Princeton, NJ: Princeton University Press.

Feinberg, John. 2001. *No one like him: The doctrine of God.* Wheaton, IL: Crossway Books.

Ferre, Frederick. 1961. *Language, Logic and God.* New York: Harper & Bros.

Fiddes, Paul S. 1988. *The creative suffering of God.* Oxford: Clarendon Press.

_____. 1989. *Past event and present salvation: The Christian idea of atonement.* Oxford: Oxford University Press.

_____. 2000. *Participating in God: A pastoral doctrine of the Trinity.* Louisville, KY: Westminster John Knox Press.

Finlan, Stephen. 2005. *Problems With Atonement: The origins of, and controversy about, the Atonement doctrine.* Collegeville, MN: Liturgical Press.

Flemming, Dean. 2005. *Contextualization in the New Testament: Patterns for theology and mission.* Downers Grove, IL: InterVarsity Press.

Ford, David F. 1989. 'Kosuke Koyama: A passionate God for Asia'. In *The modern theologians: An introduction to Christian theology in the twentieth century,* ed. David F. Ford, Oxford: Basil Blackwell, pp. 225-29.

Forde, Gerhard O. 1997. *On being a theologian of the cross: Reflections on Luther's Heidelberg Disputation, 1518.* Grand Rapids, MI: Eerdmans.

Forsyth, P. T. 1909. *The person and place of Jesus Christ.* London: Independent Press.

_____. 1917. *The justification of God.* London: Independent Press.

_____. 1948. *The cruciality of the Cross.* London: Independent Press.

Foster, Michael Dylan. 2006. 'Strange games and enchanted science: The mystery of kokkuri'.*Journal of Asian Studies* 65(2), (May), 251-75.

Fuchida, Mitsuo. 1953. *From Pearl Harbor to Golgotha.* San Jose, CA: Sky Pilots Press.

Fujita, Neil S. 1991. *Japan's Encounter with Christianity: The Catholic mission in pre-modern Japan.* New York: Paulist Press.

Fujimoto, Masaru. 2003. 'Black ships of 'shock and awe.'' *The Japan Times* June 1, 2003: www.japantimes.co.jp/community/2003/06/01/general/black-ships-of-shock-and-awe/ [accessed September 13, 2020].

Fukada, Robert. 1984. 'Remembering the dead: Practical issues'. *Japanese Religions* 13(2), 1-10.

Funaki, Shin. 1957. 'The significance of the Old Testament concept of "losing face"'. M.A. thesis. Wheaton Graduate School.

Furuya, Yasuo. 1997. 'Epilogue'. In *A History of Japanese Theology,* ed. Furuya Yasuo. Grand Rapids, MI: Eerdmans, pp. 141-46.

_____. 1998. 'Postwar Protestant missionary work in Japan: A retrospective account and theological appraisal'. *Japan Christian Review* 64, 20-27.

Furuya, Yasuo 古屋安雄. 1985. *Shūkyō no shingaku* 宗教の神学 (Theology of Religions). Kyoto: Jordan Press.

_____. 2003. *Nihon no kirisutokyō* 日本のキリスト教 (*Japanese Christianity*). Tokyo: Kyōbunkwan.

Gallagher, Kenneth T. 1962. *The Philosophy of Gabriel Marcel.* New York: Fordham University Press.

Gavrilyuk, Paul L. 2004. *The suffering of the impassible God: The dialectics of patristic thought.* Oxford: Oxford University Press.

Geertz, Clifford. 1973. *The Interpretation of Cultures: Selected essays by Clifford Geertz.* New York: Basic Books.

Germany, Charles H. 1965. *Protestant theologies in modern Japan: A history of* dominant theological currents from 1920-1960. Tokyo: International Institute for the Study of Religions.

Gessel, Van C. 1979. 'The literature of Kojima Nobuo, Yasuoka Shotaro, and Endo Shusaku: Cripples, clods, and cowards in contemporary Japanese fiction'. Ph.D. thesis. Columbia University.

_____. 1982. 'Postscript: Fact and truth in *The Samurai'*. In Shusaku Endo, *The Samurai.* London: Peter Owen, pp. 268-72.

_____. 1999. 'Hearing God in Silence: The fiction of Endo Shusaku'. *Christianity and Literature* 48(2), (Winter), 149-64.

Gilliland, Dean S. 1989. 'Contextual theology as incarnational mission'. In *The Word among us: Contextualizing mission for theology today*, ed. Dean S. Gilliland. Dallas, TX: Word Publishing, pp. 9-31.

Gittins, Anthony J. 1993. *Bread for the Journey: The mission of transformation and the transformation of mission.* Maryknoll, NY: Orbis.

Glaser, Barney G., and Anselm L. Strauss. 1967. *The discovery of grounded theory: Strategies for qualitative research.* Chicago, IL: Aldine.

Goodwin, Janet R. 1989. 'Shooing the dead to paradise'. *Japanese Journal of Religious Studies* 16(1), 63-80.

Gordon, Andrew. 2003. *A Modern History of Japan: From Tokugawa times to the present.* New York: Oxford University Press.

Green, Joel B., and Mark D. Baker. 2000. *Recovering the scandal of the Cross: Atonement in New Testament and contemporary contexts.* Downers Grove, IL: InterVarsity Press.

Green, Julien. 1996 [1929]. *The Dark Journey.* Trans. Vyvyan Holland. Dallas, TX: Texas Bookman.

Greene, Graham. 2005 [1929]. *The Man Within.* London: Penguin.

Gunton, Colin E. 1989. *The Actuality of the Atonement: A study of metaphor, rationality and the Christian tradition.* Edinburgh: T & T Clark.

Hagiwara, Takao. 1993. 'The role of the mother in modern Japanese literature: The case of Shūsaku Endō'. *British Columbia Asian Review* 7(1), (Winter 1993/94), 54-63.

Hall, Douglas J. 1987. 'Rethinking Christ: Theological reflections on Shusaku Endo's *Silence'*. *Journal of Theology for Southern Africa* 60(1), (Sep), 254-67.

Hammer, Joshua. 2006. *Yokohama Burning: The deadly 1923 earthquake and fire that forged the path to World War II.* New York: Free Press.

Hanazono, Yukio. 2006. 'Interview by Christian Broadcasting Network'. *Christian Information Service News* 66, 3.

Harada, Tasuku. 1914. *The Faith of Japan.* New York: Macmillan.

Hargreaves, Cecil. 1972. *The Gospel in a World Context.* London: Bible Reading Fellowship.

Harrington, Ann M. 1993. *Japan's Hidden Christians.* Chicago, IL: Loyola University Press.

Harris, R. Laird Harris, Gleason L. Archer Jr., and Bruce K. Waltke. 1980. *The theological wordbook of the Old Testament.* In BibleWorks 7. Norfolk, VA: BibleWorks. CD-ROM.

Hashimoto, Akio. 1992. 'Theology of the pain of God: An analysis and evaluation of Kazoh Kitamori's (1916-) work in Japanese Protestantism'. Ph.D. thesis. Concordia Seminary.

Hartshorne, Charles. 1948. *The Divine Relativity: A social conception of God.* New Haven, CT: Yale University Press.

Heisig, James W. 2004. 'Nishida's medieval bent'. *Japanese Journal of Religious Studies* 31(1), 55-72.

Hengel, Martin. 1977. *Crucifixion in the ancient world and the folly of the message of the cross*. Philadelphia, PA: Fortress Press.

Heschel, Abraham J. 2001 [1962]. *The Prophets*. New York: HarperCollins.

Hesselgrave, David J., and Edward Rommen. 1989. *Contextualization: Meanings, methods, and models*. Grand Rapids, MI: Baker.

Hesselink, I. John ジョン・ヘッセリンク. 1966. 'Seihō ni mado o hiraita nihon no shingaku' 西方に窓を開いた日本の神学 (Windows of Japanese Christian thought opened to the West). *Nihon no shingaku (Theological Studies in Japan)* 1(5), 96-103. Annual Report on Theology for The Japan Society of Christian Studies.

Hick, John. 1982. *God has many names*. Philadelphia, PA: Westminster.

_____. 1985. *Problems of religious pluralism*. New York: St. Martin's Press.

Hick, John ジョン・ヒック. 1986 [1982]. *Kami wa ōku no namae o motsu: Atarashii shūkyō teki tagen* 神は多くの名前をもつ―新しい宗教的多元 (*God has many names*). Trans. Mase Hiromasa 間瀬啓允. Tokyo: Iwanami shoten.

_____. 1990 [1985]. *Shūkyō tagen shugi: Shūkyō rikai no paradaimu henkan* 宗教多元主義―宗教理解のパラダイム変換 (*Problems of religious pluralism*). Translated by Mase Hiromasa 間瀬啓允. Tokyo: Hōzōkan.

Hiebert, Paul G. 1985. *Anthropological insights for missionaries*. Grand Rapids, MI: Baker.

_____. 1994. *Anthropological reflections on missiological issues*. Grand Rapids, MI: Baker.

_____. 1999. *Missiological implications of epistemological shifts: Affirming truth in a modern/postmodern world*. Harrisburg, PA: Trinity Press International.

_____. 2003. *Transforming Worldviews*. Unpublished manuscript.

Hill, Charles E. and Frank A. James III, eds. 2004. *The Glory of the Atonement: Biblical, historical and practical perspectives*. Downers Grove, IL: InterVarsity Press.

Hill, David. 1967. *Greek words and Hebrew meanings: Studies in the semantics of soteriological terms*. Cambridge: Cambridge University Press.

Hitt, Russell T. 1965. *Sensei: The life story of Irene Webster-Smith*. New York: Harper & Row.

Holtrop, Pieter N. 2000. 'Ōtsu and Chāmundā: Love and suffering in Shusaku Endo's novel "Deep River"'. In *Mit dem fremden leben: Perspektiven einer theologie der konvivenz, band 2*, ed. Dieter Becker and Andreas Feldtkeller, Erlangen: Erlangen Verlag für Mission und Ökumene, pp. 67-50.

The Holy Bible, New International Version. 1984. Colorado Springs, CO: International Bible Society.

Horikoshi, Nobuji 堀越暢治. 1986. *Nihonjin no kokoro to kirisutokyō* 日本人の心とキリスト教 (*The Japanese Mind and Christianity*). Tokyo: Word of Life Press.

Houston, James M. 2002. *The Mentored Life: From individualism to personhood*. Colorado Springs: CO: NavPress.

_____, ed. 2006. *Letters of faith through the seasons*, vol. 1. Colorado Springs, CO: Honor Books.

Hunsberger, George R. 1998. *Bearing the witness of the Spirit: Lesslie Newbigin's theology of cultural plurality*. Grand Rapids, MI: Eerdmans.

Hwa, Yung. 1997. *Mangoes or bananas? The quest for an authentic Asian Christian theology*. Oxford: Regnum.

Iglehart, Charles W. 1959. *A century of Protestant Christianity in Japan*. Rutland, VT: Charles E. Tuttle.

Inagaki, Hisakazu, and J. Nelson Jennings. 2000. *Philosophical theology and East-West dialogue*. Amsterdam: Rodopi.

Inoue, Yōji. 井上洋治. 1990. *Nihon to Iesu no kao* 日本とイエスの顔 (*Japan and the Face of Jesus*). Tokyo: United Church of Christ in Japan Press.

Ion, A. Hamish. 2003. 'The cross under an imperial sun: Imperialism, nationalism, and Japanese Christianity, 1895-1945'. In *Handbook of Christianity in Japan*, ed. Mark R. Mullins. Leiden: Brill, pp. 69-100.

Irvin, Dale T., and Akintunde E. Akinade. 1996. 'Foreword' to *The agitated mind of God: The theology of Kosuke Koyama*, ed. Dale T. Irvin and Akintunde E. Akindade. Maryknoll, NY: Orbis, pp. ix-xiii.

Ishida, Manabu. 1994. 'Doing theology in Japan: The alternative way of reading the Scriptures as the book of sacred drama in dialogue with Minjung theology'. *Missiology: An International Review* 22(1), (Jan), 55-63.

James, Frank A., III. 2004. 'The Atonement in church history'. In *The glory of the Atonement: Biblical, historical and practical perspectives*, ed. Charles Hill and Frank A. James III. Downers Grove, IL: InterVarsity Press, pp. 209-19.

Jenkins, Philip. 2002. *The Next Christendom: The coming of global Christianity*. Oxford: Oxford University Press.

Jennings, L. Nelson. 2003. 'Theology in Japan'. In *Handbook of Christianity in Japan*, ed. Mark R. Mullins. Leiden: Brill, pp. 181-203.

_____. 2005. *Theology in Japan: Takakura Tokutaro (1885-1934)*. Lanham, MD: University Press of America.

Johnson, Elizabeth A. 1994. 'Jesus and Salvation'. *Catholic Theological Society of America Proceedings* 49 (June), 1-18.

Johnston, William. 1994. 'Endo and Johnston talk of Buddhism and Christianity'. *America* 171(16), 18-20.

Kadowaki, Kakichi 門脇佳吉. 1997. *Nihon no shūkyō to kirisuto no michi* 日本の宗教 とキリストの道 (*Japanese religions and the way of Christ*). Tokyo: Iwanami shoten.

Kagawa, Toyohiko. 1931. *The religion of Jesus and love the law of life*. Trans. Helen F. Topping and J. Fullerton Gressitt. Chicago, IL: The John C. Winston Company.

_____. 1934. *Christ and Japan*. Trans. William Axling. New York: Friendship Press.

_____. 1935. *Meditations on the Cross*. Trans. Helen F. Topping and Marion R. Draper. Chicago, IL: Willett, Clark & Company.

Kähler, Martin. 1956 [1892]. *Der sogenannte historische Jesus und der geschichtliche, biblische Christus*. München: Chr. Kaiser.

Kaiser, Stefan. 1996. 'Translations of Christian terminology into Japanese 16-19th centuries: Problems and solutions'. In *Japan and Christianity: Impact and responses*, ed. John Breen and Mark Williams. New York: St. Martin's Press, pp. 8-29.

Kant, Immanuel. 1960 [1793]. *Religion within the limits of reason alone*. Trans. Theodore M. Greene and Hoyt H. Hudson. New York: Harper & Row.

Kauffman, Richard A. 2007. 'Suffering love'. *Christianity Today* 51(3), (Mar), 71.

Kierkegaard, Søren. 1992 [1843]. *Either/Or: A fragment of life*. Trans. Alastair Hannay. London: Penguin.

Kishimoto, Hideo 岸本英夫. 1961. *Shūkyōgaku* 宗教学 (*Religious studies*). Tokyo: Taimeidō.

Kitamori, Kazo. 1972. 'The problem of pain in Christology'. Trans. Raymond Hammer. In *Christ and the younger churches*, ed. Georg F. Vicedom. London: SPCK, pp. 83-90.

Kitamori, Kazō. 1969. 'Is "Japanese theology" possible?' Trans. Utsunomiya Hidekazu.

Northeast Asia Journal of Theology, 2 (Sep), 76-89.

_____. 1984. 'Christianity and other religions in Japan'. *Japan Christian Quarterly* 50(1), (Winter), 23-30.

Kitamori, Kazoh. 1965. *Theology of the pain of God.* Translator not listed. Richmond, VA: John Knox.

_____. 1976. 'Book review. Jürgen Moltmann, *The crucified God: The cross of Christ as the foundation and criticism of Christian theology*', translated by R.A. Wilson and John Bowden, New York: Harper & Row, 1974. *Christian Scholar's Review* 5(4), 387-89.

_____. 2005. *Theology of the Pain of God.* Translator not listed. Eugene, OR: Wipf & Stock.

Kitamori, Kazō. 北森嘉蔵. 1940. *Jūjika no shu: Kyōgigaku no tame no kakusho* 十字架の主—教義学のための覚書 (*Lord of the Cross: A primer in dogmatics*). Tokyo: Shinseido.

_____. 1943. *Shingaku to shinjō* 神学と信条 (*Theology and creeds*). Tokyo: Nagasaki shoten.

_____. 1946. *Kami no itami no shingaku* 神の痛みの神学 (*Theology of the pain of God*). Tokyo: Shinkyō shuppansha.

_____. 1950. *Konnichi no shingaku: kindai yori gendai e* 今日の神学—近代より現代へ (*Contemporary theology: From recent times to the present day*). Tokyo: Kōbundō.

_____. 1953. *Kyūsai no ronri* 救済の論理 (*The logic of salvation*). Tokyo: Kyōbunkwan.

_____. 1956. *Kami to ningen* 神と人間 (*God and humanity*). Tokyo: Gendai bungeisha.

_____. 1958. *Kami no itami no shingaku* 神の痛みの神学 (*Theology of the pain of God*). 5th ed. Tokyo: Shinkyō shuppansha.

_____. 1959a. *Gendaijin to kirisutokyō* 現代人とキリスト教 (*Modern Humanity and Christianity*). Tokyo: Kōbundō.

_____. 1959b. *Shingaku nyūmon* 神学入門 (*An Introduction to Theology*). Tokyo: Shinkyō shuppansha.

_____. 1960a. *Shingakuteki jiden I* 神学的自伝 I (*Theological autobiography I*). Tokyo: Kyōbunkwan.

_____. 1960b. *Shūkyōkaigaku no shingaku* 宗教改革の神学 (*The Theology of the Reformation*). Tokyo: Shinkyō shuppansha.

_____. 1966. *Ai ni okeru jiyū no mondai: Rutā "kirisutosha no jiyū" o chūshin toshite* 愛における自由の問題—ルター「キリスト者の自由」を中心として (*The problem of freedom in love: Concerning Luther's "Freedom of the Christian"*). Tokyo: Tōkai University Press.

_____. 1968. *Shingakuteki jiden II* 神学的自伝 II (Theological autobiography II). Tokyo: Kyōbunkwan.

_____. 1981. *Jijōsareta kami* 自乗された神 (*God overcoming God*). Tokyo: Nihon no bara shuppansha.

_____. 1985. *Tetsugaku to kami* 哲学と神 (*Philosophy and God*). Tokyo: Nihon no bara shuppansha.

_____. 1986. *Kami no itami no shingaku* 神の痛みの神学 (*Theology of the pain of God*). Kōdansha pocketbook edition (7th ed.) Tokyo: Kōdansha.

_____. 1991. *Ureinaki kami* 愁いなき神 (*Weeping God*). Tokyo: Kōdansha.

_____. 1995. *Nihonjin to seisho* 日本人と聖書 (*The Japanese and the Bible*). Tokyo: Kyōbunkwan.

_____. 1999 [1937]. *Kirisuto ni okeru kami no ninshiki* キリストにおける神の認識 (Knowledge of God in Christ). Graduation thesis. Japan Lutheran Seminary. Published in *"Kami no itami" no rokujūnen: Kitamori Kazō bokushi kinenshi* 『神の痛み』の六十年ー北森嘉蔵牧師記念誌 (*Sixty years of "the pain of God": In memory of Pastor Kitamori Kazō*), ed. Kumazawa Yoshinobu. Tokyo: Chitose Funabashi Church, pp. 70-185.

_____. 2000. *Zetsumyō no shinri* 絶妙の真理 (*Wondrous truth*). Tokyo: Kyōbunkwan.

_____. 2002. *Seisho hyakuwa* 聖書百話 (*A hundred lessons from the Bible*). Tokyo: Kōdansha.

Knitter, Paul F. 1985. *No other name? A critical survey of Christian attitudes toward the world religions*. Maryknoll, NY: Orbis.

_____. 1996. *Jesus and the other names: Christian mission and global responsibility*. Maryknoll, NY: Orbis.

Kopf, Gereon. 2004. 'Between identity and difference: Three ways of reading Nishida's non-dualism'. *Japanese Journal of Religious Studies* 31(1), 73-103.

Koyama, Kosuke. 1955. 'St. Augustine's view of the inner structure of sinful man examined in the light of his conception of order'. M.A. thesis. Princeton Theological Seminary.

_____. 1959. 'What does it mean to have a God? According to Luther's second commentary on the first twenty-two psalms (*Operationes in Psalmos, 1519-1521*): A study of the theology of faith and the theology of immediacy'. Ph.D. thesis. Princeton Theological Seminary.

_____. 1971a. 'A letter to Murray Rogers from Kosuke Koyama'. In *Missionary service in Asia today: A report on a consultation held by the Asia Methodist Advisory Committee, February 18-23, 1971*, ed. East Asia Christian Conference. Hong Kong: Chinese Christian Literature Council, pp. 130-41.

_____. 1971b. 'What makes a missionary? Towards crucified mind not crusading mind'. In *Missionary service in Asia today: A report on a consultation held by the Asia Methodist Advisory Committee, February 18-23, 1971*, ed. East Asia Christian Conference. Hong Kong: Chinese Christian Literature Council, pp. 66-75.

_____. 1972. 'The "wrath of God" and the Thai *theologia gloriae*'. In *Christ and the younger churches: Theological contributions from Asia, Africa, and Latin America*, ed. Georg F. Vicedom. London: SPCK.

_____. 1974a. 'Barefoot in an ascending elevator: A meditation: Culture and religion at the meeting point between the curve-mind and the straight-mind'. In *On language, culture, and religion: In honor of Eugene A. Nida*, ed. Matthew Black and William A. Smalley. The Hague: Mouton, pp. 213-36.

_____. 1974b. *Waterbuffalo theology*. Maryknoll, NY: Orbis.

_____. 1975a. *50 meditations*. Belfast: Christian Journals Ltd.

_____. 1975b. *Theology in Contact: Six reflections on God's word and man's life in God's world*. Madras, India: Christian Literature Society.

_____. 1976. *No handle on the cross: An Asian meditation on the crucified mind*. Maryknoll, N.Y.: Orbis.

_____. 1979a. *50 meditations*. Maryknoll, NY: Orbis.

_____. 1979b. *Three mile an hour God: Biblical reflections*. London: SCM Press.

_____. 1980a. 'Foreword by an Asian theologian'. In *Asian Christian theology:*

Emerging themes, ed. Douglas J. Elwood. Philadelphia, PA: Westminster Press, pp. 13-15.

_____. 1980b. *Three mile an hour God: Biblical reflections*. Maryknoll, NY: Orbis.

_____. 1981. 'Ritual of limping dance: A botanical observation'. *Union Seminary Quarterly Review* 36, Supplementary Issue, 91-104.

_____. 1984a. *Mount Fuji and Mount Sinai: A pilgrimage in theology*. London: SCM Press.

_____. 1984b. 'The Asian approach to Christ'. *Missiology: An International Review* 22(4), (Oct), pp. 435-47.

_____. 1985. *Mount Fuji and Mount Sinai: A critique of idols*. Maryknoll, NY: Orbis.

_____. 1987. 'The suffering God'. *Perspectives* 2(3), 4-6.

_____. 1989a. 'Kagawa, Toyohiko'. In *The perennial dictionary of world religions*, ed. Keith Crim. New York: HarperCollins, p. 397.

_____. 1989b. 'Uchimura Kanzo'. In *The perennial dictionary of world religions*, ed. Keith Crim. New York: HarperCollins, p. 772.

_____. 1992a. 'Sharing the good news of what God is doing today'. In *The scandal of the Cross: Evangelism and mission today*, ed. Wendy S. Robins and Gillian Hawney. London: The United Society for the Propagation of the Gospel, pp. 36-42

_____. 1992b. 'The eucharist: ecumenical and ecological'. *Ecumenical Review* 44(1), (Jan), pp. 80-90.

_____. 1993a. '"Extend hospitality to strangers." A missiology of *theologia crucis*.' *Currents in Theology and Mission* 20(3), (Aug), 165-76.

_____. 1993b. 'New world – new creation: Mission in power and faith'. *Mission Studies* 10(1 and 2), 59-77.

_____. 1993c. 'Participation of culture in the transfiguration of humanity'. *Asia Journal of Theology* 7(2), 214-30.

_____. 1993d. 'The crucified Christ challenges human power'. In *Asian faces of Jesus*, ed. R. S. Sugirtharajah. Maryknoll, NY: Orbis, pp. 149-62.

_____. 1993e. 'Theological education: Its unities and diversities'. *Theological Education* 30, supplement I (Autumn), 87-105.

_____. 1994a. 'Openness-in-pain: The search for a new missiology'. *National Christian Council Review* 94(4), 200-207.

_____. 1994b. 'The theology of the cross and the self-consciousness of the church'. *Asia Journal of Theology* 8(1), 2-12.

_____. 1995. 'Father, forgive …' *Ecumenical Review* 47(3), (Jul), 268-77.

_____. 1997a. 'Jesus Christ, who has gone to the utter periphery'. In *Constructive Christian theology in the worldwide church*, ed. William R. Barr. Grand Rapid, MI: Eerdmans, pp. 492-99.

_____. 1997b. 'My pilgrimage in mission'. *International Bulletin of Missionary Research* 21(2), (Apr), pp. 55-59.

_____. 1999. *Water buffalo theology*. 25th ann. ed. Maryknoll, NY: Orbis.

Koyama, Kōsuke 小山晃佑. 1982. *Jisoku go kiro no kami (shōyaku)* 時速五キロの神 (抄訳) (*Five kilometer an hour God: Selected passages*). Trans. Mochizuki Ken'ichirō. Tokyo: Dōshinsha.

_____. 1996. *Sakareta kami no sugata* 裂かれた神の姿 (*The shape of a broken God*). Trans. Iwahashi Tsunehisa 岩橋常久. Tokyo: United Church of Christ in Japan Press.

Koyama, Kosuke and Esther Stine. 1980. *"Where are you?" God asked: Reflections on a mosaic of biblical images of mission*. New York: United Presbyterian Church in the USA.

Kōyama, Kosuke 小山晃佑, and Hara Michiko 原みち子. 1988. *Josanfu wa kami o osoreteita node* 助産婦は神を畏れていたので (For the midwives feared God). Tokyo: Dōshinsha.

Kraft, Charles H. 2005. *Christianity in culture: A study in biblical theologizing in cross-cultural perspective*. 25th ann. ed. Maryknoll, NY: Orbis.

Kraft, Charles H., and Tom N. Wisley, eds. 1979. *Readings in dynamic indigeneity*. Pasadena, CA: William Carey Library.

Kraus, C. Norman. 1987. 'Cross of Christ – Dealing with shame and guilt'. *Japan Christian Quarterly* 53(4), (Fall), 221-27.

_____. 2004. *Jesus Christ our Lord: Christology from a disciple's perspective*. Rev. ed. Eugene, OR: Wipf and Stock.

Kress, Robert. 1982. *A Rahner handbook*. Atlanta, GA: John Knox Press.

Kumano, Yoshitaka 熊野義孝. 1932. *Benshōhōteki shingaku gairon* 弁証法的神学概論 (*Introduction to dialectical theology*). Tokyo: Shinseidō.

Kuribayashi, Teruo. 1987. 'A theology of the crown of thorns: Toward the liberation of the Asian outcasts'. Ph.D. thesis. Union Theological Seminary.

Kuribayashi, Teruo 栗林輝夫. 1991. *Ibara no shingaku: Hisabetsu buraku kaihō to kirisutokyō* 荊冠の神学ー被差別部落解放とキリスト教 (*Theology of the crown of thorns: Liberation of the discriminated-against buraku and Christianity*). Tokyo: Shinkyō shuppansha.

Kuwada, Hidenobu 桑田秀延. 1933. *Benshōhōteki shingaku* 辯證法的神学 (*Dialectical theology*). Tokyo: Kirisutokyō shisō sōsho kankōkai.

Kumazawa, Yoshinobu 熊澤義宣, ed. 1999. *"Kami no itami" no rokujūnen: Kitamori Kazō bokushi kinenshi* 『神の痛み』の六十年ー北森嘉蔵牧師記念誌 (*Sixty years of "the pain of God": In memory of Pastor Kitamori Kazō*). Tokyo: Chitose Funabashi Church.

Küster, Volker. 2001. *The many faces of Jesus Christ: Intercultural Christology*. Trans. John Bowden. Maryknoll, NY: Orbis.

Kwok, Pui Lan. 1984. 'God weeps with our pain'. *East Asia Journal of Theology* 2, 228-32.

Lao Tzu Tao Te Ching 老子道德經. 1974 [6th century B.C.]. In *The canon of reason and virtue*, ed. D. T. Suzuki and Paul Carus. La Salle, Open Court, pp. 27-65.

The last samurai. 2004. Dir. Edward Zwick. DVD. Burbank, CA: Warner Brothers. DVD.

Lee, Archie Chi Chung. 2005. 'Contextual theology in East Asia'. In *The modern theologians: An introduction to Christian theology since 1918*, ed. David F. Ford and Rachel Muers. Oxford: Blackwell, pp. 518-22.

Lee, Jaecheon. 2002. 'Toward an Asian contextual theology: A critical study of Kosuke Koyama's theology and ethics'. Ph.D. thesis. Drew University.

Lee, Jung Young. 1974. *God suffers for us: A systematic inquiry into a concept of divine passibility*. The Hague: Martinus Nijhoff.

Lee, Moonjang. 1995. 'Re-configuration of Western theology in Asia'. *Mission Round Table* 1(1), (Jan), 27-31.

Lee, Robert. 1989. 'Rebirth of an emperor'. *Areopagus: A Living Encounter With Today's Religions* 2(3), 16-19.

Lewis, C. S. 1960. *The Four Loves*. New York: Harcourt, Brace & World.

Long, Kathryn. 2006. 'More than meets the eye: An historical perspective on "The end of the spear"'. Paper presented at the Annual Meeting of the North Central Region of the Evangelical Missiological Society, Trinity Evangelical Divinity School, Deerfield, IL.

Luther, Martin. 1826 [1519-1521]. *Martin Luther's complete commentary on the first twenty-two psalms*, Vols. I and II. Trans. Henry Cole. London: Simpkin and Marshall.

_____. 1883- [1517-]. *D. Martin Luthers werke. Kritische gesamtausgabe* (Weimarer Ausgabe). Weimar: Hermann Böhlau.

_____. 1962a [1517]. 'Lectures on the epistle to the Hebrews 1517-1518'. In *Luther: Early theological works*, Ed. and Trans. James Atkinson. Philadelphia, PA: Westminster, pp. 27-250,

_____. 1962b [1518]. 'Disputation held at Heidelberg'. In *Luther: Early theological works*, Ed. and Trans. James Atkinson. Philadelphia, PA: Westminster, pp. 276-307.

_____. 1979 [1535]. *Commentary on Galatians*. Trans. Erasmus Middleton. Grand Rapids, MI: Kregel.

MacArthur, Douglas. 1964. *Reminiscences*. New York: McGraw-Hill.

MacDonald, George. 1867. *Unspoken sermons Series One*. London: Alexander Strahan.

_____. 1885. *Unspoken sermons Second Series*. London: Longmans, Green & Co.

Marcel, Gabriel. 1950. *The mystery of being: 1. Reflection and mystery*. Trans. G. S. Fraser. Chicago, IL: Henry Regnery.

Martin, Joseph Moody. 1981. 'Gutierrez, Koyama, and Mbiti: Gaining curriculum insights from an analysis and comparison of three ways to contextualize theology'. Ph.D. thesis. Georgia State University.

Mase-Hasegawa, Emi. 2004. 'Spirit of Christ inculturated: A theological theme implicit in Shusaku Endo's literary works'. T.D. dissertation. Lund University.

Mathy, Francis. 1974. 'Shusaku Endo: The second period'. *The Japan Christian Quarterly* 40(4), (Fall), 214-20.

Matsumoto, Paul. 1985. 'The missiological implications of shame in the Japanese world view'. Th.M. thesis. Fuller Theological Seminary.

Matsuoka, Fumitaka. 1982. 'The Christology of Shusaku Endo'. *Theology Today* (October), 294-99.

Mauriac, François. 1937 [1936]. *Life of Jesus*. Trans. Julie Kernan. New York: Longmans, Green and Co.

_____. 2005 [1932]. *Vipers' tangle*. Trans. Gerard Hopkins. Chicago, IL: Loyola Press.

McCool, Gerald A. 1977. *Catholic theology in the nineteenth century: The quest for a unitary method*. New York: Seabury Press.

_____. 1994. *The Neo-Thomists*. Milwaukee, WI: Marquette University Press.

McFarland, H. Neill. 1967. *The rush hour of the gods: A study of new religious movements in Japan*. New York: Macmillan.

McGregor, Geddes. 1975. *He who lets us be: A theology of love*. New York: Seabury Press.

McGrath, Alister E. 1990. *Luther's theology of the cross: Martin Luther's theological breakthrough*. Grand Rapids, MI: Baker.

_____. 1997. *Christian Theology: An introduction*. 2d ed. Oxford: Blackwell.

McKnight, Scot. 2005. *Jesus and His Death: Historiography, the historical Jesus, and Atonement theory*. Waco, TX: Baylor University Press.

McWilliams, Warren. 1980. 'Divine suffering in contemporary theology'. *Scottish Journal of Theology* 33(1), (Winter), 35-53.

_____. 1981. 'The pain of God in the theology of Kazoh Kitamori'. *Perspectives in Religious Studies* 8(3), (Fall), 184-200.

Michalson, Carl. 1960. *Japanese Contributions to Christian Theology*. Philadelphia, PA: Westminster.

Michell, David J. 1988. 'William S. Clark of Sapporo: Pioneer educator and church planter in Japan'. D.Miss. dissertation. Trinity Evangelical Divinity School.

The middle length sayings (Majjhima-Nikaya), vol. 1. 1967. Trans. I. B. Horner. London: Pali Text Society.

Milne, Bruce. 1998. *Know the Truth: A handbook of Christian belief*. Rev. ed. Downers Grove, IL: InterVarsity Press.

Minoda, Muneki 蓑田胸喜. 1938. *Nishida tetsugaku no hōhō ni tsuite* 西田哲学の方法に就いて (On the methodology of Nishida Philosophy). *Genri Nippon* 原理日本 14: 3-22.

Miura, Ayako 三浦綾子. 1968. *Shiokari tōge* 塩狩峠 (*Shiokari Pass*). Tokyo: Shinchōsha.

_____. 2000 [1964]. *Hyōten (jō) zoku* 氷点（上）続 (*Freezing point: upper sequel*). 67th ed. Tokyo: Kadogawa bunko.

_____. 2000 [1964]. *Hyōten (ge) zoku* 氷点（下）続 (*Freezing point: lower sequel*). 67th ed. Tokyo: Kadogawa bunko.

_____. 2001 [1964]. *Hyōten (jō)* 氷点（上）(*Freezing point I*). 66th ed. Tokyo: Kadogawa bunko.

_____. 2001 [1964]. *Hyōten (ge)* 氷点（下）(*Freezing point II*). 66th ed. Tokyo: Kadogawa bunko.

Miura, Hiroshi. 1996. *The life and thought of Kanzo Uchimura (1861-1930)*. Grand Rapids, MI: Eerdmans.

Miyahira, Nozomu. 2000. *Towards a theology of the concord of God: A Japanese perspective on the Trinity*. Carlisle, Cumbria: Paternoster.

Moltmann, Jürgen. 1967. *Theology of hope: On the ground and the implications of a Christian eschatology*. Trans. James W. Leitsch. London: SCM Press.

_____. 1972. *Der gekreuzigte Gott*. München: Christian Kaiser Verlag.

_____. 1975. 'The trinitarian history of God'. *Theology* 78(666), (Dec), 632-46.

_____. 1985. *God in creation: A new theology of creation and the Spirit of God*. Trans. Margaret Kohl. San Francisco: Harper & Row.

_____. 1992. *The Spirit of life: A universal affirmation*. Trans. Margaret Kohl. Minneapolis, MN: Fortress Press.

_____. 1993 [1974]. *The crucified God: The cross of Christ as the foundation and criticism of Christian theology*. Trans. R. A. Wilson and John Bowden. Minneapolis, MN: Fortress Press.

_____. 1993 [1975]. *The church in the power of the Spirit: A contribution to messianic ecclesiology*. Trans. Margaret Kohl. Minneapolis, MN: Fortress Press.

Moran, J. F. 1993. *The Japanese and the Jesuits: Alessandro Valignano in sixteenth-century Japan*. London: Routledge.

Morimoto, Anri. 2003. 'The (more or less) same light but from different lamps: The post-pluralist understanding of religion from a Japanese perspective'. *International Journal for Philosophy of Religion* 53(3), (Jun), 163-80.

_____. 2005. 'Foreword' to Kazoh Kitamori, *Theology of the Pain of God*, Eugene, OR: Wipf & Stock, pp. 1-4.

Morimoto, Anri 森本あんり. 2004. *Ajia shingaku kōgi: Gurōbarukasuru kontekusuto no shingaku* アジアの神学講義―グローバル化するコンテクストの神学 (*Lectures in Asian theology: Theology in a globalizing context*). Tokyo: Sōbunsha.

Morris, Leon. 1955. *The Apostolic Preaching of the Cross*. London: Tyndale.
_____. 1965. *The Cross in the New Testament*. Carlisle, Cumbria, U.K.:
Paternoster.
_____. 1983. *The Atonement: Its meaning and significance*. Downers Grove,
IL: InterVarsity Press.
Morse, Merrill. 1991. *Kosuke Koyama: A model for intercultural theology*. Frankfurt:
Peter Lang.
Mouw, Richard J. 2001. 'Violence and the Atonement'. *Books & Culture* 7(1), (Jan/Feb),
12-17.
Mullins, Mark R. 1998a. *Christianity made in Japan: A study of indigenous movements*.
Honolulu: University of Hawai'i Press.
_____. 1998b. 'What about the ancestors? Some Japanese Christian responses
to Protestant individualism'. *Studies in World Christianity* 4(1), 41-64.
_____. 2006. 'Japanese Christianity'. In *Nanzan guide to Japanese religions*,
ed. Paul L. Swanson and Clark Chilson. Honolulu, HI: University of Hawai'i Press,
pp. 115-28.
Murray, John. 1962. *The Atonement*. Philadelphia, PA: Reformed and Presbyterian
Publishing.
Nakamura, Hajime. 1964. *Ways of Thinking of Eastern Peoples: India, China, Tibet,
Japan*. Rev. English translation, ed. Philip P. Weiner. Honolulu, HI: East-West Center
Press.
Nakamura, Satoshi 中村敏. 2000. *Nihon ni okeru fukuinha no rekishi: Mō hitotsu no
nihon kirisutokyō shi* 日本における福音派の歴史ーもう一つの日本キリスト教
史 (*History of evangelicalism in Japan: Another Japanese Christian history*).
Tokyo: Word of Life Press.
Natori, Junichi. 1957. *Historical stories of Christianity in Japan*. Tokyo: Hokuseido.
Netland, Harold A. 2001. *Encountering religious pluralism: The challenge to Christian
faith and mission*. Downers Grove, IL: InterVarsity Press.
_____. 2006. 'Introduction: Globalization and theology today'. In *Globalizing
theology: Belief and practice in an era of world Christianity*, ed. Craig Ott and
Harold A. Netland. Grand Rapids, MI: Baker, pp. 14-34.
Netland, John T. 1999. 'From resistance to *kenosis*: Reconciling cultural difference in
the fiction of Endo Shusaku'. *Christianity and Literature* 48(2), 177-93.
Neuhaus, Richard John. 2000. *Death on a Friday afternoon: Meditations on the last
words of Jesus from the cross*. New York: Basic Books.
Newbigin, Lesslie. 1989. *The gospel in a pluralist society*. Grand Rapids, MI:
Eerdmans.
Ngien, Dennis. 1995. *The suffering of God according to Martin Luther's "theologia
crucis"*. Vancouver, B.C.: Regent College Publishing.
_____. 1997. 'The God who suffers'. *Christianity Today* 41(2), (Feb), 38-46.
Nicholls, Bruce. 1979. *Contextualization: A theology of gospel and culture*. Downers
Grove, IL: InterVarsity Press.
Nishida, Kitarō. 1990 [1911]. *An inquiry into the good*. Trans. Abe Masao and
Christopher Ives. New Haven, CT: Yale University Press.
Nishida, Kitarō 西田幾多郎. 1911. *Zen no kenkyū* 善の研究 (*An inquiry into the
good*). Tokyo: Kōdōkan.
_____. 1978-89 [1940]. 'Nihon bunka no mondai 日本文化の問題 (The
problem of Japanese culture)'. In *Nishida Kitarō zenshū* 西田幾多郎全集 (*The
collected works of Nishida Kitarō*), 3d and 4th eds. Tokyo: Iwanami Shoten. 12: pp.
275-383.

Nishitani, Keiji. 1991. *Nishida Kitarō*. Trans. Yamamoto Seisaku and James W. Heisig. Berkeley, CA: University of California Press.

Nitobe, Inazō. 1900. *Bushido*. Philadelphia, PA: Leeds & Biddle Co.

Nnamani, Amuluche Gregory. 1995. *The paradox of a suffering God: On the classical, modern-Western, and Third World struggles to harmonise the incompatible attributes of the trinitarian God*. Frankfurt: Peter Lang.

Noble, Colin. 1991. 'Endo Shusaku's Jesus: An introduction to a Japanese Christology'. *CRUX* 27(4), (Dec), 28-32.

_____. 1992. 'Endo Shusaku's Jesus: Analysis of a Japanese Christology'. *CRUX* 28(1), (Mar), 6-13.

Nomachi, Shinri 野町真理. 1999. '"Kami no itami no shingaku" no kirisuto chūshinteki rikai: Kirisutosha no seikatsu ni okeru kunan no sekkyokuteki no imi o motomete 「神の痛みの神学」のキリスト中心的理解―キリスト者の生活における苦難の積極的の意味を求めて(A christocentric understanding of "the pain of God theology": Seeking positive meaning in suffering in the life of a Christian)'. Graduation thesis. Tokai Theological Seminary, Nagoya, Japan.

Noro, Yoshio. 1955. *Impassibilitas Dei*. Th.D. dissertation. Union Theological Seminary.

Nuding, Norman H. 1966. 'The book shelf: *Theology of the pain of God*, by Kazoh Kitamori'. *Japan Christian Quarterly* 32(3), (Jul), 223-24.

Odagaki, Masaya. 1997. 'Theology after 1970'. In *A history of Japanese theology*, ed. Furuya Yasuo. Grand Rapids, MI: Eerdmans, pp. 113-40.

Okumura, Ichirō 奥村一郎. 2001. *Inori no kokoro: Ai no ibuki* 祈りの心―愛の息吹 (*The heart of prayer: The breath of love*). Tokyo: Kairyūsha.

Ooms, Herman. 1976. 'A structural analysis of Japanese ancestral rites and beliefs'. In *Ancestors*, ed. William H. Newell. The Hague: Mouton, pp. 61-90.

Operation Japan: Edition 2000. 2000. Tokyo: Operation Japan Publishing Company and Japan Evangelical Missionary Association.

Operation World: 21st century edition. 2001. Carlisle, Cumbria, U.K.: Paternoster.

Otto, Randall E. 1991. 'Japanese religion in Kazoh Kitamori's theology of the pain of God', *Encounter* 52(1), (Winter), pp. 33-48.

An outline of Shinto teachings. 1958. Tokyo: Jinja Honcho.

Owen, John. 1959 [1648]. *The death of death in the death of Christ*. Edinburgh: Banner of Truth.

Packer, J. I. 1974. 'What did the Cross achieve? The logic of penal substitution'. *Tyndale Bulletin* 25, 3-45.

Pannenberg, Wolfhart. 1968. *Jesus: God and man*. Trans. Lewis L. Wilkins and Duane A. Priebe. London: SCM Press.

Park, A. Sung. 1989. 'Theology of *han* (The abyss of *han*)'. *Quarterly Review* 9(1), (Spring), 48-62.

Parratt, John. 2000. 'Kazoh Kitamori's theology of the pain of God revisited'. In *Mit dem fremden leben: Perspektiven einer theologie der konvivenz, band 2*, ed. Dieter Becker and Andreas Feldtkeller. Erlangen: Erlangen Verlag für Mission und Ökumene, pp. 141-50.

Patton, Michael Quinn. 2002. *Qualitative research and evaluation methods*. 3d ed. Thousand Oaks, CA: Sage Publications.

Peterson, Eugene H. 2005. *Christ plays in ten thousand places: A conversation in spiritual theology*. Grand Rapids, MI: Eerdmans.

Pfleiderer, Georg. 2005. 'The Atonement'. In *Trinitarian soundings in systematic theology*, ed. Paul Louis Metzger. London: T & T Clark, pp. 127-38.

Phan, Peter C. 2003. *In our own tongues: Perspectives from Asia on mission and inculturation*. Maryknoll, NY: Orbis.

Phillips, James M. 1981. *From the rising of the sun: Christians and society in contemporary Japan*. Maryknoll, NY: Orbis.

Pike, Kenneth L. 1967 [1954]. *Language in relation to a unified theory of the structure of behavior*. 2d ed. The Hague: Mouton & Co.

Piryns, Ernest D. 1987. 'Japanese theology and inculturation'. *Journal of Ecumenical Studies* 24(4), (Fall), 535-56.

Prang, Margaret. 1995. *Caroline Macdonald of Japan: A heart at leisure from itself.* Vancouver, B.C.: University of British Columbia Press.

Priest, Robert J. 1994. 'Missionary elenctics: Conscience and culture'. *Missiology: An International Review* 22(3), (Jul), 291-315.

_____. 2006. '"Experience-near" theologizing in diverse human contexts'. In *Globalizing theology: Belief and practice in an era of world Christianity*, ed. Craig Ott and Harold A. Netland. Grand Rapids, MI: Baker, pp. 180-95.

Rahner, Karl. 1997. *The Trinity*. Trans. Joseph Donceel. New York: Crossroad.

Ramachandra, Vinoth. 1996. *The recovery of mission: Beyond the pluralist paradigm*. Grand Rapids, MI: Eerdmans.

Reinsma, Luke M. 1999. 'Shusaku Endo's river of life'. *Christianity and Literature* 48(2), (Fall), 195-211.

Report of the Secretary of the Navy, December 4, 1852. Washington, D.C.: Navy Historical Center.

Ritter, Heinrich. 1898. *A History of Protestant Missions in Japan*. Tokyo: The Methodist Publishing House.

Ro, Bong Rin. 2001. 'Pain of God theology'. In *Evangelical dictionary of theology*, 2d edn. Ed. Walter A. Elwell. Grand Rapids, MI: Baker, pp. 883-84

Robinson, H. Wheeler. 1939. *Suffering, human and divine*. New York: Macmillan and Co.

Ross, Andrew. 1994. *A Vision Betrayed: The Jesuits in Japan and China 1542-1742*. Maryknoll, NY: Orbis.

Rozendaal, Lois Eleanor. 1958. 'Philosophy of education for lay leaders in the church school'. M.R.E. thesis. Princeton Theological Seminary.

Sacks, James Lee. 1992. 'The dynamics of shame in Japanese chronically absent students: A study of the theological-psychological meaning and pastoral implications of shame in caring for chronically absent students'. Th.D. dissertation.Luther Northwestern Theological Seminary.

Sadowitz, Chris. 2004. 'Recognizing world view and its relationship to real gospel presentation and understanding'. *Occasional Bulletin of the Evangelical Missiological Society* 17(2), 1-4.

Saeki, P. Yoshiro. 1951. *The Nestorian documents and relics in China*. 2^d ed. Tokyo: Maruzen.

Sanneh, Lamin. 1989. *Translating the Message: The missionary impact on culture*. Maryknoll, NY: Orbis.

Sano, Hitoshi. 1999. 'The transformation of Father Rodrigues in Shusaku Endo's *Silence*'. *Christianity and Literature* 48(2), (Fall), 165-75.

Sato, Toshio. 1996. 'The second generation'. In *A History of Japanese Theology*, ed. Yasuo Furuya. Grand Rapids, MI: Eerdmans, pp. 43-82.

Satō, Saku 佐藤朔. 1940. *Furansu bungaku sobyō* フランス文学素描 (*A sketch of French literature*). 11th ed. Tokyo: Seikōsha.

Satō, Shigehiko 佐藤繁彦. 1918. *Wakaki Rūteru* 若きルーテル (*Young Luther*).

Tokyo: Keiseisha.

_____. 1961. *Rōmasho kōkai ni arawareshi Ruttā no konpon shishō* 羅馬書講解に現われしルッたーの根本思想 (*Luther's elemental thoughts on Romans*). Rev. ed. Tokyo: Seibunsha.

Schmiechen, Peter. 2005. *Saving Power: Theories of atonement and forms of the church.* Grand Rapids, MI: Eerdmans.

Schnabel, Eckhard J. 2004a. *Early Christian Mission*, vol 1: *Jesus and the twelve.* Downers Grove, IL: InterVarsity Press.

_____. 2004b. *Early Christian Mission*, vol 2: *Paul and the early Church.* Downers Grove, IL: InterVarsity Press.

Schneider, Bernardin, OFM. 2003. 'Bible translations'. In *Handbook of Christianity in Japan*, ed. Mark R. Mullins. Leiden: Brill, pp. 205-25.

Schuchert, Richard A. 1978. 'Translator's preface' to Shusaku Endo. *A Life of Jesus.* New York: Paulist Press, pp. 3-5.

Schütte, Josef Franz. [1980] 1985. *Valignano's mission principles for Japan.* Vol. I. Trans. John J. Coyne. St Louis, MO: Institute of Jesuit Sources.

Schwarz, Hans. 2005. *Theology in a Global Context: The last two hundred years.* Grand Rapids, MI: Eerdmans.

Seattle University. 2001. 'Renowned theologian Kosuke Koyama named visiting ecumenical theologian at Seattle University': www.seattleu.edu/home/news_events/news/news_detail.asp?elYear=2001&elID=521 2002111820. [No longer publicly available].

Seelye, Julius H. 1873. *The way, the truth, and the life: Lectures to educated Hindus.* Bombay, India: Education Society's Press.

Seelye, Julius Hawley. ジュリオス・エイチ・シーレー. 1881. *Shūkyō yōron* 宗教要論 (*A treatise on religion*). Trans. Kozaki Hiromichi 小崎弘道. Tokyo: Jūjiya.

Shenk, Wilbert R. 1999. *Changing frontiers of mission.* Maryknoll, NY: Orbis.

Sherrill, Michael John. 2003. 'Christian churches in the postwar period'. In *Handbook of Christianity in Japan*, ed. Mark R. Mullins. Leiden: Brill, pp. 163-80.

Shimazono, Susumu. 2003. 'New religions and Christianity'. In *Handbook of Christianity in Japan*, ed. Mark R. Mullins. Leiden: Brill, pp. 277-94.

Shorrock, Tim. 2004a. 'Red flags and Christian soldiers (Part I)'. *The Interpreter*, no. 72, (February 1, 2004), 1-2. The US Navy Japanese/Oriental Language School Archival Project, University of Colorado at Boulder.

_____. 2004b. 'Red flags and Christian soldiers (Part III)'. *The Interpreter*, no. 73A, (March 15, 2004), 1. The US Navy Japanese/Oriental Language School Archival Project, University of Colorado at Boulder.

Shorter, Aylward. 1988. *Toward a Theology of Inculturation.* Maryknoll, NY: Orbis.

Shriver, Donald W., Jr. 1996. 'An afterword: A personal tribute to Kosuke Koyama'. In *The agitated mind of God*, ed. Dale T. Irvin and Akintunde E. Akinade. Maryknoll, NY: Orbis, pp. 225-30.

Song, Choan-Seng. 1979. *Third-eye Theology: Theology in formation in Asian settings.* Rev. ed. Maryknoll, NY: Orbis.

Song, Taesuk Raymond. 2009. 'Shame and guilt in the Japanese culture: A study of lived experiences of Japanese emerging generation and its relation to the church mission in Japan'. Ph.D. thesis. Trinity Evangelical Divinity School.

Spae, Joseph J. 1971. *Japanese religiosity.* Tokyo: Oriens Institute for Religious Research.

Spurgeon, Terry, comp. 1987. *Howard and Gwen Norman papers.* Special Collections, The Library of the University of British Columbia.

Stott, John W. 1986. *The Cross of Christ*. Downers Grove, IL: InterVarsity Press.

Strauss, Anselm, and Juliet Corbin. 1998. *Basics of qualitative research: Techniques and procedures for developing grounded theory*. Thousand Oaks, CA: Sage Publications.

Strauss, Steve. 2006. 'The role of context in shaping theology'. In *Contextualization and syncretism: Navigating cultural currents*, ed. Gailyn Van Rheenen. Pasadena, CA: William Carey Library, pp. 99-128.

Tagawa, Kenzō 田川健三. 1988. *Shūkyō towa nanika* 宗教とは何か (*What is religion?*). Tokyo: Daiwa shobō.

Takakura, Tokutarō 高倉徳太郎. 1921. *Onchō no ōkoku* 恩寵の王国 (*Kingdom of grace*). Kamakura, Kanagawa Pref.: Seisho kensansha.

_____. 1925. *Onchō to shinjitsu* 恩寵と真実 (*Grace and faithfulness*). Tokyo: Nagasaki shoten.

_____. 1926. *Onchō to shōmei* 恩寵と召命 (*Grace and calling*). Tokyo: Nagasaki shoten.

_____. 1927. *Fukuinteki kirisutokyō* 福音的基督教 (*Evangelical Christianity*). Tokyo: Nagasaki shoten.

Takayanagi, Shun'ichi. 1979. 'Between fact and truth – Endō Shūsaku's powerless Jesus'. *The Japan Missionary Bulletin* 33(11), (Nov), 608-14.

Takenaka, Masao. 1986. *God is rice: Asian culture and Christian faith*. Geneva: World Council of Churches.

_____. 2002. *When the bamboo bends: Christ and culture in Japan*. Geneva: World Council of Churches.

Takizawa, Katsumi 滝沢克己. 1964. *Bukkyō to kirisutokyō* 佛教與基督教 (*Buddhism and Christianity*). Kyoto: Hōzōkan.

Tanabe, Hajime. 1986 [1946]. *Philosophy as metanoetics*. Trans. Takeuchi Yoshinori. Berkeley, CA: University of California Press.

Tanabe, Hajime 田邊元. 1946. *Zangedō toshite no tetsugaku* 懺悔道としての哲学 (*Philosophy as metanoetics*). Tokyo: Iwanami shoten.

_____. 1963-64 [1930]. 'Nishida sensei no oshie o aogu 西田先生の教えを仰ぐ(A humble request for clarification and guidance from the teachings of Professor Nishida).' In *Tanabe Hajime zenshū* 田辺元全集 (*The collected works of Tanabe Hajime*) Tokyo: Chikuma Shobō, 4:305-28.

Tang, Edmond. 2004. 'East Asia'. In *An introduction to Third World theologies*, ed. John Parratt. Cambridge: Cambridge University Press.

TEF Staff. 1972. *Ministry in context: The third mandate programme of the theological education fund (1970-77)*. Bromley, Kent, U.K.: Theological Education Fund.

Thelle, Notto R. 1987. *Buddhism and Christianity in Japan: From conflict to dialogue, 1854-1899*. Honolulu, HI: University of Hawaii Press.

Thomas, Linda E. *Anthropology, mission, and the African woman*. Chicago, IL: CCGM Publications.

Tiénou, Tite. 1983. 'Biblical foundations: An African study'. *Evangelical Review of Theology* 7(1), (Jan), 89-101.

Tillich, Paul. 1953. *Systematic Theology*, vol. 1. London: James Nesbit.

_____. 1964. *Christianity and the encounter of the world religions*. New York: Columbia University Press.

Tomioka, Kōichirō 富岡幸一郎. 2001. *Uchimura Kanzō* 内村鑑三 (*Uchimura Kanzō*). Tokyo: Itsuki shōbō.

Tosaka, Jun 戸坂潤. 1966 [1932]. 'Kyōto gakuha no tetsugaku 京都学派の哲学 (The Kyoto school of philosophy)'. In *Tosaka Jun zenshū* 戸坂潤全集 (*The collected works of Tosaka Jun)*. Tokyo: Keisō Shobō, 3:171-76.

Trudgill, Peter. 1983. *Sociolinguistics: An introduction to language and society*. Rev. ed. Harmondsworth: Penguin.

Tsuchiya, Hiroshi. 2000. '"Religious studies" in Japan and future prospects'. Trans. Paul S. Swanson. *Nanzan Bulletin* 24(1), 8-21.

Tsunoda, Ryusaku, Wm. Theodore de Bary, and Donald Keene, comp. 1958. *Sources of Japanese Tradition*. New York: Columbia University Press.

Uchida, Kazuhiko. 1991. 'Religious pluralism and the uniqueness of Jesus Christ'. Paper presented at the Asia Theological Association Consultation in Manila, Philippines.

Uchimura, Kanzō. 1895. *How I Became a Christian: Out of my diary*. Tokyo: Keiseisha.

Uchimura Kanzō 内村鑑三. 1980-84 [1901]. 'Mukyōkairon 無教会論 (Theory of Non-church Christianity)'. In *Uchimura Kanzō zenshū* 内村全集 (*The complete works of Uchimura Kanzō*), vol. 9. Tokyo: Iwanami Shoten, pp. 71-74.

_____. 1980-84 [1920]. 'Nihonteki kirisutokyō 日本的基督教 (Japanese Christianity)'. In *Uchimura Kanzō zenshū* 内村全集 (*The complete works of Uchimura Kanzō*), vol. 25. Tokyo: Iwanami Shoten, pp. 592-93.

Uemura, Masahisa. 植村正久. 1932. *Uemura Masahisa zenshū, dai yon kan* 植村正久全集第四巻 (*The complete works of Uemura Masahisa*, vol. 4). Tokyo: Kankokai.

_____. 1948 [1901]. *Reisei no kiki* 霊性の危機 (*The spiritual crisis*). Tokyo: Keiseisha.

_____. 1972. *Uemura Masahisa sekkyō shū* 植村正久説教集 (*Sermons of Uemura Masahisa*). Tokyo: Shinkyō shuppansha.

van Buren, Paul. 1972. *The Edges of Language*. London: SCM Press.

Vanhoozer, Kevin J. 1999. '"But that's your interpretation": Realism, reading, and reformation'. *Modern Reformation* 8(4), (Jul/Aug), 21-28.

_____. 2004. 'The Atonement in Postmodernity: Guilt, goats and gifts'. In *The glory of the Atonement: Biblical, historical and practical perspectives*, ed. Charles Hill and Frank A. James III. Downers Grove, IL: InterVarsity Press, pp. 367-404.

_____. 2005. *The drama of doctrine: A canonical-linguistic approach to Christian theology*. Louisville, KY: Westminster John Knox Press.

_____. 2006. 'Imprisoned or free? Text, status, and theological interpretation in the master/slave discourse of Philemon'. In *Reading Scripture with the Church: Toward a hermeneutic for theological interpretation*, ed. A. K. M. Adam, Stephen E. Fowl, Kevin J. Vanhoozer, and Francis Watson. Grand Rapids, MI: Baker, pp. 51-93

Varley, H. Paul. 1984. *Japanese Culture*. 3d ed. Honolulu, HI: University of Hawaii Press.

Vining, Elizabeth Gray. 1990 [1952]. *Windows for the Crown Prince*. Rutland, VT: Charles E. Tuttle.

Volf, Miroslav. 1996. *Exclusion and Embrace: A theological exploration of identity, otherness, and reconciliation*. Nashville, TN: Abingdon, 1996.

_____. 2004. 'Christianity and Violence'. *Reflections* 91(1), (Winter), 16-22.

von Loewenich, Walther. 1954. *Luthers theologia crucis*. 4th ed. München: Kaiser-Verlag.

Walls, Andrew F. 1996. *The missionary movement in Christian history: Studies in the transmission of faith*. Maryknoll, NY: Orbis.

_____. 2002. *The cross-cultural process in Christian history: Studies in the transmission and appropriation of faith*. Maryknoll, NY: Orbis.

Waltke, Bruce Kenneth. 1958. 'The theological significations of *vAnti,* and *`Upe,r* in the New Testament'. Th.D. dissertation. Dallas Theological Seminary.

Warfield, Benjamin Breckinridge. 1950. *The Person and Work of Christ*, ed. Samuel G. Craig. Philadelphia, PA: Presbyterian & Reformed Publishing Co.

Wargo, Robert J. J. 2005. *The logic of nothingness: A study of Nishida Kitarō*. Honolulu, HI: University of Hawai'i Press.

Watanabe, Hidetoshi 渡辺英俊. 1986. *Gendai no senkyō to seisho kaishaku* 現代の宣教と聖書解釈 (Contemporary missions and biblical exegesis). Tokyo: Shinkyō shuppansha.

Weaver, J. Denny. 2001. *The Nonviolent Atonement*. Grand Rapids, MI: Eerdmans.

Weinandy, Thomas G. 2000. *Does God Suffer?* Notre Dame, IN: University of Notre Dame Press.

Whiteman, Darrell L. 1997. 'Contextualization: The theory, the gap, the challenge'. *International Bulletin of Missionary Research* 21(1), (Jan), 2-7.

Whorf, Benjamin Lee. 1956. 'The relation of habitual thought and behavior to language'. In *Language, thought, and reality: Selected writings of Benjamin Lee Whorf*, ed. John B. Carol. Cambridge, MA: MIT Press, pp. 134-159.

Williams, Daniel Day. 1967. *What present day theologians are thinking*. 3d ed. New York: Harper & Row.

Williams, Mark B. 1999. *Endō Shūsaku: A literature of reconciliation*. London: Routledge.

_____. 2002. 'Endō Shūsaku: Death and Rebirth in *Deep River*'. *Christianity and Literature* 51(2), (Fall), 219-39.

_____. 2003. 'Bridging the divide: Writing Christian faith (and doubt) in modern Japan'. In *Handbook of Christianity in Japan*, ed. Mark R. Mullins. Leiden: Brill, pp. 295-320.

Willis, Elizabeth. 1992. 'Christ as eternal companion: A study in the Christology of Shusaku Endo'. *Scottish Journal of Theology* 45, 85-100.

Winter, Michael. 1995. *The Atonement*. Collegeville, MN: Liturgical Press.

Wolff, Hans Walter. 1974. *Anthropology of the Old Testament*. Mifflintown, PA: Sigler.

Wood, Robert W., ed. 1961. 'Tillich encounters Japan'. *Japanese Religions* 2(2 and 3), (May), 48-75.

Woodard, William P. 1972. *The Allied Occupation of Japan 1945-1952 and Japanese Religions*. Leiden: Brill.

Wright, N. T. 1992. *The New Testament and the People of God*. Minneapolis, MN: Fortress Press.

Yagi, Seiichi. 1997. 'The third generation, 1945-1970'. In *A History of Japanese Theology*, ed. Furuya Yasuo. Grand Rapids, MI: Eerdmans, pp. 83-111.

Yamamori, Tetsunao. 1974. *Church Growth in Japan: A study in the development of eight denominations 1859-1939*. South Pasadena, CA: William Carey Library.

Yamamoto, Kanō. 1966. 'Theology in Japan: Main trends in our time'. *Japan Christian Quarterly* 32(1), (Winter), 37-47.

Yanagida, Tomonobu 柳田友信. 1958. *Nihon kirisutoshi* 日本基督史 (History of Christianity in Japan). Appendix to E. E. Cairns, *Kirisuto kyōkaishi: Ima kara gendai made* 基督教会史ー初代から現代まで (Christianity through the centuries), E. E. Cairns. Tokyo: Seishotosho kankōkai, pp. 619-87.

Yancey, Philip. 2003. *Soul Survivor: How thirteen unlikely mentors helped my faith survive the church*. New York: Doubleday.

Yeow, Choo Lak. 2004. 'Theological education in South East Asia, 1957-2002'. *International Bulletin of Missionary Research* 28(1), (Jan), 26-29.

Yoshida Reiji. 2007. 'Sex slave history erased from texts; '93 apology next?' Mar 11, 2007. *The Japan Times* (online edition):

https://www.japantimes.co.jp/news/2007/03/11/national/sex-slave-history-erased-fro
m-texts-93-apology-next/. [accessed Sep 30, 2020].
Yusa, Michiko. 2002. *Zen and Philosophy: An intellectual biography of Nishida Kitarō.*
Honolulu, HI: University of Hawai'i Press.
Zizioulas, John D. 1985. *Being as Communion: Studies in personhood and the Church.*
Crestwood, NY: St Vladimir's Seminary Press.

Personal Communication:
Stephen Bevans, SVD. The Louis J. Lutzbetak, SVD Professor of Mission and Culture,
Catholic Theological Union, Chicago, IL.
Marva Dawn. Teaching Fellow of Spiritual Theology, Regent College, Vancouver, B.C.
Tim Dearborn. Associate Director for Faith and Development, World Vision
International, Monrovia, CA.
James Houston. Board of Governors' Professor of Spiritual Theology, Regent College,
Vancouver, B.C.
John Howes. Professor Emeritus of Asian Studies, University of British Columbia,
Vancouver, B.C.
Koyama Kōsuke. John D. Rockefeller Jr. Professor Emeritus of Ecumenical Studies,
Union Theological Seminary, New York, NY.
Harold Netland. Professor of Philosophy of Religion and Intercultural Studies and
Naomi A. Fausch Chair of Missions, Trinity Evangelical Divinity School, Deerfield,
IL.
James Packer. Board of Governors' Professor of Systematic and Historical Theology,
Regent College, Vancouver, B.C.
Robert Solomon. Bishop, The Methodist Church in Singapore.
Tite Tiénou. Senior Vice-President of Education, Academic Dean and Professor of
Missions, Trinity Evangelical Divinity School, Deerfield, IL.
Kevin Vanhoozer. Research Professor of Systematic Theology, Trinity Evangelical
Divinity School, Deerfield, IL.